HOW TO USE THIS BOOK

Each flashcard introduces a Spanish word or sentence with its pronunciation underneath. The meaning in English is also presented, along with a picture to help increase memory retention. Some nouns are presented with the article el or la (the) to show their gender (el = masculine, la = feminine). At the bottom of some cards there are notes corresponding to the following categories:

g *Grammar:* They include important grammar issues to note, such as the gender of nouns where it may need to be specified.

p *Pronunciation:* Some words are pronounced differently across Spanish speaking countries. These variations in pronunciation are specified where applicable.

v *Verbs:* Underneath each verb, there is an example sentence along with its translation.

c *Culture:* Where appropriate, a cultural note related to the word or expression on the card is given.

Tips: In general, Spanish nouns end in -o if they're masculine and in -a if they're feminine. Any exceptions will be specified on a Grammar note.
* As a general rule, to form the plural of nouns and adjectives, add -s if they end in a vowel, and -es if they end in a consonant.

Pronunciation Guide

Transcription	*English example*	*Spanish word*	*Sample transcription*
ah	father	aro	**ah**-roh
ee	see	aquí	ah-**kee**
eh	egg	sed	**sehd**
oh	okay	oso	**oh**-soh
oo	too	usted	oos-**tehd**
h	help	jamón	hah-**mohn**
g	gap	gato	**gah**-toh
y	yes	llama	**yah**-mah
ch	church	escuchar	ehs-koo-**chahr**
yah	yard	esquiar	ehs-**kyahr**
yeh	yes	invierno	een-**byehr**-noh
yoh	yogurt	natación	nah-tah-**syohn**

Pronunciation Guide

Transcription	*English example*	*Spanish word*	*Sample transcription*
wah	want	agua	**ah**-gwah
weh	when	puente	**pwehn**-teh
ey	they	béisbol	**beys**-bohl
ay	eye	hay	**ay**
rr	grr	perro	**peh**-rroh
ow	cow	flauta	**flow**-tah
b	boy	bar ver	**bahr** **behr**

***Note:** In the transcription, the syllables in bold font mark where the word carries the stress.*

** The consonants not shown on the table generally have the same sound in both languages.*

Days *(Los días)*

The days of the week in Spanish are:

Lunes	(**loo**-nehs)	Monday
Martes	(**mahr**-tehs)	Tuesday
Miércoles	(**myehr**-koh-lehs)	Wednesday
Jueves	(**hweh**-behs)	Thursday
Viernes	(**byehr**-nehs)	Friday

Months *(Los meses)*

The months in Spanish are:

Enero	(eh-**neh**-roh)	January
Febrero	(feh-**breh**-roh)	February
Marzo	(**mahr**-soh)	March
Abril	(ah-**breel**)	April
Mayo	(**mah**-yoh)	May
Junio	(**hoo**-nyoh)	June
Julio	(**hoo**-lyoh)	July
Agosto	(ah-**gohs**-toh)	August
Septiembre	(sehp-**tyehm**-breh)	September
Octubre	(ohk-**too**-breh)	October
Noviembre	(noh-**byehm**-breh)	November
Diciembre	(dee-**syehm**-breh)	December

Note: *The days and the months in Spanish are masculine.*

Pronouns (Los pronombres)

A pronoun is a word that takes the place of a noun. In Spanish, the personal pronouns are:

Yo	(**yoh**)	I
Tú	(**too**)	You (informal)
Usted	(oos-**tehd**)	You (formal)
Él	(**ehl**)	He
Ella	(**eh**-yah)	She
Nosotros/as	(noh-**soh**-trohs/trahs)	We
Ustedes	(oos-**teh**-dehs)	You (plural)
Vosotros/as*	(boh-**soh**-trohs/trahs)	You (plural)
Ellos/as	(**eh**-yohs/yahs)	They

Possessive adjectives *(Los adjetivos posesivos)*

Possessive adjectives sit before a noun to show possession or ownership. In Spanish, they are:

Mi (**mee**)	My
Tu (**too**)	Your (informal)
Su (**soo**)	Your (formal, singular and plural), his, her, their
Nuestro/a (**nwehs**-troh)	Our
Vuestro/a* (**bwehs**-troh)	Your (plural)

** Used in Spain only.*

Prepositions *(Las preposiciones)*

Prepositions show the relationship between pronouns and nouns and other elements in a sentence. Some Spanish prepositions are:

a	(**ah**)	at, to
bajo	(**bah**-hoh)	under
con	(**kohn**)	with
de	(**deh**)	of, from
desde	(**dehs**-deh)	from, after, since
en	(**ehn**)	in, on, at
entre	(**ehn**-treh)	among, between
para	(**pah**-rah)	for, in order to
por	(**pohr**)	by, for
sin	(**seen**)	without

Conjunctions *(Las conjunciones)*

Conjunctions are connecting or linking words. Some conjunctions in Spanish are:

cuando	(**kwahn**-doh)	when
pero	(**peh**-roh)	but
porque	(**pohr**-keh)	because
que	(**keh**)	that,
because		
si	(**see**)	if
y	(**ee**)	and
o	(**oh**)	or

Cardinal numbers *(Los números cardinales)*

In Spanish, some cardinal numbers are:

0 cero (**seh**-roh)
1 uno (**oo**-noh)
2 dos (**dohs**)
3 tres (**trehs**)
4 cuatro (**kwah**-troh)
5 cinco (**seen**-koh)
6 seis (**seyhs**)
7 siete (**syeh**-teh)
8 ocho (**oh**-choh)
9 nueve (**nweh**-beh)
10 diez (**dyehs**)
11 once (**ohn**-seh)
12 doce (**doh**-seh)
13 trece (**treh**-seh)
14 catorce (kah-**tohr**-seh)
15 quince (**keen**-seh)
16 dieciséis (dyeh-see-**seys**)
17 diecisiete (dyeh-see-**syeh**-teh)
18 dieciocho (dyeh-**syoh**-choh)
19 diecinueve (dyeh-see-**nweh**-beh)
20 veinte (**beyn**-teh)
21 veintiuno (beyn-**tyoo**-noh)
22 veintidós (beyn-tee-**dohs**)
30 treinta (**treyn**-tah)
31 treinta y uno (**treyn**-tah ee oo-noh)

Ordinal numbers *(Los números cardinales)*

In Spanish, some cardinal numbers are:

first	primero	(pree-**meh**-roh)
second	segundo	(seh-**goon**-doh)
third	tercero	(tehr-**seh**-roh)
fourth	cuarto	(**kwahr**-toh)
fifth	quinto	(**keen**-toh)

Verb Conjugations

Some useful verbs in the present tense are:

ser (to be)

soy	I am	somos	we are
eres	you are (informal)	sóis*	you (plural) are
es	you are (formal), he is, she is	son	you (plural) are, they are

estar (to be - location, state, condition)

estoy	I am	estamos	we are
estás	you are (informal)	estáis*	you (plural) are
está	you are (formal), he is, she is	están	you (plural) are, they are

ir (to go)

voy	I go	vamos	we go
vas	you go (informal)	váis*	you (plural) go
va	you go (formal), he goes, she goes	van	you (plural) go, they go

hacer (to do, to make)

hago	I do	hacemos	we do
haces	you do (informal)	hacéis*	you (plural) do
hace	you do (formal), he does, she does	hacen	you (plural) do, they do

tener (to have)

tengo	I have	tenemos	we have
tienes	you have (informal)	tenéis*	you (plural) have
tiene	you have (formal), he has, she has	tienen	you (plural) have, they have

** Used in Spain only.*

Verb Conjugations

Regular -ar verbs
Drop -ar and add -o, -as, -a, -amos, áis, -an

hablar (to talk, to speak)

hablo	I talk	hablamos	we talk
hablas	you talk (informal)	habláis*	you (plural) talk
habla	you talk (formal), he talks, she talks	hablan	they talk

Regular -er verbs
Drop -er and add -o, -es, -e, -emos, éis, -en

comer (to eat)

como	I eat	comemos	we eat
comes	you eat (informal)	coméis*	you (plural) eat
come	you eat (formal), he eats, she eats	comen	they eat

Regular -ir verbs
Drop -ir and add -o, -es, -e, -imos, ís, -en

vivir (to live)

vivo	I live	vivimos	we live
vives	you live (informal)	vivís*	you (plural) live
vive	you live (formal), he lives, she lives	viven	they live

** Used in Spain only.*

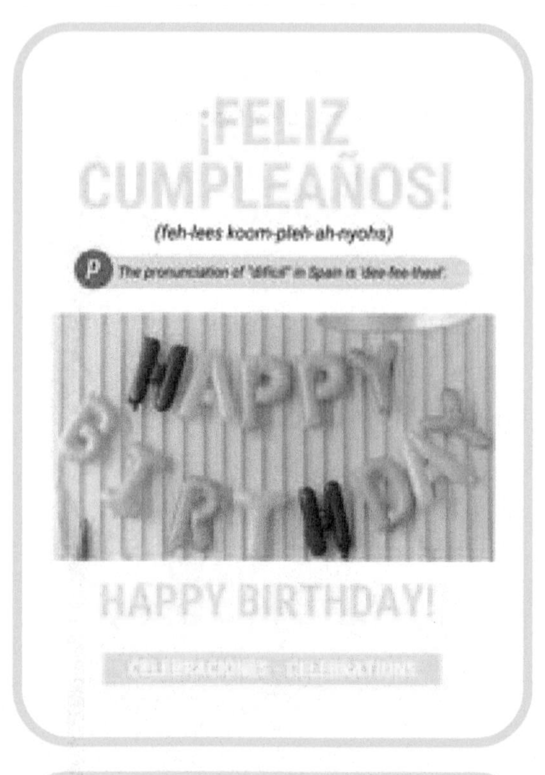
¡FELIZ CUMPLEAÑOS!
(feh-lees koom-pleh-ah-nyohs)
p
The pronunciation of "difícil" in Spain is 'dee-fee-theel'.
HAPPY BIRTHDAY!
CELEBRACIONES - CELEBRATIONS

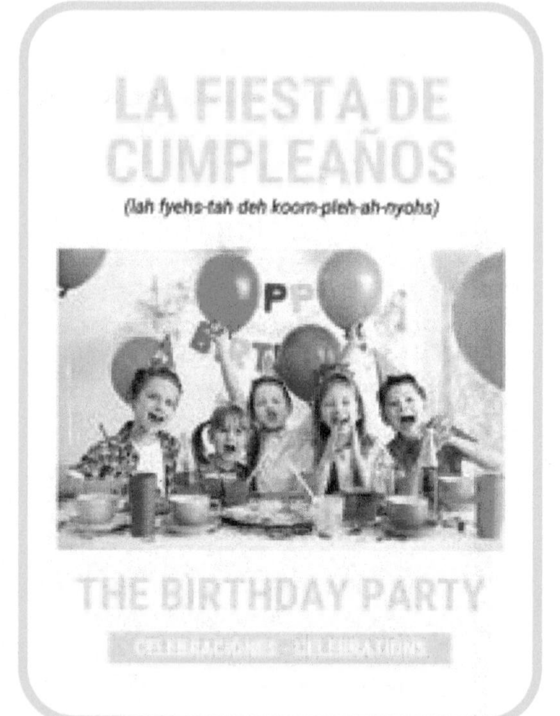
LA FIESTA DE CUMPLEAÑOS
(lah fyehs-tah deh koom-pleh-ah-nyohs)
THE BIRTHDAY PARTY
CELEBRACIONES - CELEBRATIONS

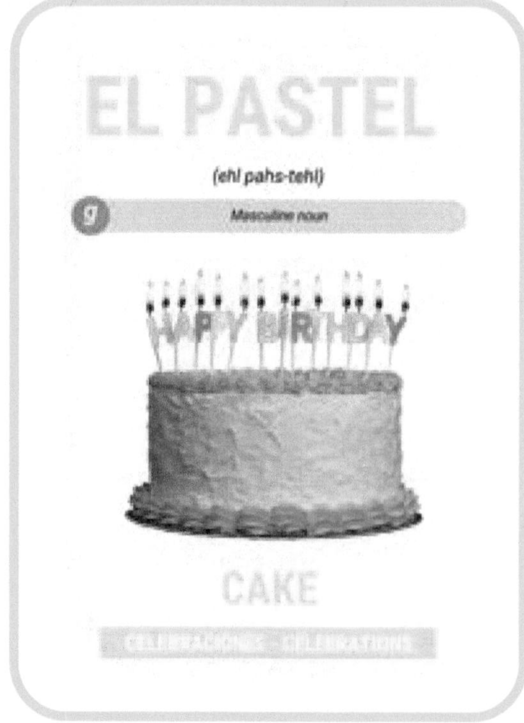
EL PASTEL
(ehl pahs-tehl)
g
Masculine noun
HAPPY BIRTHDAY
CAKE
CELEBRACIONES - CELEBRATIONS

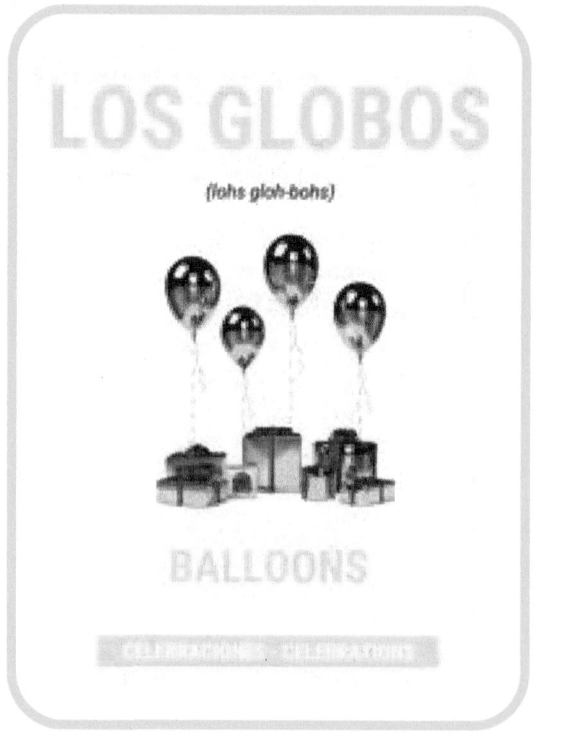
LOS GLOBOS
(lohs gloh-bohs)
BALLOONS
CELEBRACIONES - CELEBRATIONS

LAS SERPENTINAS
(lahs sehr-pehn-tee-nahs)
STREAMERS
CELEBRACIONES - CELEBRATIONS

EL CONFETI
(ehl kohm-feh-tee)
g
Masculine noun
CONFETTI
CELEBRACIONES - CELEBRATIONS

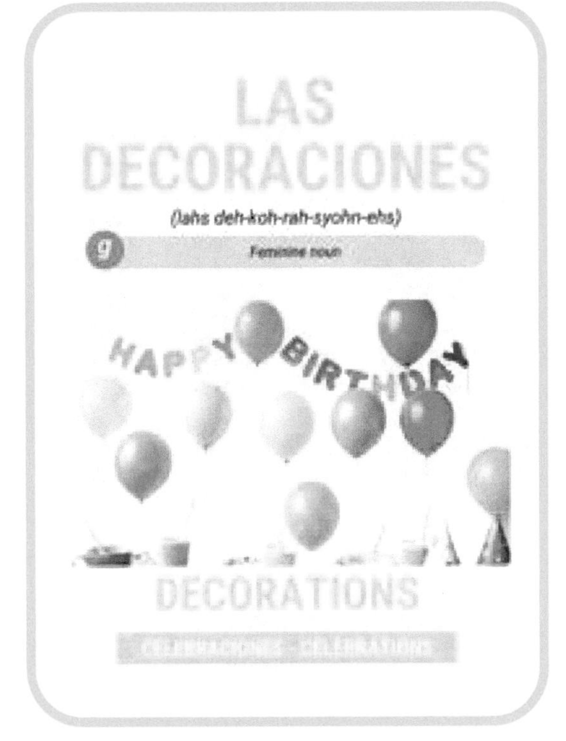
LAS DECORACIONES
(lahs deh-koh-rah-syohn-ehs)
g
Feminine noun
HAPPY BIRTHDAY
DECORATIONS
CELEBRACIONES - CELEBRATIONS

LOS GORROS
(lohs goh-rrohs)
PARTY HATS
CELEBRACIONES - CELEBRATIONS

LOS REGALOS

(lohs rreh-gah-lohs)

PRESENTS

CELEBRACIONES - CELEBRATIONS

LAS VELAS

(lahs beh-lahs)

CANDLES

CELEBRACIONES - CELEBRATIONS

LOS JUEGOS

(lohs hweh-gohs)

GAMES

CELEBRACIONES - CELEBRATIONS

LAS BEBIDAS

(lahs beh-bee-dahs)

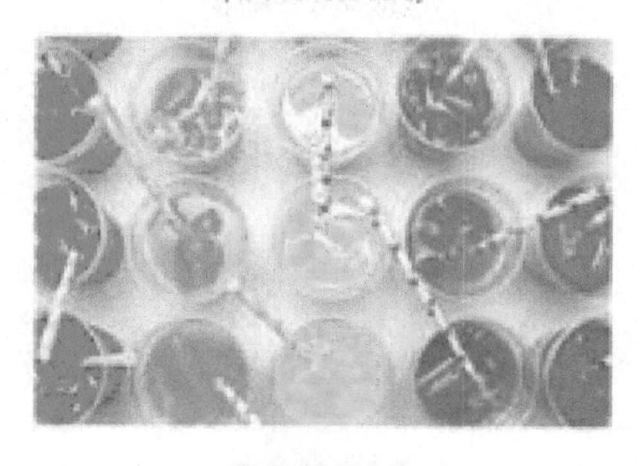

DRINKS

CELEBRACIONES - CELEBRATIONS

LA COMIDA

(lah koh-mee-dah)

FOOD

CELEBRACIONES - CELEBRATIONS

LA MÚSICA

(lah moo-see-kah)

MUSIC

CELEBRACIONES - CELEBRATIONS

BAILAR

(bay-lahr)

V — Bailo salsa y bachata / I dance salsa and bachata

TO DANCE

CELEBRACIONES - CELEBRATIONS

EL CUMPLEAÑERO / LA CUMPLEAÑERA

(ehl koom-plah-nyeh-roh / lah koom-plah-nyeh-rah)

BIRTHDAY BOY / BIRTHDAY GIRL

CELEBRACIONES - CELEBRATIONS

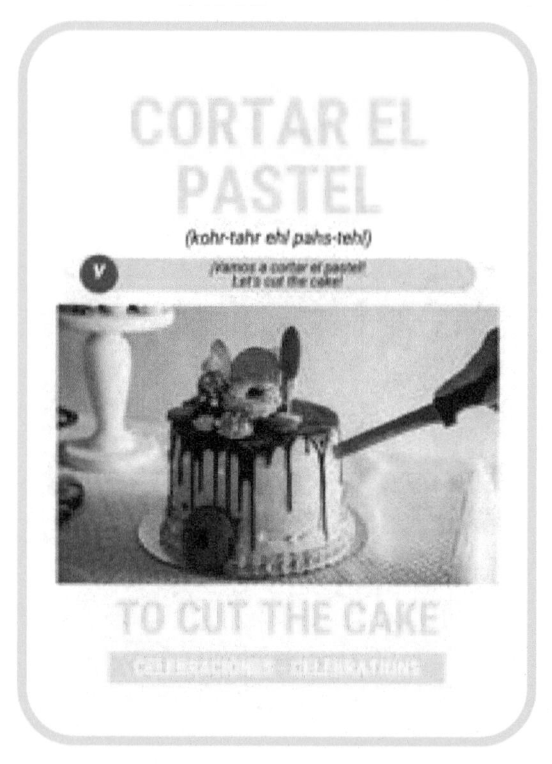
CORTAR EL PASTEL
(kohr-tahr ehl pahs-tehl)
V
¡Vamos a cortar el pastel!
Let's cut the cake!
TO CUT THE CAKE
CELEBRACIONES - CELEBRATIONS

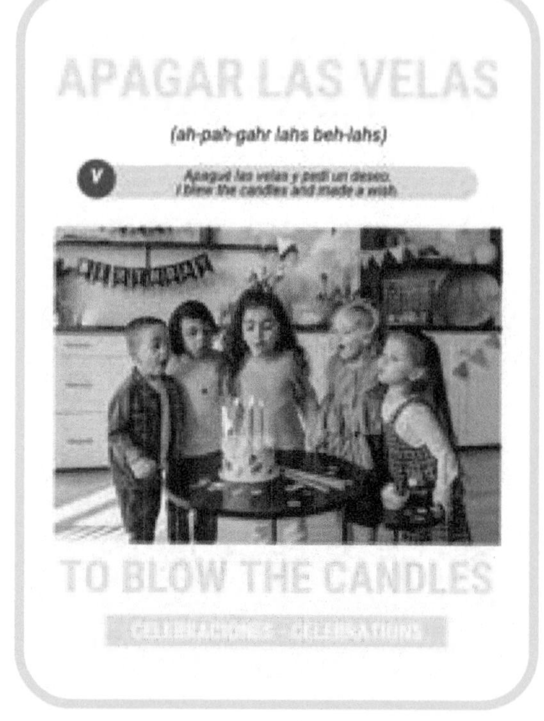
APAGAR LAS VELAS
(ah-pah-gahr lahs beh-lahs)
V
Apagué las velas y pedí un deseo.
I blew the candles and made a wish.
TO BLOW THE CANDLES
CELEBRACIONES - CELEBRATIONS

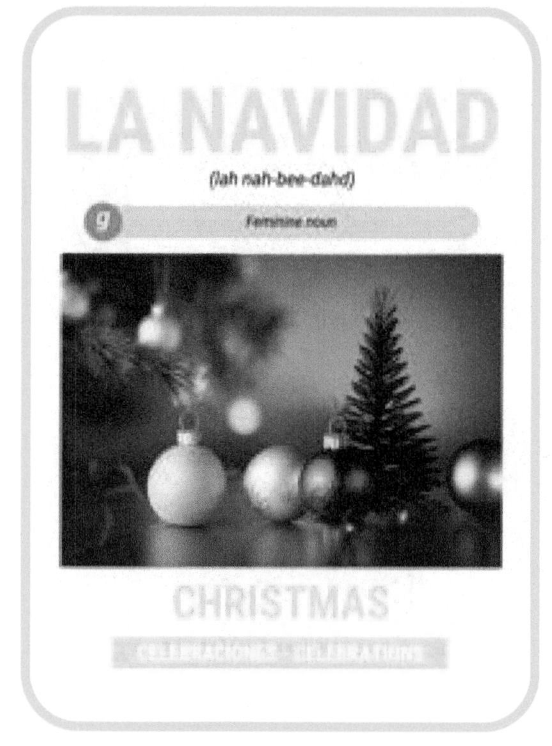
LA NAVIDAD
(lah nah-bee-dahd)
g
Feminine noun
CHRISTMAS
CELEBRACIONES - CELEBRATIONS

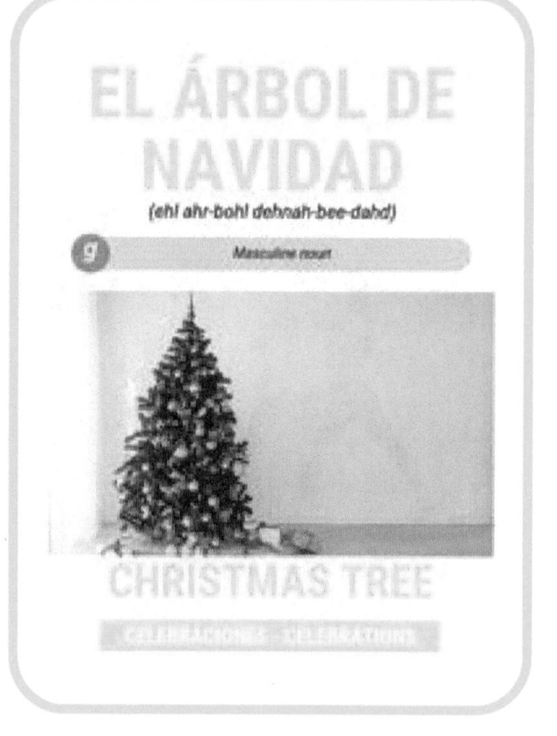
EL ÁRBOL DE NAVIDAD
(ehl ahr-bohl dehnah-bee-dahd)
g
Masculine noun
CHRISTMAS TREE
CELEBRACIONES - CELEBRATIONS

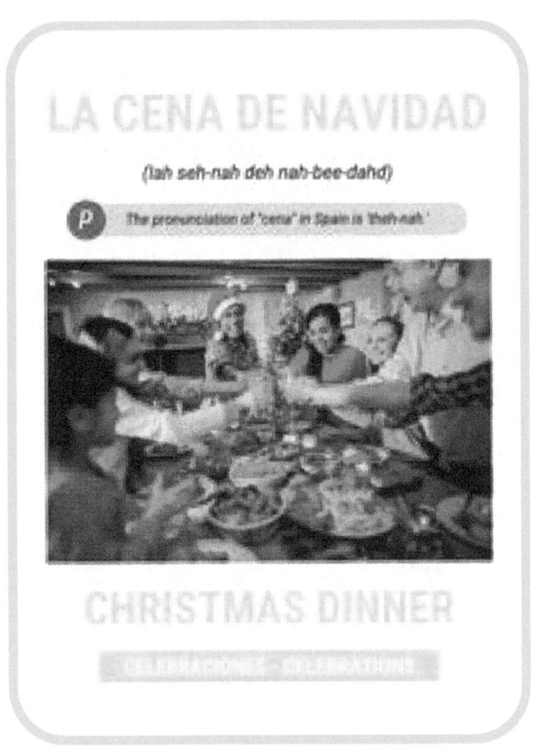
LA CENA DE NAVIDAD
(lah seh-nah deh nah-bee-dahd)
P
The pronunciation of "cena" in Spain is 'theh-nah.'
CHRISTMAS DINNER

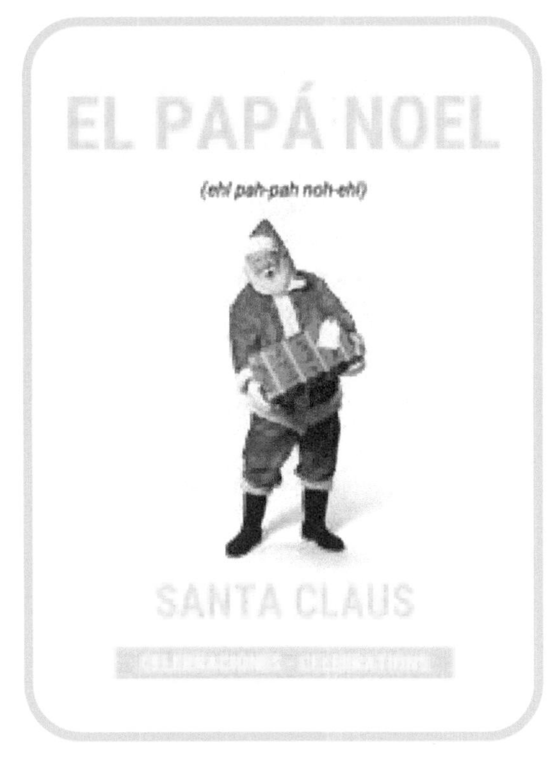
EL PAPÁ NOEL
(ehl pah-pah noh-ehl)
SANTA CLAUS

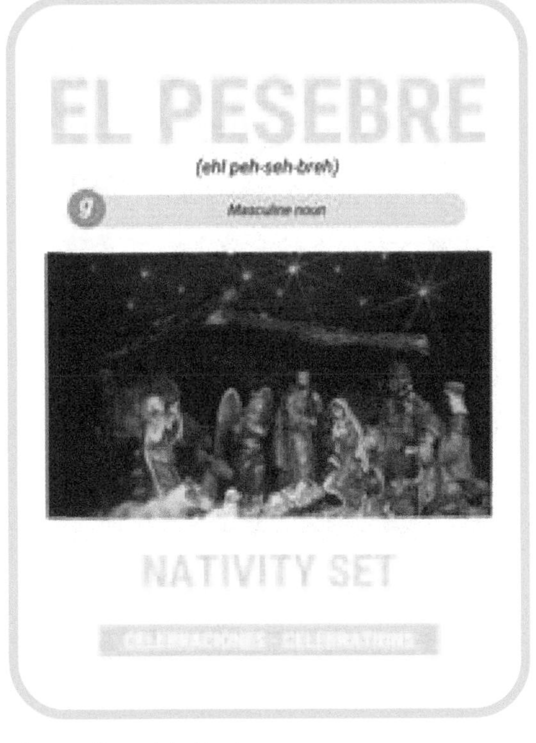
EL PESEBRE
(ehl peh-seh-breh)
g
Masculine noun
NATIVITY SET

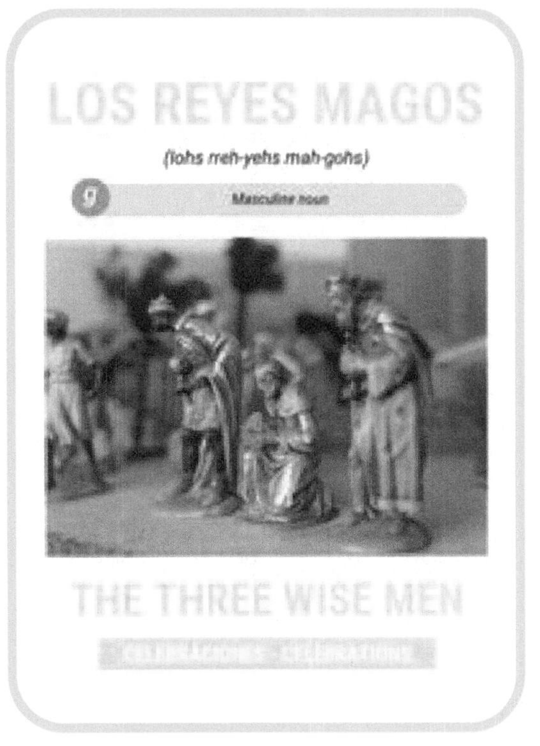
LOS REYES MAGOS
(lohs reh-yehs mah-gohs)
g
Masculine noun
THE THREE WISE MEN

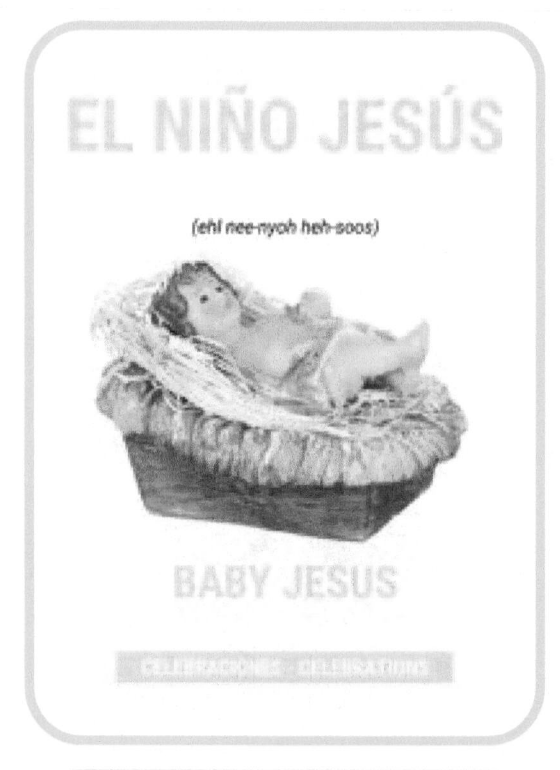
EL NIÑO JESÚS
(ehl nee-nyoh heh-soos)
BABY JESUS
CELEBRACIONES - CELEBRATIONS

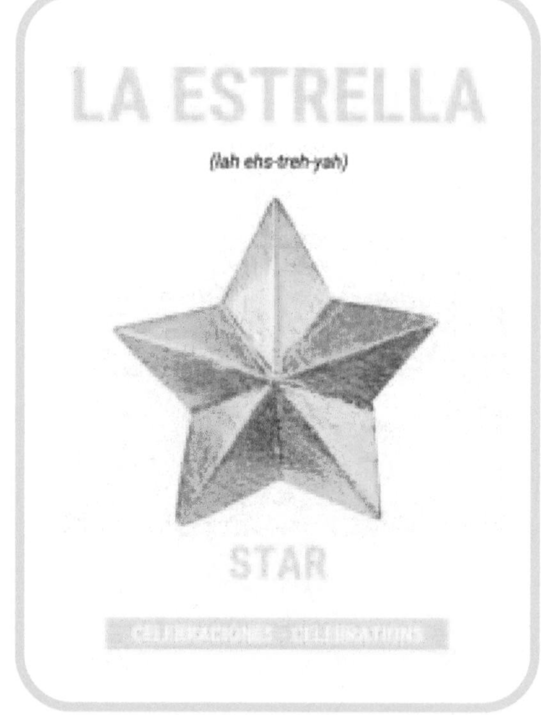
LA ESTRELLA
(lah ehs-treh-yah)
STAR
CELEBRACIONES - CELEBRATIONS

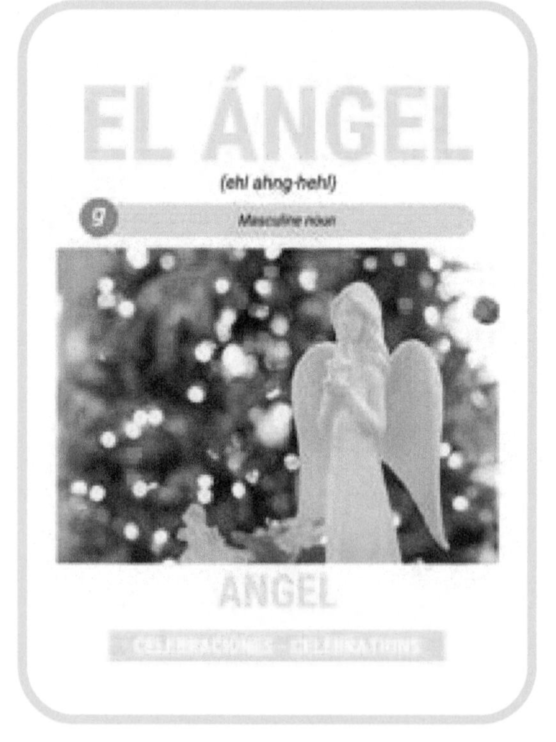
EL ÁNGEL
(ehl ahng-hehl)
g
Masculine noun
ANGEL
CELEBRACIONES - CELEBRATIONS

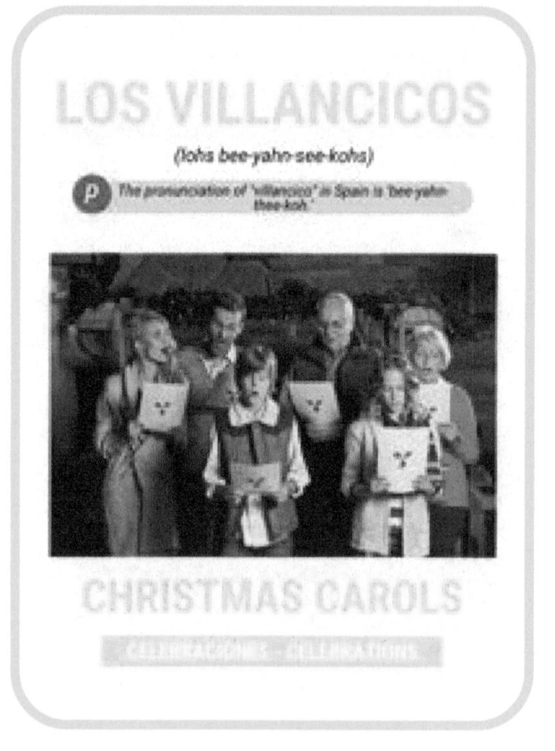
LOS VILLANCICOS
(lohs bee-yahn-see-kohs)
p
The pronunciation of "villancico" in Spain is "bee-yahn-thee-koh."
CHRISTMAS CAROLS
CELEBRACIONES - CELEBRATIONS

¡FELIZ NAVIDAD!
(feh-lees nah-bee-dahd)
p
The pronunciation of "feliz" in Spain is "feh-leeth."
MERRY CHRISTMAS!
CELEBRACIONES - CELEBRATIONS

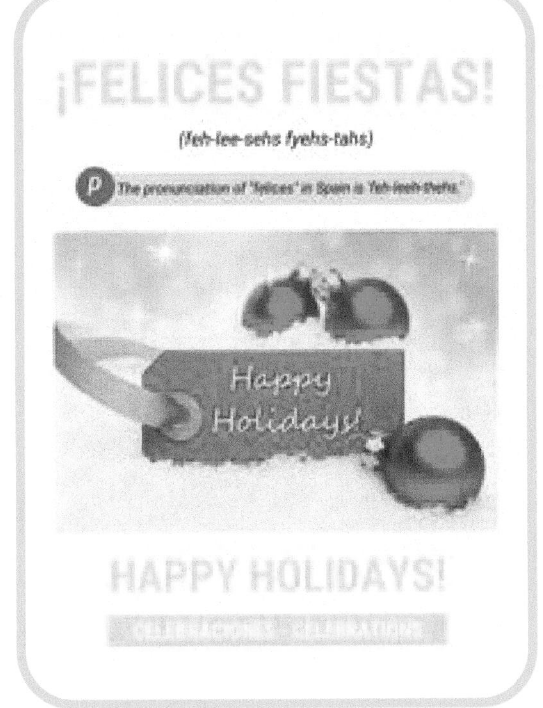

¡FELICES FIESTAS!
(feh-lee-sehs fyehs-tahs)
p
The pronunciation of "felices" in Spain is "feh-leeh-thehs."
Happy Holidays!
HAPPY HOLIDAYS!
CELEBRACIONES - CELEBRATIONS

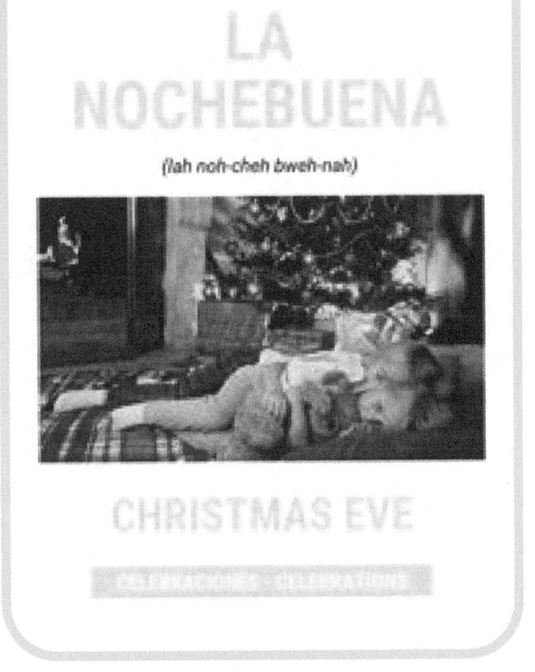

LA NOCHEBUENA
(lah noh-cheh bweh-nah)
CHRISTMAS EVE
CELEBRACIONES - CELEBRATIONS

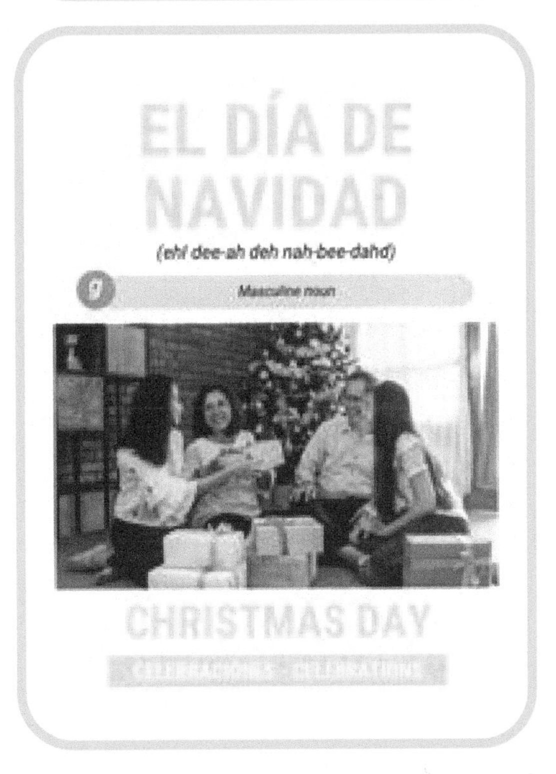

EL DÍA DE NAVIDAD
(ehl dee-ah deh nah-bee-dahd)
g
Masculine noun
CHRISTMAS DAY
CELEBRACIONES - CELEBRATIONS

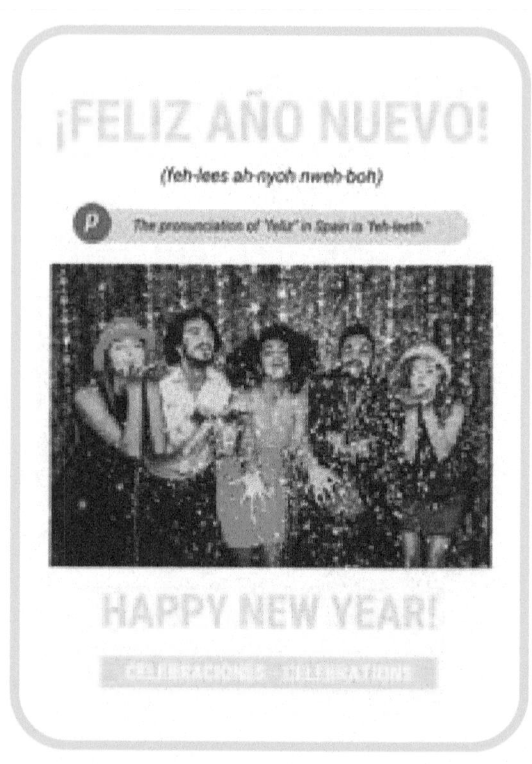
¡FELIZ AÑO NUEVO!
(feh-lees ah-nyoh nweh-boh)
P
The pronunciation of "feliz" in Spain is "feh-leeth."
HAPPY NEW YEAR!
CELEBRACIONES - CELEBRATIONS

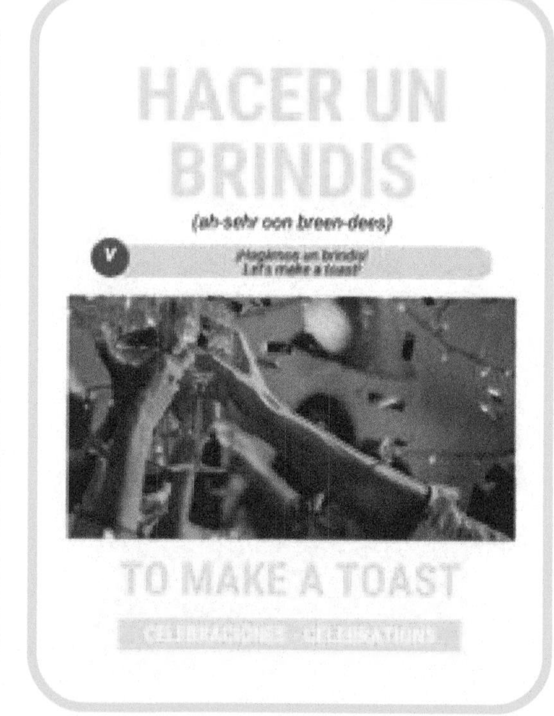
HACER UN BRINDIS
(ah-sehr oon breen-dees)
V
¡Hagamos un brindis!
Let's make a toast!
TO MAKE A TOAST
CELEBRACIONES - CELEBRATIONS

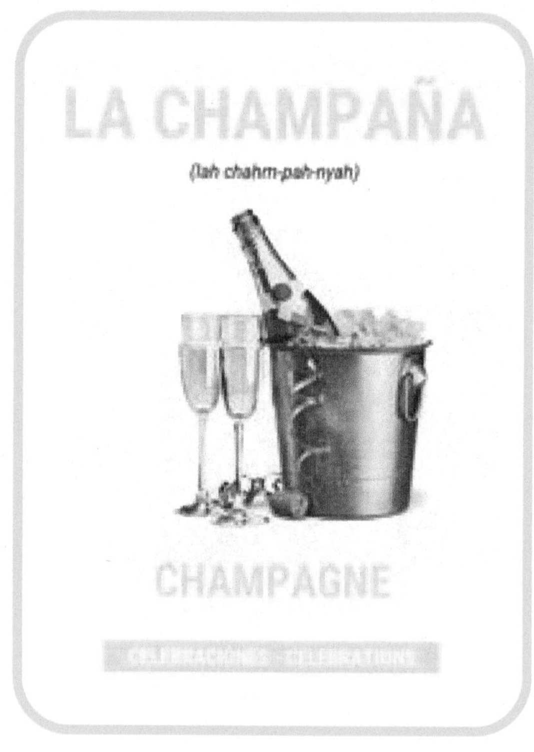
LA CHAMPAÑA
(lah chahm-pah-nyah)
CHAMPAGNE
CELEBRACIONES - CELEBRATIONS

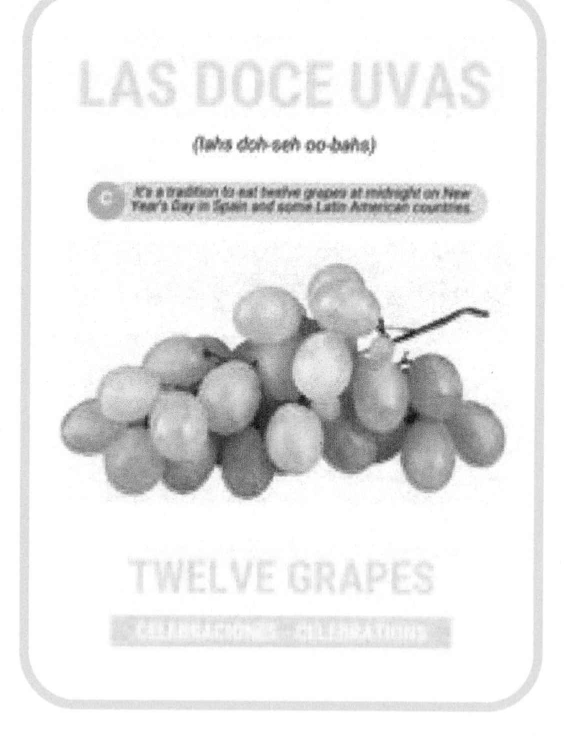
LAS DOCE UVAS
(lahs doh-seh oo-bahs)
C
It's a tradition to eat twelve grapes at midnight on New Year's Day in Spain and some Latin American countries.
TWELVE GRAPES
CELEBRACIONES - CELEBRATIONS

LA MEDIANOCHE
(lah meh-dyah-noh-cheh)
g
Feminine noun
MIDNIGHT

LOS FUEGOS ARTIFICIALES
(lohs fweh-gohs ahr-teefee-syahl-ehs)
p
The pronunciation of "artificiales" in Spain is "ahr-tee-fee-thyahl-ehs."
FIREWORKS

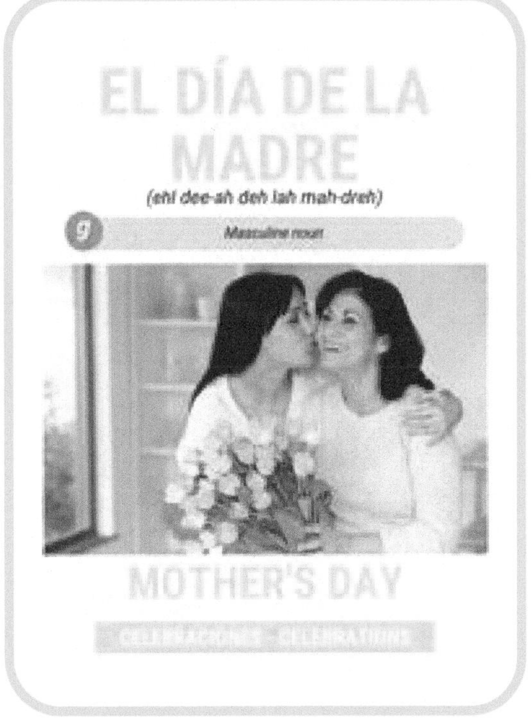
EL DÍA DE LA MADRE
(ehl dee-ah deh lah mah-dreh)
g
Masculine noun
MOTHER'S DAY

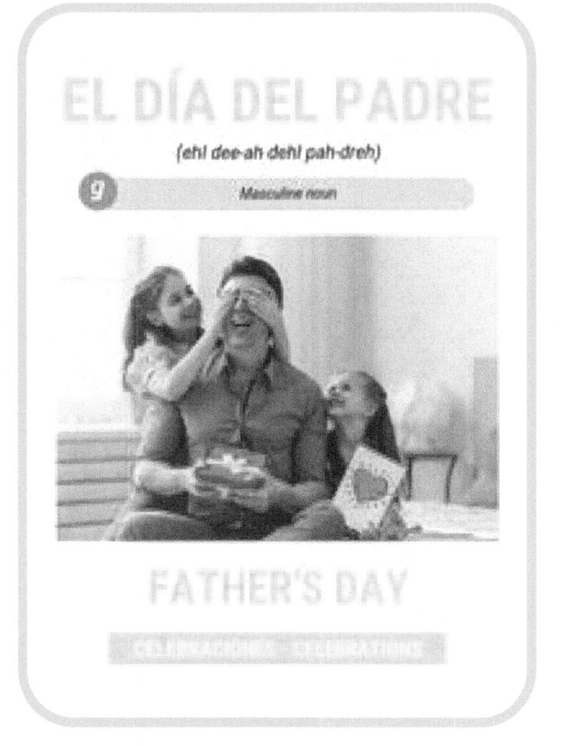
EL DÍA DEL PADRE
(ehl dee-ah dehl pah-dreh)
g
Masculine noun
FATHER'S DAY

EL ANIVERSARIO DE BODAS

(ehl ah-nee-behr-sah-ryoh deh boh-dahs)

g Masculine noun

WEDDING ANNIVERSARY

CELEBRACIONES - CELEBRATIONS

UNA BODA

(oo-nah boh-dah)

A WEDDING

CELEBRACIONES - CELEBRATIONS

LOS NOVIOS

(lohs noh-byohs)

THE BRIDE AND GROOM

CELEBRACIONES - CELEBRATIONS

LA LUNA DE MIEL

(lah loo-nah deh myehl)

g Feminine noun

HONEYMOON

CELEBRACIONES - CELEBRATIONS

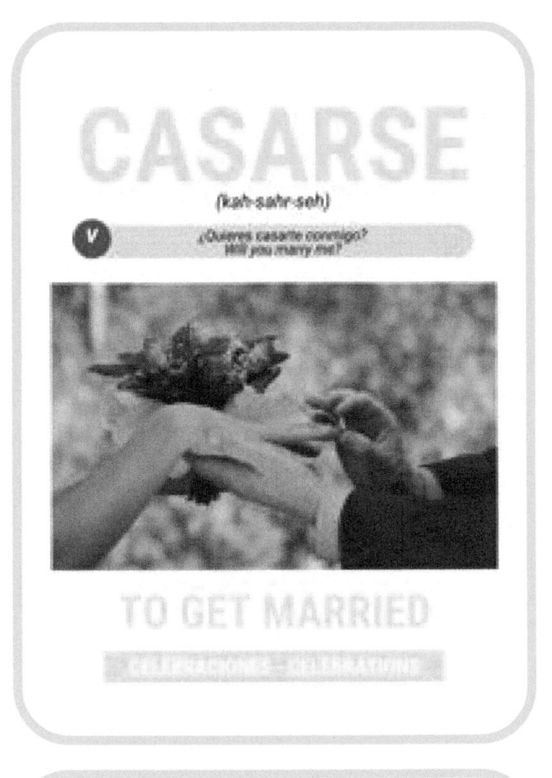
CASARSE
(kah-sahr-seh)
V
¿Quieres casarte conmigo?
Will you marry me?
TO GET MARRIED
CELEBRACIONES - CELEBRATIONS

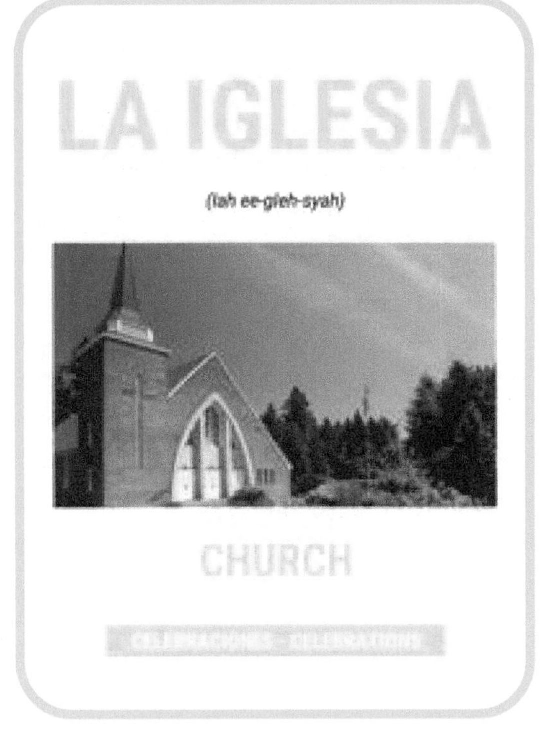
LA IGLESIA
(lah ee-gleh-syah)
CHURCH
CELEBRACIONES - CELEBRATIONS

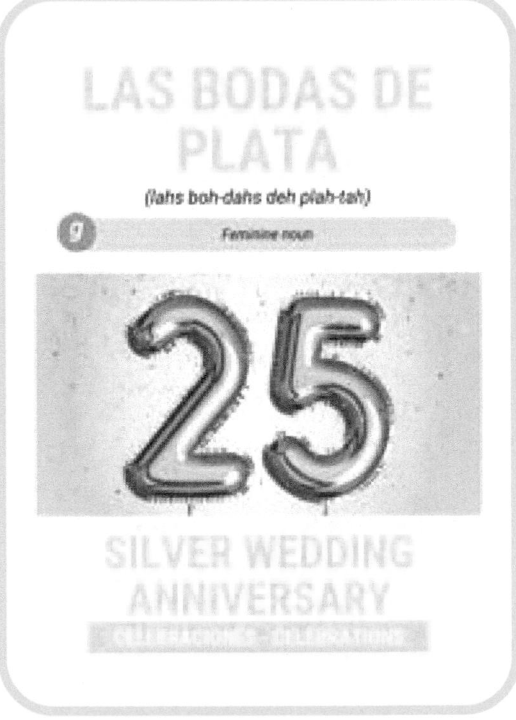
LAS BODAS DE PLATA
(lahs boh-dahs deh plah-tah)
g
Feminine noun
25
SILVER WEDDING ANNIVERSARY
CELEBRACIONES - CELEBRATIONS

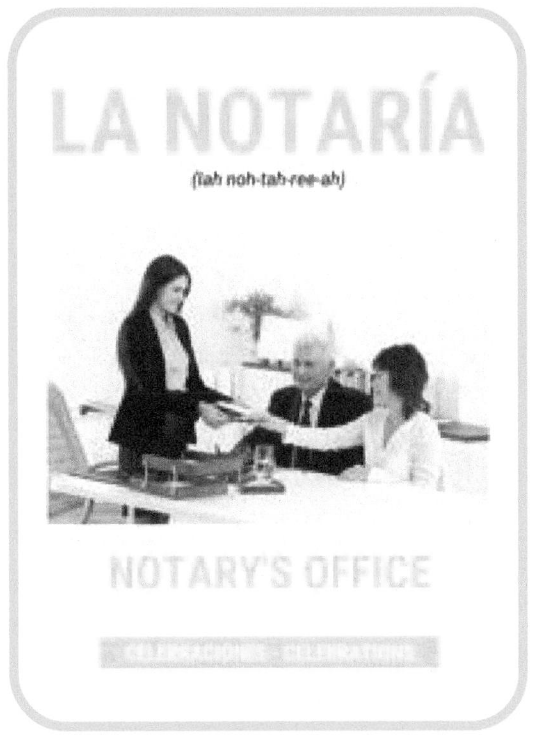
LA NOTARÍA
(lah noh-tah-ree-ah)
NOTARY'S OFFICE
CELEBRACIONES - CELEBRATIONS

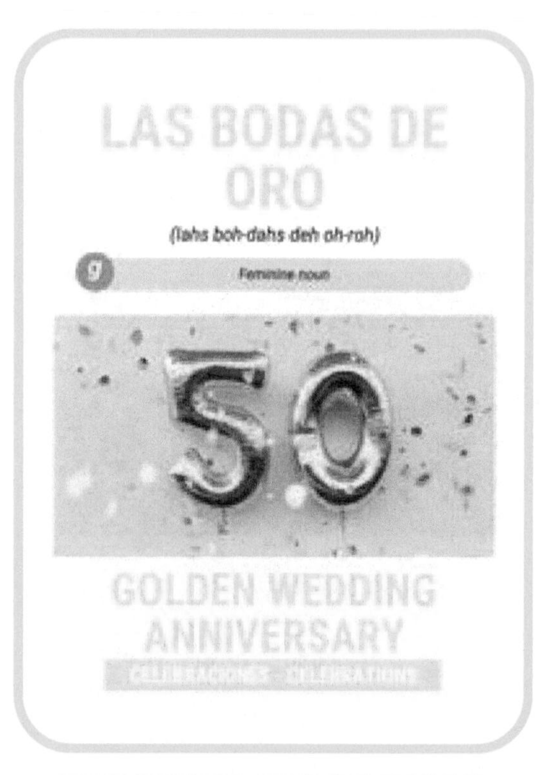
LAS BODAS DE ORO
(lahs boh-dahs deh oh-roh)
g
Feminine noun
GOLDEN WEDDING ANNIVERSARY
CELEBRACIONES · CELEBRATIONS

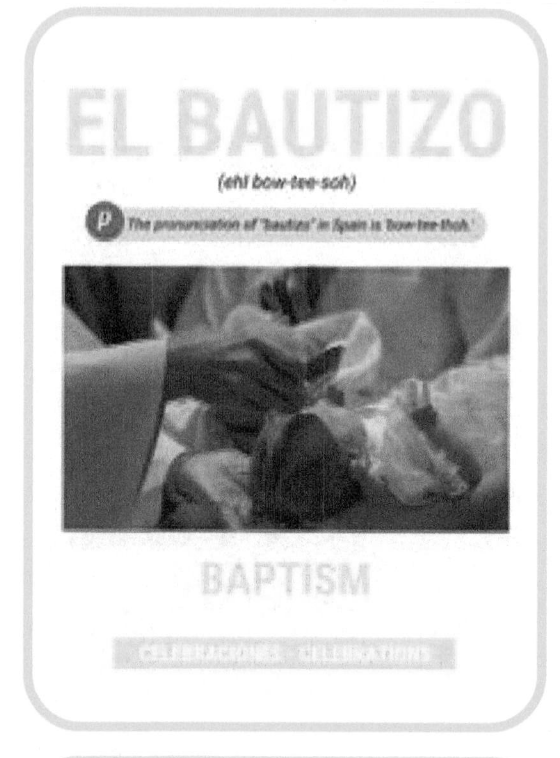
EL BAUTIZO
(ehl bow-tee-soh)
p
The pronunciation of "bautizo" in Spain is 'bow-tee-thoh.'
BAPTISM
CELEBRACIONES · CELEBRATIONS

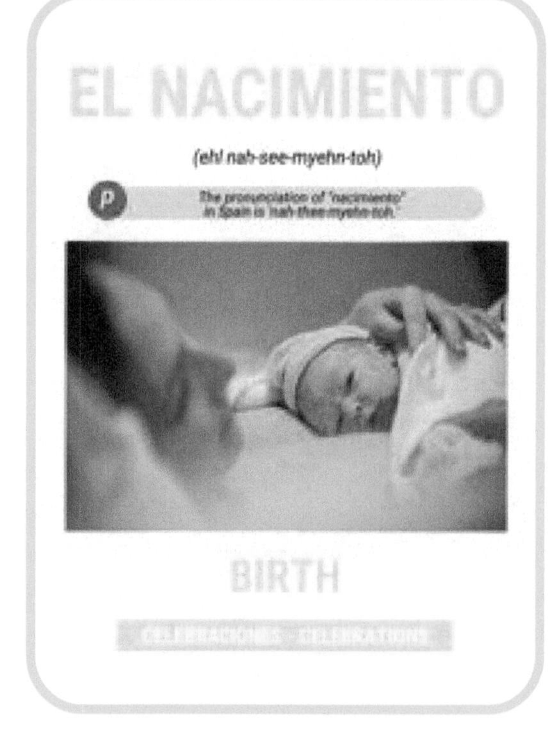
EL NACIMIENTO
(ehl nah-see-myehn-toh)
p
The pronunciation of "nacimiento" in Spain is 'nah-thee-myehn-toh.'
BIRTH
CELEBRACIONES · CELEBRATIONS

EL FUNERAL
(ehl foo-neh-rahl)
g
Masculine noun
FUNERAL
CELEBRACIONES · CELEBRATIONS

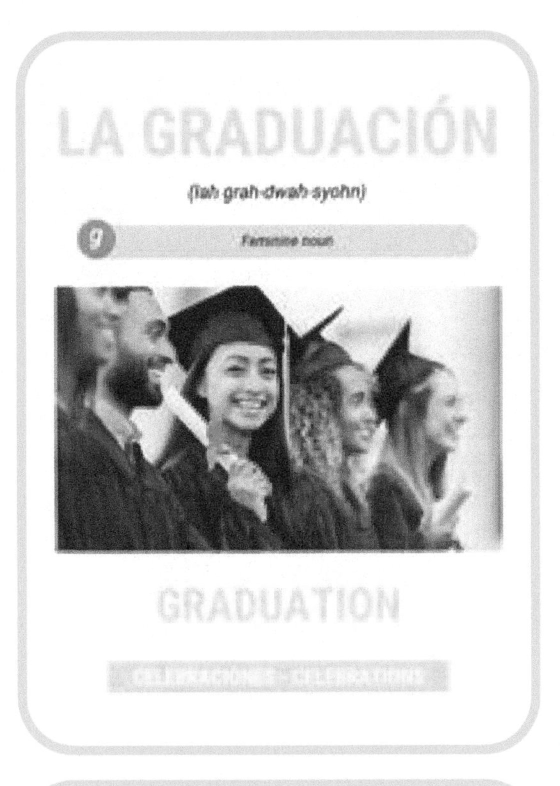
LA GRADUACIÓN
(lah grah-dwah-syohn)
g
Feminine noun
GRADUATION
CELEBRACIONES - CELEBRATIONS

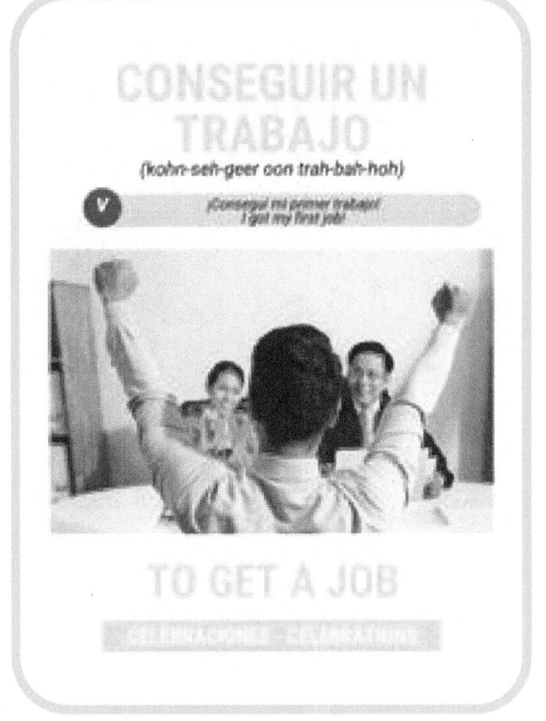
CONSEGUIR UN TRABAJO
(kohn-seh-geer oon trah-bah-hoh)
v
¡Conseguí mi primer trabajo!
I got my first job!
TO GET A JOB
CELEBRACIONES - CELEBRATIONS

LA PRIMERA COMUNIÓN
(lah pree-meh-rah koh-moo-nyohn)
g
Feminine noun
FIRST COMMUNION
CELEBRACIONES - CELEBRATIONS

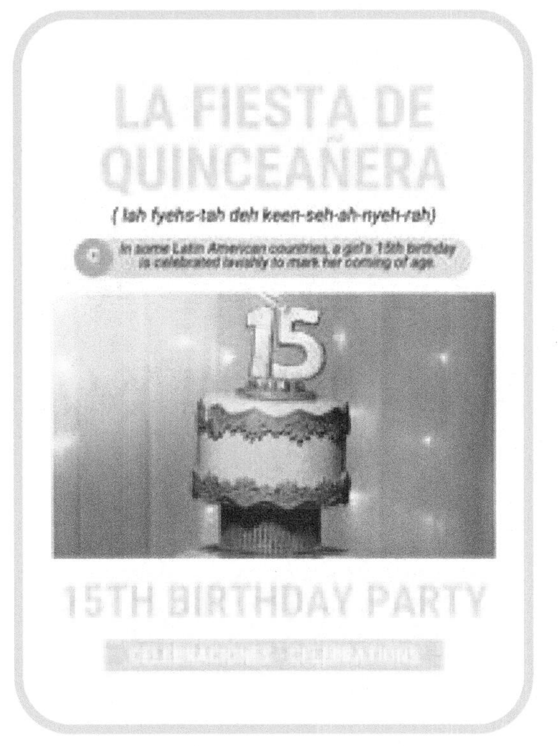
LA FIESTA DE QUINCEAÑERA
(lah fyehs-tah deh keen-seh-ah-nyeh-rah)
In some Latin American countries, a girl's 15th birthday is celebrated lavishly to mark her coming of age.
15
15TH BIRTHDAY PARTY
CELEBRACIONES - CELEBRATIONS

EL VESTIDO

(ehl behs-tee-doh)

DRESS

CELEBRACIONES - CELEBRATIONS

LAS FLORES

(lahs floh-rehs)

g Feminine noun

FLOWERS

CELEBRACIONES - CELEBRATIONS

EL BESO

(ehl beh-soh)

KISS

CELEBRACIONES - CELEBRATIONS

EL ABRAZO

(ehl ah-brah-soh)

p *The pronunciation of "abrazo" in Spain is "ah-brah-thoh."*

HUG

CELEBRACIONES - CELEBRATIONS

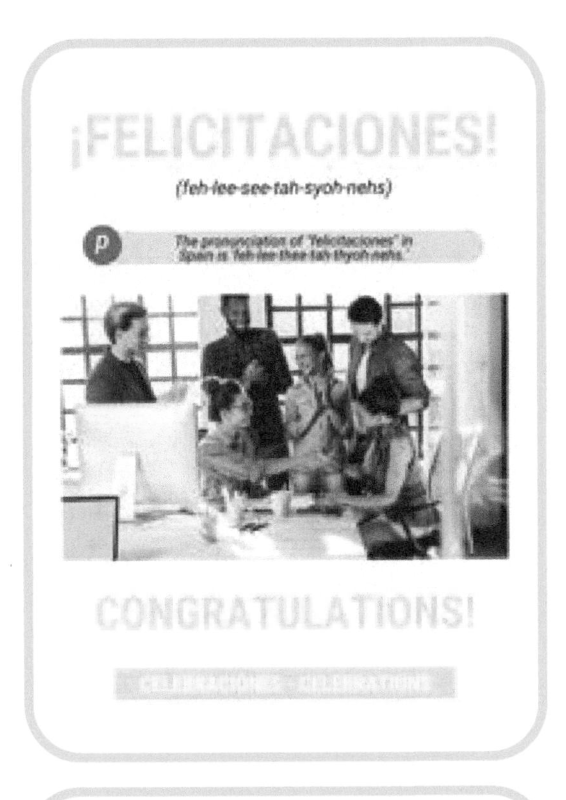
¡FELICITACIONES!
(feh-lee-see-tah-syoh-nehs)
p
The pronunciation of "felicitaciones" in Spain is 'feh-lee-thee-tah-thyoh-nehs.'
CONGRATULATIONS!
CELEBRACIONES - CELEBRATIONS

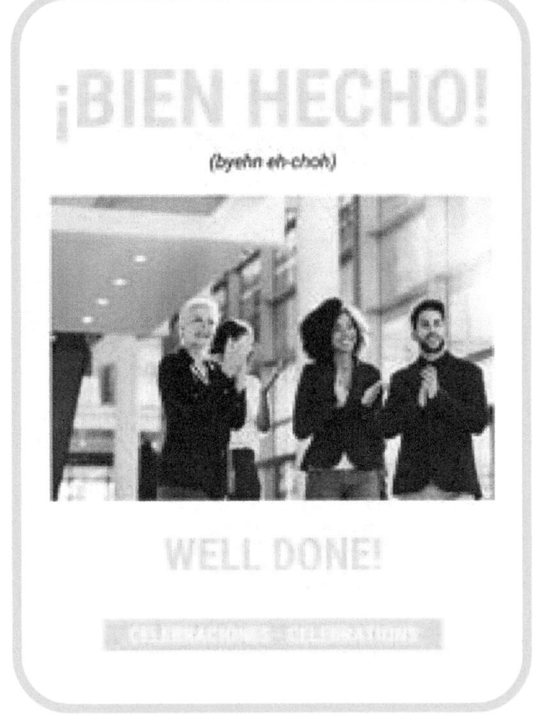
¡BIEN HECHO!
(byehn eh-choh)
WELL DONE!
CELEBRACIONES - CELEBRATIONS

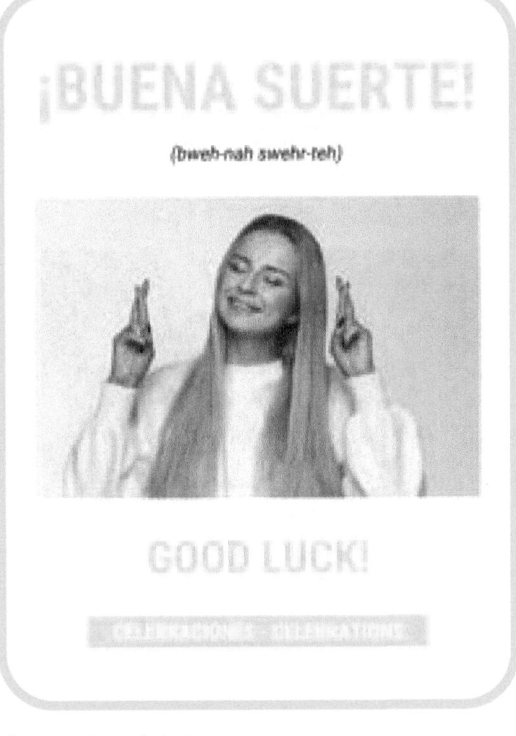
¡BUENA SUERTE!
(bweh-nah swehr-teh)
GOOD LUCK!
CELEBRACIONES - CELEBRATIONS

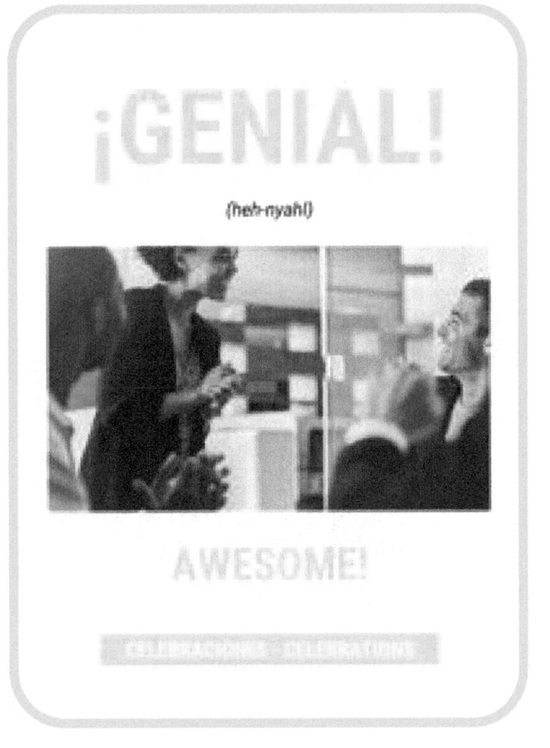
¡GENIAL!
(heh-nyahl)
AWESOME!
CELEBRACIONES - CELEBRATIONS

QUISIERA VER UN MÉDICO

(kee-syeh-rah behr oon meh-dee-koh)

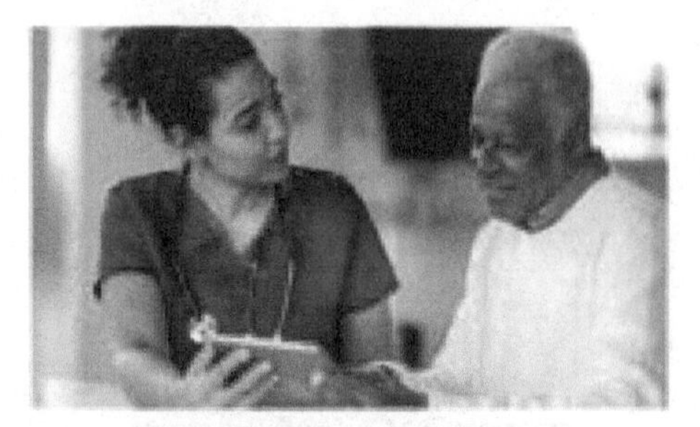

I'D LIKE TO SEE A DOCTOR

LA SALUD - HEALTH

UNA CITA

(oo-nah see-tah)

p — *The pronunciation of "cita" in Spain is 'thee-tah.'*

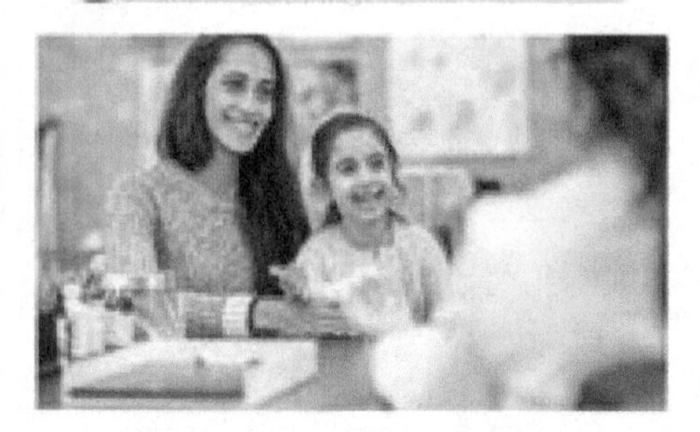

AN APPOINTMENT

LA SALUD - HEALTH

¡ES UNA EMERGENCIA!

(ehs oo-nah eh-mehr-hehn-syah)

p — *The pronunciation of "emergencia" in Spain is 'eh-mehr-hehn-thyah.'*

IT'S AN EMERGENCY!

LA SALUD - HEALTH

EL HOSPITAL

(ehl ohs-pee-tahl)

g — *Masculine noun*

HOSPITAL

LA SALUD - HEALTH

EL CENTRO DE SALUD

(ehl sehn-troh deh sah-lood)

p The pronunciation of "centro" in Spain is "thehn-troh."

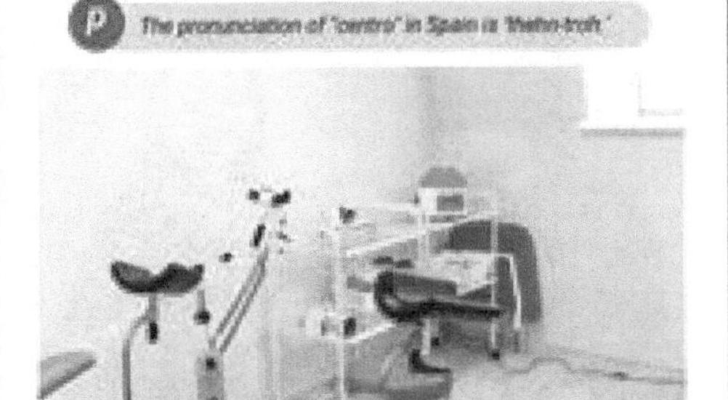

MEDICAL CENTER

LA SALUD - HEALTH

LA AMBULANCIA

(lah ahm-boo-lahn-syah)

p The pronunciation of "ambulancia" in Spain is "ahm-boo-lahn-thyah."

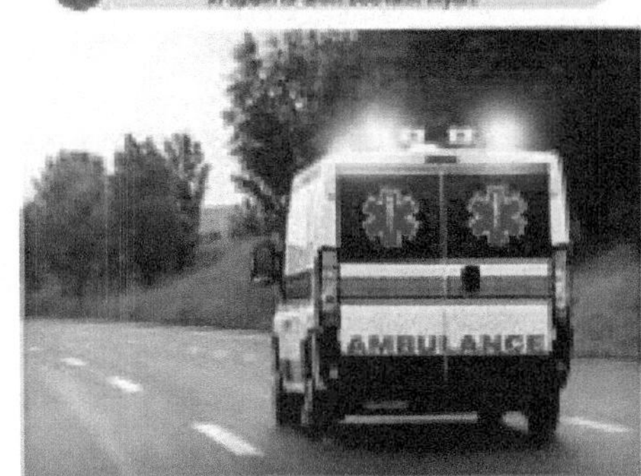

AMBULANCE

LA SALUD - HEALTH

LOS PRIMEROS AUXILIOS

(lohs pree-meh-rohs owk-see-lyohs)

g Masculine noun

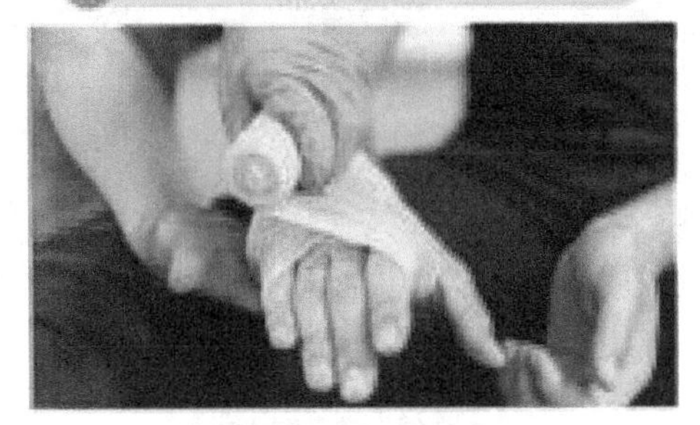

FIRST AID

LA SALUD - HEALTH

¿TIENE UN BOTIQUÍN?

(tyeh-neh oon boh-tee-keen)

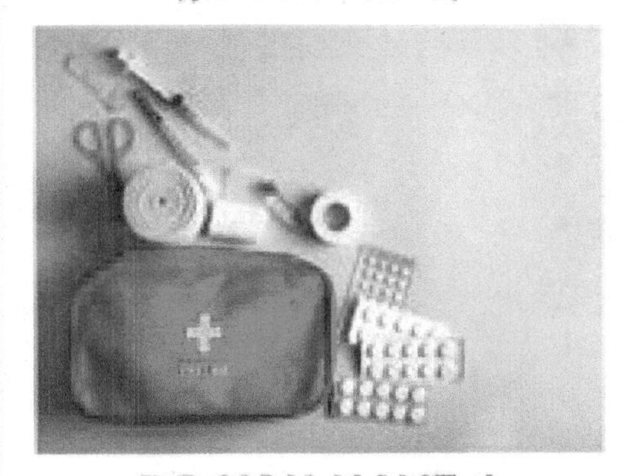

DO YOU HAVE A FIRST AID KIT?

LA SALUD - HEALTH

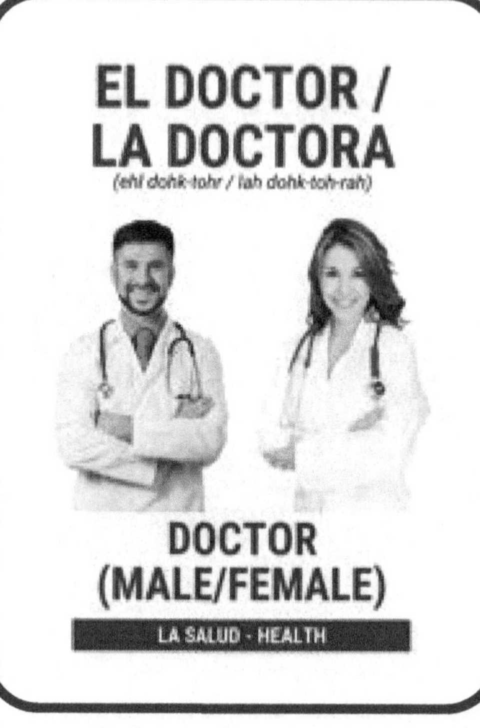
EL DOCTOR /
LA DOCTORA
(ehl dohk-tohr / lah dohk-toh-rah)
DOCTOR
(MALE/FEMALE)
LA SALUD - HEALTH

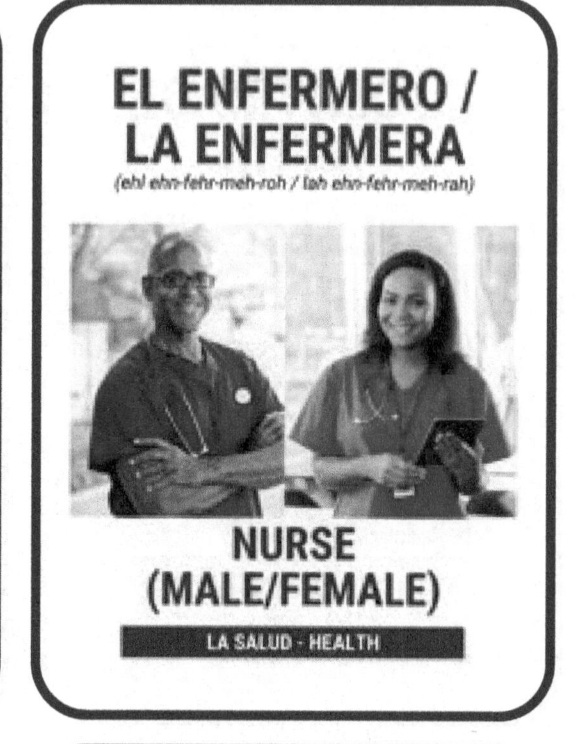
EL ENFERMERO /
LA ENFERMERA
(ehl ehn-fehr-meh-roh / lah ehn-fehr-meh-rah)
NURSE
(MALE/FEMALE)
LA SALUD - HEALTH

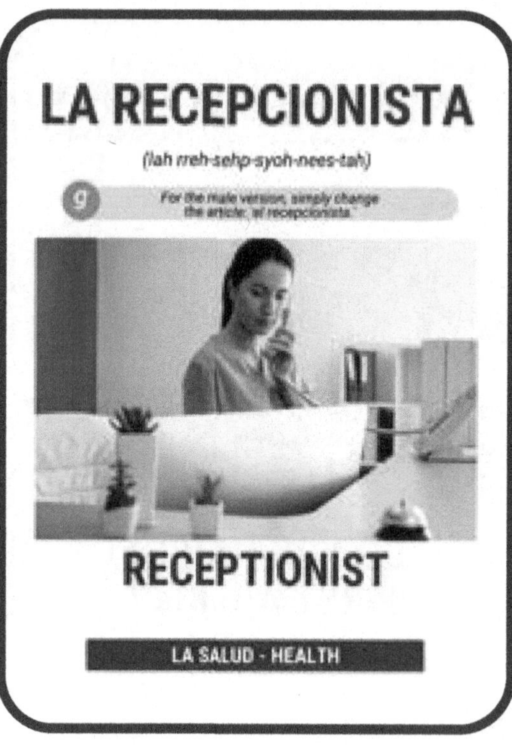
LA RECEPCIONISTA
(lah rreh-sehp-syoh-nees-tah)
g
For the male version, simply change the article: 'el recepcionista.'
RECEPTIONIST
LA SALUD - HEALTH

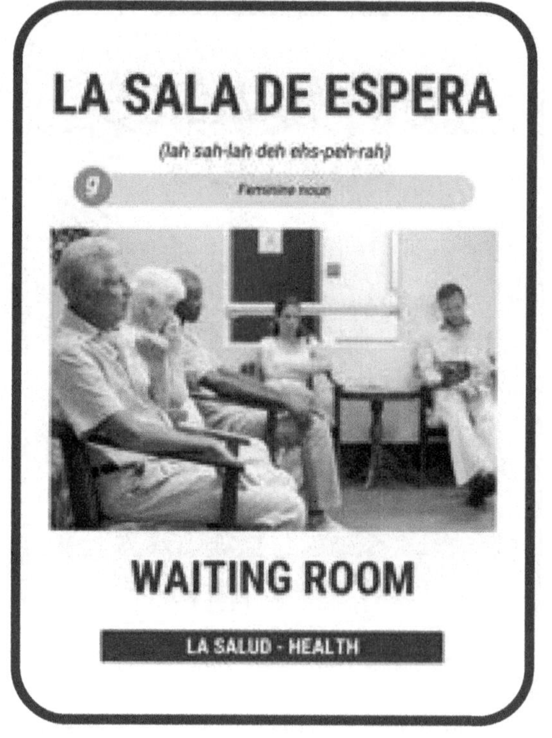
LA SALA DE ESPERA
(lah sah-lah deh ehs-peh-rah)
g
Feminine noun
WAITING ROOM
LA SALUD - HEALTH

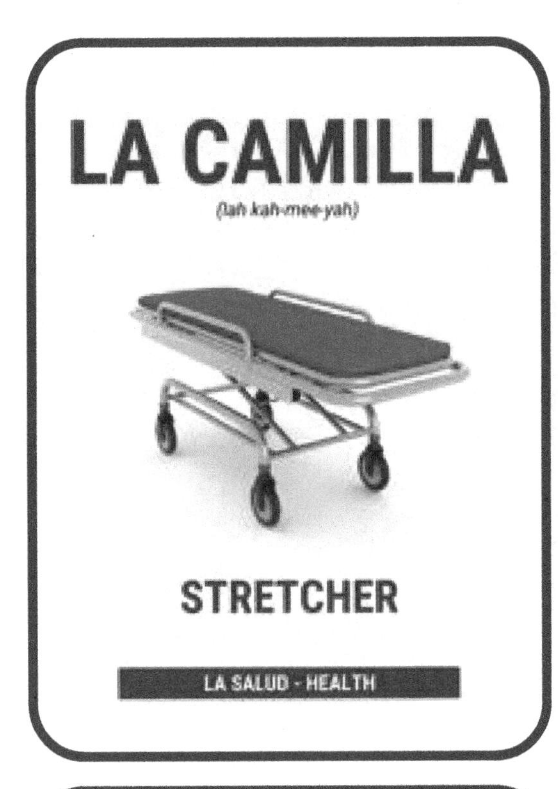
LA CAMILLA
(lah kah-mee-yah)
STRETCHER
LA SALUD - HEALTH

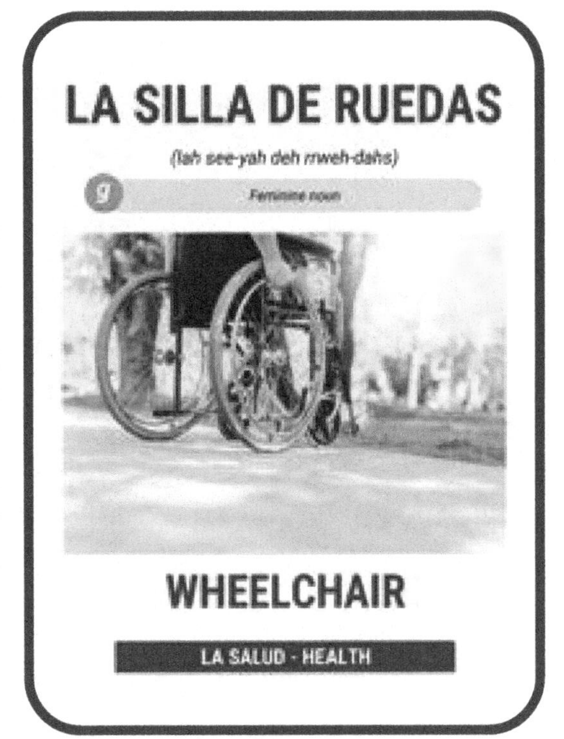
LA SILLA DE RUEDAS
(lah see-yah deh rrweh-dahs)
g
Feminine noun
WHEELCHAIR
LA SALUD - HEALTH

SOY DISCAPACITADO
(soy dees-kah-pah-see-tah-doh)
g
For the female version, simply change the ending: "soy discapacitada."
I AM DISABLED
LA SALUD - HEALTH

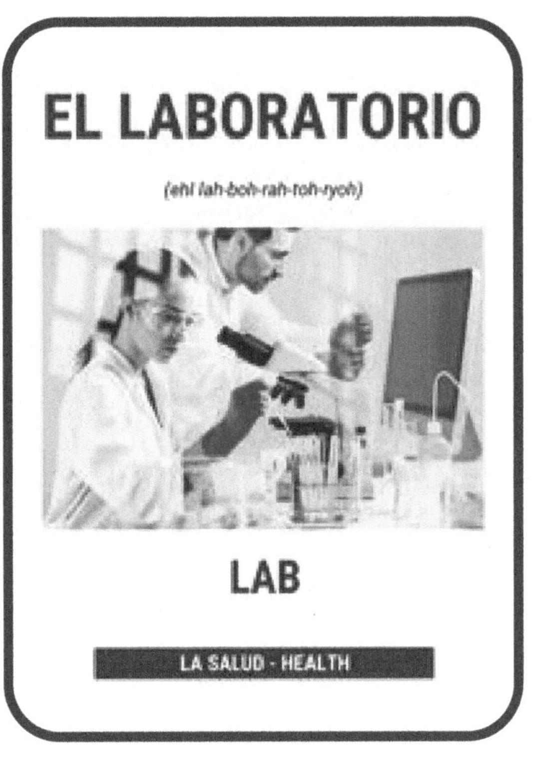
EL LABORATORIO
(ehl lah-boh-rah-toh-ryoh)
LAB
LA SALUD - HEALTH

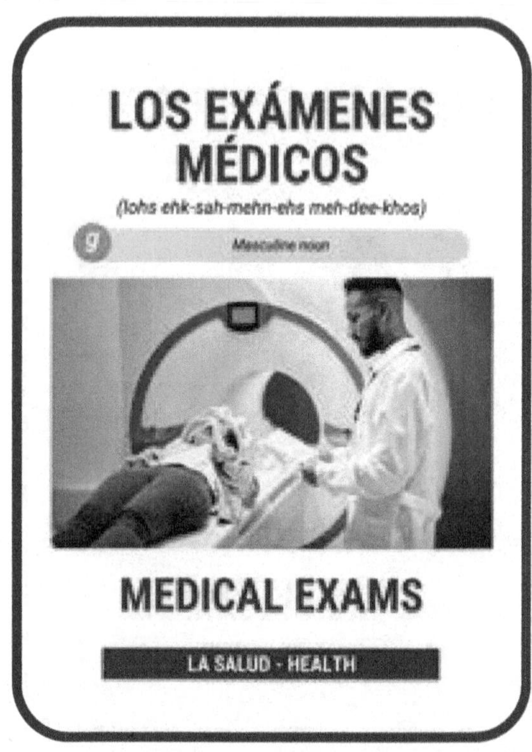
LOS EXÁMENES MÉDICOS
(lohs ehk-sah-mehn-ehs meh-dee-khos)
g
Masculine noun
MEDICAL EXAMS
LA SALUD - HEALTH

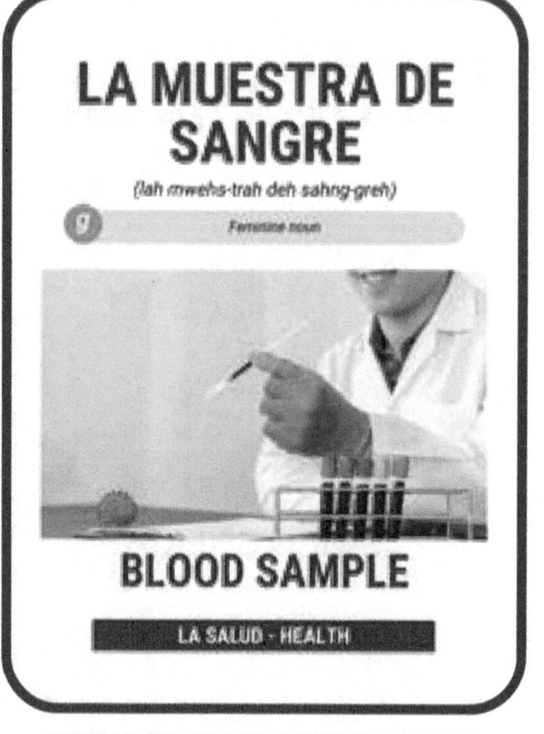
LA MUESTRA DE SANGRE
(lah mwehs-trah deh sahng-greh)
g
Feminine noun
BLOOD SAMPLE
LA SALUD - HEALTH

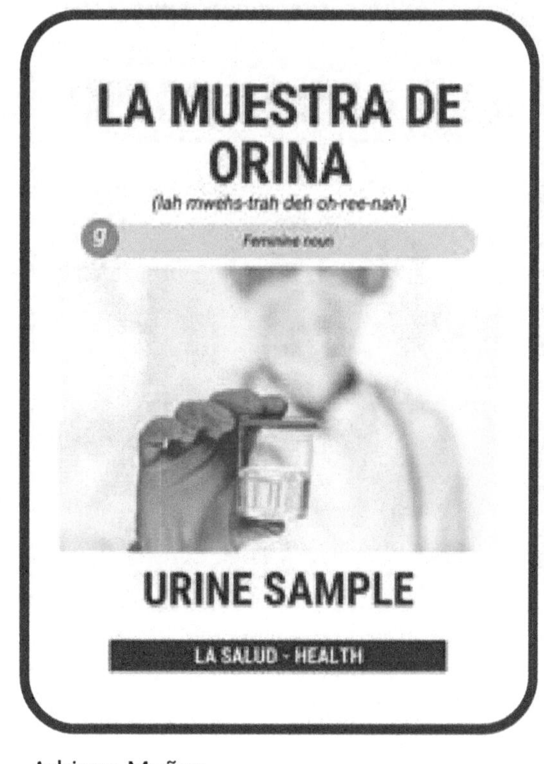
LA MUESTRA DE ORINA
(lah mwehs-trah deh oh-ree-nah)
g
Feminine noun
URINE SAMPLE
LA SALUD - HEALTH

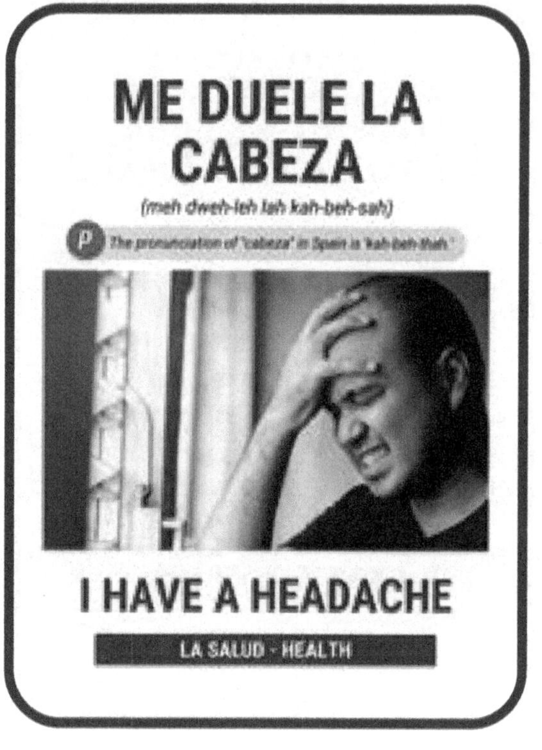
ME DUELE LA CABEZA
(meh dweh-leh lah kah-beh-sah)
p
I HAVE A HEADACHE
LA SALUD - HEALTH

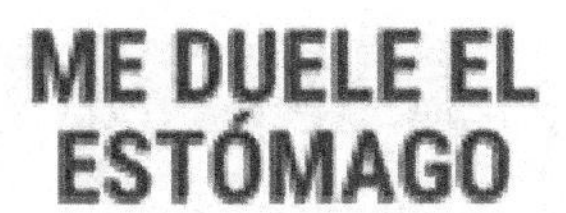

ME DUELE EL ESTÓMAGO

(meh dweh-leh ehl ehs-toh-mah-goh)

Say 'Me duele...' (it hurts) followed by a body part to indicate pain in that particular area.

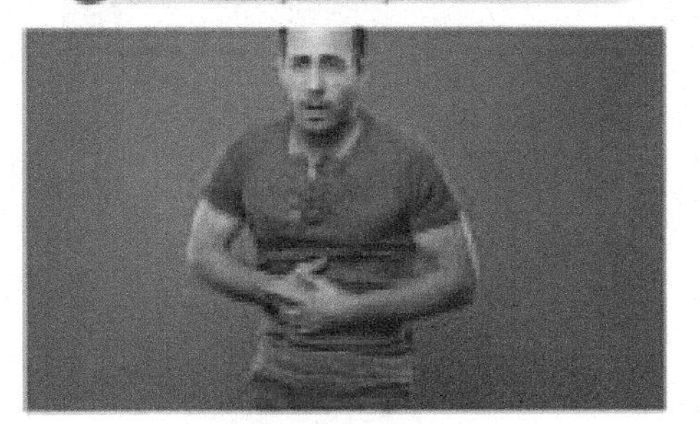

I HAVE A STOMACHACHE

LA SALUD - HEALTH

LA GARGANTA

(lah gahr-gahn-tah)

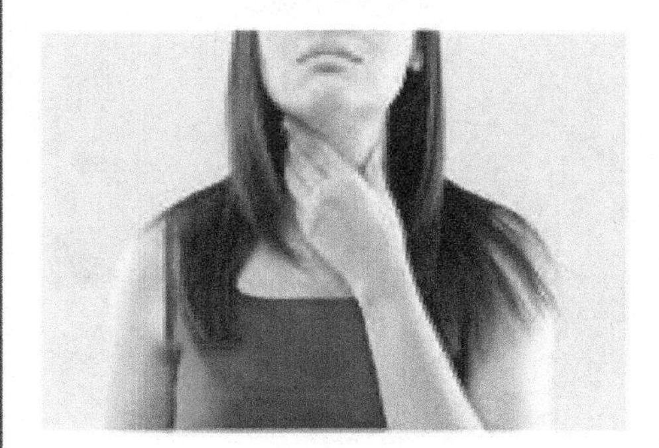

THROAT

LA SALUD - HEALTH

EL HUESO

(ehl weh-soh)

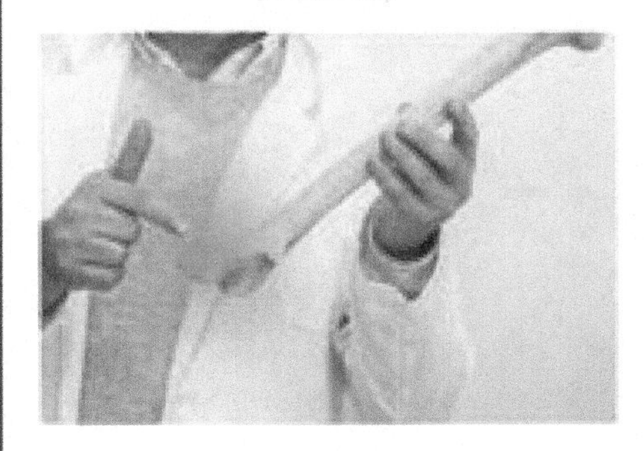

BONE

LA SALUD - HEALTH

EL MÚSCULO

(ehl moos-koo-loh)

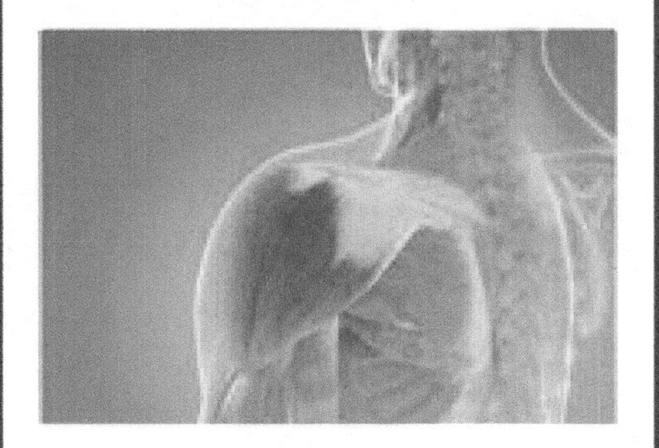

MUSCLE

LA SALUD - HEALTH

EL PELO

(ehl peh-loh)

HAIR

LA SALUD - HEALTH

LA FRENTE

(lah frehn-teh)

g Feminine noun

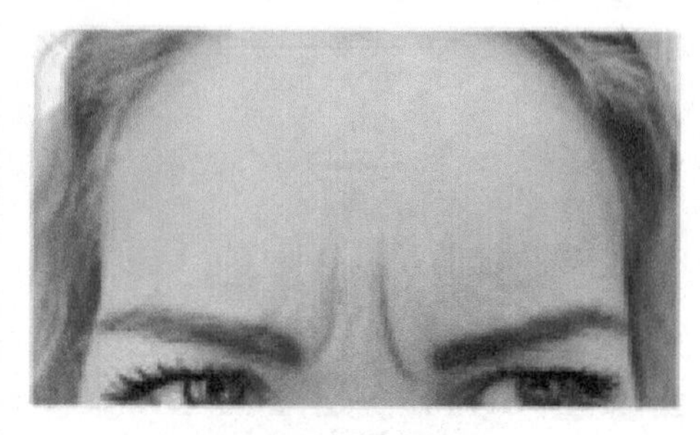

FOREHEAD

LA SALUD - HEALTH

LA NARIZ

(la nah-rees)

p *The pronunciation of "nariz" in Spain is 'nah-reeth.'*

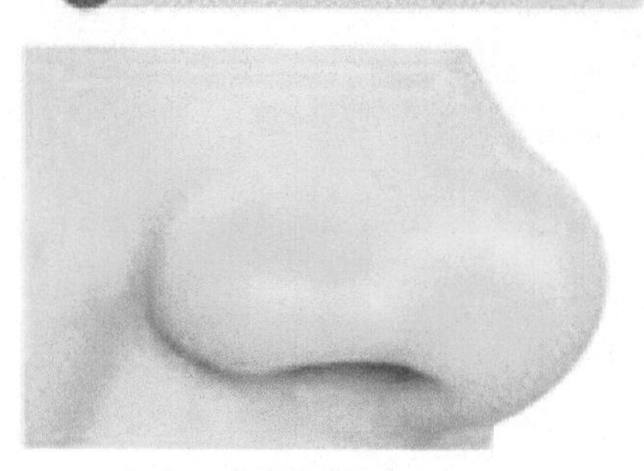

NOSE

LA SALUD - HEALTH

LA BOCA

(lah boh-kah)

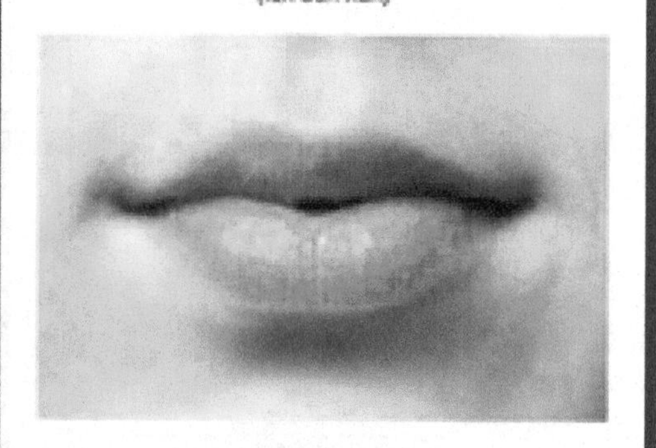

MOUTH

LA SALUD - HEALTH

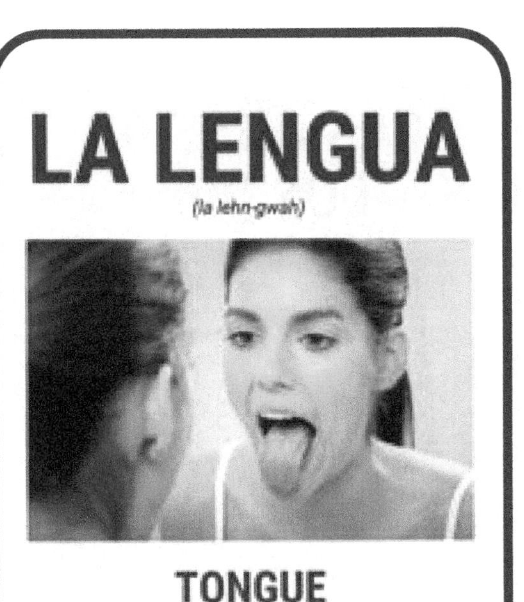
LA LENGUA
(la lehn-gwah)
TONGUE
LA SALUD - HEALTH

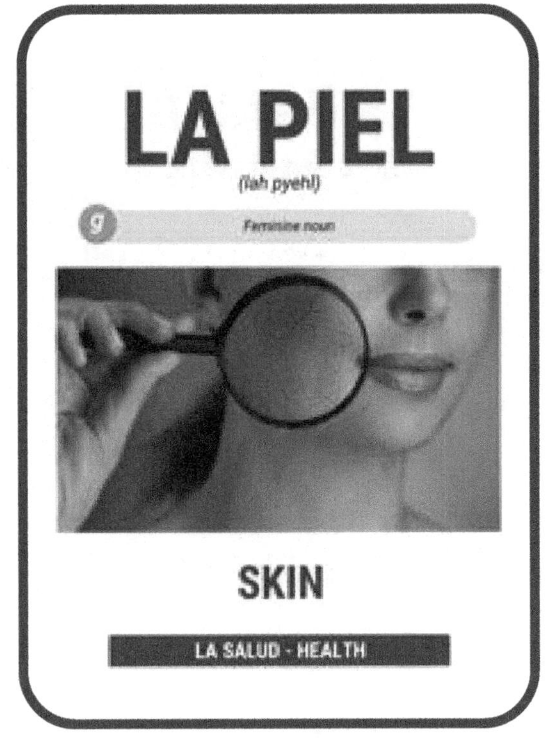
LA PIEL
(lah pyehl)
g
Feminine noun
SKIN
LA SALUD - HEALTH

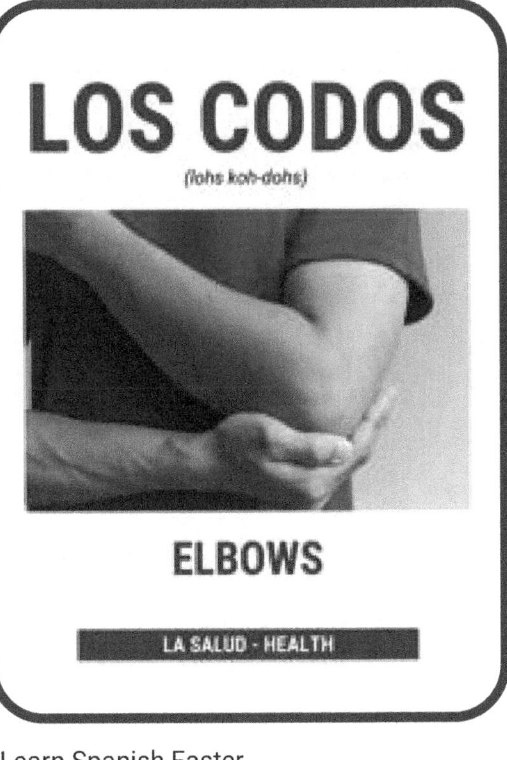
LOS CODOS
(lohs koh-dohs)
ELBOWS
LA SALUD - HEALTH

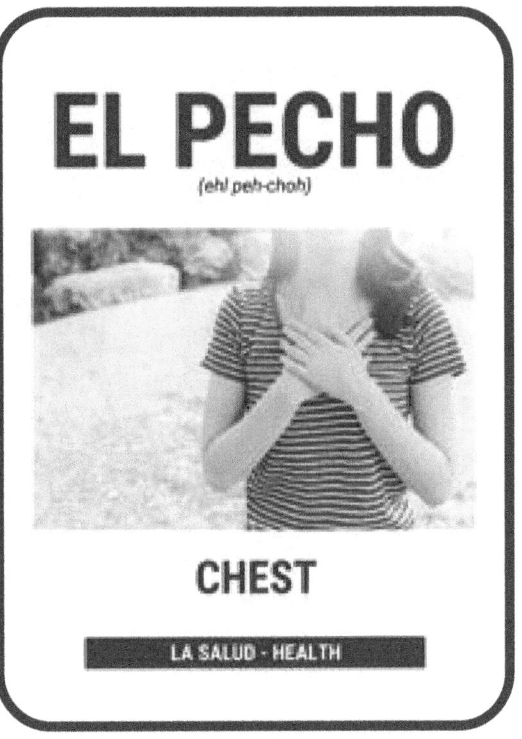
EL PECHO
(ehl peh-choh)
CHEST
LA SALUD - HEALTH

LAS UÑAS DE LAS MANOS
(lahs oo-nyahs deh lahs mah-nohs)
g
Feminine noun
FINGERNAILS
LA SALUD - HEALTH

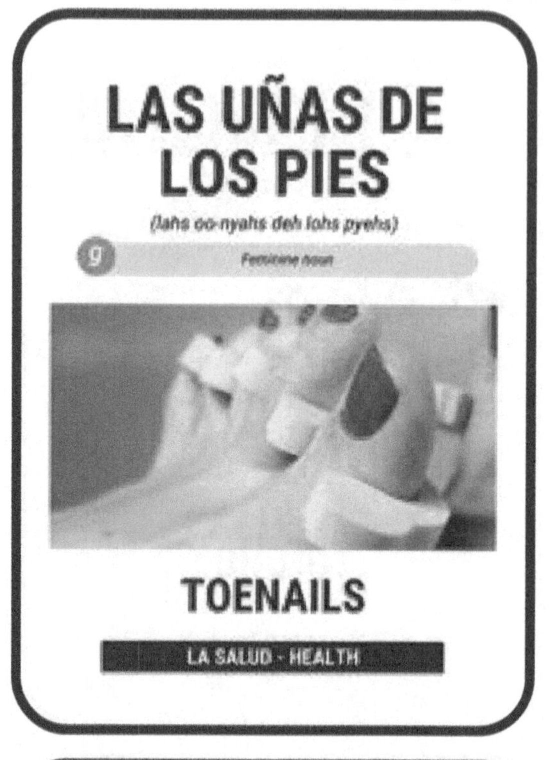
LAS UÑAS DE LOS PIES
(lahs oo-nyahs deh lohs pyehs)
g
Feminine noun
TOENAILS
LA SALUD - HEALTH

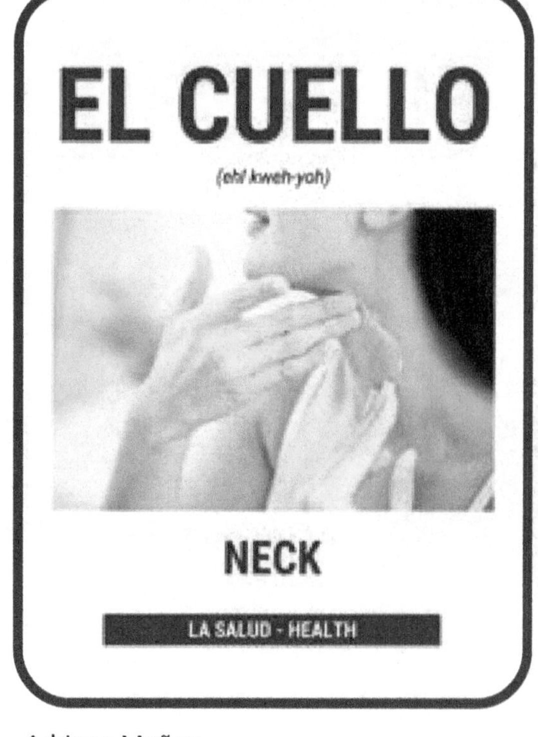
EL CUELLO
(ehl kweh-yoh)
NECK
LA SALUD - HEALTH

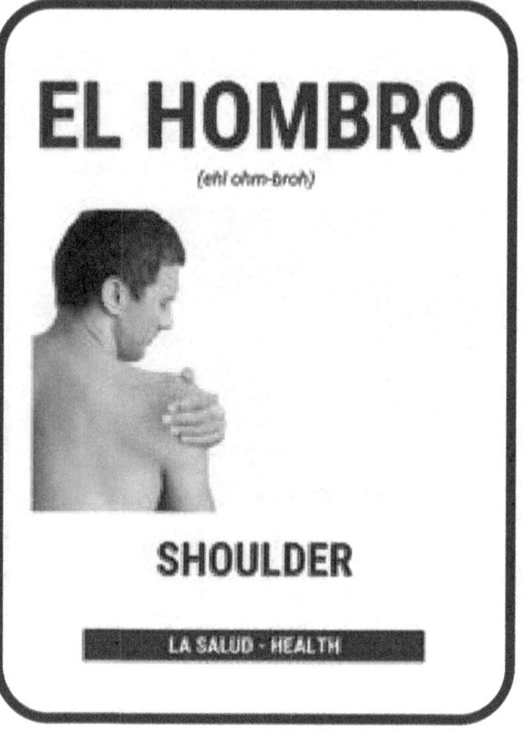
EL HOMBRO
(ehl ohm-broh)
SHOULDER
LA SALUD - HEALTH

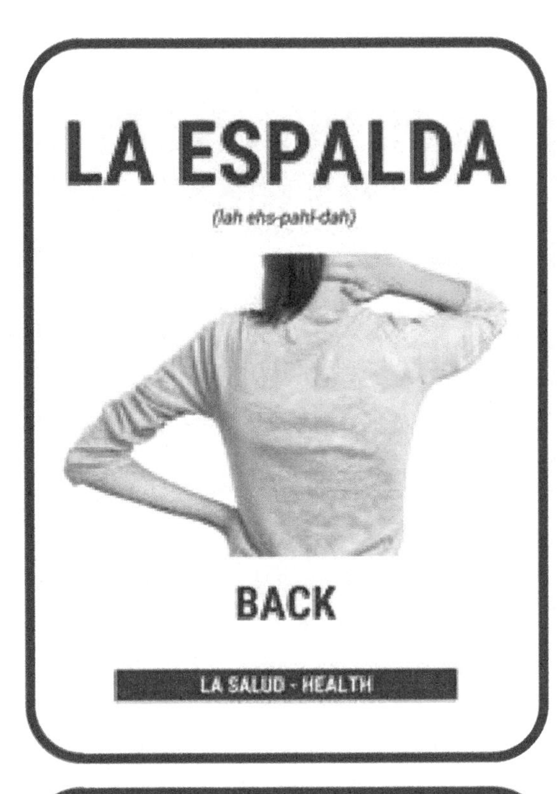
LA ESPALDA
(lah ehs-pahl-dah)
BACK
LA SALUD - HEALTH

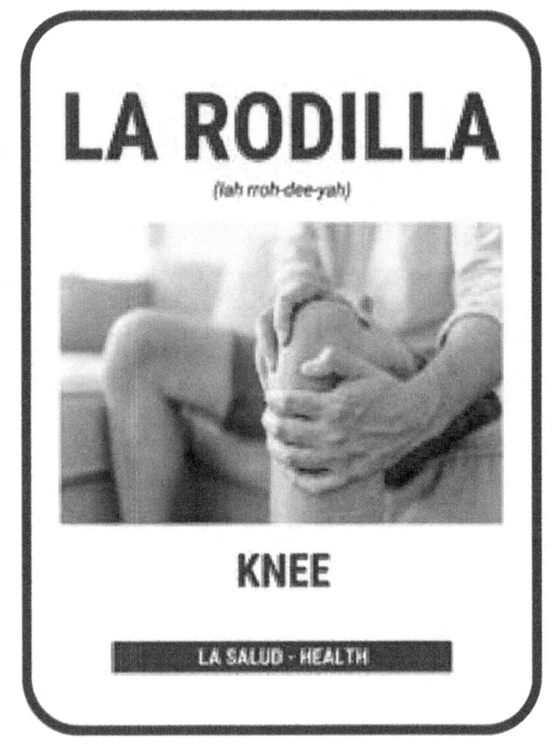
LA RODILLA
(lah rroh-dee-yah)
KNEE
LA SALUD - HEALTH

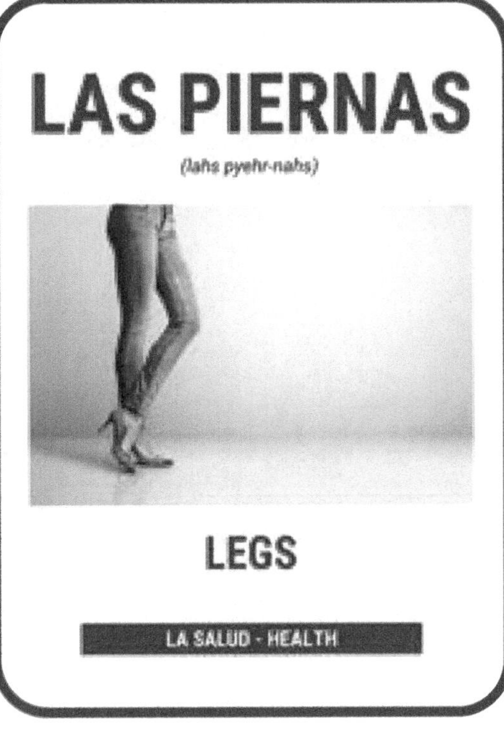
LAS PIERNAS
(lahs pyehr-nahs)
LEGS
LA SALUD - HEALTH

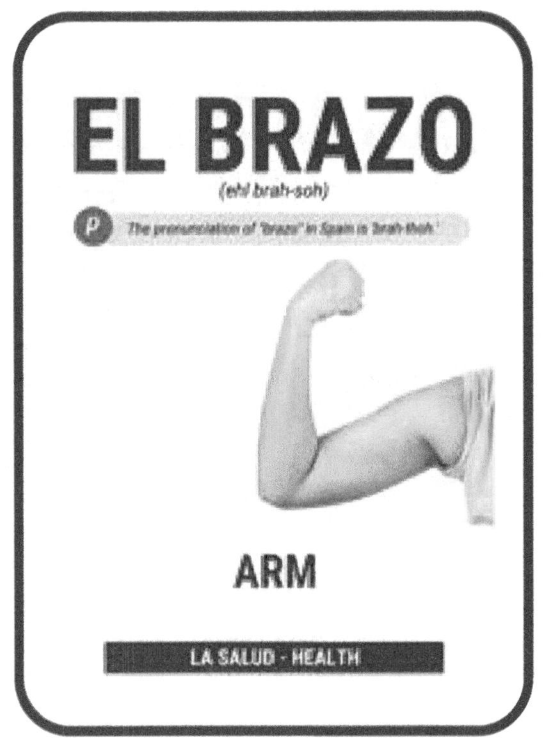
EL BRAZO
(ehl brah-soh)
ARM
LA SALUD - HEALTH

LOS DEDOS DE LAS MANOS
(lohs deh-dohs deh lahs mah-nohs)
g
Masculine noun
FINGERS
LA SALUD - HEALTH

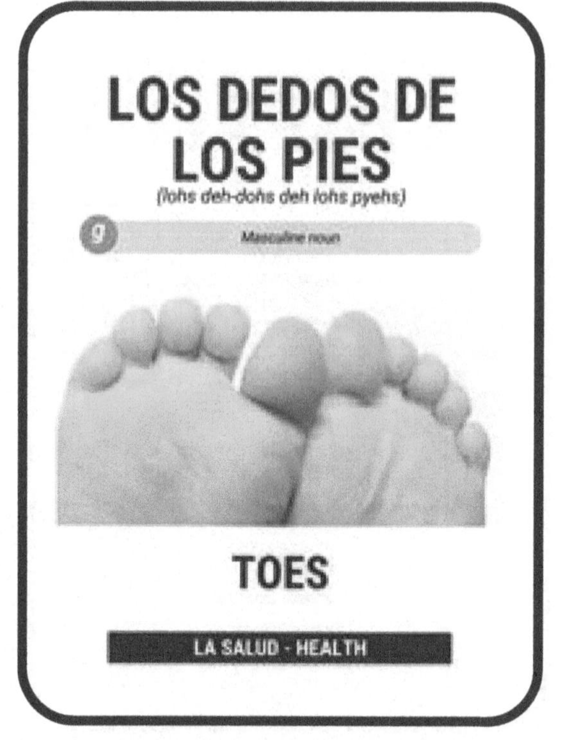
LOS DEDOS DE LOS PIES
(lohs deh-dohs deh lohs pyehs)
g
Masculine noun
TOES
LA SALUD - HEALTH

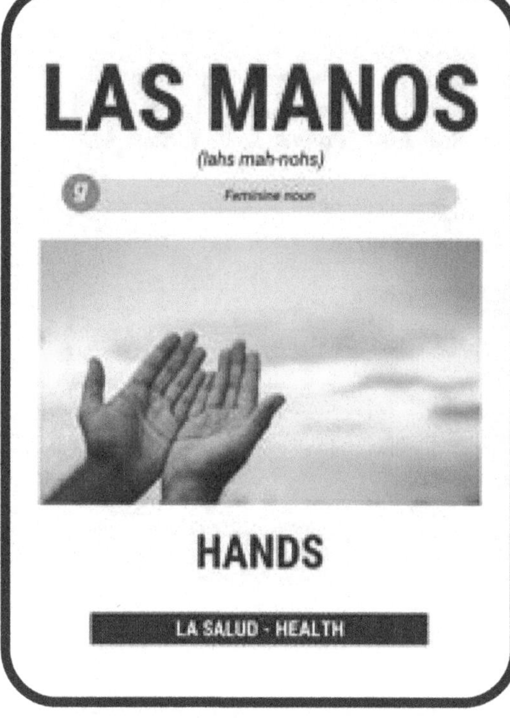
LAS MANOS
(lahs mah-nohs)
g
Feminine noun
HANDS
LA SALUD - HEALTH

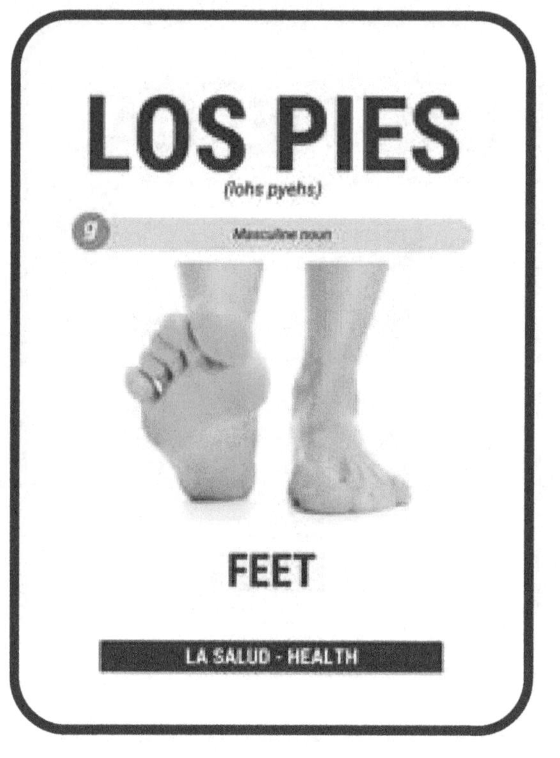
LOS PIES
(lohs pyehs)
g
Masculine noun
FEET
LA SALUD - HEALTH

NAUSEA

LA SALUD - HEALTH

EL MAREO

(ehl mah-reh-oh)

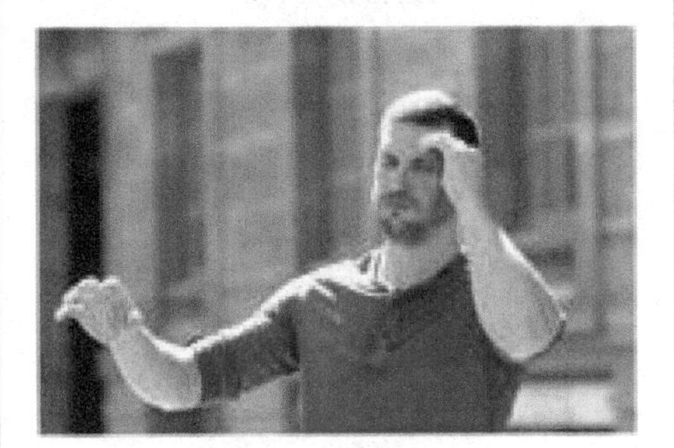

DIZZINESS

LA SALUD - HEALTH

LA FRACTURA

(lah frahk-too-rah)

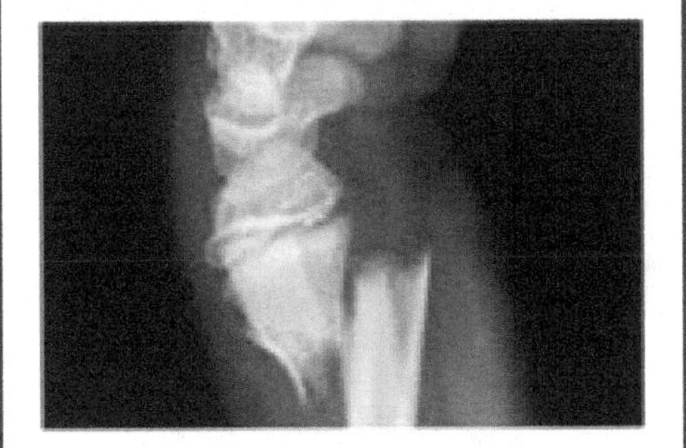

BROKEN BONE

LA SALUD - HEALTH

LOS OJOS

(lohs oh-hohs)

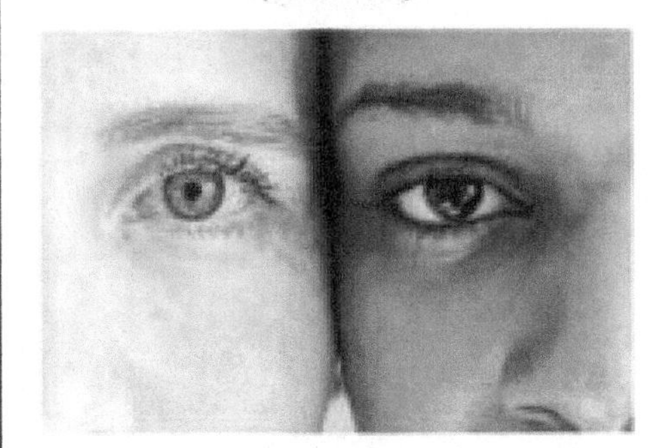

EYES

LA SALUD - HEALTH

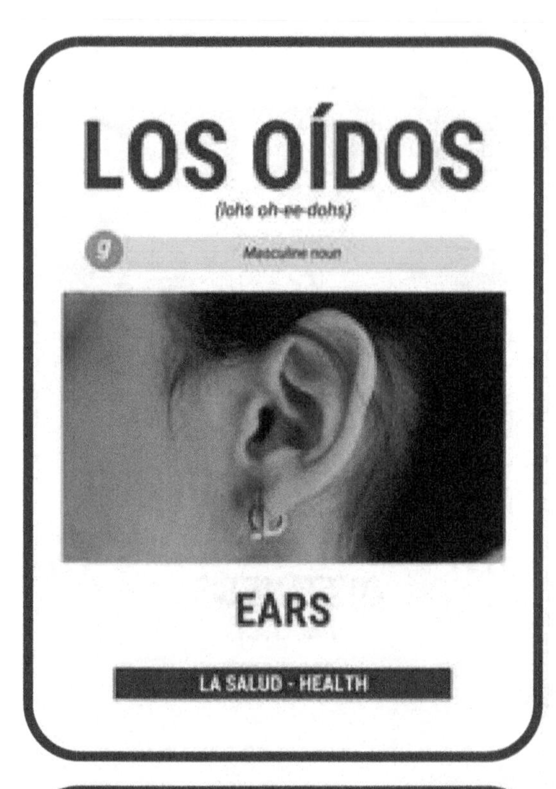
LOS OÍDOS
(lohs oh-ee-dohs)
g
Masculine noun
EARS
LA SALUD - HEALTH

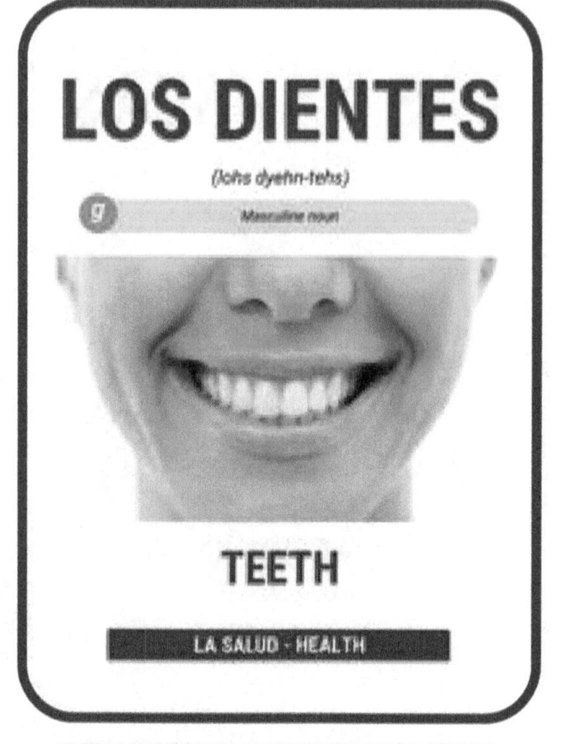
LOS DIENTES
(lohs dyehn-tehs)
g
Masculine noun
TEETH
LA SALUD - HEALTH

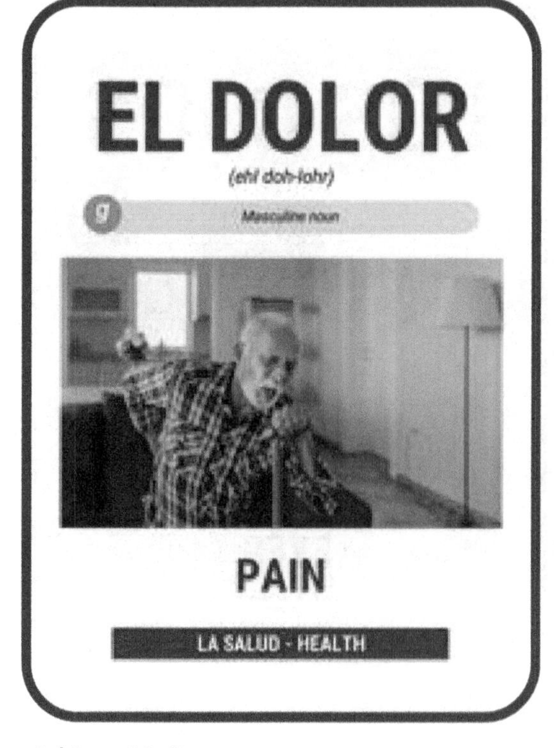
EL DOLOR
(ehl doh-lohr)
g
Masculine noun
PAIN
LA SALUD - HEALTH

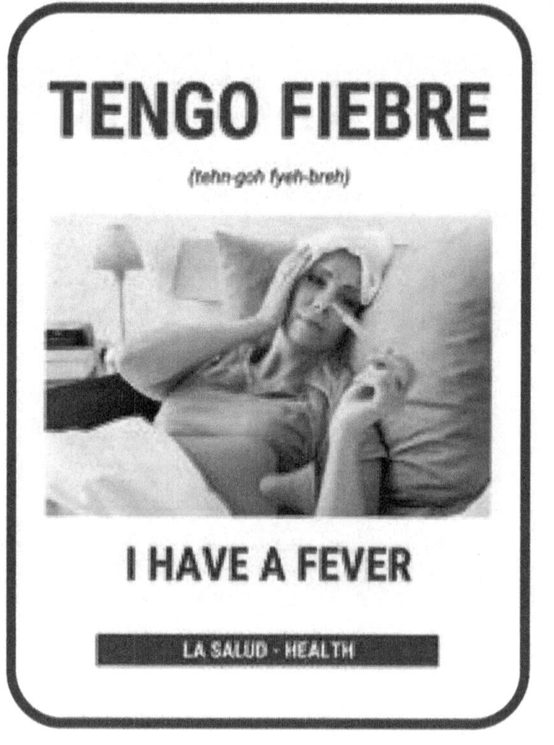
TENGO FIEBRE
(tehn-goh fyeh-breh)
I HAVE A FEVER
LA SALUD - HEALTH

TENGO ESCALOFRÍOS

(tehn-goh ehs-kah-loh-free-ohs)

I'M SHIVERING

LA SALUD - HEALTH

ME CAÍ

(meh kah-ee)

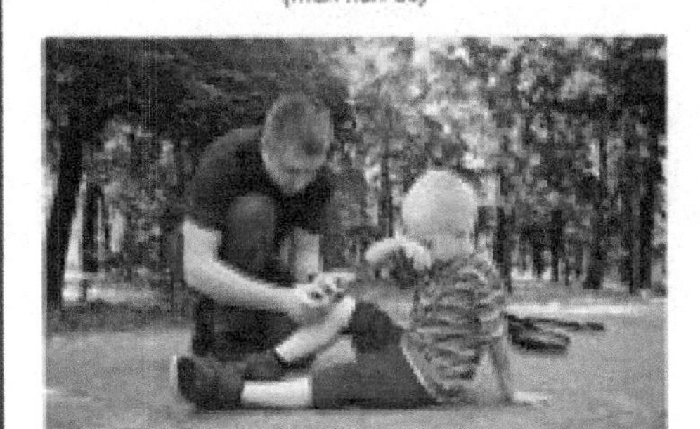

I FELL

LA SALUD - HEALTH

ME QUEMÉ

(meh keh-meh)

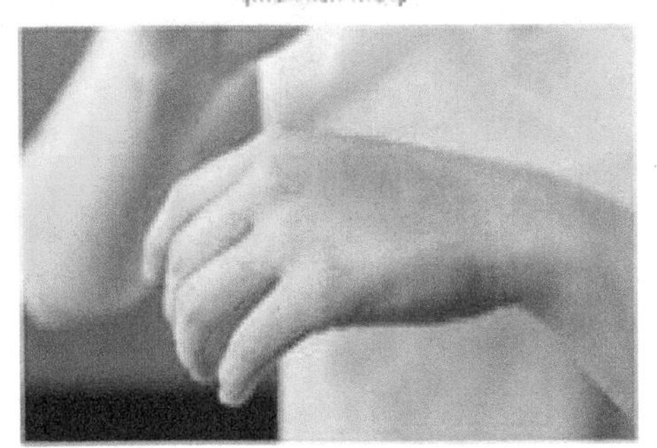

I BURNED MYSELF

LA SALUD - HEALTH

ME TORCÍ EL TOBILLO

(meh tohr-see ehl toh-bee-yoh)

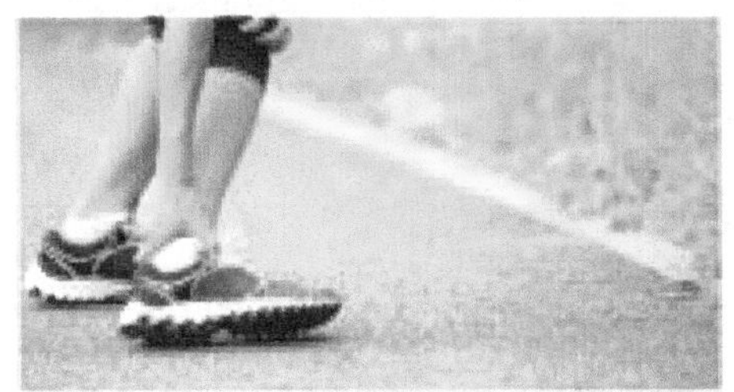

I TWISTED MY ANKLE

LA SALUD - HEALTH

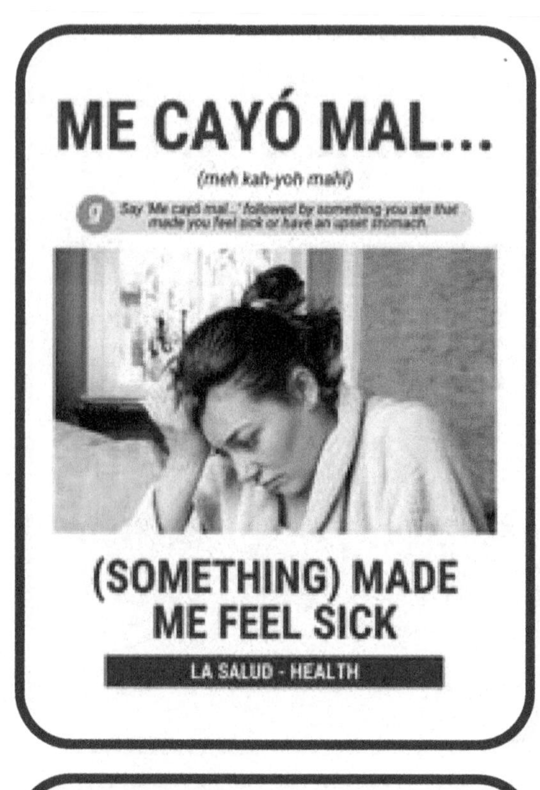
ME CAYÓ MAL...
(meh kah-yoh mahl)
g
Say 'Me cayó mal...' followed by something you ate that made you feel sick or have an upset stomach.
(SOMETHING) MADE ME FEEL SICK
LA SALUD - HEALTH

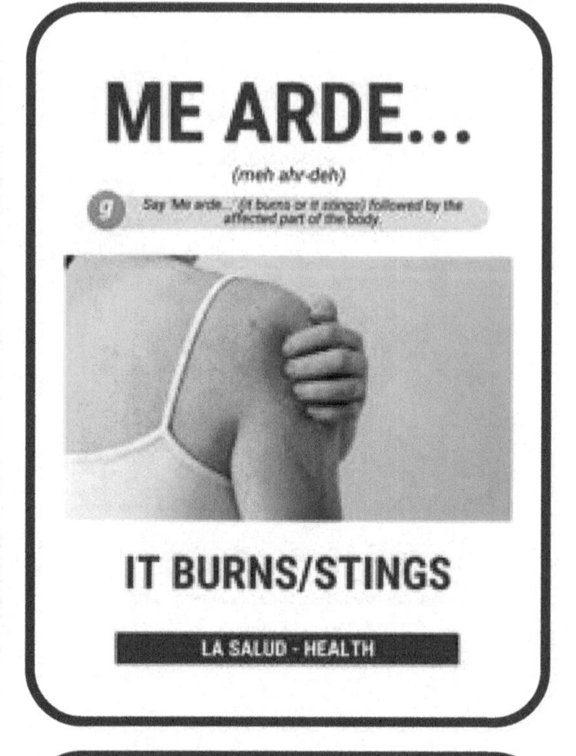
ME ARDE...
(meh ahr-deh)
g
Say 'Me arde...' (it burns or it stings) followed by the affected part of the body.
IT BURNS/STINGS
LA SALUD - HEALTH

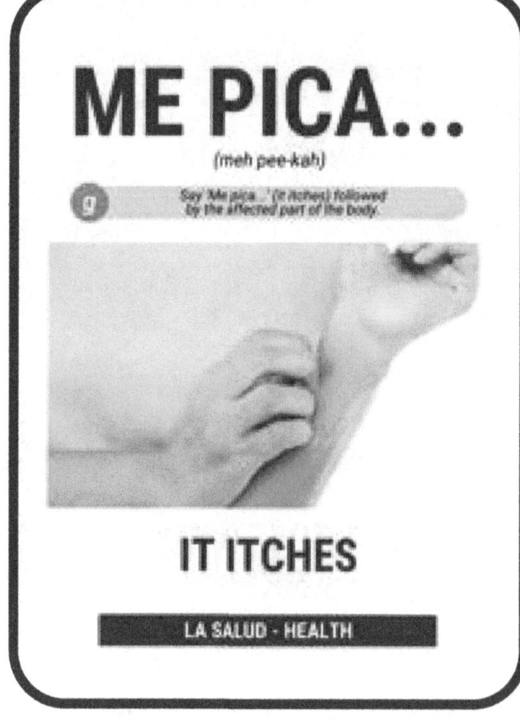
ME PICA...
(meh pee-kah)
g
Say 'Me pica...' (it itches) followed by the affected part of the body.
IT ITCHES
LA SALUD - HEALTH

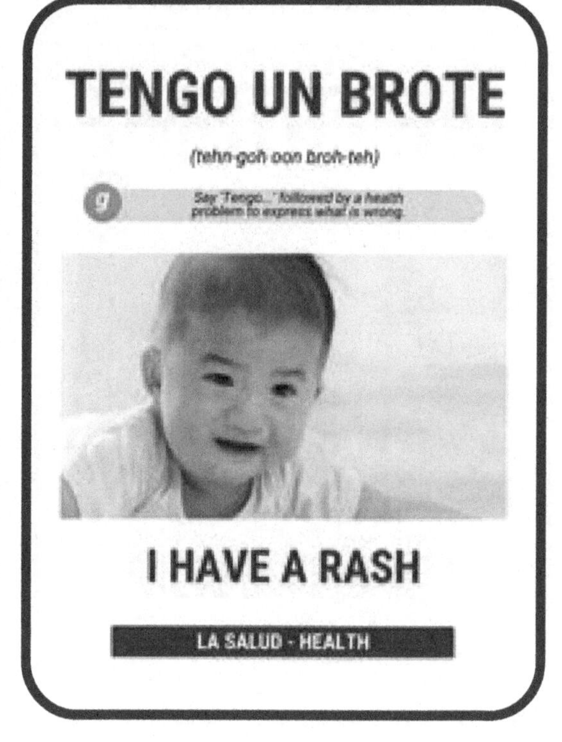
TENGO UN BROTE
(tehn-goh oon broh-teh)
g
Say 'Tengo...' followed by a health problem to express what is wrong.
I HAVE A RASH
LA SALUD - HEALTH

SOY ALÉRGICO / ALÉRGICA A...

(soy ah-lehr-hee-koh / ah-lehr-hee-kah ah)

g — Say 'Soy alérgico/a a...' followed by the thing you are allergic to.

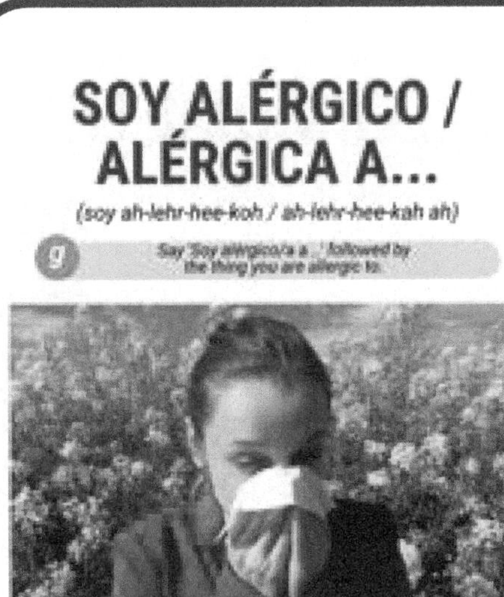

I AM ALLERGIC TO...

LA SALUD - HEALTH

LA FÓRMULA MÉDICA

(lah fohr-moo-lah meh-dee-kah)

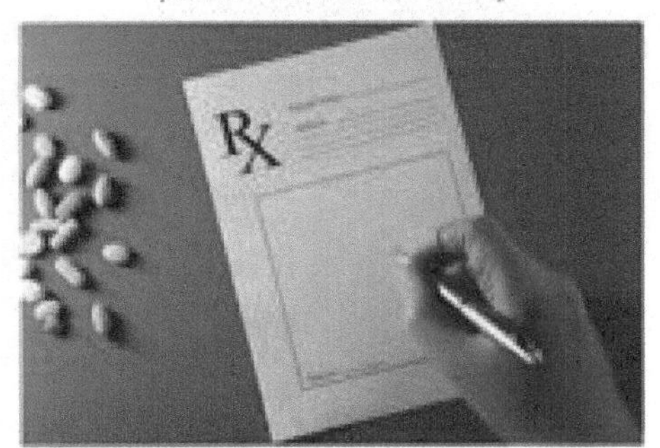

PRESCRIPTION

LA SALUD - HEALTH

LOS MEDICAMENTOS

(lohs meh-dee-kah mehn-tohs)

g — Masculine noun

MEDICINE

LA SALUD - HEALTH

LA INYECCIÓN

(lah een-yekh-syohn)

p — The pronunciation of 'inyección' in Spain is 'een-yekh-thyohn.'

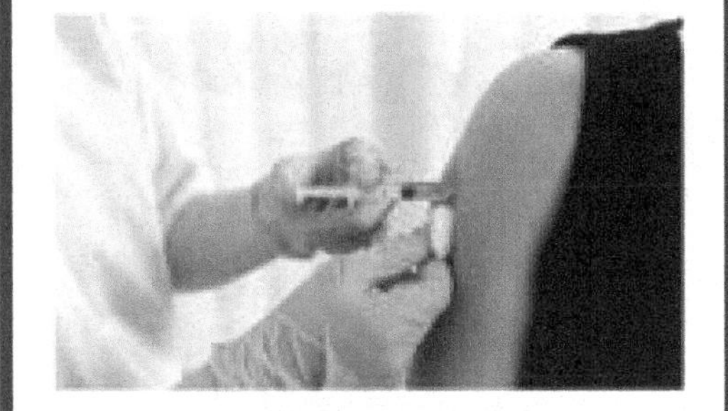

INJECTION

LA SALUD - HEALTH

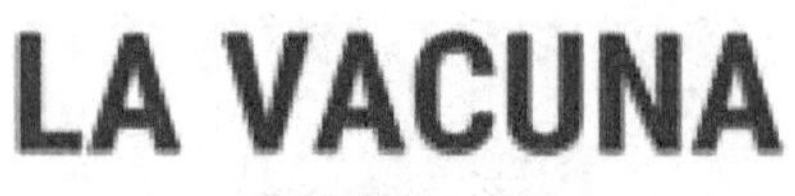

LA VACUNA

(lah bah-koo-nah)

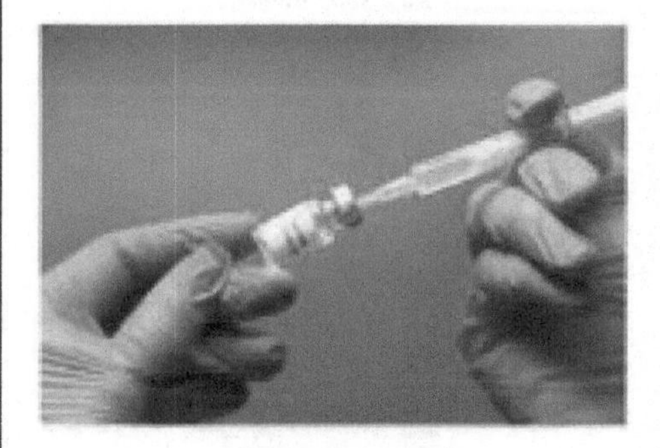

VACCINE

LA SALUD - HEALTH

EL TERMÓMETRO

(ehl tehr-moh-meh-troh)

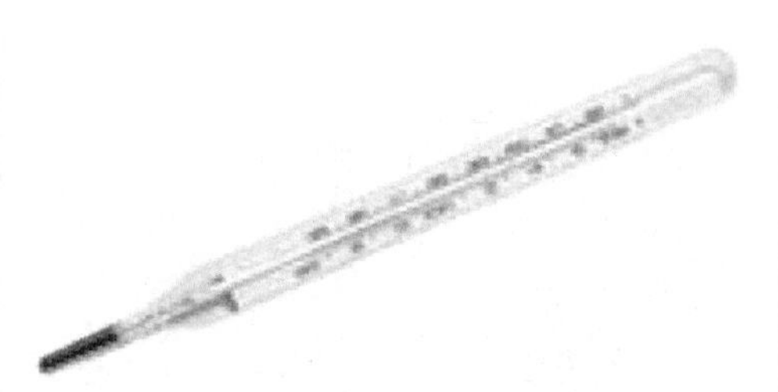

THERMOMETER

LA SALUD - HEALTH

LA CIRUGÍA

(lah see-roo-hee-ah)

The pronunciation of "cirugía" in Spain is 'thee-roo-hee-ah.'

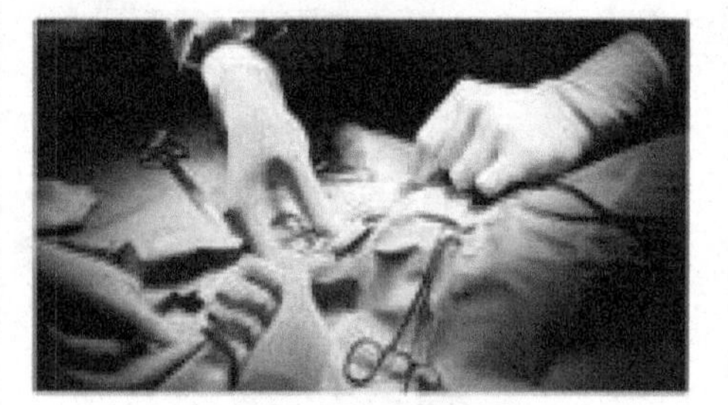

SURGERY

LA SALUD - HEALTH

LA ANESTESIA

(lah ah-nehs-teh-syah)

Feminine noun

ANESTHESIA

LA SALUD - HEALTH

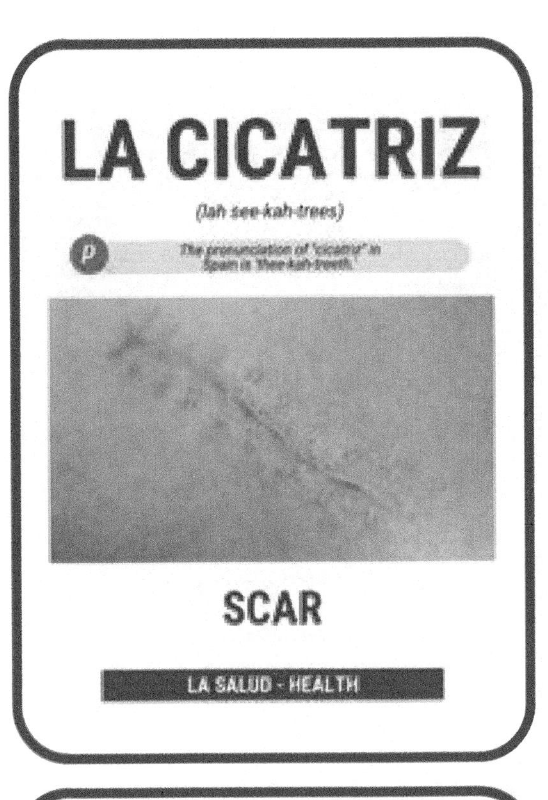
LA CICATRIZ
(lah see-kah-trees)
The pronunciation of "cicatriz" in Spain is "thee-kah-treeth."
SCAR
LA SALUD - HEALTH

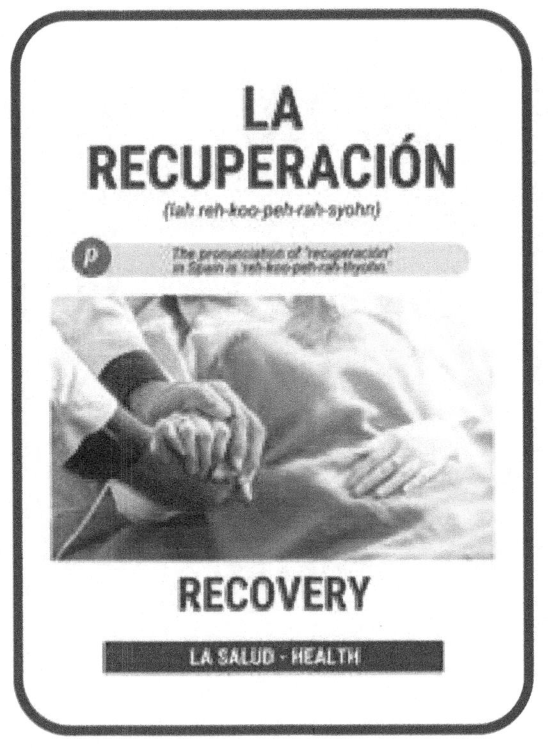
LA RECUPERACIÓN
(lah reh-koo-peh-rah-syohn)
The pronunciation of "recuperación" in Spain is "reh-koo-peh-rah-thyohn."
RECOVERY
LA SALUD - HEALTH

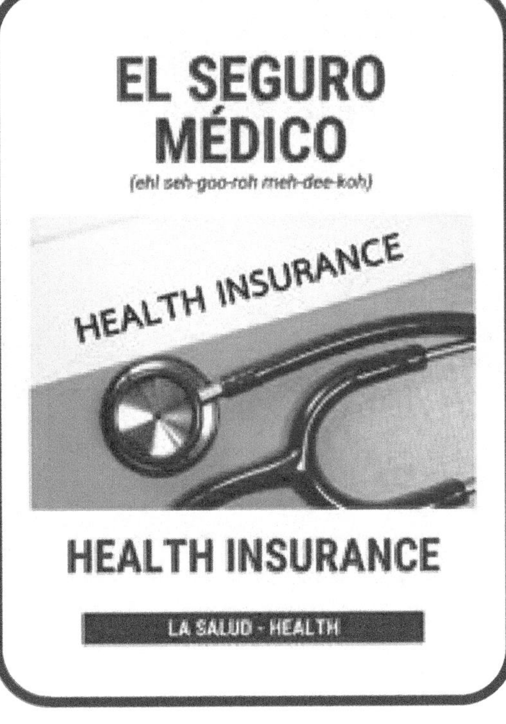
EL SEGURO MÉDICO
(ehl seh-goo-roh meh-dee-koh)
HEALTH INSURANCE
HEALTH INSURANCE
LA SALUD - HEALTH

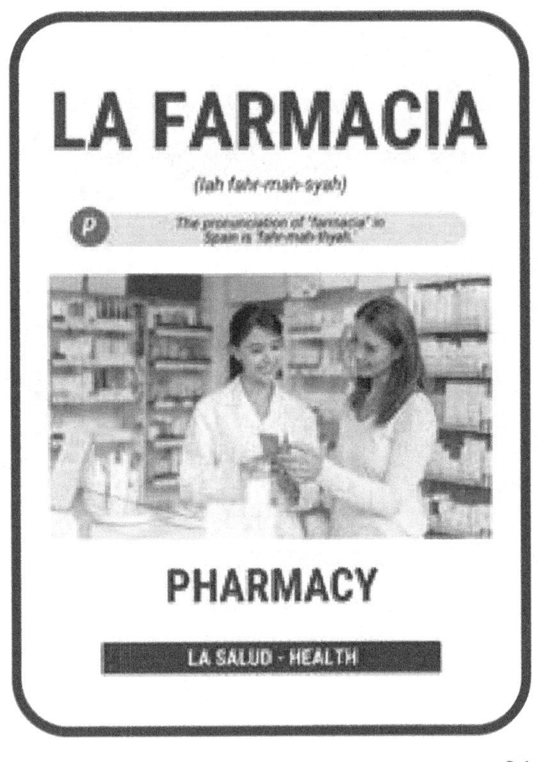
LA FARMACIA
(lah fahr-mah-syah)
The pronunciation of "farmacia" in Spain is "fahr-mah-thyah."
PHARMACY
LA SALUD - HEALTH

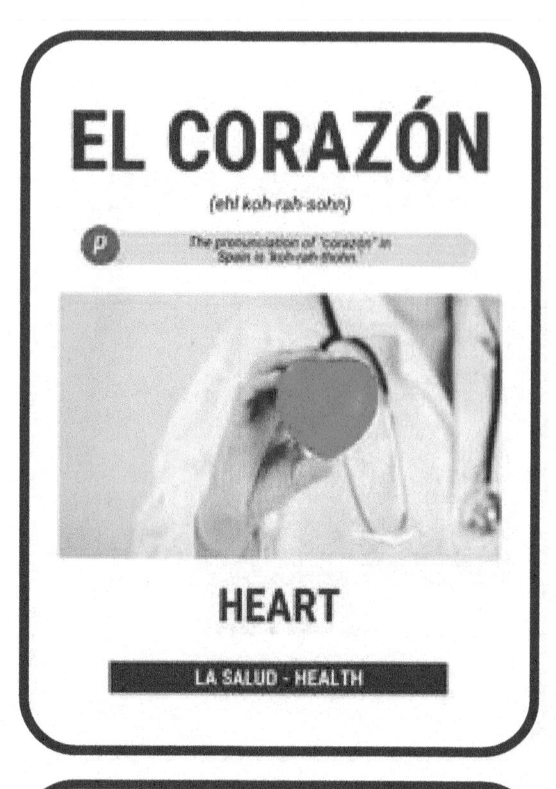
EL CORAZÓN
(ehl koh-rah-sohn)
p
The pronunciation of "corazón" in Spain is 'koh-rah-thohn.'
HEART
LA SALUD - HEALTH

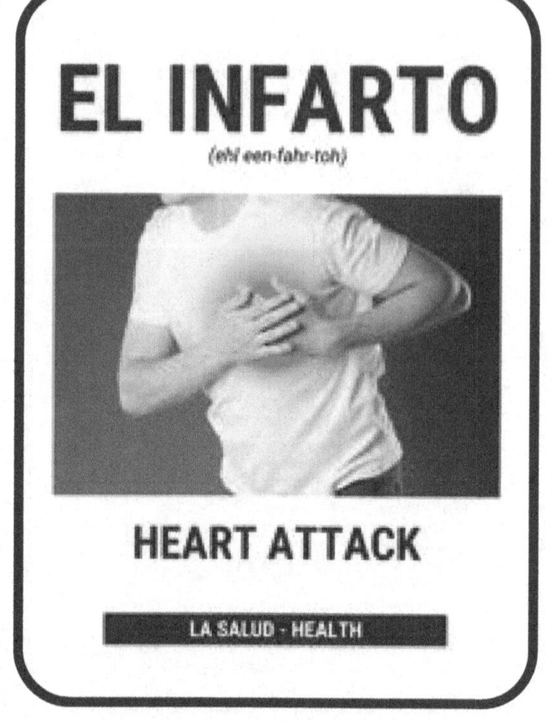
EL INFARTO
(ehl een-fahr-toh)
HEART ATTACK
LA SALUD - HEALTH

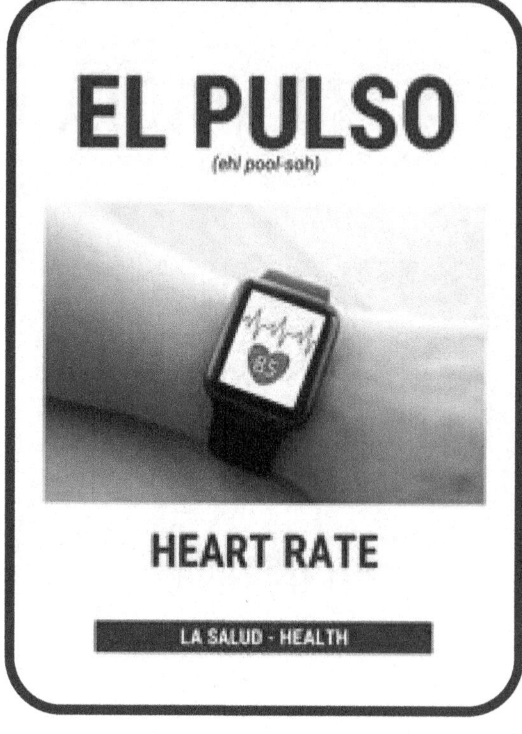
EL PULSO
(ehl pool-soh)
85
HEART RATE
LA SALUD - HEALTH

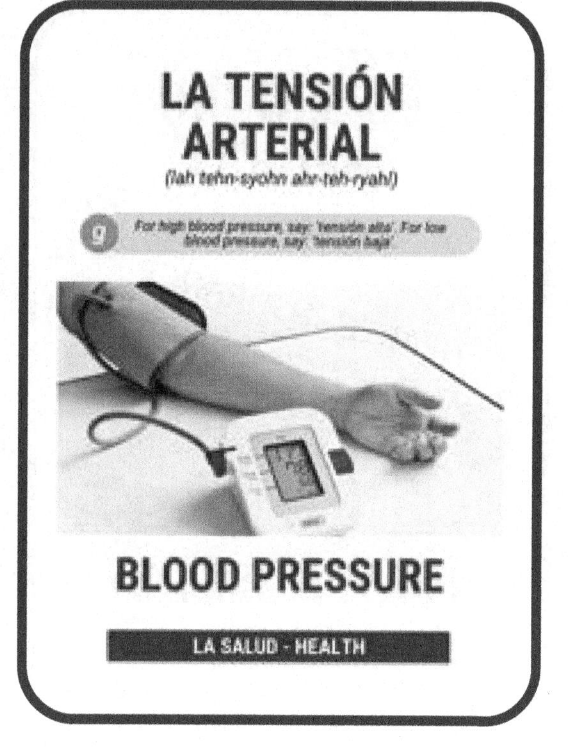
LA TENSIÓN ARTERIAL
(lah tehn-syohn ahr-teh-ryahl)
g
For high blood pressure, say: 'tensión alta'. For low blood pressure, say: 'tensión baja'.
BLOOD PRESSURE
LA SALUD - HEALTH

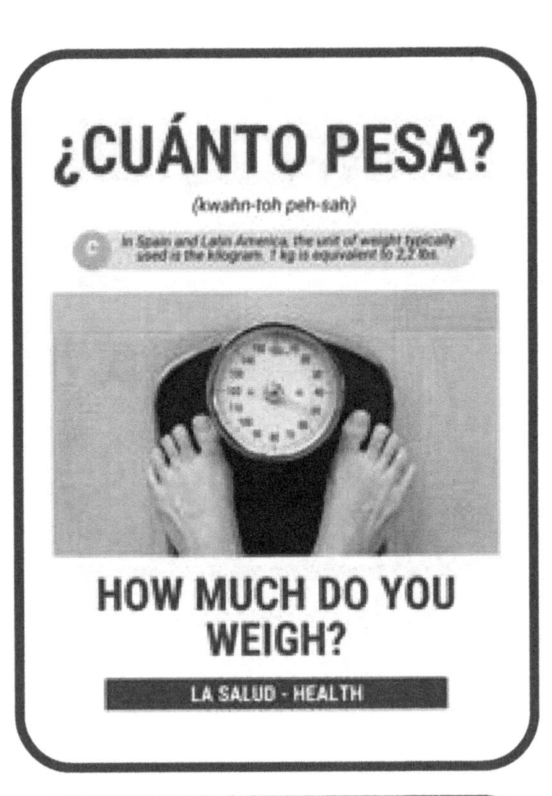
¿CUÁNTO PESA?
(kwahn-toh peh-sah)
C
In Spain and Latin America, the unit of weight typically used is the kilogram. 1 kg is equivalent to 2.2 lbs.
HOW MUCH DO YOU WEIGH?
LA SALUD - HEALTH

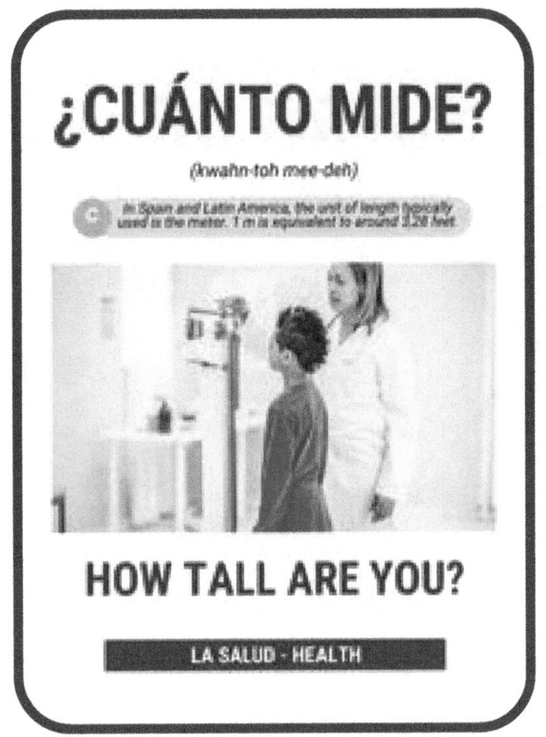
¿CUÁNTO MIDE?
(kwahn-toh mee-deh)
C
In Spain and Latin America, the unit of length typically used is the meter. 1 m is equivalent to around 3.28 feet.
HOW TALL ARE YOU?
LA SALUD - HEALTH

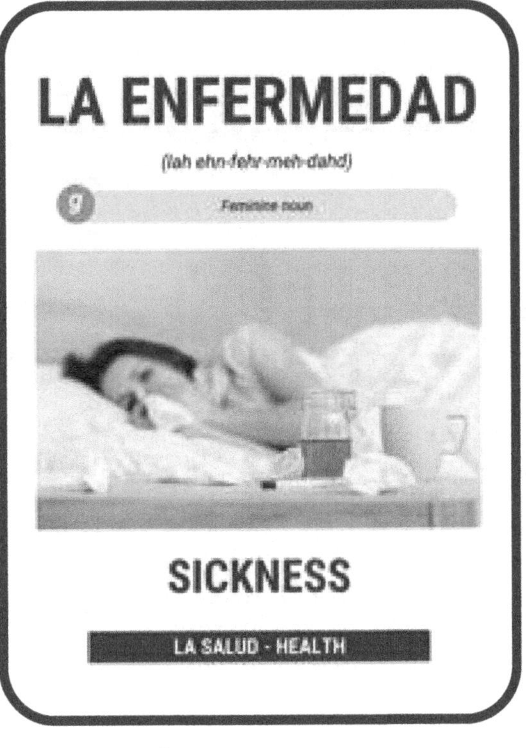
LA ENFERMEDAD
(lah ehn-fehr-meh-dahd)
g
Feminine noun
SICKNESS
LA SALUD - HEALTH

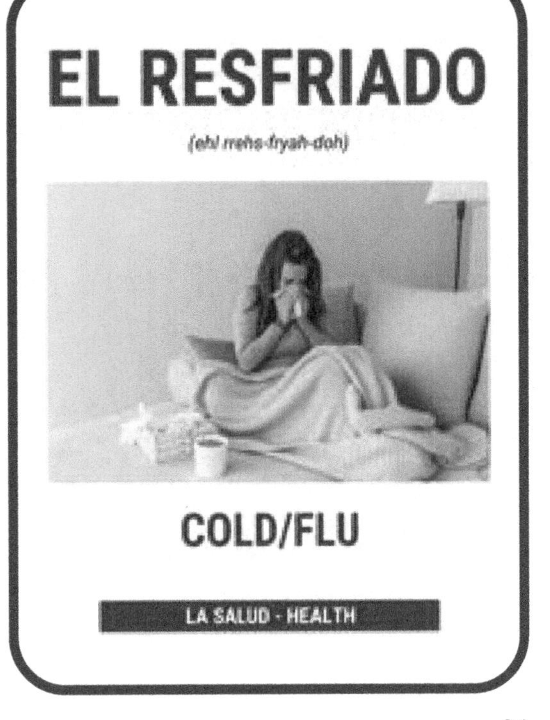
EL RESFRIADO
(ehl rehs-fryah-doh)
COLD/FLU
LA SALUD - HEALTH

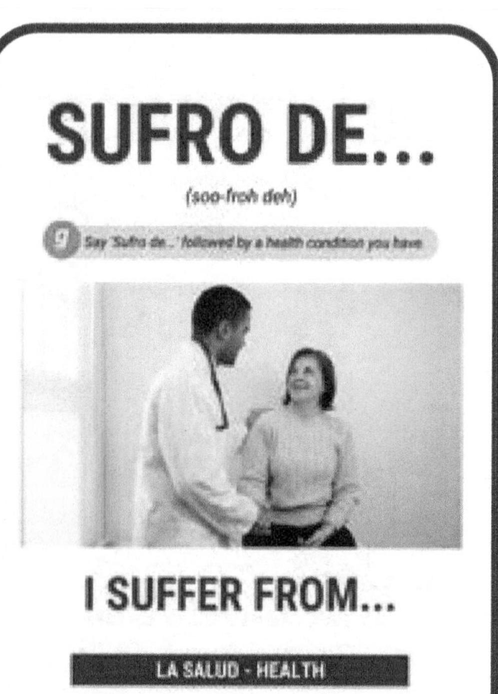
SUFRO DE...
(soo-froh deh)
g
Say 'Sufro de...' followed by a health condition you have
I SUFFER FROM...
LA SALUD - HEALTH

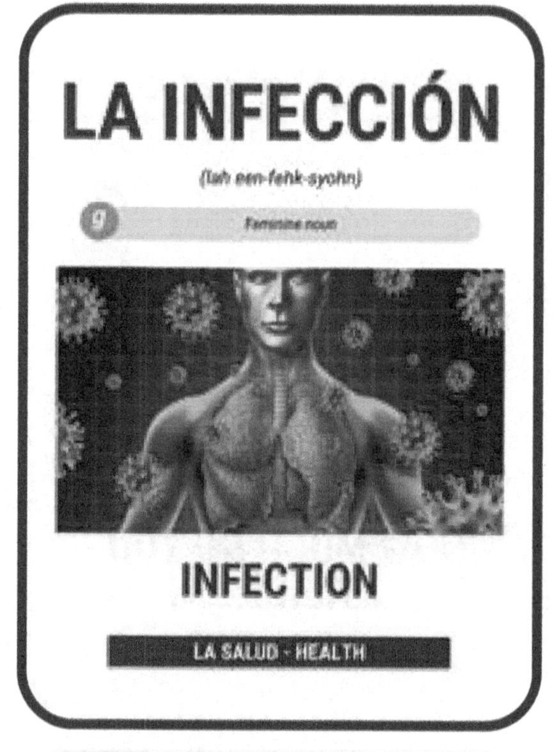
LA INFECCIÓN
(lah een-fehk-syohn)
g
Feminine noun
INFECTION
LA SALUD - HEALTH

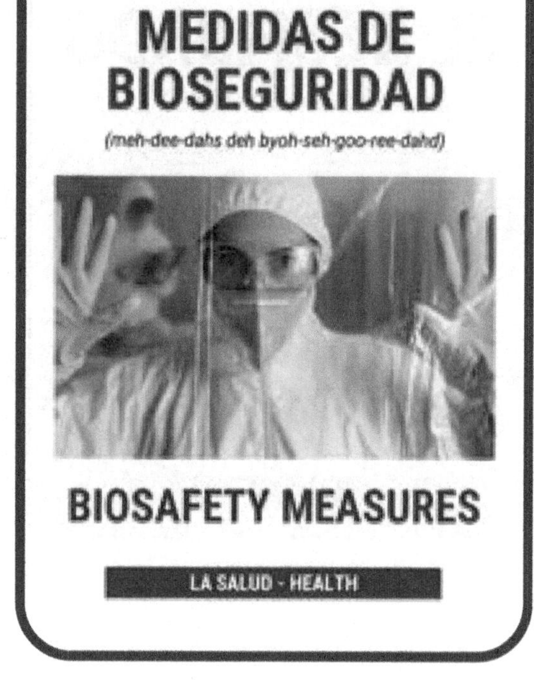
MEDIDAS DE BIOSEGURIDAD
(meh-dee-dahs deh byoh-seh-goo-ree-dahd)
BIOSAFETY MEASURES
LA SALUD - HEALTH

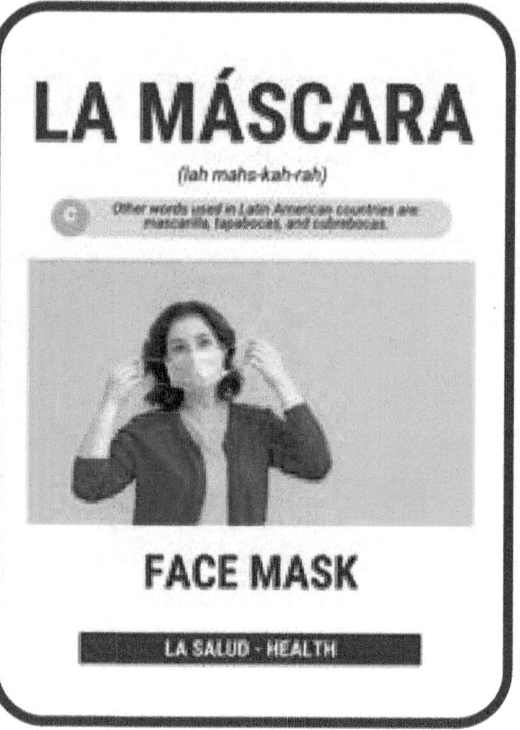
LA MÁSCARA
(lah mahs-kah-rah)
C
Other words used in Latin American countries are: mascarilla, tapabocas, and cubrebocas.
FACE MASK
LA SALUD - HEALTH

LA SALUD MENTAL

(lah sah-lood mehn-tahl)

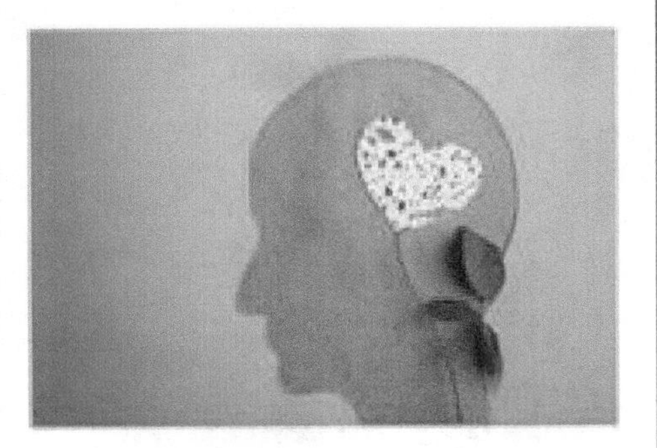

MENTAL HEALTH

LA SALUD - HEALTH

HACER EJERCICIO

(ah-sehr eh-hehr-see-syoh)

TO EXERCISE

LA SALUD - HEALTH

LOS HÁBITOS SALUDABLES

(lohs ah-bee-tohs sah-loo-dah-blehs)

HEALTHY HABITS

LA SALUD - HEALTH

LA DIETA SANA

(lah dyeh-tah sah-nah)

HEALTHY DIET

LA SALUD - HEALTH

DORMIR

(dohr-meer)

Duermo 6 horas por la noche.
I sleep 6 hours at night.

TO SLEEP

LA SALUD - HEALTH

PRACTICAR UN DEPORTE

(prahk-tee-kahr oon deh-pohr-teh)

Practicamos muchos deportes.
We practice many sports.

TO PLAY A SPORT

LA SALUD - HEALTH

MEDITAR

(meh-dee-tahr)

Meditamos siempre a la madrugada.
We always meditate at dawn.

TO MEDITATE

LA SALUD - HEALTH

DESCANSAR

(dehs-kahn-sahr)

¿Por qué no descansamos un poco?
Why don't we rest for a bit?

TO REST

LA SALUD - HEALTH

EL ESTRÉS

(ehl ehs-trehs)

g — *Masculine noun*

STRESS

LA SALUD - HEALTH

EL CANSANCIO

(ehl kahn-sahn-syoh)

p — *The pronunciation of "cansancio" in Spain is 'kahn-sahn-thyoh'.*

TIREDNESS

LA SALUD - HEALTH

LOS ANALGÉSICOS

(lohs ah-nahl-heh-see-kohs)

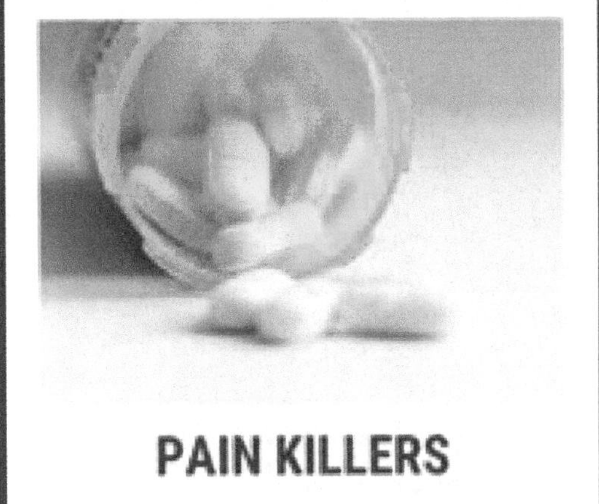

PAIN KILLERS

LA SALUD - HEALTH

LOS ANTIBIÓTICOS

(lohs ahn-tee-byoh-tee-kohs)

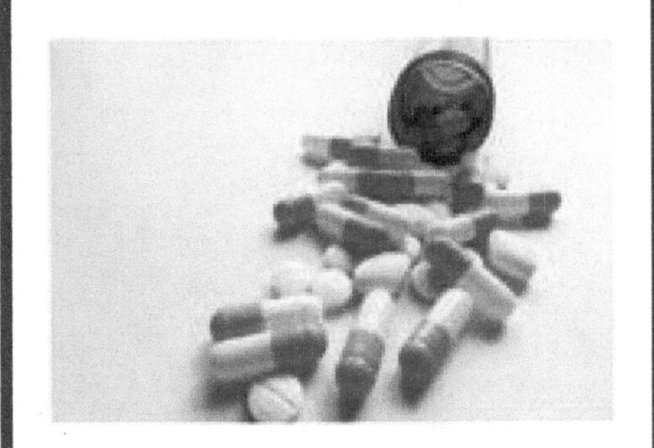

ANTIBIOTICS

LA SALUD - HEALTH

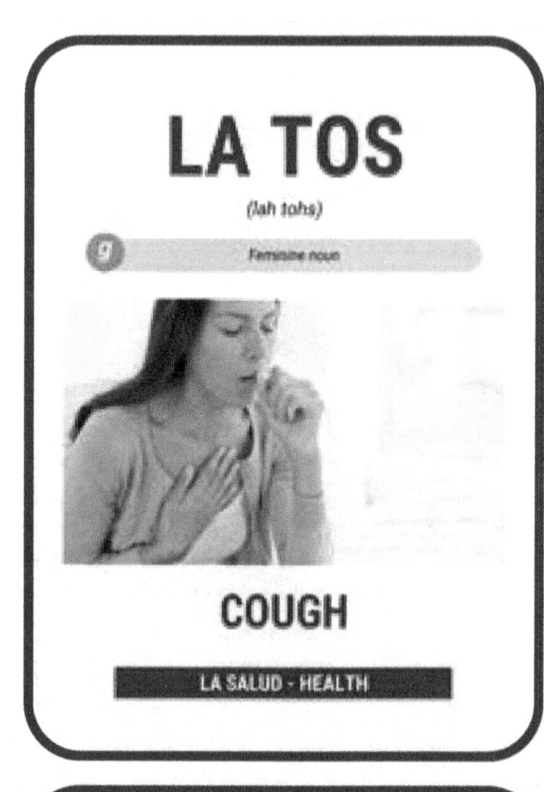
LA TOS
(lah tohs)
g
Feminine noun
COUGH
LA SALUD - HEALTH

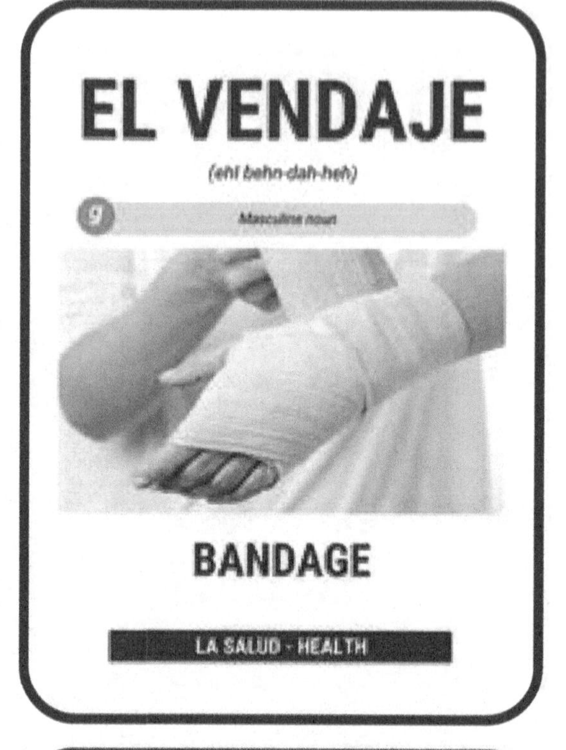
EL VENDAJE
(ehl behn-dah-heh)
g
Masculine noun
BANDAGE
LA SALUD - HEALTH

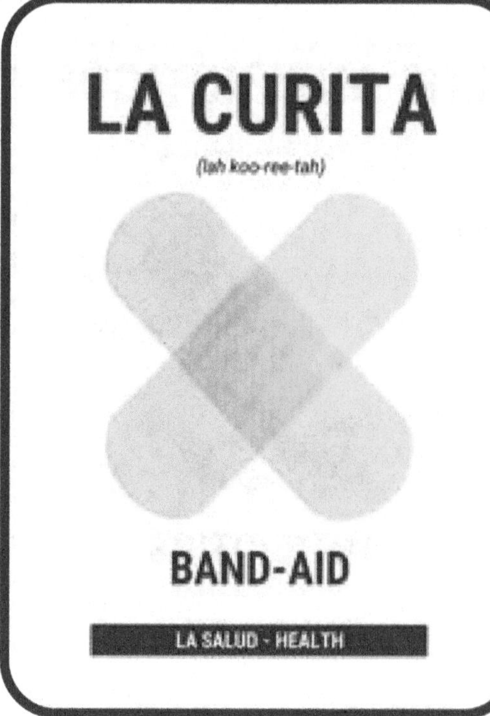
LA CURITA
(lah koo-ree-tah)
BAND-AID
LA SALUD - HEALTH

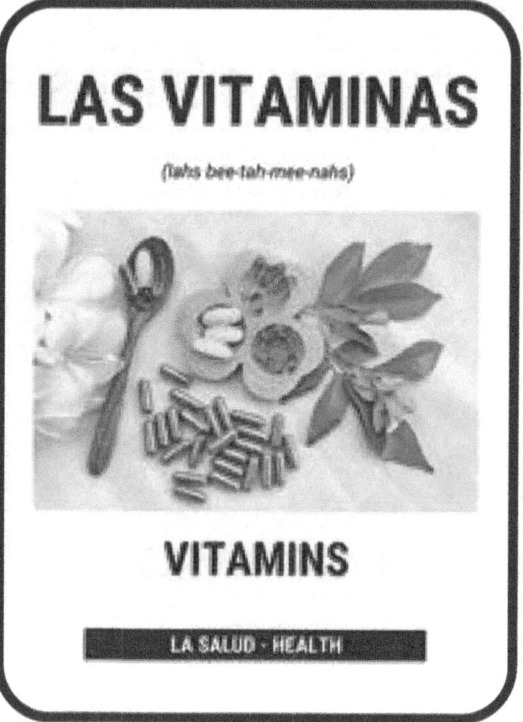
LAS VITAMINAS
(lahs bee-tah-mee-nahs)
VITAMINS
LA SALUD - HEALTH

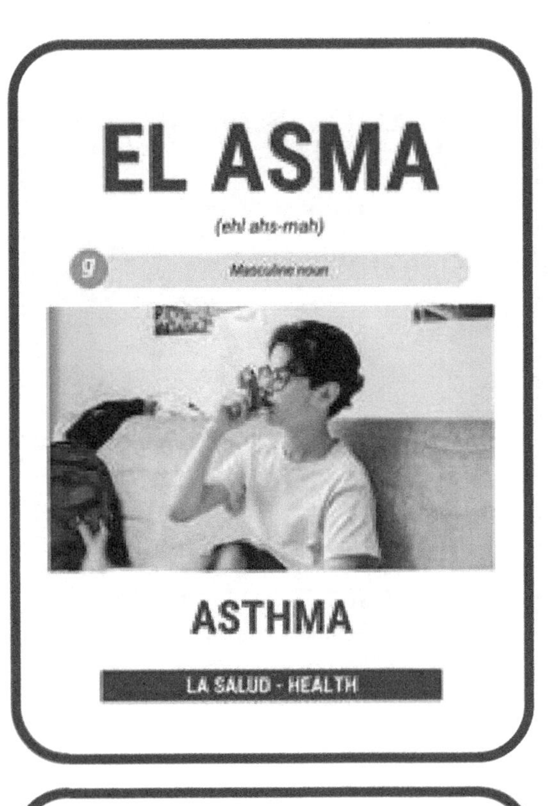
EL ASMA
(ehl ahs-mah)
g
Masculine noun
ASTHMA
LA SALUD - HEALTH

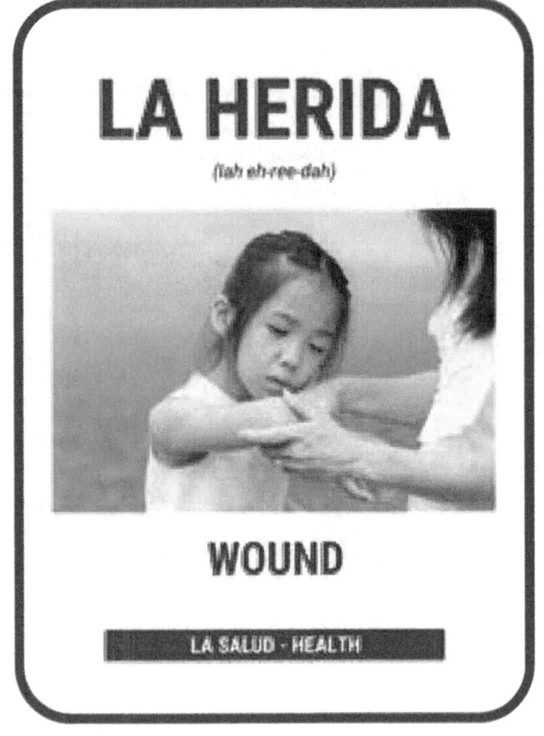
LA HERIDA
(lah eh-ree-dah)
WOUND
LA SALUD - HEALTH

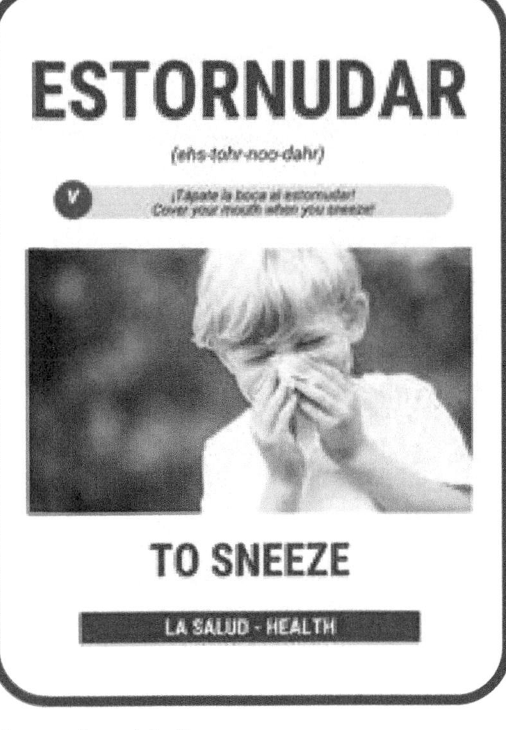
ESTORNUDAR
(ehs-tohr-noo-dahr)
v
¡Tápate la boca al estornudar!
Cover your mouth when you sneeze!
TO SNEEZE
LA SALUD - HEALTH

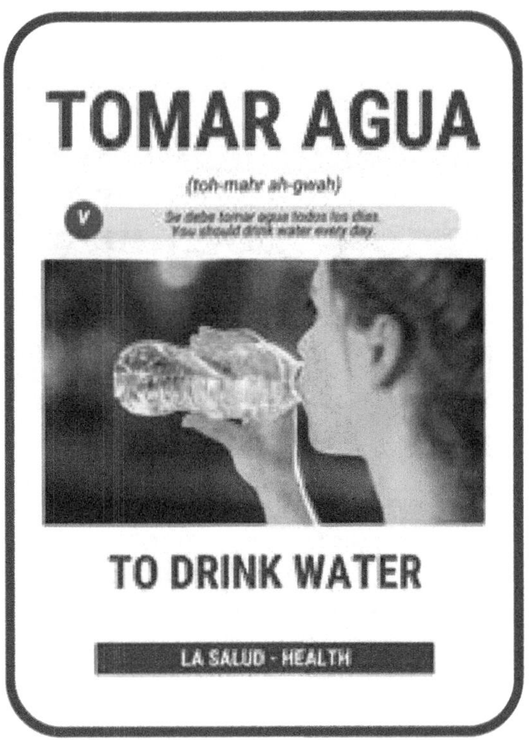
TOMAR AGUA
(toh-mahr ah-gwah)
v
Se debe tomar agua todos los días.
You should drink water every day.
TO DRINK WATER
LA SALUD - HEALTH

DEJAR DE FUMAR

(deh-hahr deh foo-mahr)

Dejé de fumar hace 6 años.
I quit smoking 6 years ago.

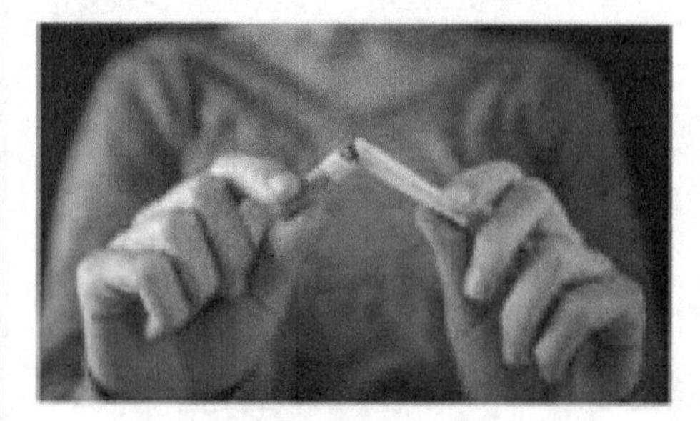

TO QUIT SMOKING

LA SALUD - HEALTH

ME SIENTO DÉBIL

(meh syehn-toh deh-beel)

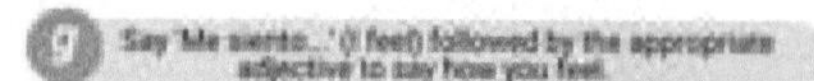

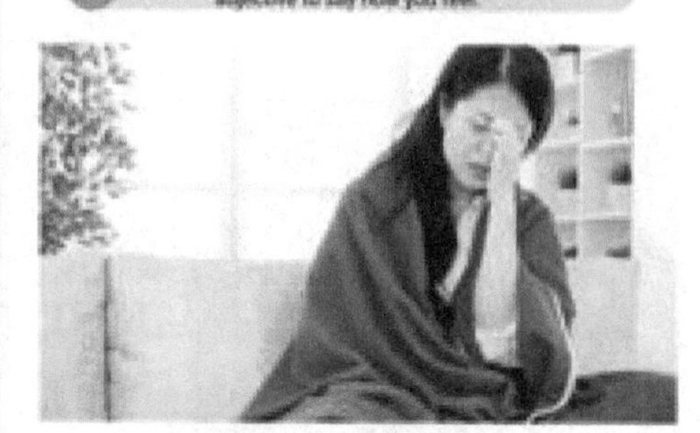

I FEEL WEAK

LA SALUD - HEALTH

¿DÓNDE PUEDO TOMAR UN TAXI?

(dohn-deh pweh-doh toh-mahr oon tahk-see)

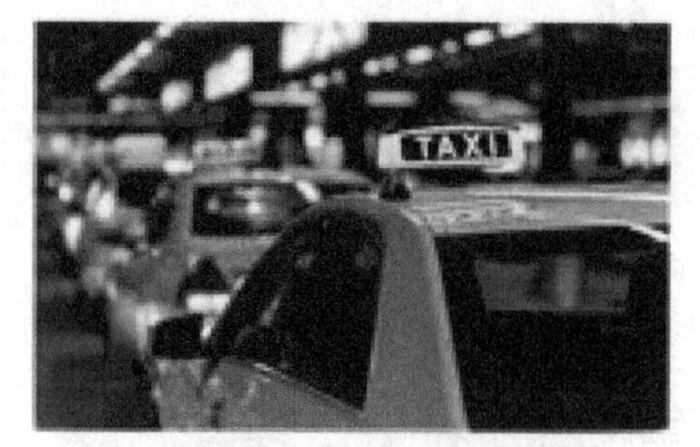

WHERE CAN I TAKE A TAXI?

VIAJANDO - TRAVELING

LA AEROLÍNEA

(lah ah-eh-roh-lee-neh-ah)

AIRLINE

VIAJANDO - TRAVELING

LA PUERTA DE EMBARQUE

(lah pwehr-tah deh ehm-bahr-keh)

BOARDING GATE

VIAJANDO - TRAVELING

EL PASABORDO

(ehl pah-sah-bohr-doh)

BOARDING PASS

VIAJANDO - TRAVELING

EL PASAPORTE

(ehl pah-sah-pohr-teh)

g *Masculine noun*

PASSPORT

VIAJANDO - TRAVELING

EL TIQUETE

(ehl tee-keh-teh)

 *Masculine noun*

PLANE TICKET

VIAJANDO - TRAVELING

EL EQUIPAJE DE MANO

(ehl eh-kee-pah-heh deh mah-noh)

g Masculine noun

CARRY-ON LUGGAGE

VIAJANDO - TRAVELING

EL EQUIPAJE DE BODEGA

(ehl eh-kee-pah-heh deh boh-deh-gah)

g Masculine noun

CHECKED LUGGAGE

VIAJANDO - TRAVELING

LA SALA DE ESPERA

(lah sah-lah deh ehs-peh-rah)

WAITING ROOM

VIAJANDO - TRAVELING

LA PLAZOLETA DE COMIDAS

(lah plah-soh-leh-tah deh koh-mee-dahs)

p The pronunciation of "plazoleta" in Spain is "plah-thoh-leh-tah."

FOOD COURT

VIAJANDO - TRAVELING

LOS RESTAURANTES

(lohs rrehs-tow-rahn-tehs)

Masculine noun

RESTAURANTS

VIAJANDO - TRAVELING

LA ESCALA

(lah ehs-kah-lah)

STOPOVER

VIAJANDO - TRAVELING

¿DÓNDE PUEDO CARGAR MI MÓVIL?

(dohn-deh pweh-doh kahr-gahr mee moh-beel)

WHERE CAN I CHARGE MY CELL PHONE?

VIAJANDO - TRAVELING

LA INFORMACIÓN DE VUELO

(lah eem-fohr-mah-syohn deh bweh-loh)

p The pronunciation of "información" in Spain is 'eem-fohr-mah-thyohn'.

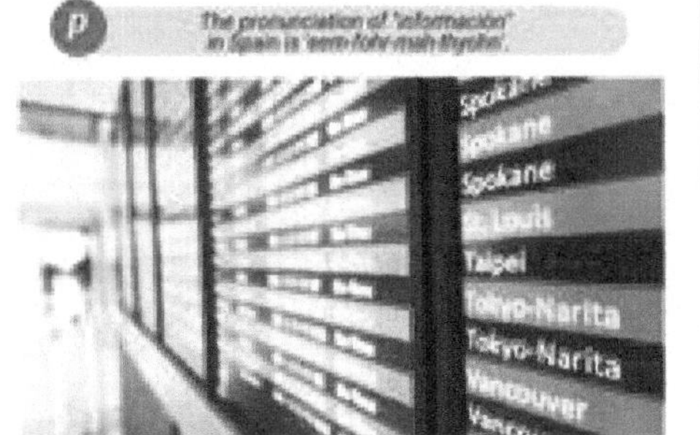

FLIGHT INFORMATION

VIAJANDO - TRAVELING

¿CUÁL ES LA HORA DE LLEGADA?

(kwahl ehs lah oh-rah deh yeh-gah-dah)

7375	9:58 AM	A10	Landed
5682	10:12 AM	B1	Now 11:00 AM
2915	10:25 AM	B12	Now 10:20 AM
281	10:42 AM	S4	Now 10:09 AM
2296	10:40 AM	C10	Now 10:43 AM
126	11:05 AM	C9	Now 10:46 AM
490	11:50 AM	S12	Now 11:45 AM
282	9:23 AM	S9	In Customs

WHAT IS THE TIME OF ARRIVAL?

VIAJANDO - TRAVELING

¿CUÁL ES LA HORA DE SALIDA?

(kwahl ehs lah oh-rah deh sah-lee-dah)

WHAT IS THE TIME OF DEPARTURE?

VIAJANDO - TRAVELING

LA HORA DE EMBARQUE

(lah oh-rah deh ehm-bahr-keh)

BOARDING TIME

VIAJANDO - TRAVELING

EL CONTROL DE INMIGRACIÓN

(ehl kohn-trohl deh een-mee-grah-syohn)

P The pronunciation of 'inmigración' in Spain is 'een-mee-grah-thyohn.'

IMMIGRATION CONTROL

VIAJANDO - TRAVELING

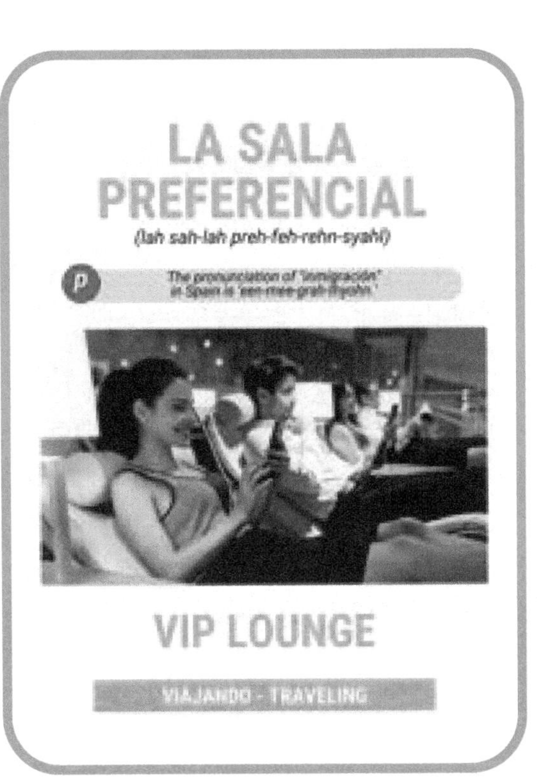
LA SALA PREFERENCIAL
(lah sah-lah preh-feh-rehn-syahl)
p
The pronunciation of "inmigración" in Spain is 'een-mee-grah-thyohn.'
VIP LOUNGE
VIAJANDO - TRAVELING

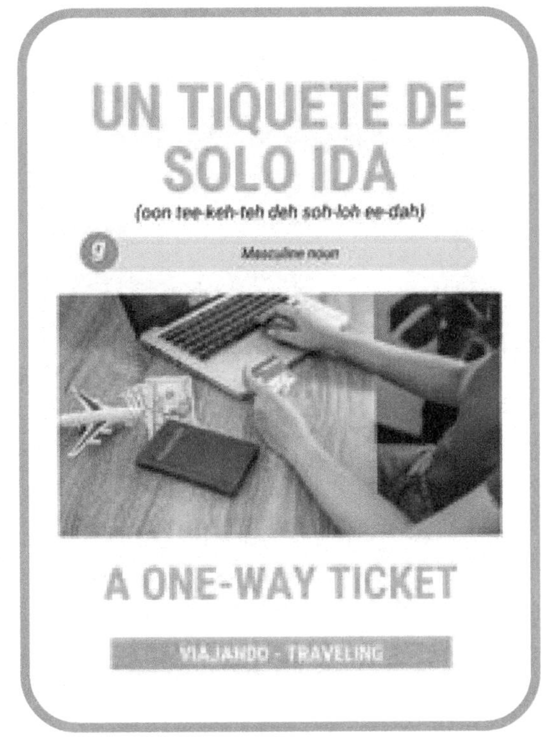
UN TIQUETE DE SOLO IDA
(oon tee-keh-teh deh soh-loh ee-dah)
g
Masculine noun
A ONE-WAY TICKET
VIAJANDO - TRAVELING

UN TIQUETE DE IDA Y VUELTA
(oon tee-keh-teh deh ee-dah ee bwehl-tah)
g
Masculine noun
SURNAME
12 7A
7B
A ROUND-TRIP TICKET
VIAJANDO - TRAVELING

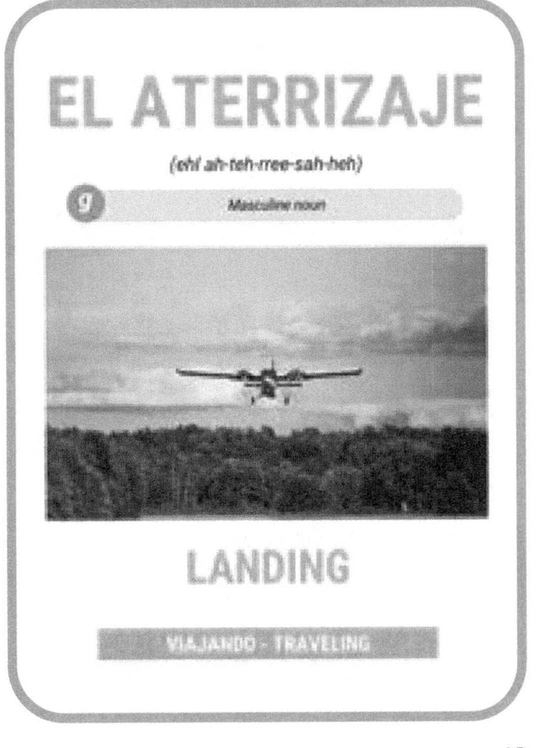
EL ATERRIZAJE
(ehl ah-teh-rree-sah-heh)
g
Masculine noun
LANDING
VIAJANDO - TRAVELING

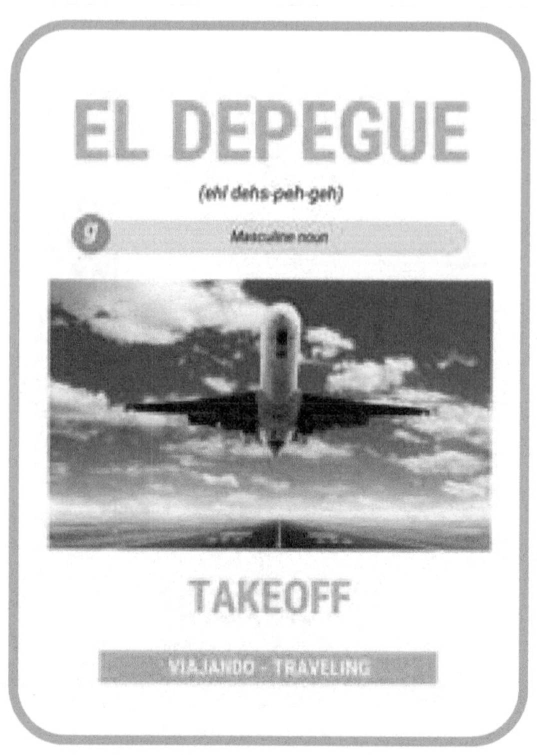
EL DEPEGUE
(ehl dehs-peh-geh)
g
Masculine noun
TAKEOFF
VIAJANDO - TRAVELING

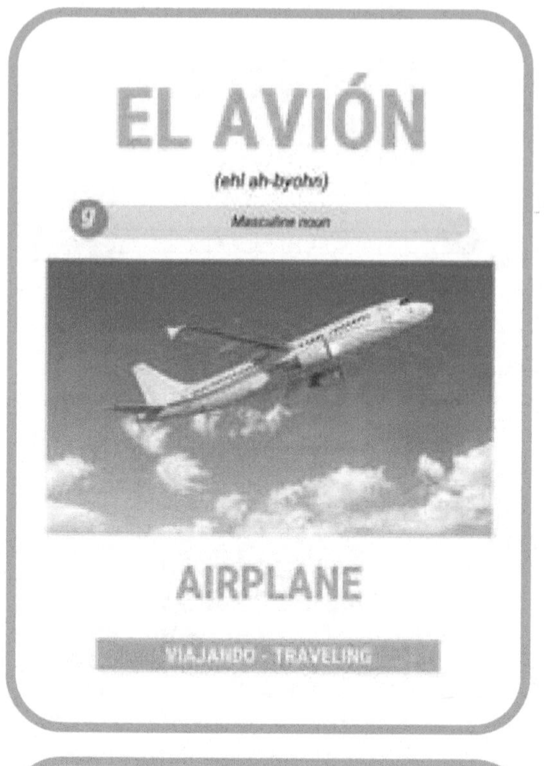
EL AVIÓN
(ehl ah-byohn)
g
Masculine noun
AIRPLANE
VIAJANDO - TRAVELING

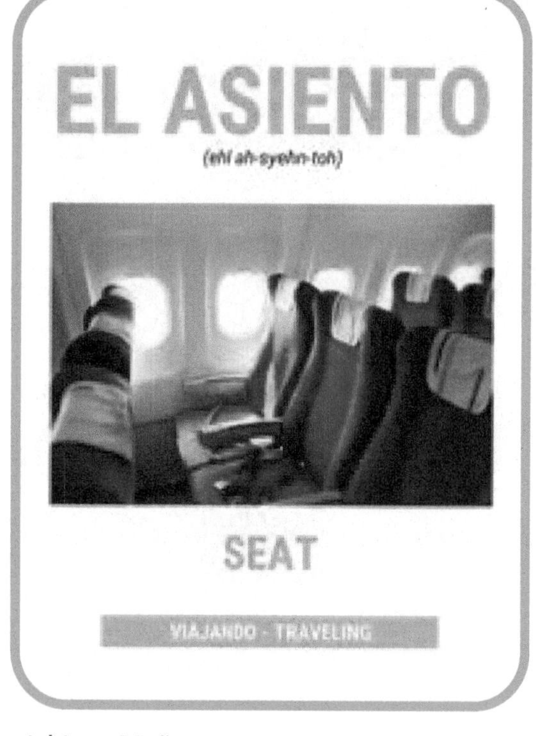
EL ASIENTO
(ehl ah-syehn-toh)
SEAT
VIAJANDO - TRAVELING

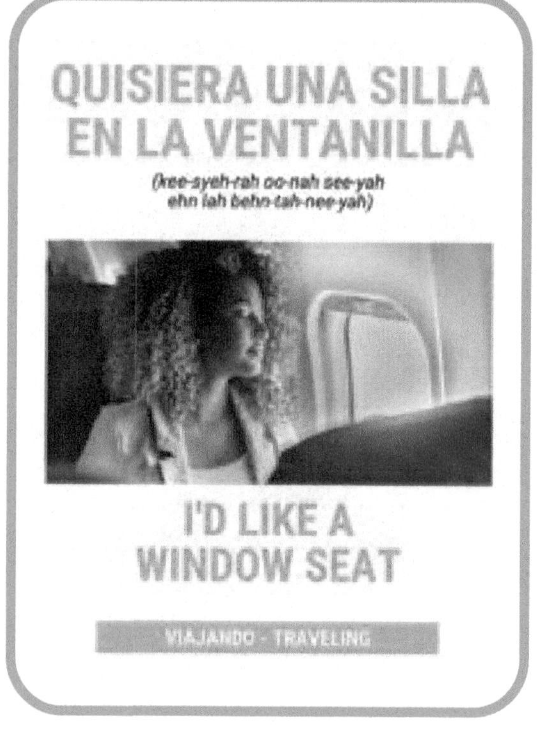
QUISIERA UNA SILLA
EN LA VENTANILLA
(kee-syeh-rah oo-nah see-yah
ehn lah behn-tah-nee-yah)
I'D LIKE A
WINDOW SEAT
VIAJANDO - TRAVELING

QUISIERA UNA SILLA EN EL PASILLO

(kee-syeh-rah oo-nah see-yah ehn ehl pah-see-yoh)

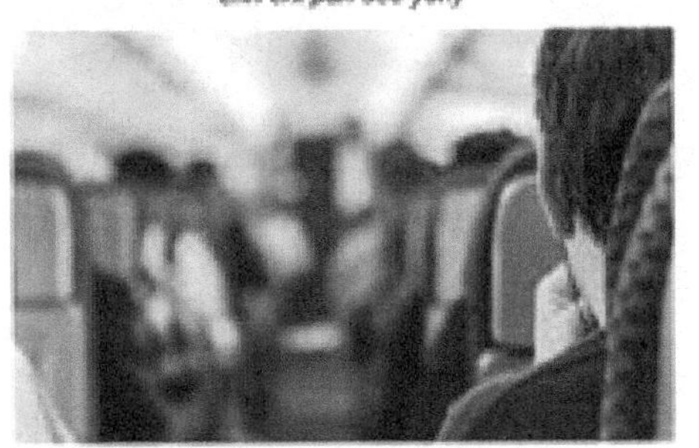

I'D LIKE AN AISLE SEAT

VIAJANDO - TRAVELING

EL VUELO ESTÁ RETRASADO

(ehl bweh-loh ehs-tah rreh-trah-sah-doh)

THE FLIGHT IS DELAYED

VIAJANDO - TRAVELING

EL VUELO FUE CANCELADO

(ehl bweh-loh fweh kahn-seh-lah-doh)

P — *The pronunciation of "cancelado" in Spain is 'kahn-theh-lah-doh'.*

THE FLIGHT WAS CANCELED

VIAJANDO - TRAVELING

LA SALIDA DE EMERGENCIA

(lah sah-lee-dah deh eh-mehr-hen-syah)

P — *The pronunciation of "emergencia" in Spain is 'eh-mehr-hen-thyah'.*

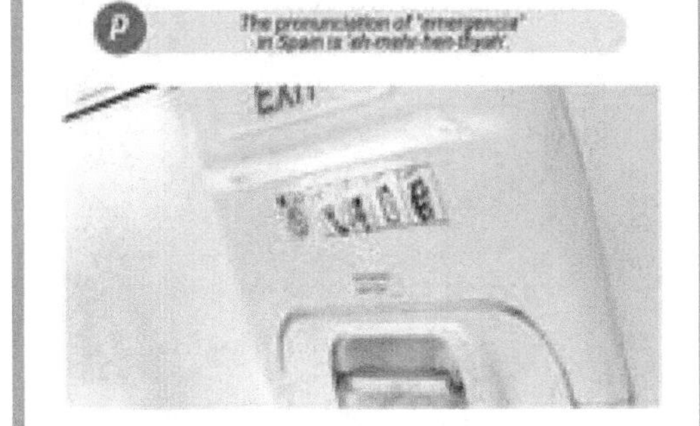

EMERGENCY EXIT

VIAJANDO - TRAVELING

LA COMIDA A BORDO

(lah koh-mee-dah ah bohr-doh)

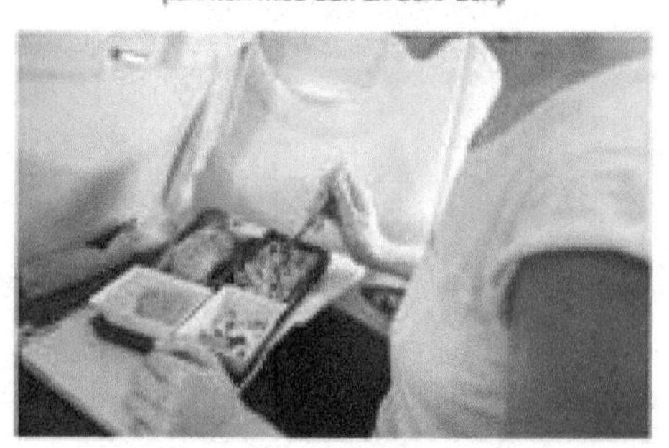

PLANE MEAL

VIAJANDO - TRAVELING

EL ENTRETENIMIENTO A BORDO

(ehl ehn-treh-teh-nee-myehn-toh ah bohr-doh)

FLIGHT ENTERTAINMENT

VIAJANDO - TRAVELING

LA VENTANILLA

(lah behn-tah-nee-yah)

WINDOW

VIAJANDO - TRAVELING

EL ALA

(ehl ah-lah)

g Feminine noun

WING

VIAJANDO - TRAVELING

LOS BAÑOS

(lohs bah-nyohs)

TOILETS

VIAJANDO - TRAVELING

VIAJO EN PRIMERA CLASE

(byah-hoh ehn pree-meh-rah klah-seh)

I TRAVEL IN FIRST CLASS

VIAJANDO - TRAVELING

VIAJAS EN CLASE EJECUTIVA

(byah-hahs ehn klah-seh eh-heh-koo-tee-bah)

YOU TRAVEL IN BUSINESS CLASS

VIAJANDO - TRAVELING

VIAJAMOS EN CLASE TURISTA

(byah-hah-mohs ehn klah-seh too-rees-tah)

WE TRAVEL IN ECONOMY CLASS

VIAJANDO - TRAVELING

EL PILOTO

(ehl pee-loh-toh)

g For the female version, simply change the article: 'la piloto.'

PILOT

VIAJANDO - TRAVELING

LA ASISTENTE DE VUELO

(lah ah-sees-tehn-teh deh bweh-loh)

g For the male version, simply change the article: 'el asistente.'

FLIGHT ATTENDANT

VIAJANDO - TRAVELING

LA ADUANA

(lah ah-dwah-nah)

CUSTOMS

VIAJANDO - TRAVELING

EL AEROPUERTO

(ehl ah-eh-roh-pwehr-toh)

AIRPORT

VIAJANDO - TRAVELING

LOS PASAJEROS

(lohs pah-sah-heh-rohs)

PASSENGERS

VIAJANDO - TRAVELING

EL VUELO DE CONEXIÓN

(ehl bweh-loh deh koh-nehk-syohn)

CONNECTING FLIGHT

VIAJANDO - TRAVELING

LA RECOGIDA DEL EQUIPAJE

(lah reh-koh-hee-dah dehl eh-kee-pah-heh)

BAGGAGE CLAIM

VIAJANDO - TRAVELING

EL DESTINO

(ehl dehs-tee-noh)

DESTINATION

VIAJANDO - TRAVELING

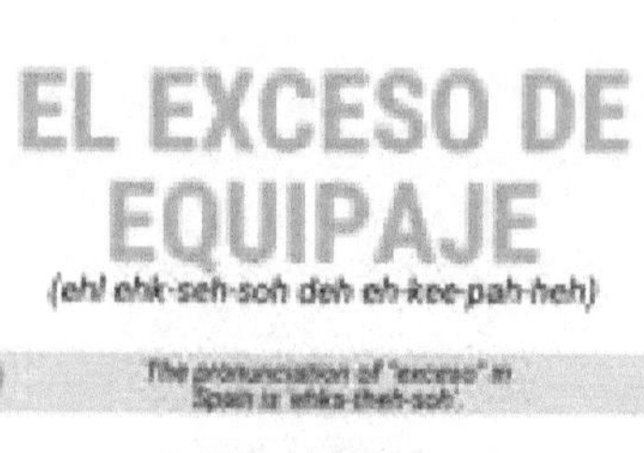

EL EXCESO DE EQUIPAJE

(ehl ehk-seh-soh deh eh-kee-pah-heh)

P The pronunciation of "exceso" in Spain is 'ehks-theh-soh'.

EXCESS BAGGAGE

VIAJANDO - TRAVELING

EL NÚMERO DE VUELO

(ehl noo-meh-roh deh bweh-loh)

105 Dresden
34 Bremen
73 Hongkong
481 London-City Airport
322 Sankt Petersburg
468 Amsterdam
423 Paris-Ch De Gaulle
63 Stockholm

FLIGHT NUMBER

VIAJANDO - TRAVELING

UN VUELO DIRECTO

(oon bweh-loh dee-rehk-toh)

DIRECT FLIGHT

VIAJANDO - TRAVELING

LA TURBULENCIA

(lah toor-boo-lehn-syah)

P The pronunciation of "turbulencia" in Spain is 'toor-boo-lehn-thyah'.

TURBULENCE

VIAJANDO - TRAVELING

EL TRANSPORTE

(ehl trahns-pohr-teh)

Masculine noun

TRANSPORT

VIAJANDO - TRAVELING

EL TRANSPORTE PÚBLICO

(ehl trahns-pohr-teh poo-blee-koh)

Masculine noun

PUBLIC TRANSPORT

VIAJANDO - TRAVELING

LA LANCHA

(lah lahn-chah)

SPEED BOAT

VIAJANDO - TRAVELING

EL BARCO

(ehl bahr-koh)

BOAT

VIAJANDO - TRAVELING

EL CRUCERO

(ehl kroo-seh-roh)

The pronunciation of "crucero" in Spain is 'kroo-theh-roh'

CRUISE SHIP

VIAJANDO - TRAVELING

UNAS BALSAS

(oo-nahs bahl-sahs)

SOME RAFTS

VIAJANDO - TRAVELING

EL TREN

(ehl trehn)

TRAIN

VIAJANDO - TRAVELING

EL METRO

(ehl meh-troh)

SUBWAY

VIAJANDO - TRAVELING

LA CAMIONETA

(lah kah-myoh-neh-tah)

VAN

VIAJANDO - TRAVELING

QUISIERA ALQUILAR UN AUTO

(kee-syeh-rah ahl-kee-lahr oon ow-toh)

I'D LIKE TO RENT A CAR

VIAJANDO - TRAVELING

VAMOS A PIE

(bah-mohs ah pyeh)

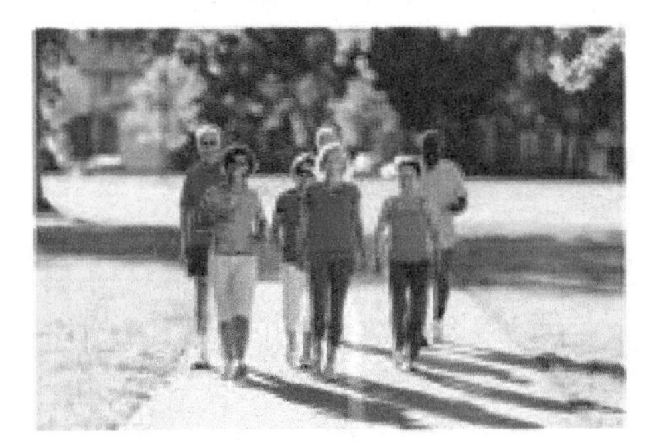

WE GO BY FOOT

VIAJANDO - TRAVELING

ALOJARSE

(ah-loh-har-seh)

V 
Nos alojamos en un hostal.
We stayed in a hostal.

TO STAY IN A HOTEL

VIAJANDO - TRAVELING

(ehl oh-tehl)

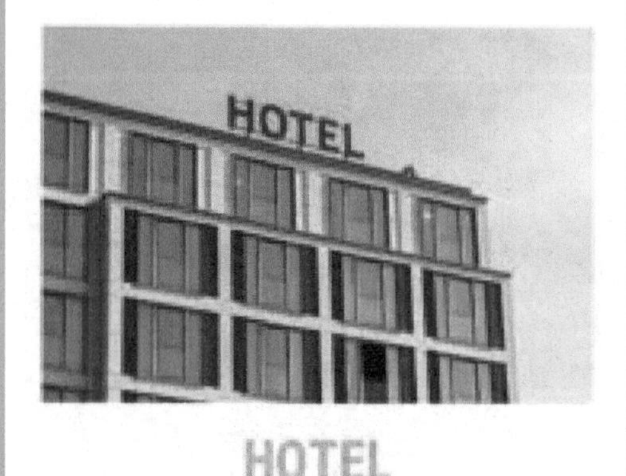

HOTEL

VIAJANDO - TRAVELING

EL HOSTAL

(ehl ohs-tahl)

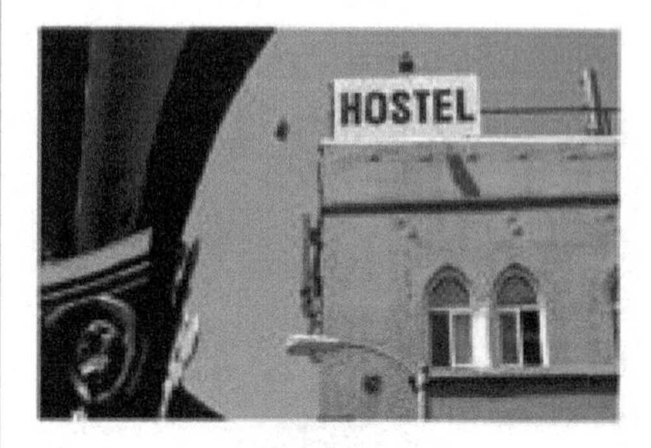

HOSTEL

VIAJANDO - TRAVELING

DESAYUNO INCLUIDO

(dehs-ah-yoo-noh eeng-klwee-doh)

BREAKFAST INCLUDED

VIAJANDO - TRAVELING

EL PARQUE

(ehl pahr-keh)

g Masculine noun

PARK

VIAJANDO - TRAVELING

EL PARQUE DE DIVERSIONES

(ehl pahr-keh deh dee-behr-syoh-nehs)

AMUSEMENT PARK

VIAJANDO - TRAVELING

EL PARQUE NATURAL

(ehl pahr-keh nah-too-rahl)

g — *Masculine noun*

NATURAL PARK

VIAJANDO - TRAVELING

EL ZOOLÓGICO

(ehl soh-oh-loh-hee-koh)

p — *The pronunciation of "zoológico" in Spain is 'thoh-oh-loh-hee-koh'.*

ZOO

VIAJANDO - TRAVELING

EL CENTRO COMERCIAL

(ehl sehn-troh koh-mehr-syahl)

g — *Masculine noun*

SHOPPING MALL

VIAJANDO - TRAVELING

LOS MUSEOS

(lohs moo-seh-ohs)

MUSEUMS

VIAJANDO - TRAVELING

LAS AGUAS TERMALES

(lahs ah-gwahs tehr-mah-lehs)

HOT SPRINGS

VIAJANDO - TRAVELING

LOS LAGOS

(lohs lah-gohs)

LAKES

VIAJANDO - TRAVELING

LOS RÍOS

(lohs rree-ohs)

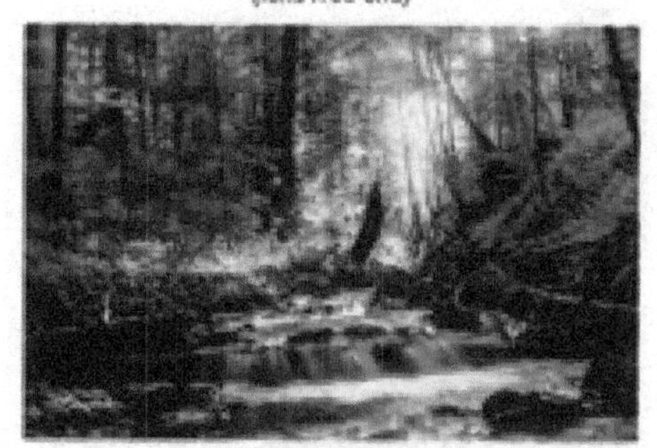

RIVERS

VIAJANDO - TRAVELING

LAS PLAYAS

(lahs plah-yahs)

BEACHES

VIAJANDO - TRAVELING

EL SITIO PARA ACAMPAR

(ehl see-tyoh pah-rah ah-kahm-pahr)

g — *Masculine noun*

CAMPING SITE

VIAJANDO - TRAVELING

EL MERCADO

(ehl mehr-kah-doh)

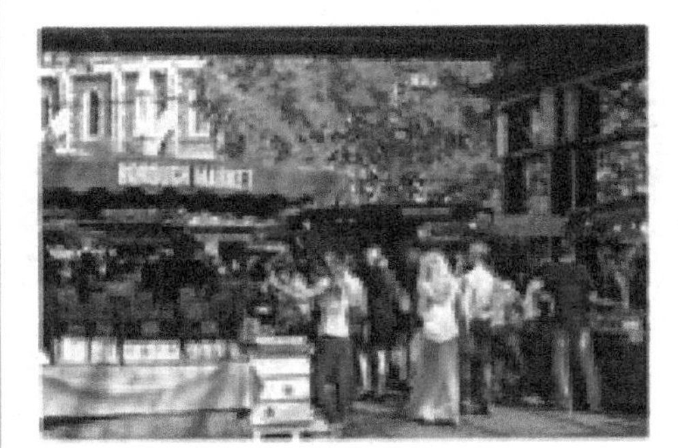

MARKET

VIAJANDO - TRAVELING

TOMAR UN AUTOBÚS

(toh-mahr oon ow-toh boos)

v — *Tomamos un autobús para ir al centro.*
We took a bus to go to the city center.

TO TAKE A BUS

VIAJANDO - TRAVELING

ALQUILAR UNA BICICLETA

(ahl-kee-lahr oo-na bee-see-kleh-tah)

Hoy vamos a alquilar bicicletas.
We're going to rent bikes today.

TO RENT A BIKE

VIAJANDO - TRAVELING

LA CALLE

(lah kah-yeh)

g — Masculine noun

STREET

VIAJANDO - TRAVELING

ESTOY PERDIDO / ESTOY PERDIDA

(ehs-toy pehr-dee-doh / ehs-toy pehr-dee-dah)

g — * Perdido = male
Perdida = female

I'M LOST

VIAJANDO - TRAVELING

¿DÓNDE ESTÁ...?

(dohn-deh ehs-tah)

g — Say 'Dónde está...' followed by the place you are looking for.

WHERE IS...

VIAJANDO - TRAVELING

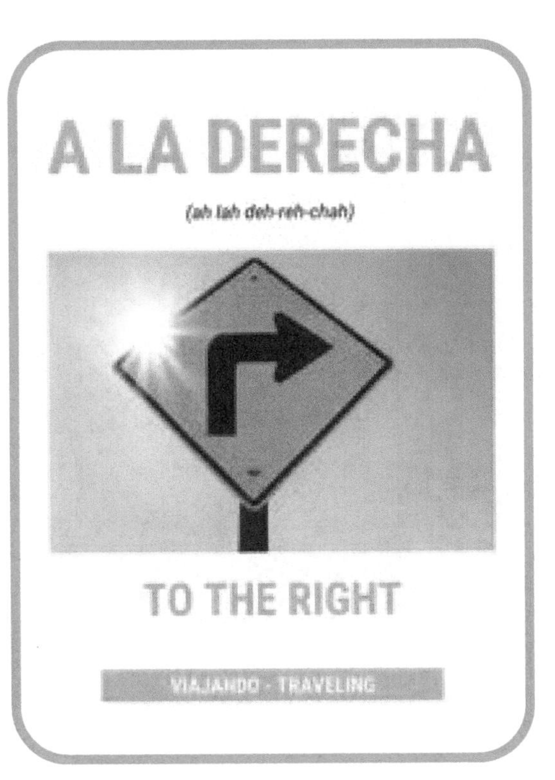
A LA DERECHA
(ah lah deh-reh-chah)
TO THE RIGHT
VIAJANDO - TRAVELING

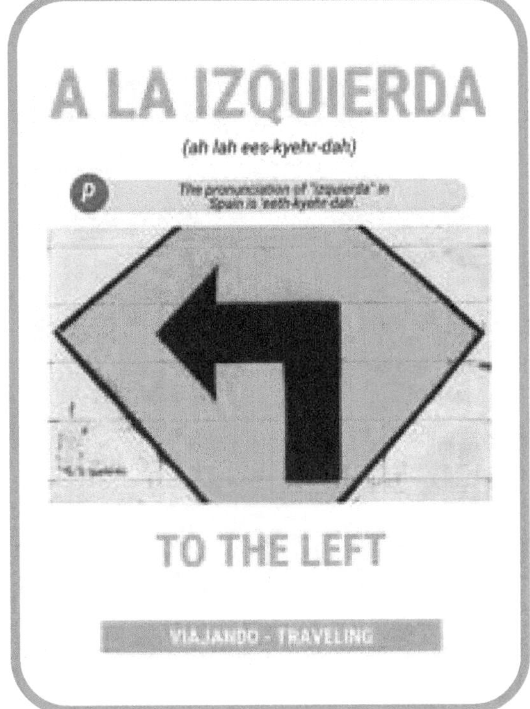
A LA IZQUIERDA
(ah lah ees-kyehr-dah)
P
The pronunciation of "izquierda" in Spain is 'eeth-kyehr-dah'.
TO THE LEFT
VIAJANDO - TRAVELING

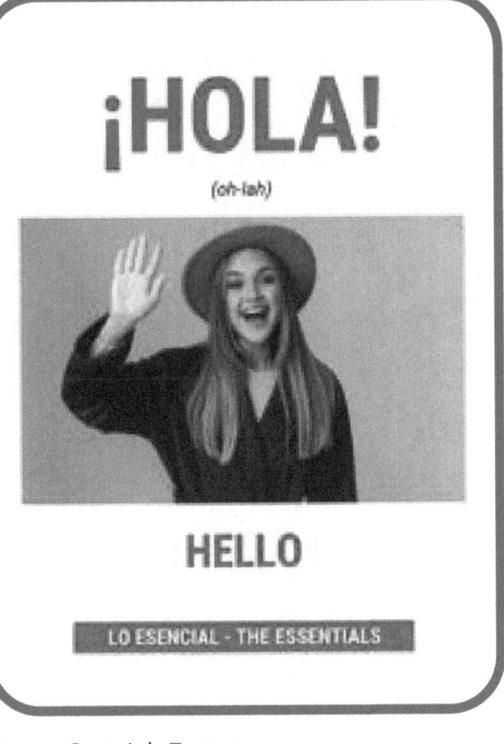
¡HOLA!
(oh-lah)
HELLO
LO ESENCIAL - THE ESSENTIALS

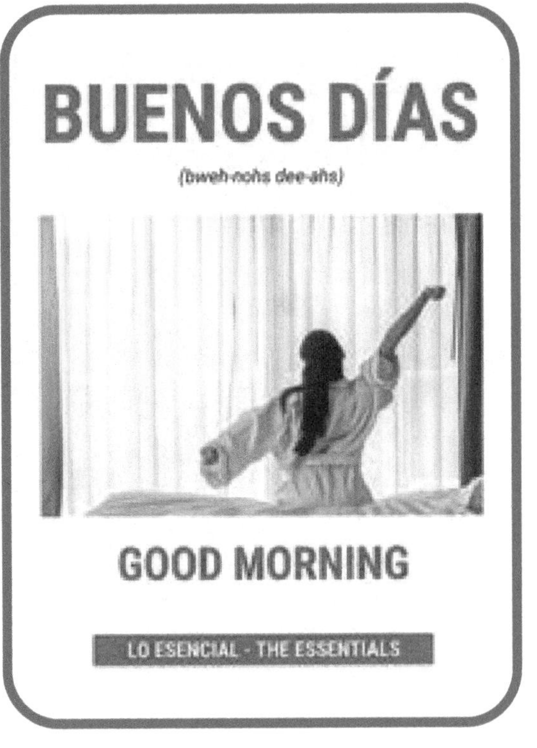
BUENOS DÍAS
(bweh-nohs dee-ahs)
GOOD MORNING
LO ESENCIAL - THE ESSENTIALS

BUENAS TARDES

(bweh-nahs tahr-dehs)

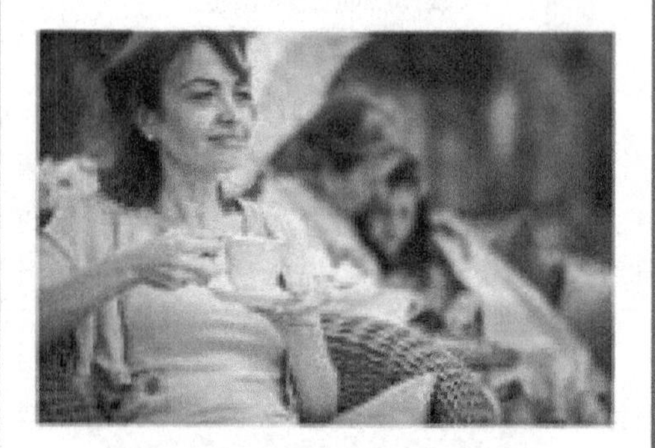

GOOD AFTERNOON

LO ESENCIAL - THE ESSENTIALS

BUENAS NOCHES

(bweh-nahs noh-chehs)

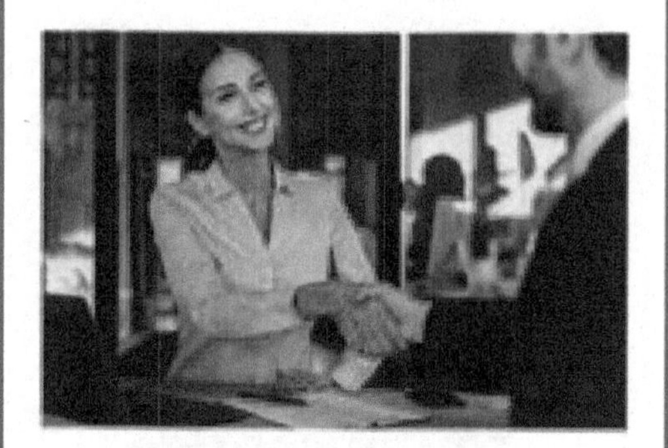

GOOD EVENING

LO ESENCIAL - THE ESSENTIALS

¿CÓMO ESTÁS?

(koh-moh ehs-tahs)

g For the formal version, say: ¿Cómo está?

HOW ARE YOU?

LO ESENCIAL - THE ESSENTIALS

MUCHO GUSTO

(moo-choh goos-toh)

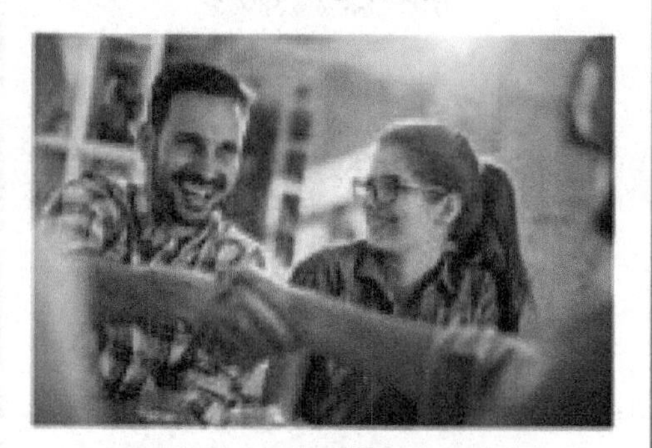

NICE TO MEET YOU

LO ESENCIAL - THE ESSENTIALS

ESTOY BIEN

(ehs-toy byehn)

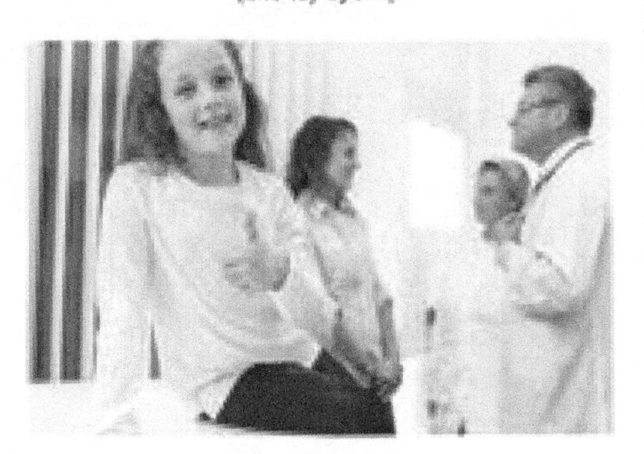

I'M FINE

LO ESENCIAL - THE ESSENTIALS

NO ESTOY TAN BIEN

(noh ehs-toy tahn byehn)

I'M NOT SO GOOD

LO ESENCIAL - THE ESSENTIALS

¿Y TÚ?

(ee too)

For the formal version, say: ¿Y usted?

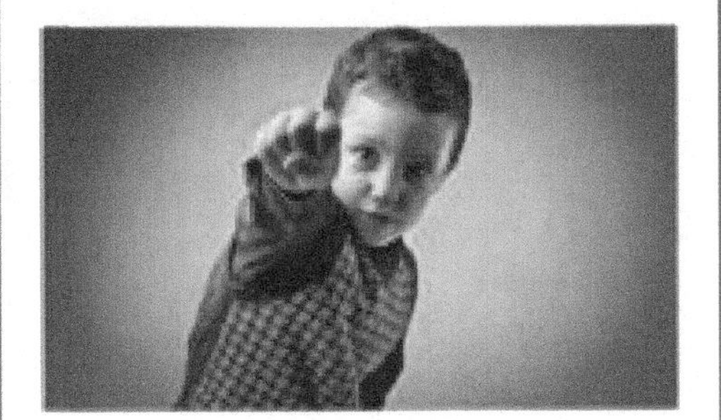

AND YOU?

LO ESENCIAL - THE ESSENTIALS

¿QUÉ TE PASA?

(keh teh pah-sah)

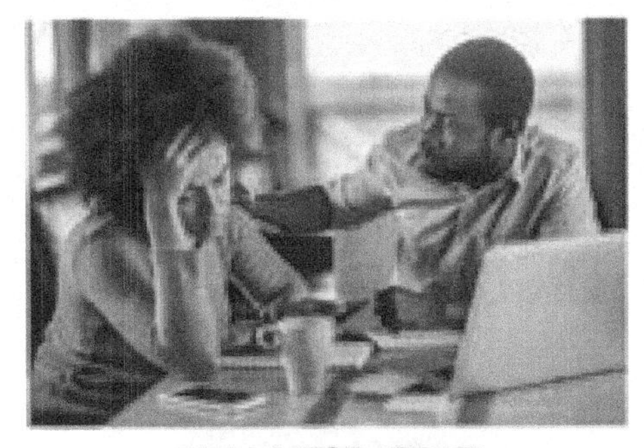

WHAT'S THE MATTER?

LO ESENCIAL - THE ESSENTIALS

SOY DE...

(soy deh)

I'M FROM...

LO ESENCIAL - THE ESSENTIALS

¿DE DÓNDE ERES?

(deh dohn-deh eh-rehs)

For the formal version, say: ¿De dónde es?

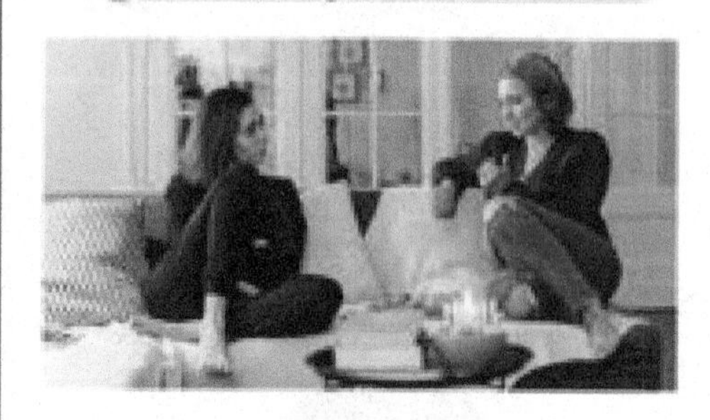

WHERE ARE YOU FROM?

LO ESENCIAL - THE ESSENTIALS

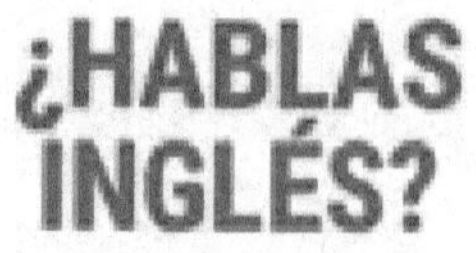

¿HABLAS INGLÉS?

(ah-blahs een-glehs)

For the formal version, say: ¿Habla inglés?

DO YOU SPEAK ENGLISH?

LO ESENCIAL - THE ESSENTIALS

¿ENTIENDES?

(ehn-tyehn-dehs)

For the formal version, say: ¿Entiende?

DO YOU UNDERSTAND?

LO ESENCIAL - THE ESSENTIALS

(noh ehn-tyehn-doh)

I DON'T UNDERSTAND

LO ESENCIAL - THE ESSENTIALS

¿PUEDES AYUDARME?

(pweh-dehs ah-yoo-dahr-meh

For the formal version, say: ¿Puede ayudarme?

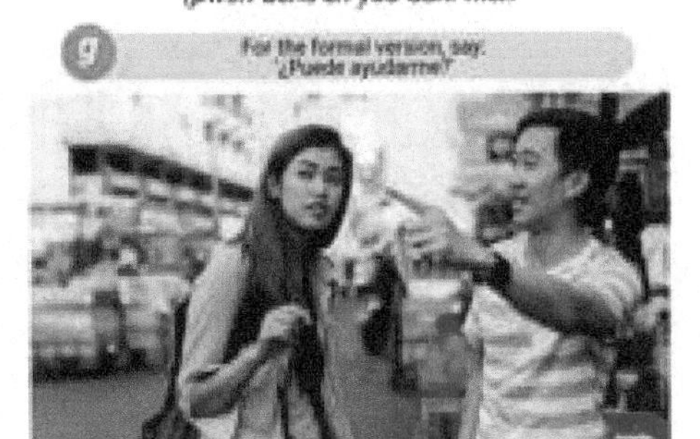

CAN YOU HELP ME?

LO ESENCIAL - THE ESSENTIALS

¿PUEDES REPETIR?

(pweh-dehs reh-peh-teer)

For the formal version, say: ¿Puede repetir?

CAN YOU REPEAT?

LO ESENCIAL - THE ESSENTIALS

¿QUÉ SIGNIFICA ESO?

(keh seeg-nee-fee-kah eh-soh)

WHAT DOES THAT MEAN?

LO ESENCIAL - THE ESSENTIALS

ESTOY APRENDIENDO ESPAÑOL

(ehs-toy ah-prehn-dyehn-doh ehs-pah-nyohl)

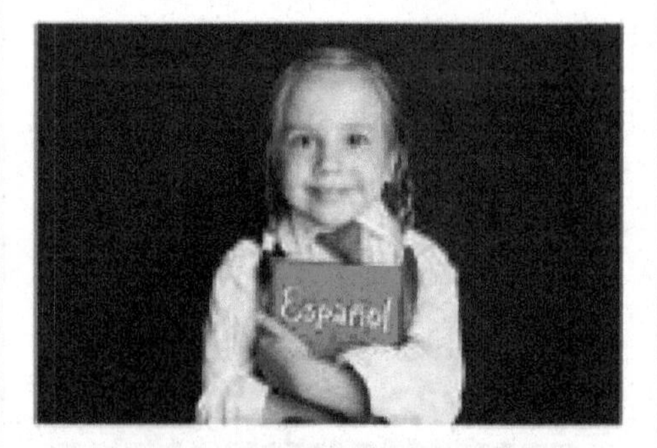

I'M LEARNING SPANISH

LO ESENCIAL - THE ESSENTIALS

¿CÓMO TE LLAMAS?

(koh-moh teh yah-mahs)

For the formal version, say: ¿Cómo se llama?

WHAT'S YOUR NAME?

LO ESENCIAL - THE ESSENTIALS

¿QUÉ HORA ES?

(keh oh-rah ehs)

WHAT TIME IS IT?

LO ESENCIAL - THE ESSENTIALS

NO SE

(noh seh)

I DON'T KNOW

LO ESENCIAL - THE ESSENTIALS

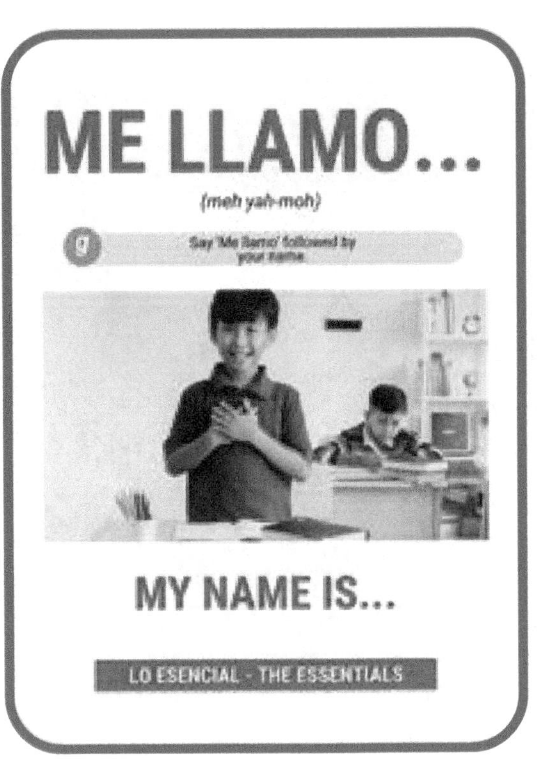
ME LLAMO...
(meh yah-moh)
Say 'Me llamo' followed by your name.
MY NAME IS...
LO ESENCIAL - THE ESSENTIALS

POR FAVOR
(pohr fah-bohr)
PLEASE
LO ESENCIAL - THE ESSENTIALS

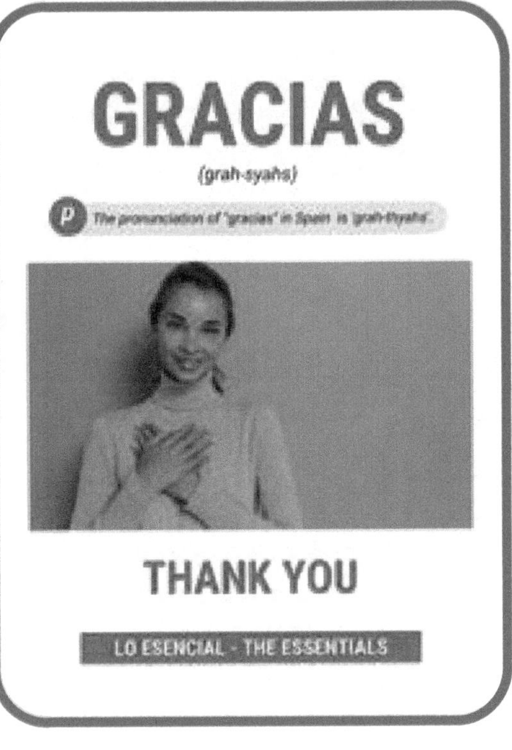
GRACIAS
(grah-syahs)
The pronunciation of "gracias" in Spain is 'grah-thyahs'.
THANK YOU
LO ESENCIAL - THE ESSENTIALS

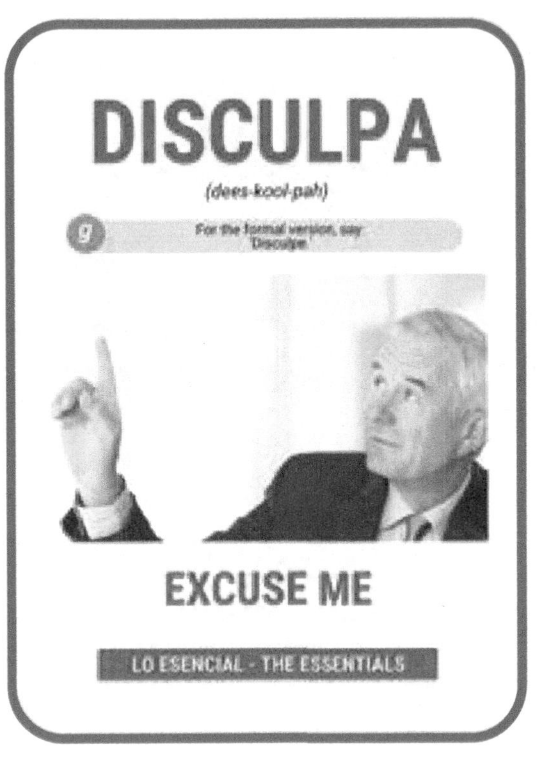
DISCULPA
(dees-kool-pah)
For the formal version, say 'Disculpe.'
EXCUSE ME
LO ESENCIAL - THE ESSENTIALS

PERDÓN

(pehr-dohn)

I'M SORRY

LO ESENCIAL - THE ESSENTIALS

ADIÓS

(ah-dyohs)

GOODBYE

LO ESENCIAL - THE ESSENTIALS

CHAO

(chah-oh)

BYE

LO ESENCIAL - THE ESSENTIALS

HASTA LUEGO

(ahs-tah lweh-goh)

SEE YOU LATER

LO ESENCIAL - THE ESSENTIALS

HASTA PRONTO

(ahs-tah prohn-toh)

SEE YOU SOON

LO ESENCIAL - THE ESSENTIALS

HASTA MAÑANA

(ahs-tah mah-nyah-nah)

SEE YOU TOMORROW

LO ESENCIAL - THE ESSENTIALS

ME GUSTARÍA...

(meh goos-tah-ree-ah)

g Say 'Me gustaría' followed by what you would like.

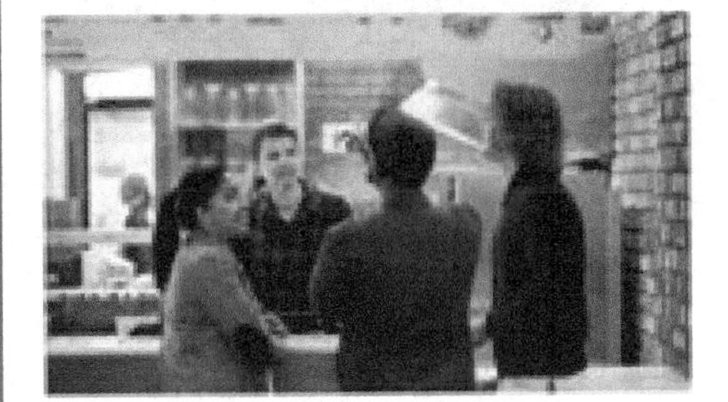

I WOULD LIKE...

LO ESENCIAL - THE ESSENTIALS

¿TIENE...?

(tyeh-neh)

g Say 'Tiene...' followed by the thing you are looking for.

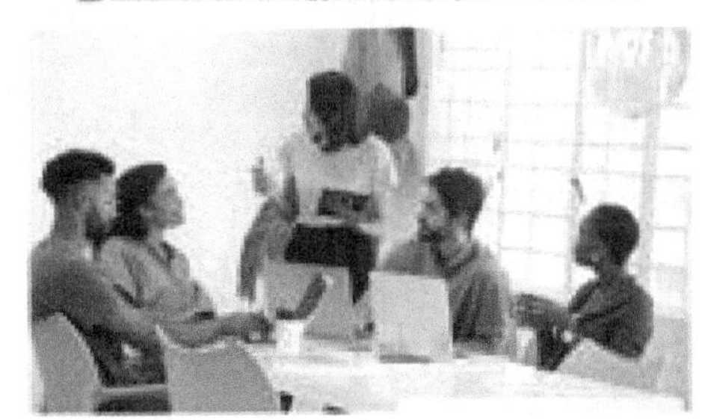

DO YOU HAVE...?

LO ESENCIAL - THE ESSENTIALS

¿ME DA...?

(meh dah)

g Say 'Me da' followed by the thing you are asking for.

CAN I HAVE...?

LO ESENCIAL - THE ESSENTIALS

¿ESTÁ CERCA?

(ehs-tah sehr-kah)

The pronunciation of 'cerca' in p Spain is 'thehr-kah'.

IS IT NEAR?

LO ESENCIAL - THE ESSENTIALS

¿ESTÁ LEJOS?

(ehs-tah leh-hohs)

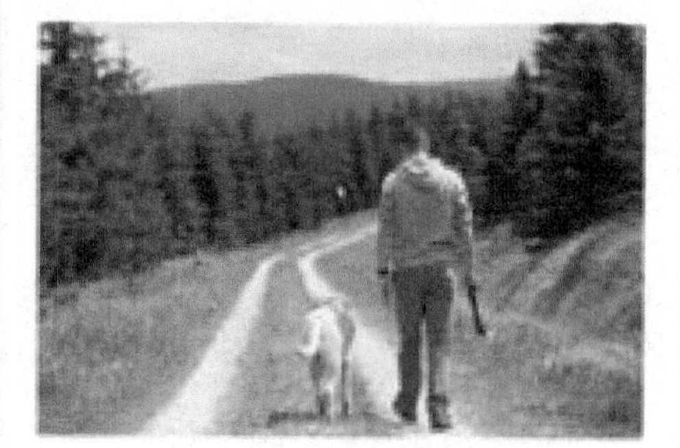

IS IT FAR?

LO ESENCIAL - THE ESSENTIALS

EL CAJERO AUTOMÁTICO

(ehl kah-heh-roh ow-toh-mah-tee-koh)

ATM

LO ESENCIAL - THE ESSENTIALS

EL BANCO

(ehl bahn-koh)

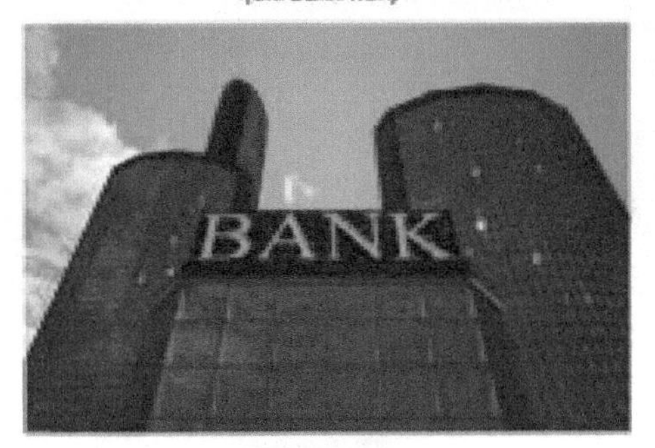

BANK

LO ESENCIAL - THE ESSENTIALS

LA CASA DE CAMBIO

(lah kah-sah deh kahm-byoh)

g Feminine noun

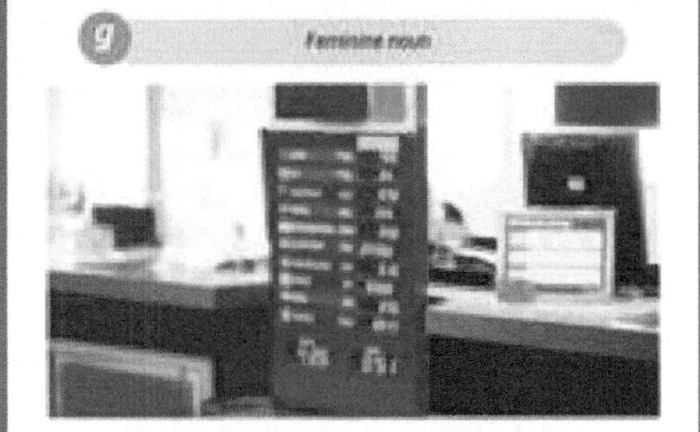

MONEY EXCHANGE

LO ESENCIAL - THE ESSENTIALS

EL DINERO

(ehl dee-neh-roh)

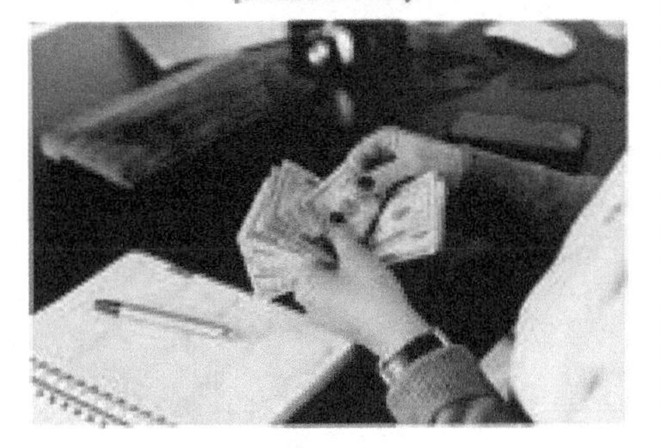

MONEY

LO ESENCIAL - THE ESSENTIALS

EL EFECTIVO

(ehl eh-fehk-tee-boh)

CASH

LO ESENCIAL - THE ESSENTIALS

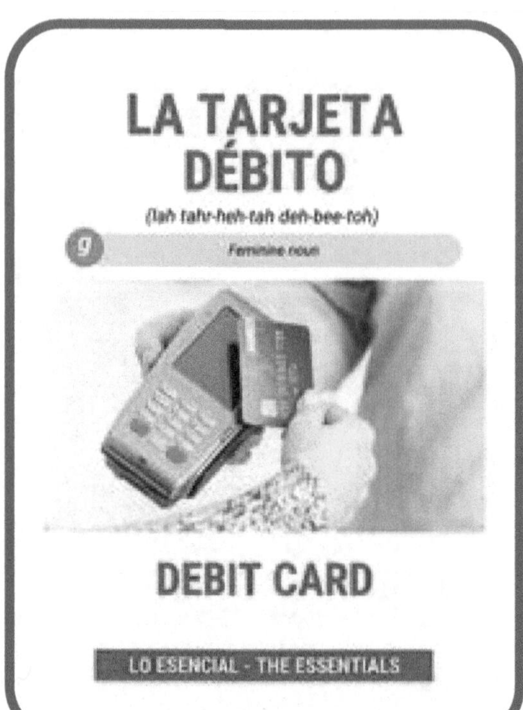
LA TARJETA DÉBITO
(lah tahr-heh-tah deh-bee-toh)
g
Feminine noun
DEBIT CARD
LO ESENCIAL - THE ESSENTIALS

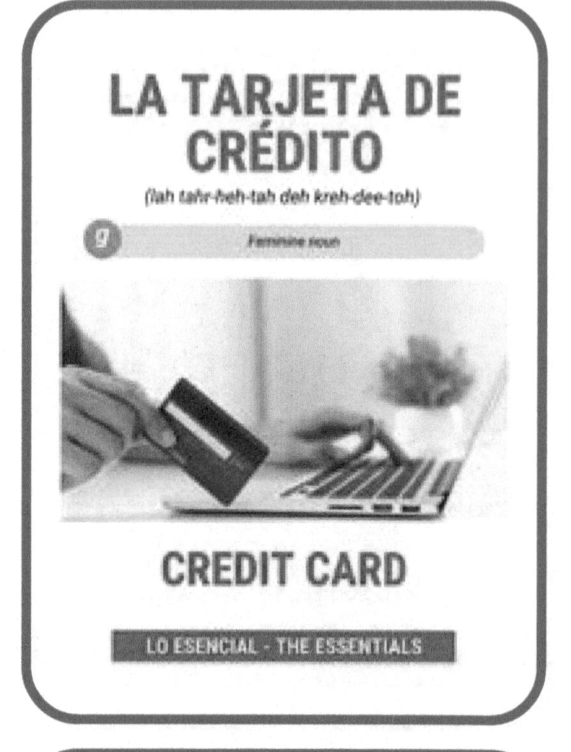
LA TARJETA DE CRÉDITO
(lah tahr-heh-tah deh kreh-dee-toh)
g
Feminine noun
CREDIT CARD
LO ESENCIAL - THE ESSENTIALS

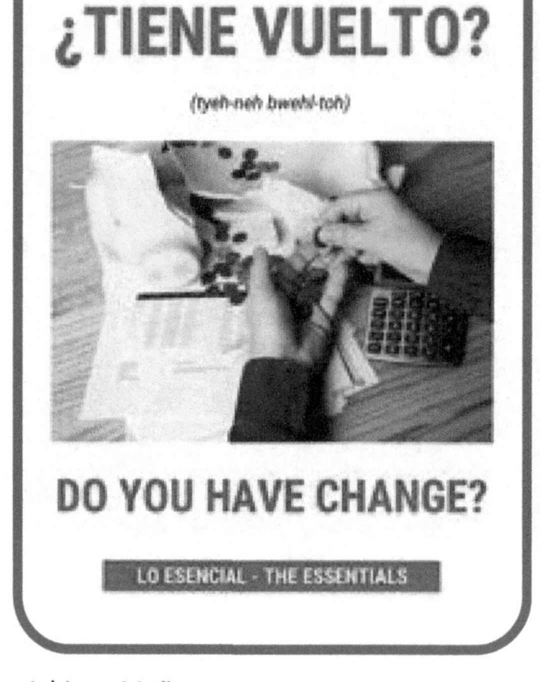
¿TIENE VUELTO?
(tyeh-neh bwehl-toh)
DO YOU HAVE CHANGE?
LO ESENCIAL - THE ESSENTIALS

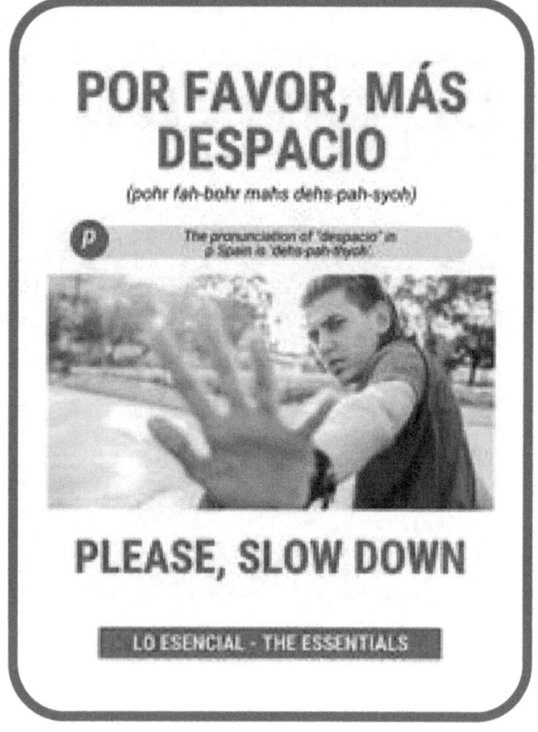
POR FAVOR, MÁS DESPACIO
(pohr fah-bohr mahs dehs-pah-syoh)
p
The pronunciation of "despacio" in Spain is 'dehs-pah-thyoh'.
PLEASE, SLOW DOWN
LO ESENCIAL - THE ESSENTIALS

¿CÓMO SE PRONUNCIA?

(koh-moh seh proh-noon-syah)

The pronunciation of "pronuncia" in Spain is 'proh-noon-thyah'.

HOW IS IT PRONOUNCED?

LO ESENCIAL - THE ESSENTIALS

GRACIAS POR TU AYUDA

(grah-syahs pohr too ah-yoo-dah)

For the formal version, say: 'Gracias por su ayuda.'

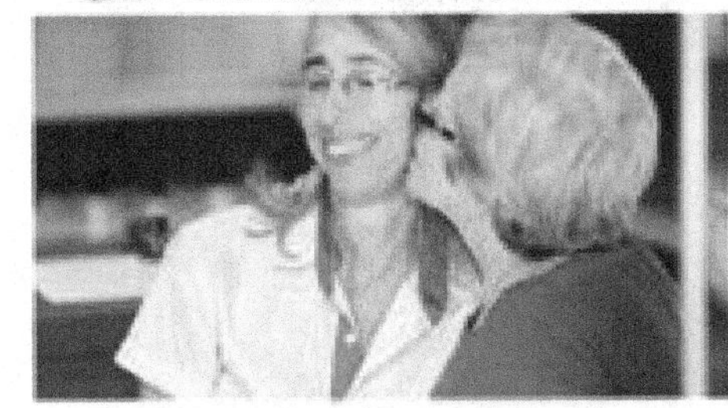

THANK YOU FOR YOUR HELP

LO ESENCIAL - THE ESSENTIALS

¿HAY ALGÚN BAR POR AQUÍ?

(ay ahl-goon bahr pohr ah-kee)

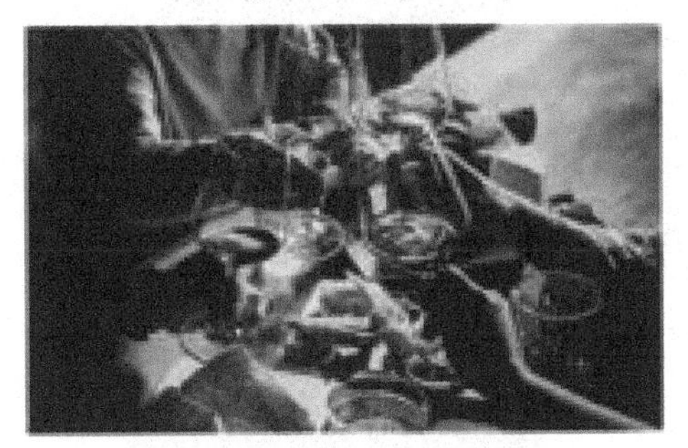

IS THERE A BAR AROUND HERE?

LO ESENCIAL - THE ESSENTIALS

¿ME PODRÍA RECOMENDAR...?

(meh poh-dryah reh-koh-mehn-dahr)

Say 'Me podría recomendar' followed by the thing you would like to be advised about.

COULD YOU RECOMMEND...?

LO ESENCIAL - THE ESSENTIALS

AQUÍ
(ah-kee)

HERE

LO ESENCIAL - THE ESSENTIALS

ALLÁ
(ah-yah)

THERE

LO ESENCIAL - THE ESSENTIALS

DETRÁS
(deh-trahs)

BEHIND

LO ESENCIAL - THE ESSENTIALS

ADELANTE
(ah-deh-lahn-teh)

AHEAD

LO ESENCIAL - THE ESSENTIALS

EN LA ESQUINA

(ehn lah ehs-kee-nah)

IN THE CORNER

LO ESENCIAL - THE ESSENTIALS

DAR LA VUELTA

(dahr lah bwehl-tah)

TURN AROUND

LO ESENCIAL - THE ESSENTIALS

A UNA CUADRA

(ah oo-nah kwah-drah)

IN ONE BLOCK

LO ESENCIAL - THE ESSENTIALS

GIRAR

(hee-rahr)

V

TO TURN

LO ESENCIAL - THE ESSENTIALS

(kyehn)

WHO?

LO ESENCIAL - THE ESSENTIALS

¿POR QUÉ?

(pohr-keh)

WHY?

LO ESENCIAL - THE ESSENTIALS

¿QUÉ?

(keh)

WHAT?

LO ESENCIAL - THE ESSENTIALS

¿CÓMO?

(koh-moh)

HOW?

LO ESENCIAL - THE ESSENTIALS

(kwahn-toh)

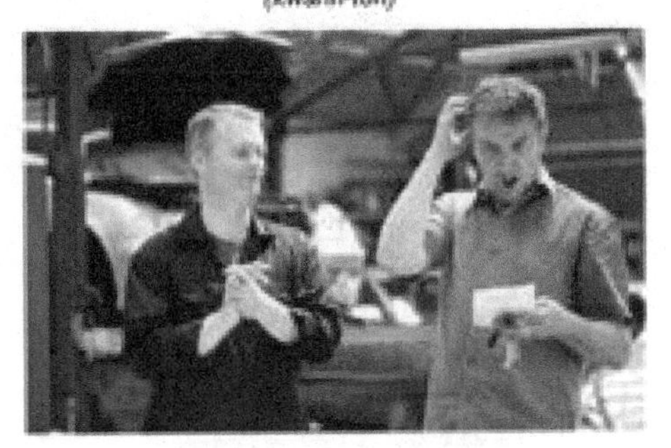

HOW MUCH?

LO ESENCIAL - THE ESSENTIALS

¿CUÁNTOS? / ¿CUÁNTAS?

(kwahn-tohs / kwahn-tahs)

Select 'cuántos' or 'cuántas' depending on the gender of what you are asking about: ¿Cuántos gatos? or ¿Cuántas gatas? (How many male/female cats?)

HOW MANY?

LO ESENCIAL - THE ESSENTIALS

¿CADA CUÁNTO?

(kah-dah kwahn-toh)

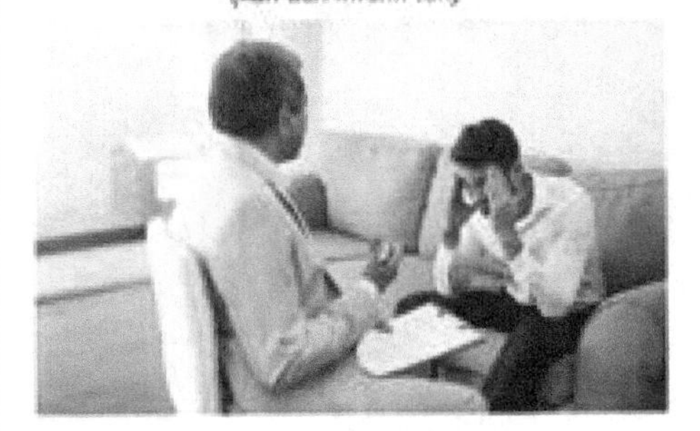

HOW OFTEN?

LO ESENCIAL - THE ESSENTIALS

¿POR CUÁNTO TIEMPO?

(pohr kwahn-toh tyehm-poh)

FOR HOW LONG?

LO ESENCIAL - THE ESSENTIALS

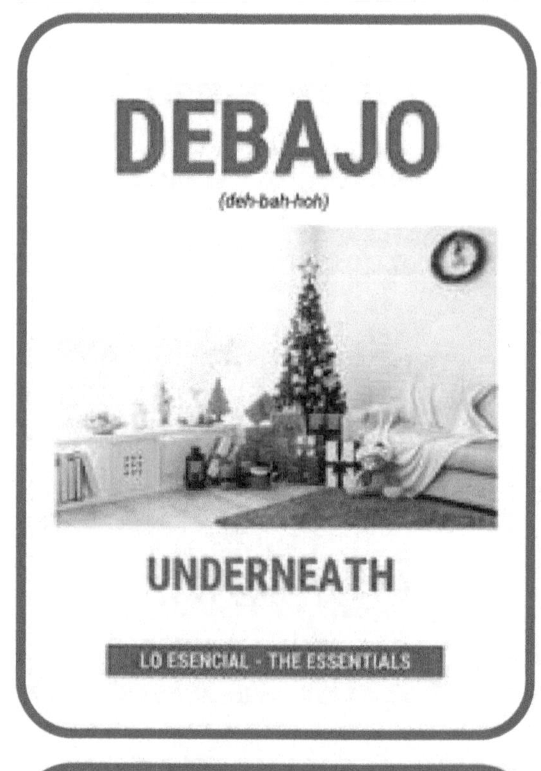
DEBAJO
(deh-bah-hoh)
UNDERNEATH
LO ESENCIAL - THE ESSENTIALS

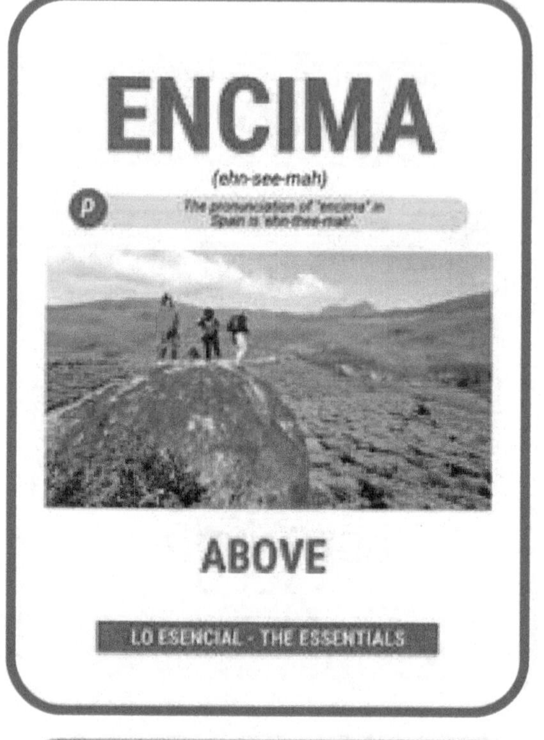
ENCIMA
(ehn-see-mah)
P
The pronunciation of 'encima' in Spain is 'ehn-thee-mah'.
ABOVE
LO ESENCIAL - THE ESSENTIALS

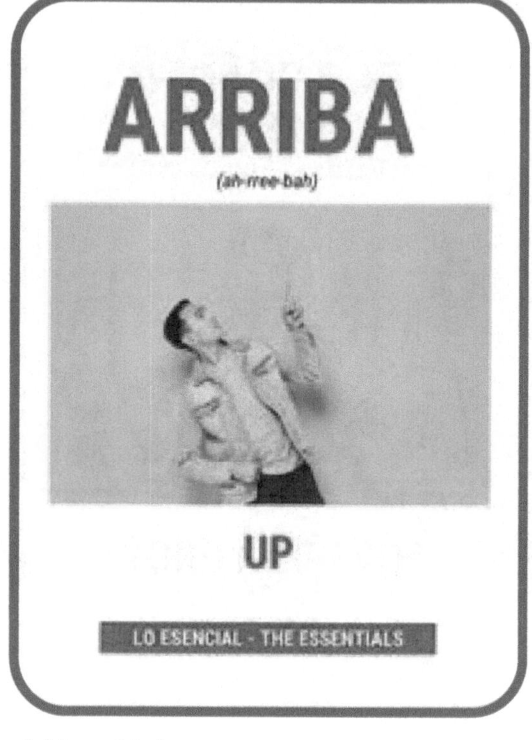
ARRIBA
(ah-rree-bah)
UP
LO ESENCIAL - THE ESSENTIALS

ABAJO
(ah-bah-hoh)
DOWN
LO ESENCIAL - THE ESSENTIALS

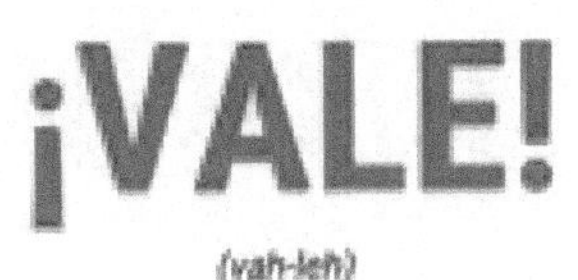

(vah-leh)

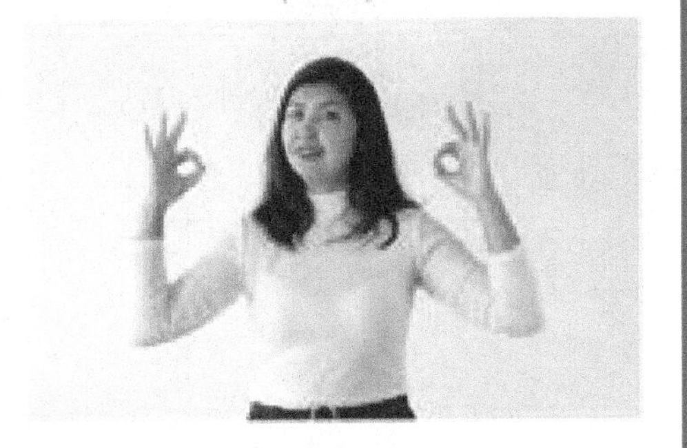

OKAY!

LO ESENCIAL - THE ESSENTIALS

¡DIOS MÍO!

(dyohs mee-oh)

OH MY GOD!

LO ESENCIAL - THE ESSENTIALS

¡AY!

(ay)

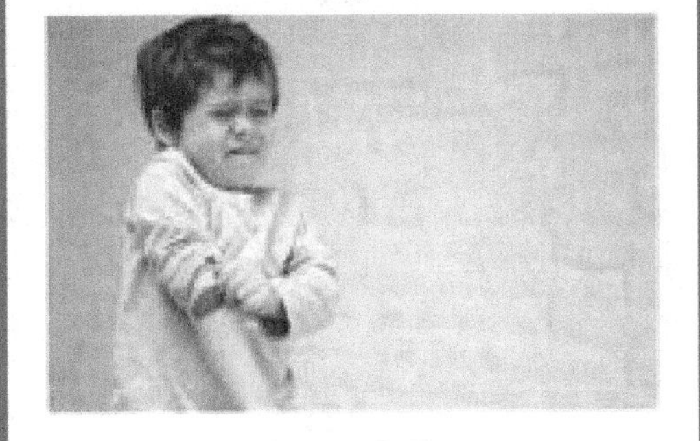

OUCH!

LO ESENCIAL - THE ESSENTIALS

¡OYE!

(oh-yeh)

HEY!

LO ESENCIAL - THE ESSENTIALS

¡BRAVO!

(brah-boh)

WELL DONE!

LO ESENCIAL - THE ESSENTIALS

¡CUIDADO!

(kwee-dah-doh)

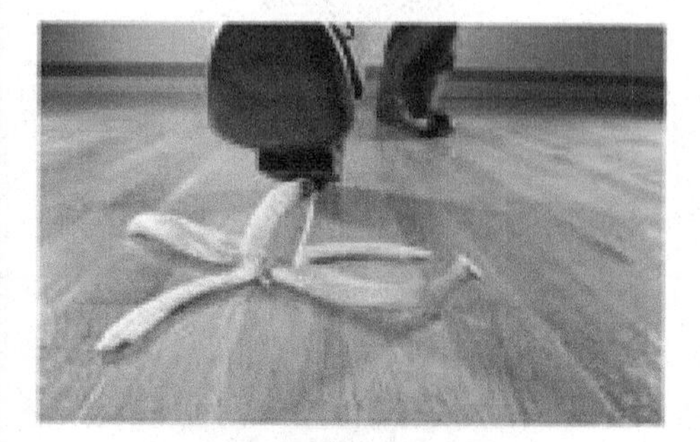

WATCH OUT!

LO ESENCIAL - THE ESSENTIALS

¡AJÁ!

(ah-hah)

YEAH!

LO ESENCIAL - THE ESSENTIALS

¡QUÉ LÁSTIMA!

(keh lahs-tee-mah)

WHAT A SHAME!

LO ESENCIAL - THE ESSENTIALS

PUES...

(pwehs)

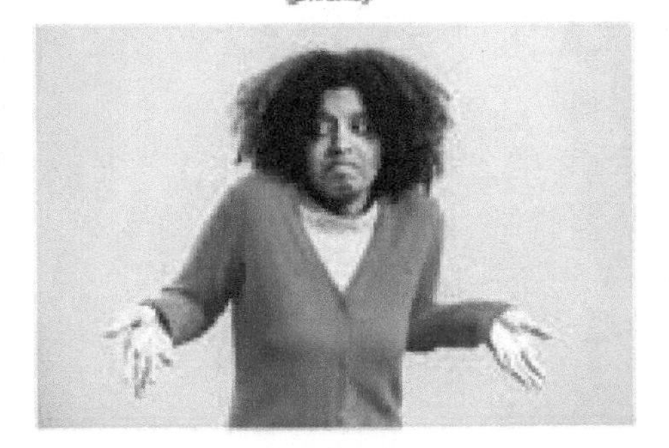

WELL...

LO ESENCIAL - THE ESSENTIALS

PERO...

(peh-roh)

BUT...

LO ESENCIAL - THE ESSENTIALS

¡POR SUPUESTO!

(pohr soo-pwehs-toh)

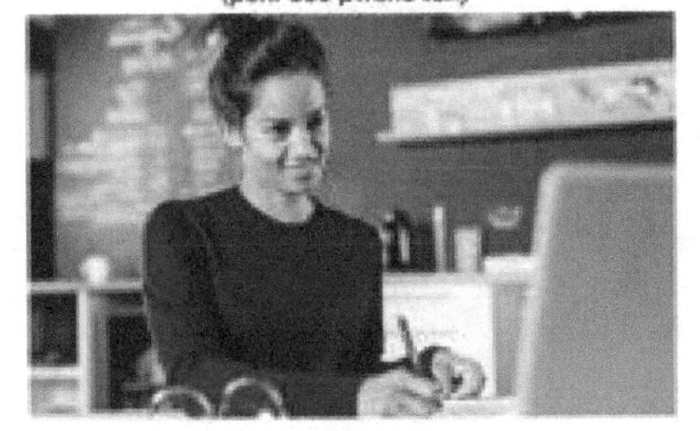

OF COURSE!

LO ESENCIAL - THE ESSENTIALS

¿SABES?

(sah-behs)

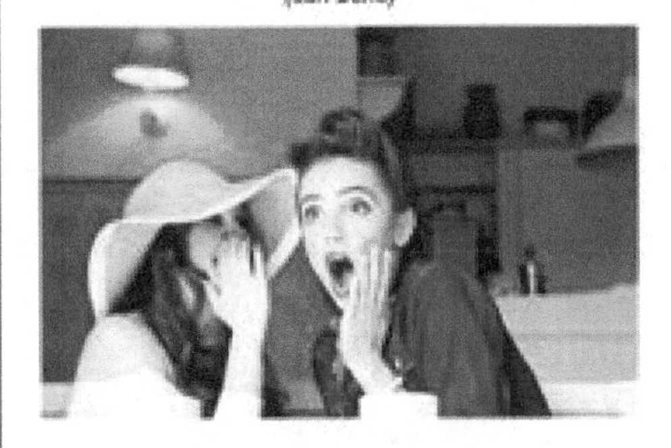

YOU KNOW?

LO ESENCIAL - THE ESSENTIALS

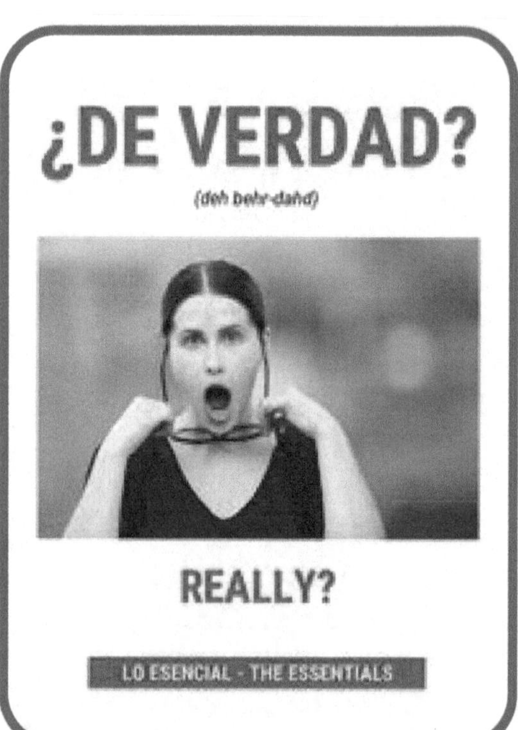
¿DE VERDAD?
(deh behr-dahd)
REALLY?
LO ESENCIAL - THE ESSENTIALS

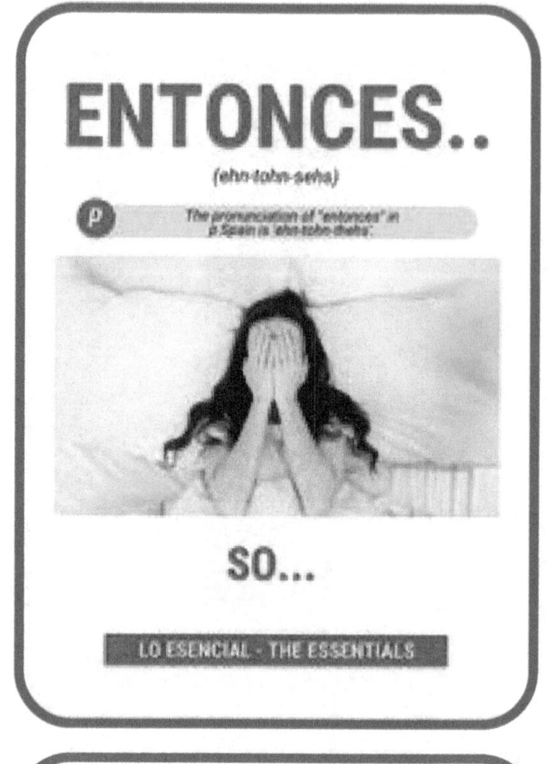
ENTONCES..
(ehn-tohn-sehs)
The pronunciation of "entonces" in Spain is 'ehn-tohn-thehs'.
SO...
LO ESENCIAL - THE ESSENTIALS

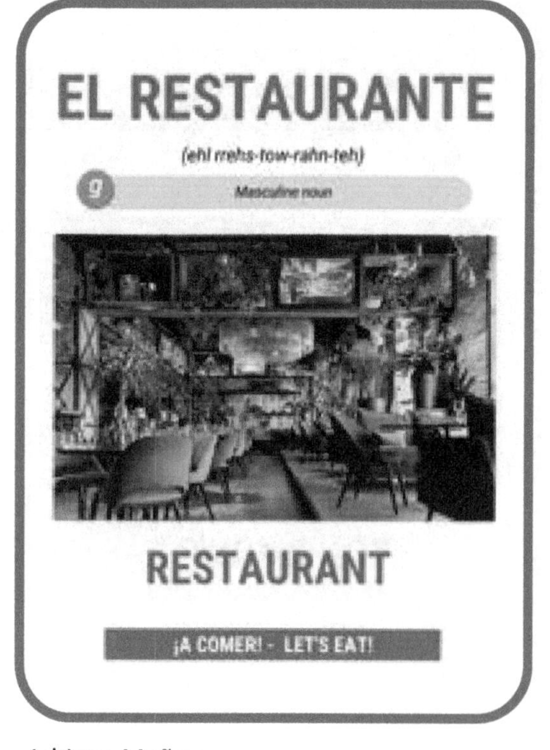
EL RESTAURANTE
(ehl rrehs-tow-rahn-teh)
g
Masculine noun
RESTAURANT
¡A COMER! - LET'S EAT!

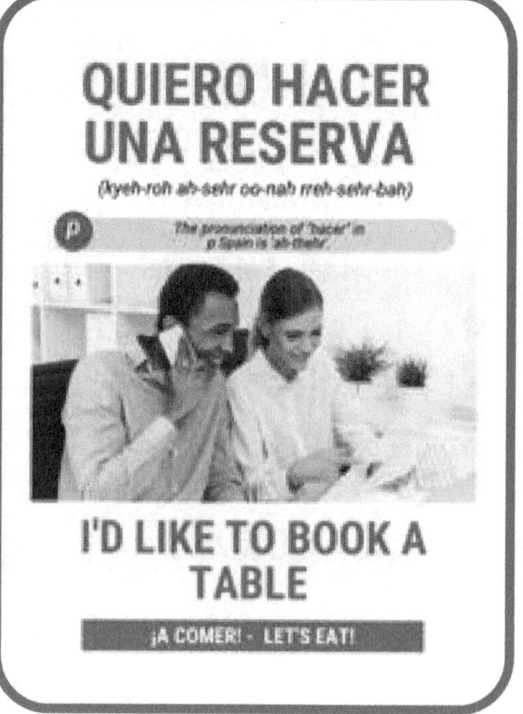
QUIERO HACER UNA RESERVA
(kyeh-roh ah-sehr oo-nah rreh-sehr-bah)
The pronunciation of "hacer" in Spain is 'ah-thehr'.
I'D LIKE TO BOOK A TABLE
¡A COMER! - LET'S EAT!

UNA MESA PARA DOS

(oo-nah meh-sah pah-rah dohs)

g Feminine noun

A TABLE FOR TWO

¡A COMER! - LET'S EAT!

QUISIERA VER EL MENÚ

(kee-syeh-rah behr ehl meh-noo)

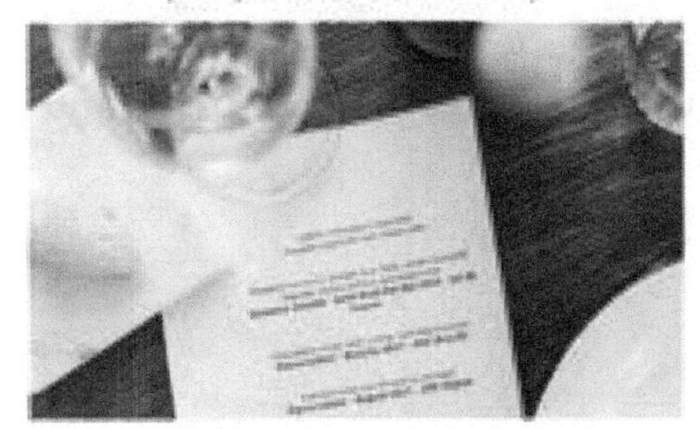

I'D LIKE TO SEE THE MENU

¡A COMER! - LET'S EAT!

¿HAY MENÚ VEGETARIANO?

(ay meh-noo beh-heh-tah-ryah-noh)

IS THERE A VEGETARIAN MENU?

¡A COMER! - LET'S EAT!

¿HAY MENÚ VEGANO?

(ay meh-noo beh-gah-noh)

IS THERE A VEGAN MENU?

¡A COMER! - LET'S EAT!

¿QUÉ ME RECOMIENDA?

(keh meh rreh-koh-myehn-dah)

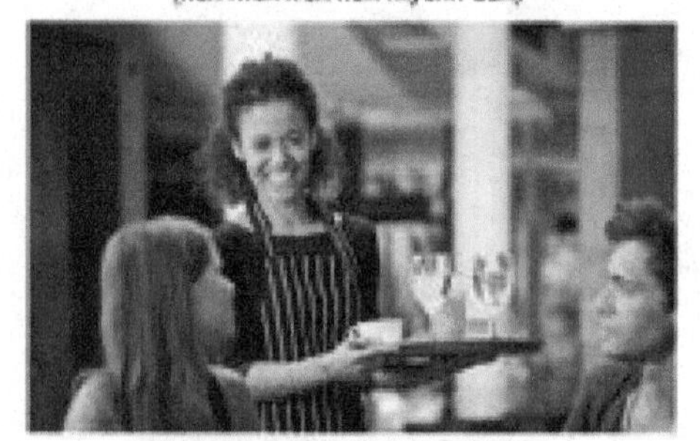

WHAT DO YOU RECOMMEND?

¡A COMER! - LET'S EAT!

LAS ENTRADAS

(lahs ehn-trah-dahs)

STARTERS

¡A COMER! - LET'S EAT!

EL PLATO PRINCIPAL

(ehl plah-toh preen-see-pahl)

g Masculine noun

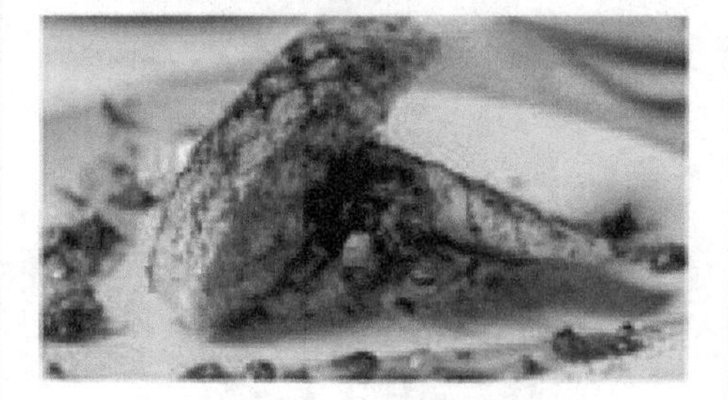

MAIN COURSE

¡A COMER! - LET'S EAT!

UNA ENSALADA

(oo-nah ehn-sah-lah-dah)

SALAD

¡A COMER! - LET'S EAT!

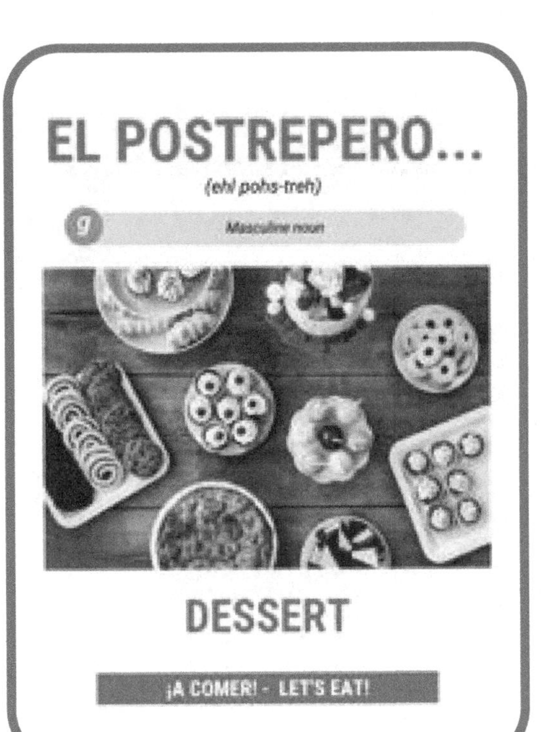
EL POSTREPERO...
(ehl pohs-treh)
g
Masculine noun
DESSERT
¡A COMER! - LET'S EAT!

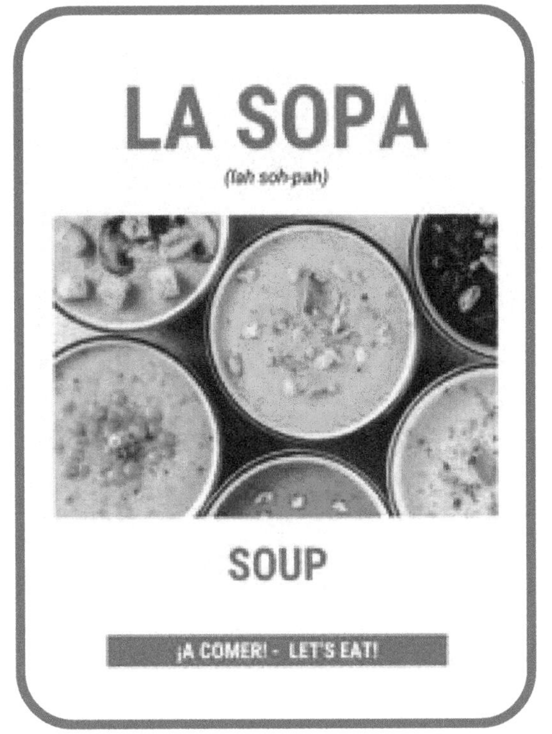
LA SOPA
(lah soh-pah)
SOUP
¡A COMER! - LET'S EAT!

LAS BEBIDAS
(lahs beh-bee-dahs)
BEVERAGES
¡A COMER! - LET'S EAT!

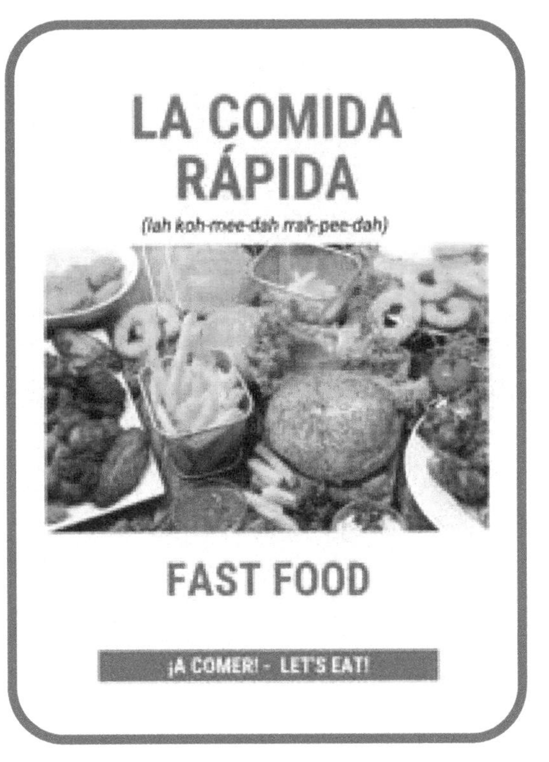
LA COMIDA RÁPIDA
(lah koh-mee-dah rrah-pee-dah)
FAST FOOD
¡A COMER! - LET'S EAT!

LA HAMBURGUESA

(lah ahm-boor-geh-sah)

HAMBURGER

¡A COMER! - LET'S EAT!

UNA PIZZA DE PEPPERONI

(oo-nah peet-sah deh peh-peh-roh-nee)

Say 'Una pizza de...' followed by the type of pizza or the toppings you want.

PEPPERONI PIZZA

¡A COMER! - LET'S EAT!

UNAS PAPAS FRITAS

(oo-nahs pah-pahs free-tahs)

In Spain, use the word 'patatas' instead of 'papas'.

FRENCH FRIES

¡A COMER! - LET'S EAT!

LOS NUGGETS DE POLLO

(lohs noo-gehts deh poh-yoh)

CHICKEN NUGGETS

¡A COMER! - LET'S EAT!

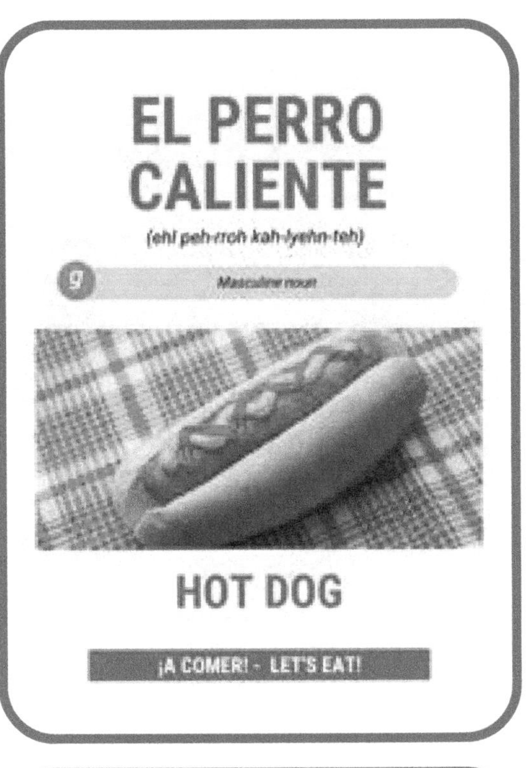
EL PERRO CALIENTE
(ehl peh-rroh kah-lyehn-teh)
HOT DOG
¡A COMER! - LET'S EAT!

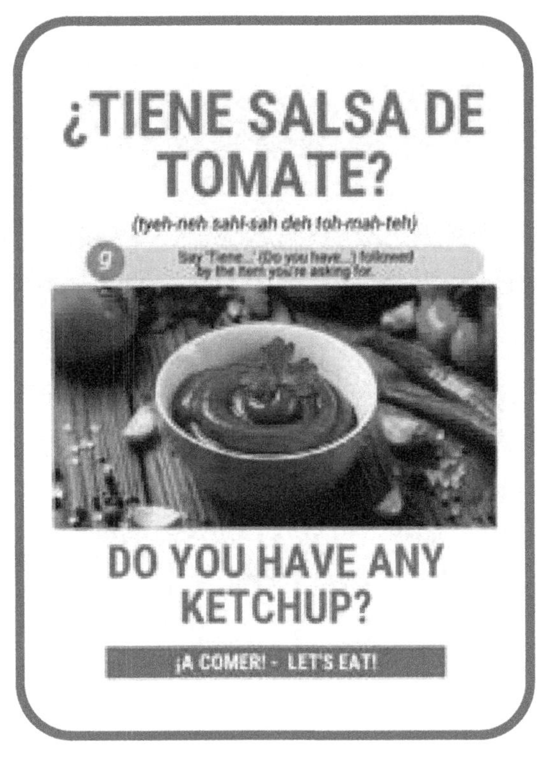
¿TIENE SALSA DE TOMATE?
(tyeh-neh sahl-sah deh toh-mah-teh)
Say "Tiene..." (Do you have...) followed by the item you're asking for.
DO YOU HAVE ANY KETCHUP?
¡A COMER! - LET'S EAT!

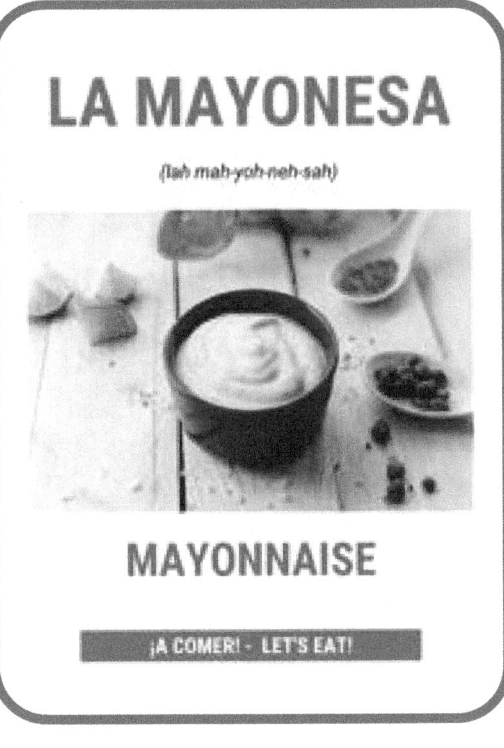
LA MAYONESA
(lah mah-yoh-neh-sah)
MAYONNAISE
¡A COMER! - LET'S EAT!

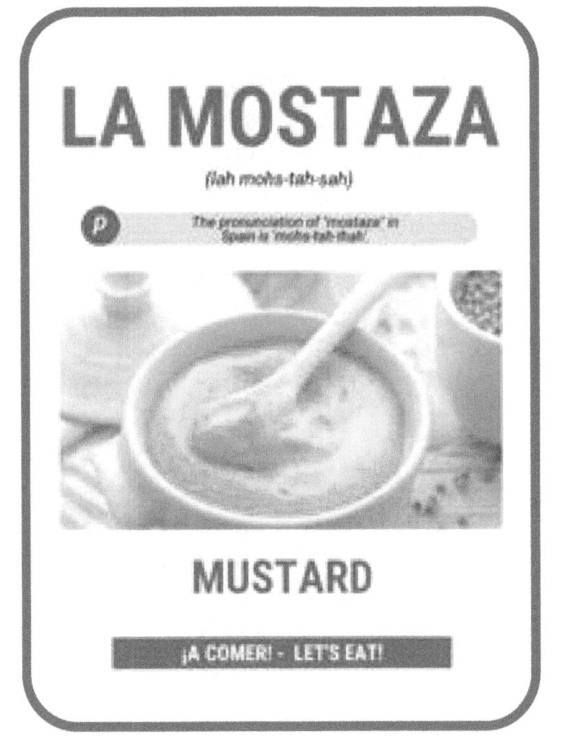
LA MOSTAZA
(lah mohs-tah-sah)
The pronunciation of "mostaza" in Spain is 'mohs-tah-thah'.
MUSTARD
¡A COMER! - LET'S EAT!

LA GASEOSA

(lah gah-seh-oh-sah)

SODA

¡A COMER! - LET'S EAT!

EL POLLO

(ehl poh-yoh)

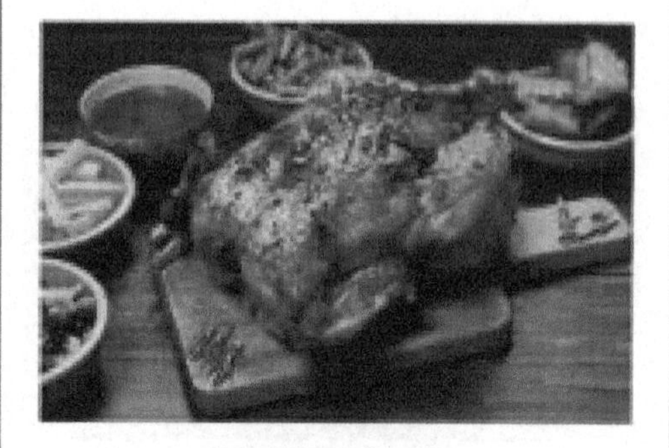

CHICKEN

¡A COMER! - LET'S EAT!

LA RES

(lah rrehs)

g — *Feminine noun*

BEEF

¡A COMER! - LET'S EAT!

EL CERDO

(ehl sehr-doh)

p — *The pronunciation of "cerdo" in Spain is 'thehr-doh'.*

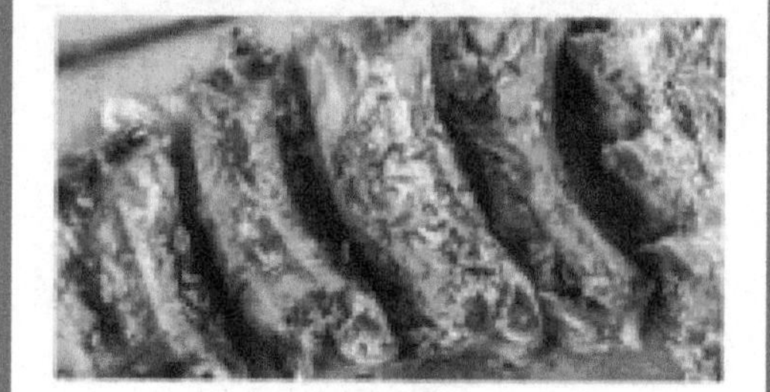

PORK

¡A COMER! - LET'S EAT!

LA CARNE DE...

(lah kahr-neh deh)

(TYPE OF) MEAT

¡A COMER! - LET'S EAT!

EL PESCADO

(ehl pehs-kah-doh)

FISH

¡A COMER! - LET'S EAT!

LOS MARISCOS

(lohs mah-rees-kohs)

SEAFOOD

¡A COMER! - LET'S EAT!

EL ARROZ

(ehl ah-rrohs)

p *The pronunciation of "arroz" in Spain is 'ah-rrohth'.*

RICE

¡A COMER! - LET'S EAT!

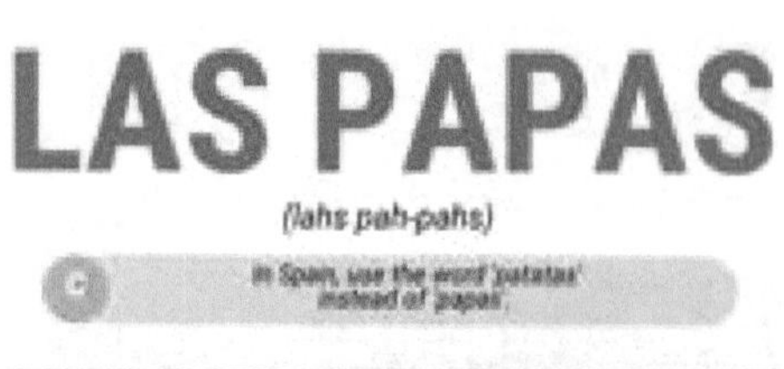

LAS PAPAS

(lahs pah-pahs)

In Spain, use the word 'patatas' instead of 'papas'.

POTATOES

¡A COMER! - LET'S EAT!

SIN CEBOLLA, POR FAVOR

(seen seh-boh-yah pohr fah-bohr)

Say 'sin' followed by the ingredient you don't want in your food.

NO ONION, PLEASE

¡A COMER! - LET'S EAT!

PARA MI...

(pah-rah mee)

Say 'para mi...' followed by your order.

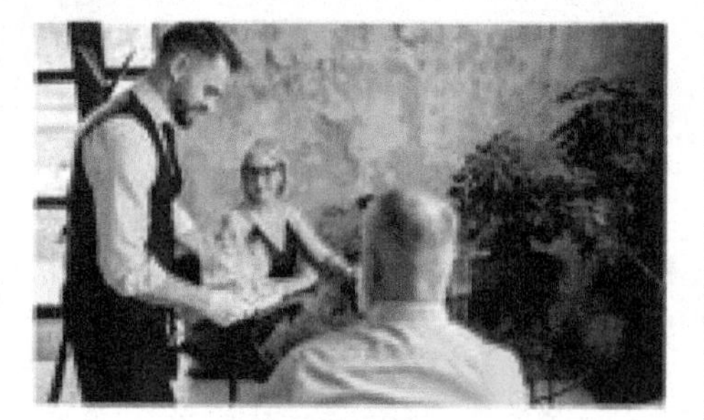

FOR ME...

¡A COMER! - LET'S EAT!

ME TRAE...

(meh trah-eh)

CAN I HAVE...

¡A COMER! - LET'S EAT!

EL AGUA SIN GAS

(ehl ah-gwah seen gahs)

g — Say 'agua con gas' if ordering sparkling water.

STILL WATER

¡A COMER! - LET'S EAT!

¿CON QUÉ VIENE?

(kohn keh byeh-neh)

WHAT DOES IT COME WITH?

¡A COMER! - LET'S EAT!

LAS BEBIDAS ALCOHOLICAS

(lahs beh-bee-dahs al-koh-oh-lee-kahs)

g — Feminine noun

ALCOHOLIC DRINKS

¡A COMER! - LET'S EAT!

UN JUGO

(oon hoo-goh)

c — In Spain, use the word 'zumo' instead of 'jugo'.

JUICE

¡A COMER! - LET'S EAT!

EL MESERO / LA MESERA

(ehl meh-seh-roh/ lah meh-seh-rah)

WAITER/WAITRESS

¡A COMER! - LET'S EAT!

¿DÓNDE ESTÁN LOS BAÑOS?

(dohn-deh ehs-tahn lohs bah-nyohs)

WHERE ARE THE TOILETS?

¡A COMER! - LET'S EAT!

LA CUENTA, POR FAVOR

(lah kwehn-tah pohr-fah-bohr)

CAN I HAVE THE BILL, PLEASE?

¡A COMER! - LET'S EAT!

EL SERVICIO ESTÁ INCLUIDO

(ehl sehr-bee-syoh ehs-tah een-klwee-doh)

SERVICE INCLUDED

¡A COMER! - LET'S EAT!

LA PROPINA

(lah proh-pee-nah)

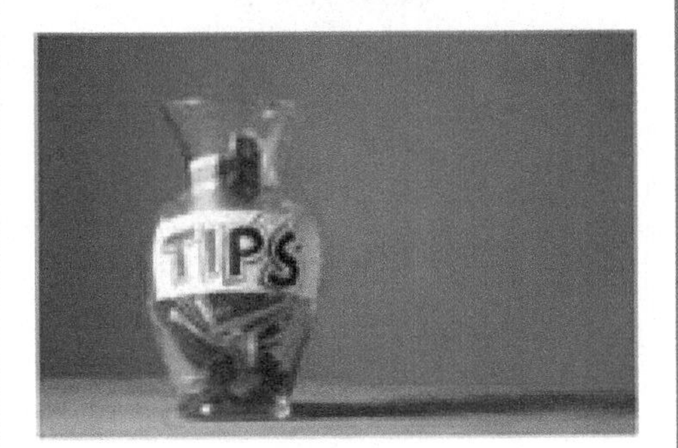

TIP

¡A COMER! - LET'S EAT!

¿ES PARA LLEVAR?

(ehs pah-rah yeh-bahr)

TO GO?

¡A COMER! - LET'S EAT!

¿PARA COMER AQUÍ?

(pah-rah koh-mehr ah-kee)

TO EAT HERE?

¡A COMER! - LET'S EAT!

¡ESTÁ DELICIOSO!

(ehs-tah deh-lee-syoh-soh)

IT'S DELICIOUS!

¡A COMER! - LET'S EAT!

¡ESTÁ MUY RICO!

(ehs-tah mwee ree-koh)

IT'S VERY GOOD!

¡A COMER! - LET'S EAT!

NO ESTÁ MUY BUENO

(noh ehs-tah mwee bweh-noh)

IT'S NOT VERY GOOD

¡A COMER! - LET'S EAT!

ESTÁ FRÍO

(ehs-tah free-oh)

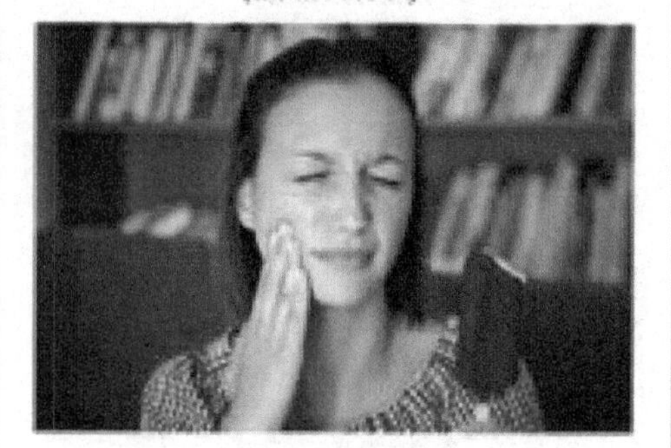

IT'S COLD

¡A COMER! - LET'S EAT!

ESTÁ MUY CALIENTE

(ehs-tah mwee kah-lyehn-teh)

IT'S VERY HOT

¡A COMER! - LET'S EAT!

ESTÁ MUY PICANTE

(ehs-tah mwee pee-kahn-teh)

IT'S VERY HOT (SPICY)

¡A COMER! - LET'S EAT!

LE FALTA SAL

(leh fahl-tah sahl)

IT NEEDS MORE SALT

¡A COMER! - LET'S EAT!

NO ESTÁ FRESCO

(noh ehs-tah frehs-koh)

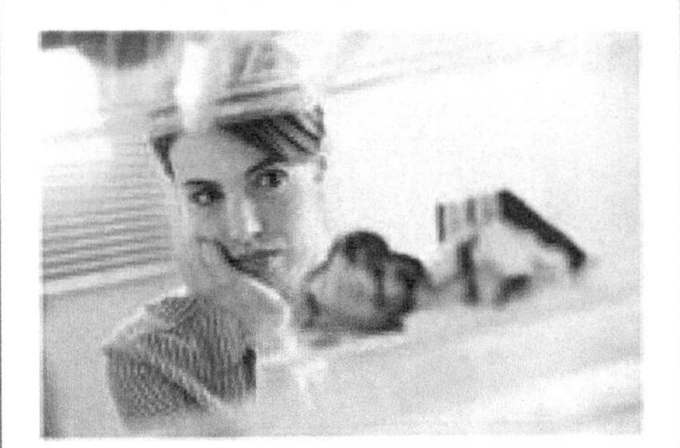

IT'S NOT FRESH

¡A COMER! - LET'S EAT!

¡SE ESTÁ TARDANDO MUCHO!

(seh ehs-tah tahr-dahn-doh moo-choh)

IT'S TAKING TOO LONG!

¡A COMER! - LET'S EAT!

EL DESAYUNO

(ehl deh-sah-yooh-noh)

BREAKFAST

¡A COMER! - LET'S EAT!

EL ALMUERZO

(ehl ahl-mwehr-soh)

C In some Latin American countries, lunch is usually the main, and biggest meal in the day

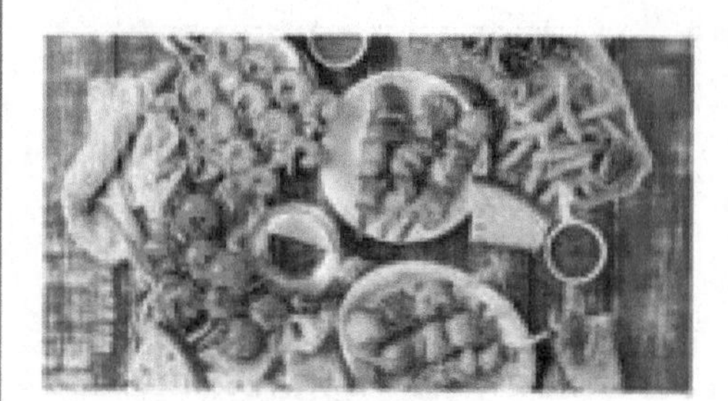

LUNCH

¡A COMER! - LET'S EAT!

CENAR

(seh-nahr)

V In Spanish, breakfast, lunch, and dinner also have verbal forms: Desayunamos tarde = We have breakfast late. Almorzamos temprano = We have lunch early. Cenamos con los amigos = We have dinner with friends.

TO HAVE DINNER

¡A COMER! - LET'S EAT!

LA CENA

(lah seh-nah)

P The pronunciation of "cena" in Spain is 'theh-nah'.

DINNER

¡A COMER! - LET'S EAT!

¿VAMOS POR UN CAFÉ?

(bah-mohs pohr oon kah-feh)

DO YOU WANT TO GO FOR A COFFEE?

¡A COMER! - LET'S EAT!

UN CAFÉ AMERICANO

(oon kah-feh ah-meh-ree-kah-noh)

A café americano is typically a black coffee mixed with water.

A BLACK COFFEE

¡A COMER! - LET'S EAT!

UN ESPRESSO

(oon ehs-preh-soh)

An espresso is typically a small, undiluted shot of coffee.

AN ESPRESSO

¡A COMER! - LET'S EAT!

UN CAFÉ CON LECHE

(oohn kah-feh kohn leh-cheh)

A LATTE

¡A COMER! - LET'S EAT!

UN CAPUCHINO

(oon kah-poo-chee-noh)

A CAPPUCCINO

¡A COMER! - LET'S EAT!

CON AZÚCAR

(kohn ah-soo-kahr)

Say 'sin azúcar' if ordering a coffee without sugar.

WITH SUGAR

¡A COMER! - LET'S EAT!

UNA PORCIÓN DE TORTA

(ooh-nah pohr-syohn deh tohr-tah)

A SLICE OF CAKE

¡A COMER! - LET'S EAT!

QUIERO ALGO DE SAL

(kyeh-roh ahl-goh deh sahl)

I'D LIKE SOMETHING SAVORY

¡A COMER! - LET'S EAT!

QUIERO ALGO DE DULCE

(kyeh-roh ahl-goh deh dool-seh)

I'D LIKE SOMETHING SWEET

¡A COMER! - LET'S EAT!

LAS VERDURAS

(lahs behr-doo-rahs)

VEGETABLES

¡A COMER! - LET'S EAT!

LAS FRUTAS

(lahs froo-tahs)

FRUITS

¡A COMER! - LET'S EAT!

LA CARNE

(lah kahr-neh)

MEAT

¡A COMER! - LET'S EAT!

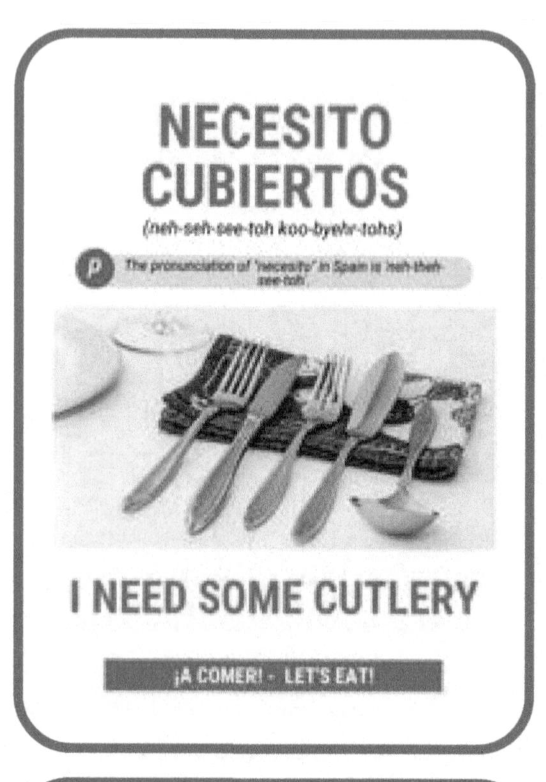
NECESITO CUBIERTOS
(neh-seh-see-toh koo-byehr-tohs)
p
The pronunciation of "necesito" in Spain is 'neh-theh-see-toh'.
I NEED SOME CUTLERY
¡A COMER! - LET'S EAT!

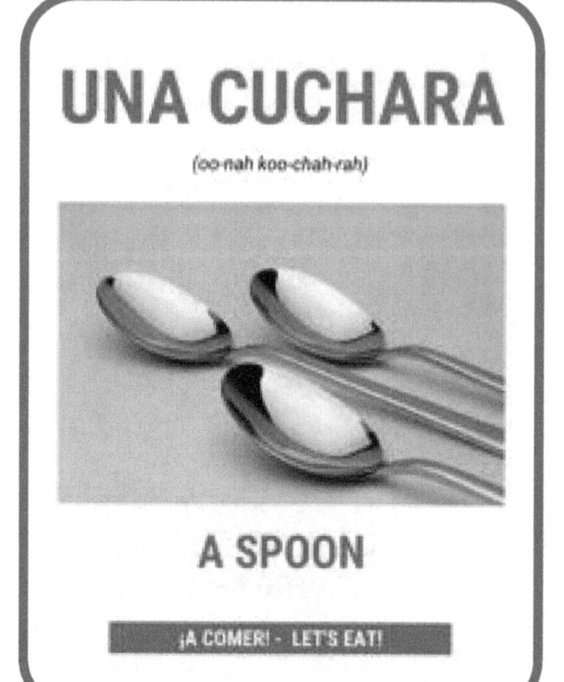
UNA CUCHARA
(oo-nah koo-chah-rah)
A SPOON
¡A COMER! - LET'S EAT!

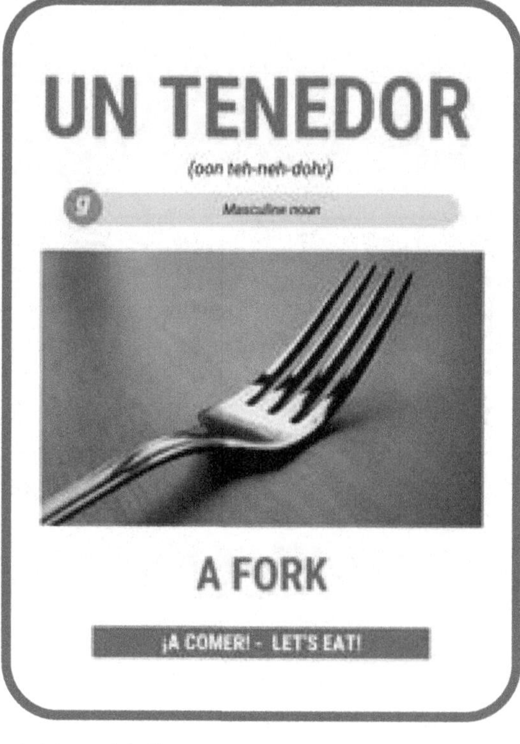
UN TENEDOR
(oon teh-neh-dohr)
g
Masculine noun
A FORK
¡A COMER! - LET'S EAT!

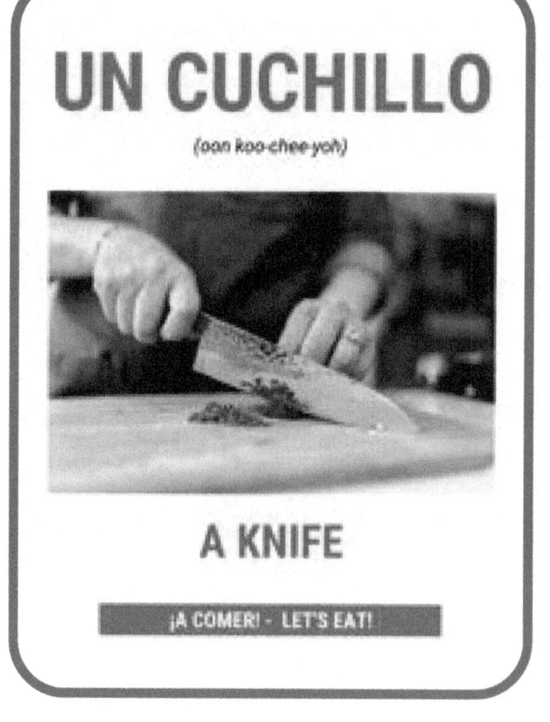
UN CUCHILLO
(oon koo-chee-yoh)
A KNIFE
¡A COMER! - LET'S EAT!

UN PLATO

(oon plah-toh)

A PLATE

¡A COMER! - LET'S EAT!

UNA TAZA

(oo-nah tah-sah)

P The pronunciation of 'taza' in Spain is 'tah-thah'.

A CUP

¡A COMER! - LET'S EAT!

UN VASO

(oon bah-soh)

A GLASS

¡A COMER! - LET'S EAT!

UNA COPA

(oo-nah koh-pah)

A GLASS (FOR WINE)

¡A COMER! - LET'S EAT!

EL VINO TINTO

(ehl bee-noh teen-toh)

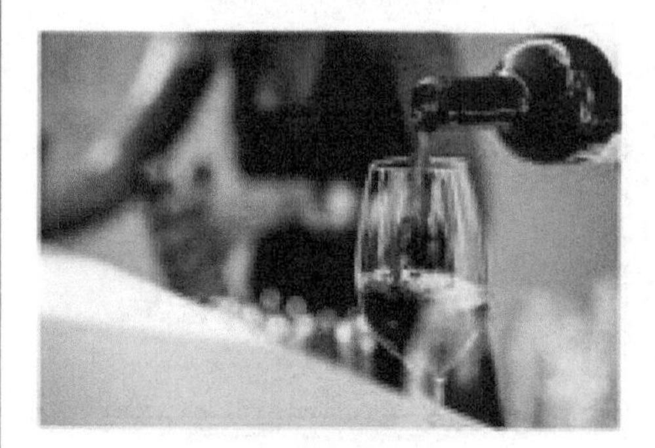

RED WINE

¡A COMER! - LET'S EAT!

EL VINO BLANCO

(ehl bee-noh blahn-koh)

WHITE WINE

¡A COMER! - LET'S EAT!

EL VINO ESPUMOSO

(ehl bee-noh ehs-poo-moh-soh)

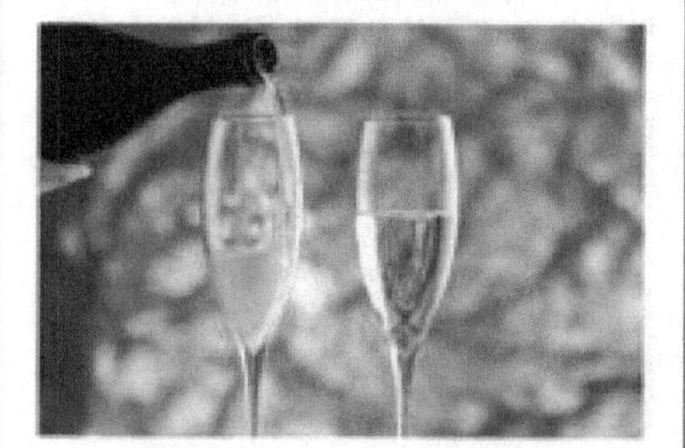

SPARKLING WINE

¡A COMER! - LET'S EAT!

LA CERVEZA

(lah sehr-beh-sah)

P The pronunciation of "cerveza" in Spain is "thehr-beh-thah".

BEER

¡A COMER! - LET'S EAT!

(lah pahs-tah)

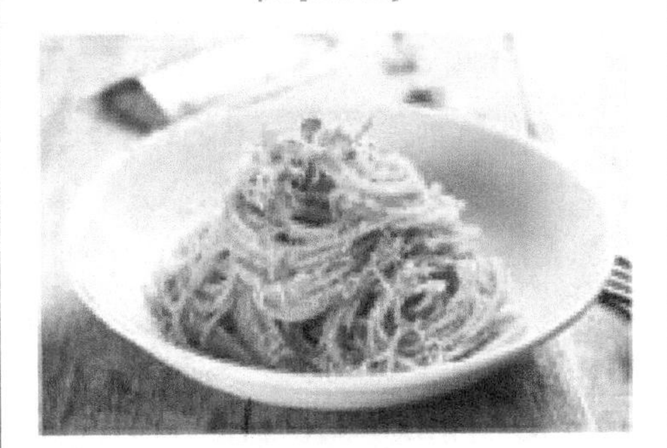

PASTA

¡A COMER! - LET'S EAT!

LA SALSA

(lah sahl-sah)

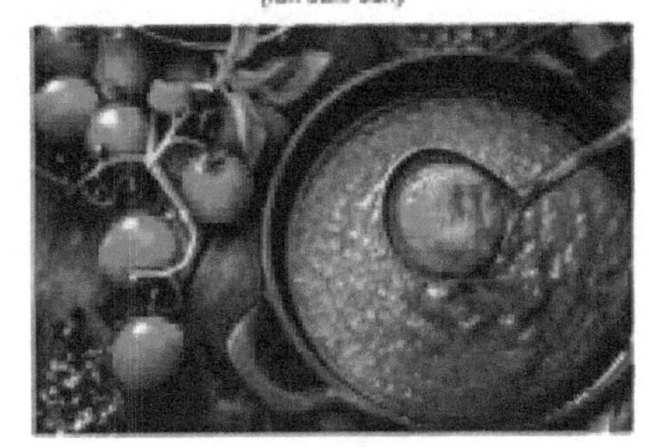

SAUCE

¡A COMER! - LET'S EAT!

LA MANTEQUILLA

(lah mahn-teh-kee-yah)

BUTTER

¡A COMER! - LET'S EAT!

EL QUESO

(ehl keh-soh)

CHEESE

¡A COMER! - LET'S EAT!

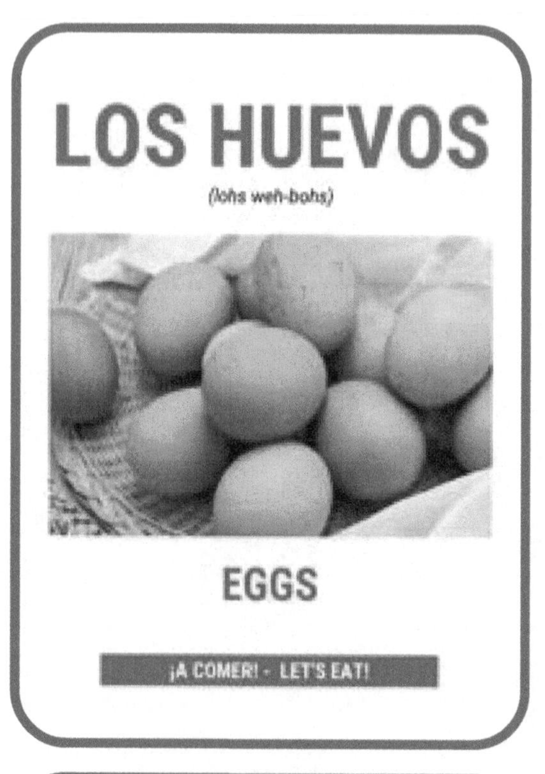
LOS HUEVOS
(lohs weh-bohs)
EGGS
¡A COMER! - LET'S EAT!

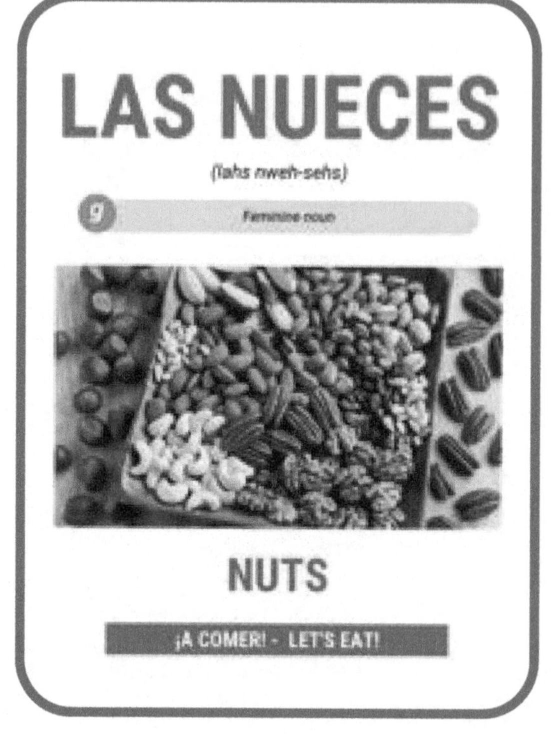
LAS NUECES
(lahs nweh-sehs)
g
Feminine noun
NUTS
¡A COMER! - LET'S EAT!

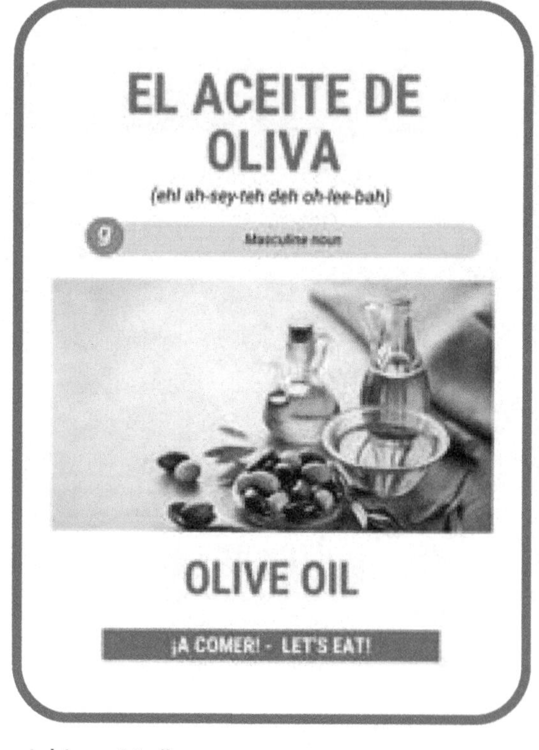
EL ACEITE DE OLIVA
(ehl ah-sey-teh deh oh-lee-bah)
g
Masculine noun
OLIVE OIL
¡A COMER! - LET'S EAT!

EL AJO
(ehl ah-hoh)
GARLIC
¡A COMER! - LET'S EAT!

LAS SEMILLAS

(lahs seh-mee-yahs)

SEEDS

¡A COMER! - LET'S EAT!

TENGO HAMBRE

(tehn-goh ahm-breh)

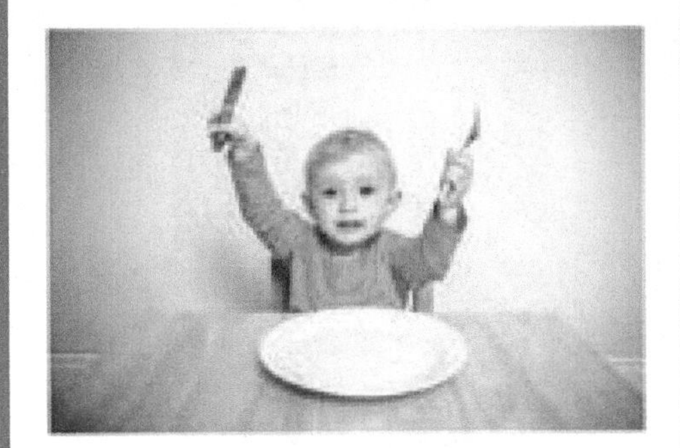

I'M HUNGRY

¡A COMER! - LET'S EAT!

TENGO SED

(tehn-goh sehd)

I'M THIRSTY

¡A COMER! - LET'S EAT!

QUIERO ALGO DE COMER

(kyeh-roh ahl-goh deh koh-mehr)

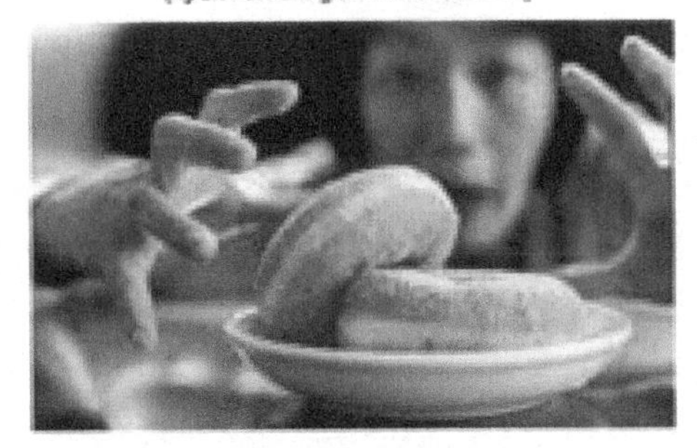

I WANT SOMETHING TO EAT

¡A COMER! - LET'S EAT!

QUIERO ALGO DE TOMAR

(kyeh-roh ahl-goh deh toh-mahr)

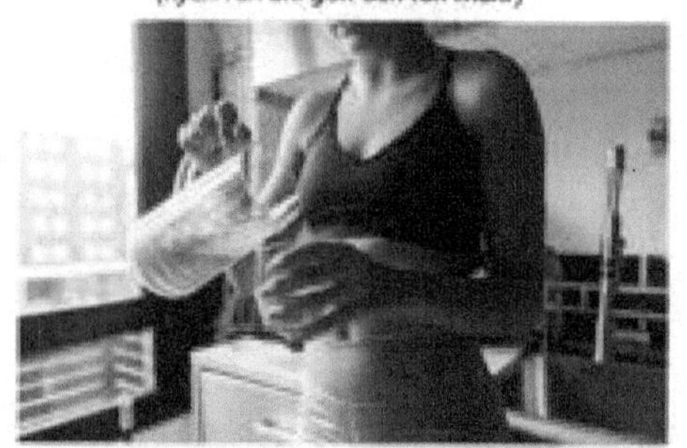

I WANT SOMETHING TO DRINK

¡A COMER! - LET'S EAT!

UN HELADO

(oon eh-lah-doh)

AN ICE CREAM

¡A COMER! - LET'S EAT!

¿QUÉ SABORES HAY?

(keh sah-boh-rehs ay)

WHAT FLAVORS ARE THERE?

¡A COMER! - LET'S EAT!

UN HELADO DE FRESA

(oon eh-lah-doh deh freh-sah)

A STRAWBERRY ICE CREAM

¡A COMER! - LET'S EAT!

UN HELADO DE CHOCOLATE

(oon eh-lah-doh deh choh-koh-lah-teh)

A CHOCOLATE ICE CREAM

¡A COMER! - LET'S EAT!

UN HELADO DE VAINILLA

(oon eh-lah-doh deh bay-nee-yah)

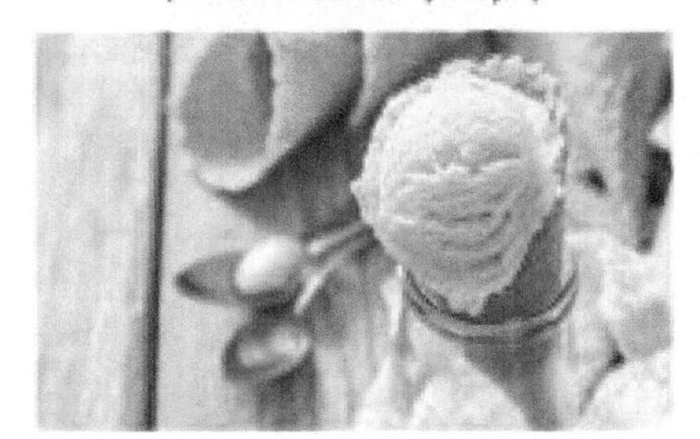

A VANILLA ICE CREAM

¡A COMER! - LET'S EAT!

UN HELADO DE FRUTOS ROJOS

(oon eh-lah-doh deh froo-tohs rroh-hos)

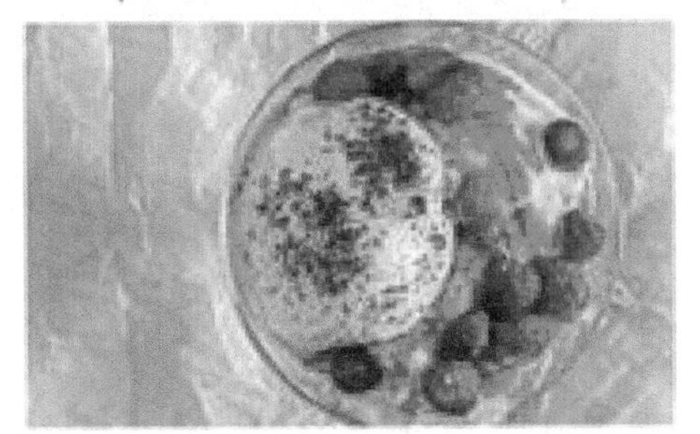

A RED BERRIES ICE CREAM

¡A COMER! - LET'S EAT!

UN HELADO DE LIMÓN

(oon eh-lah-doh deh lee-mohn)

A LEMON ICE CREAM

¡A COMER! - LET'S EAT!

¡BUEN PROVECHO!

(bwehn proh-beh-cho)

ENJOY YOUR MEAL!

¡A COMER! - LET'S EAT!

¡SALUD!

(sah-lood)

CHEERS!

¡A COMER! - LET'S EAT!

EL YOGUR

(ehl yoh-goor)

Masculine noun

YOGURT

¡A COMER! - LET'S EAT!

EL PAN

(ehl pahn)

g Masculine noun

BREAD

¡A COMER! - LET'S EAT!

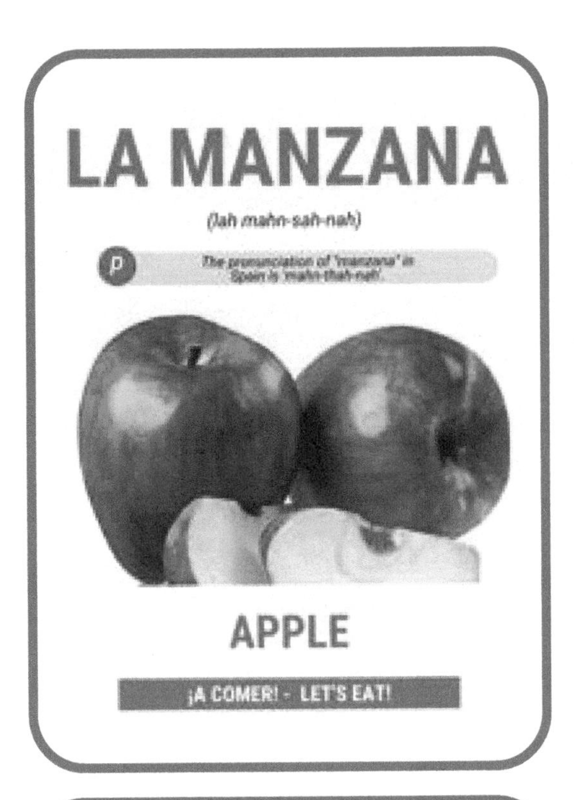
LA MANZANA
(lah mahn-sah-nah)
P
The pronunciation of "manzana" in Spain is 'mahn-thah-nah'.
APPLE
¡A COMER! - LET'S EAT!

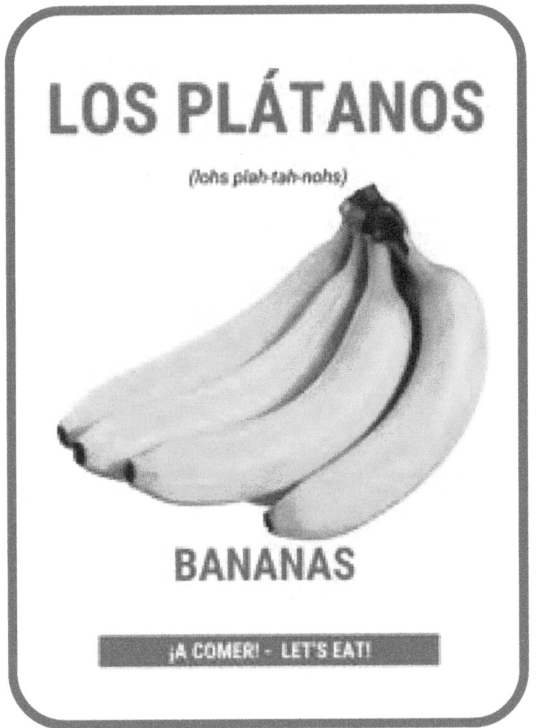
LOS PLÁTANOS
(lohs plah-tah-nohs)
BANANAS
¡A COMER! - LET'S EAT!

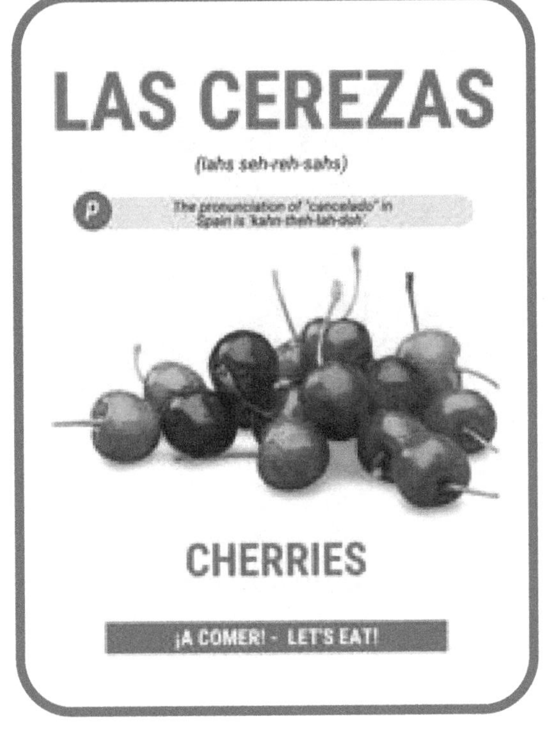
LAS CEREZAS
(lahs seh-reh-sahs)
P
The pronunciation of "cancelado" in Spain is 'kahn-theh-lah-doh'.
CHERRIES
¡A COMER! - LET'S EAT!

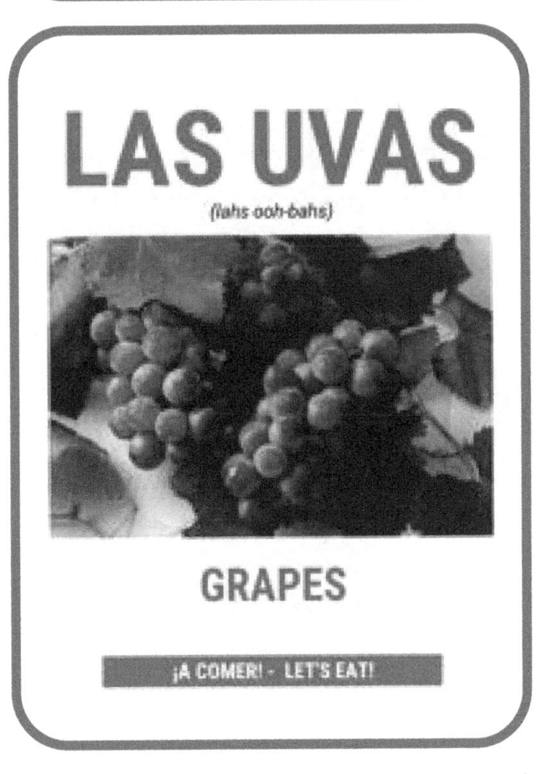
LAS UVAS
(lahs ooh-bahs)
GRAPES
¡A COMER! - LET'S EAT!

LA NARANJA
(lah nah-rahn-hah)
ORANGE
¡A COMER! - LET'S EAT!

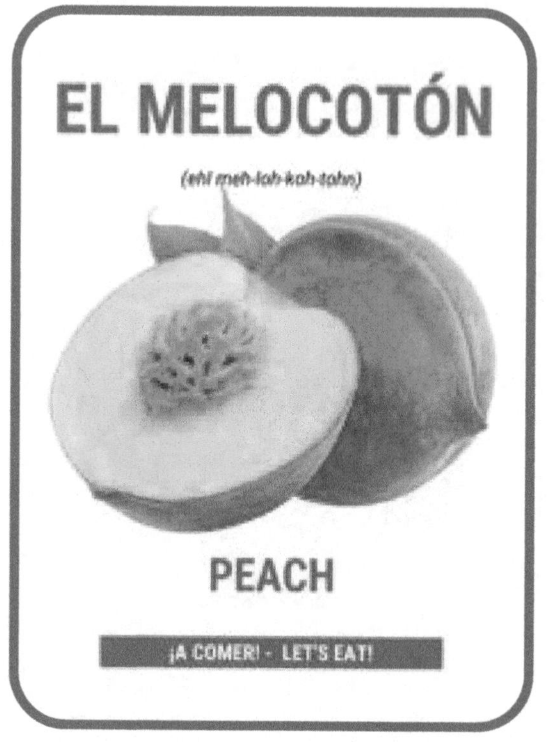
EL MELOCOTÓN
(ehl meh-loh-koh-tohn)
PEACH
¡A COMER! - LET'S EAT!

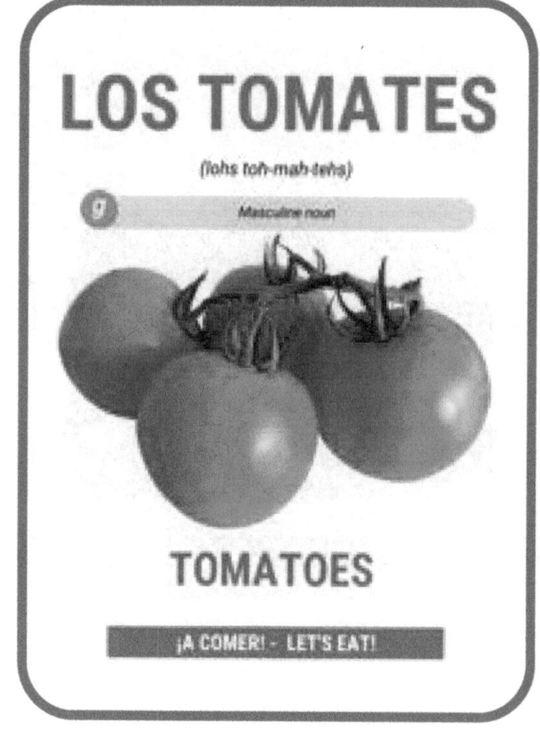
LOS TOMATES
(lohs toh-mah-tehs)
g
Masculine noun
TOMATOES
¡A COMER! - LET'S EAT!

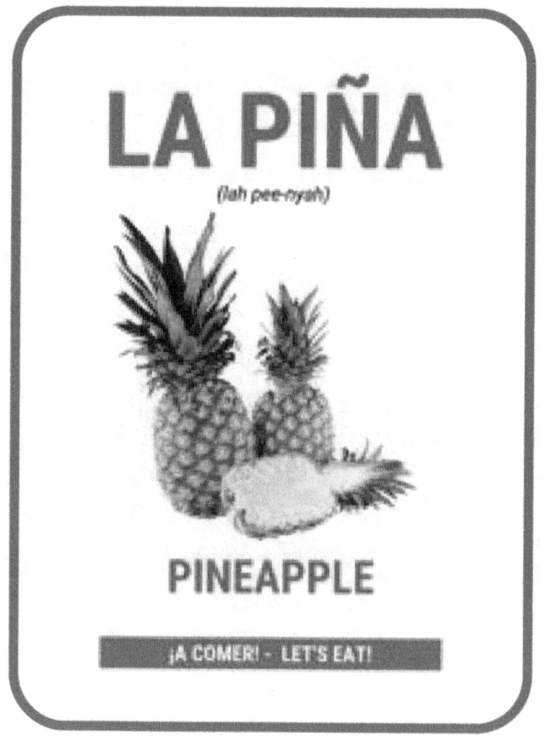
LA PIÑA
(lah pee-nyah)
PINEAPPLE
¡A COMER! - LET'S EAT!

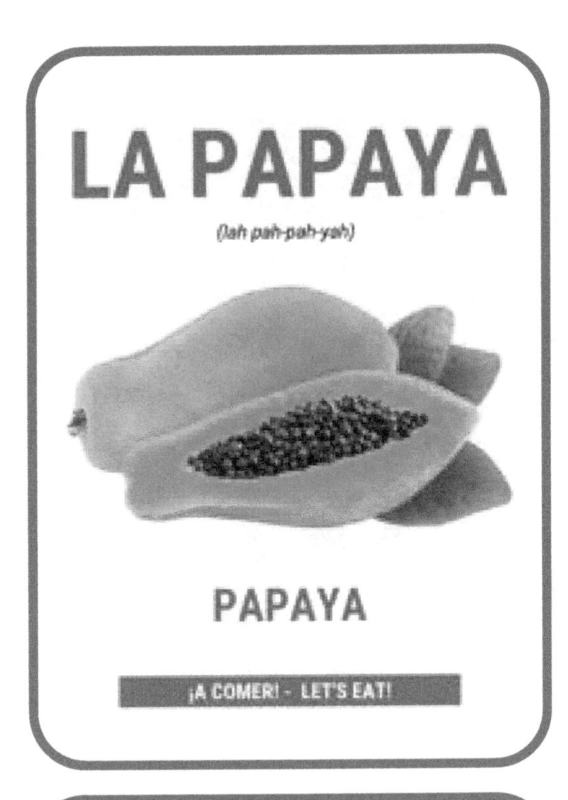
LA PAPAYA
(lah pah-pah-yah)
PAPAYA
¡A COMER! - LET'S EAT!

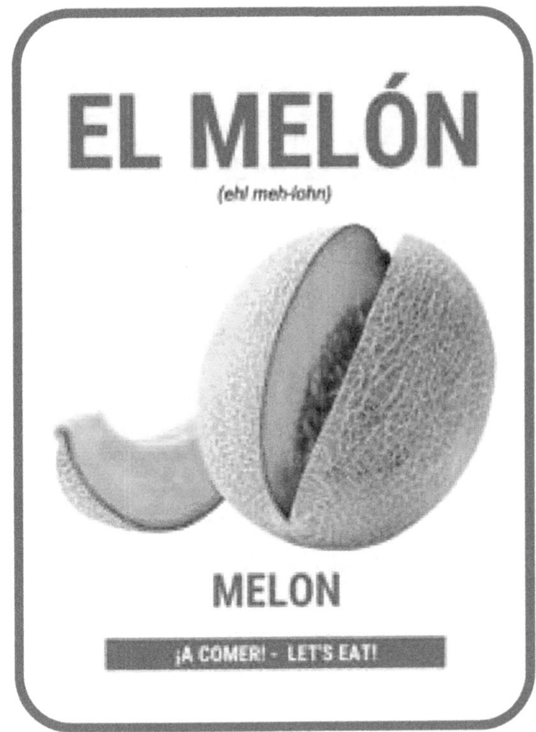
EL MELÓN
(ehl meh-lohn)
MELON
¡A COMER! - LET'S EAT!

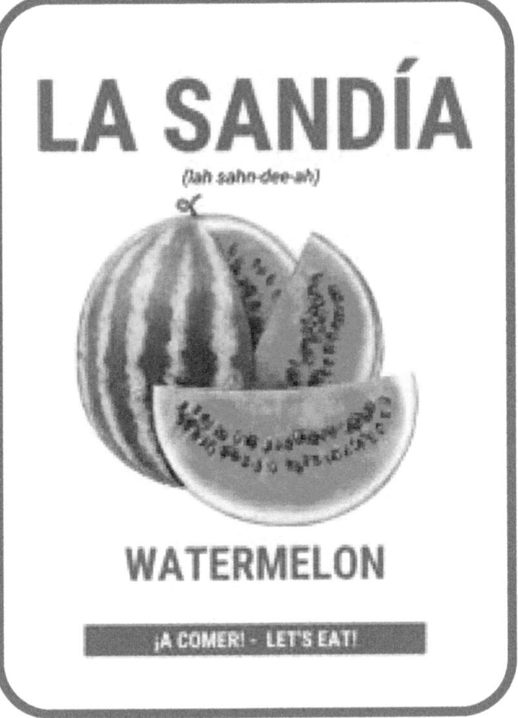
LA SANDÍA
(lah sahn-dee-ah)
WATERMELON
¡A COMER! - LET'S EAT!

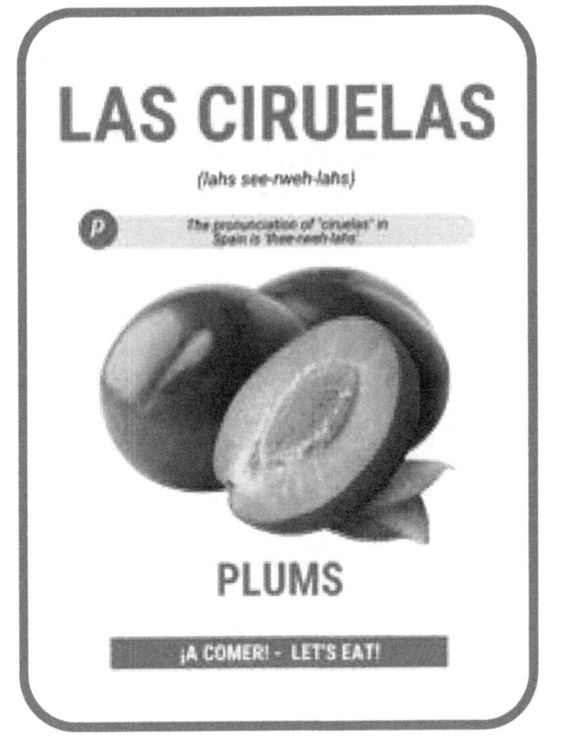
LAS CIRUELAS
(lahs see-rweh-lahs)
P
The pronunciation of "ciruelas" in Spain is "thee-rweh-lahs"
PLUMS
¡A COMER! - LET'S EAT!

LAS
FRAMBUESAS
(lahs frahm-bweh-sahs)
RASPBERRIES
¡A COMER! - LET'S EAT!

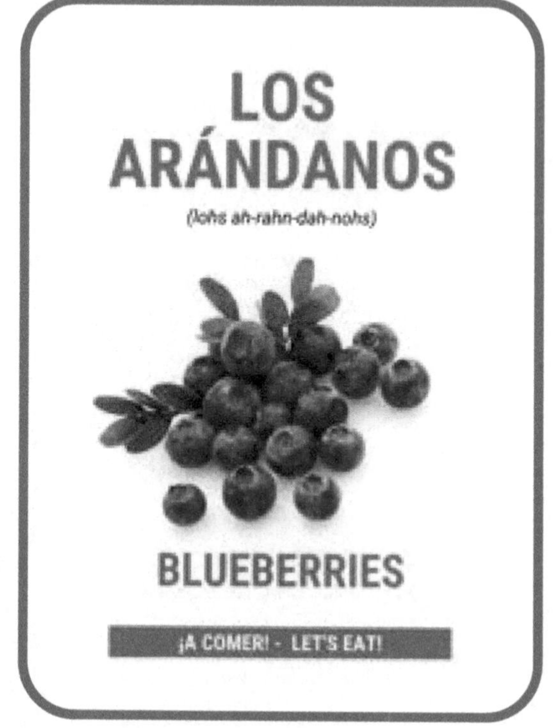
LOS
ARÁNDANOS
(lohs ah-rahn-dah-nohs)
BLUEBERRIES
¡A COMER! - LET'S EAT!

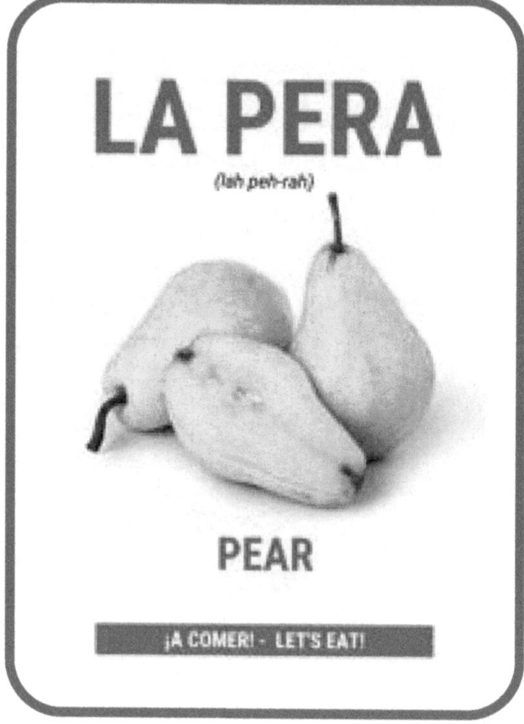
LA PERA
(lah peh-rah)
PEAR
¡A COMER! - LET'S EAT!

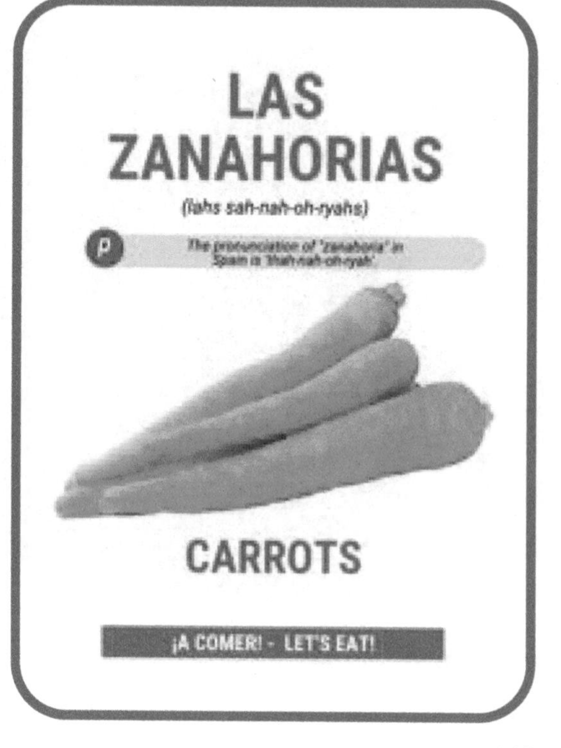
LAS
ZANAHORIAS
(lahs sah-nah-oh-ryahs)
P
The pronunciation of 'zanahoria' in Spain is 'thah-nah-oh-ryah'.
CARROTS
¡A COMER! - LET'S EAT!

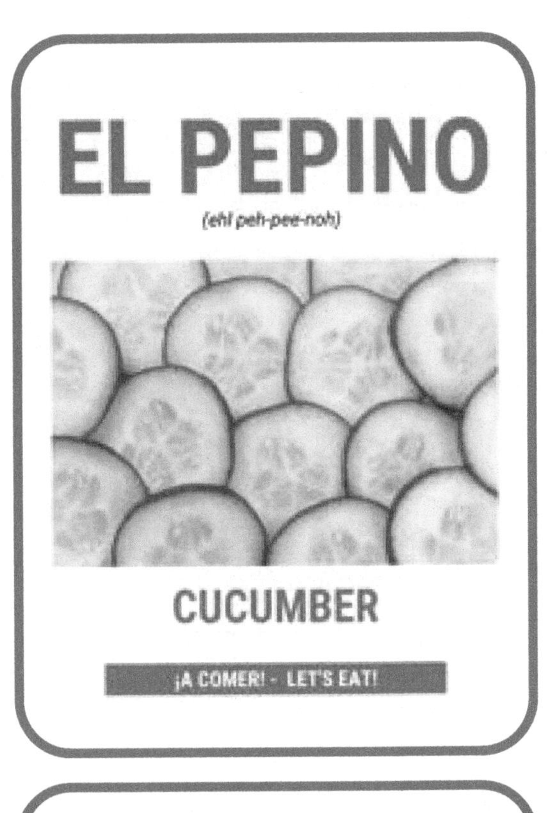
EL PEPINO
(ehl peh-pee-noh)
CUCUMBER
¡A COMER! - LET'S EAT!

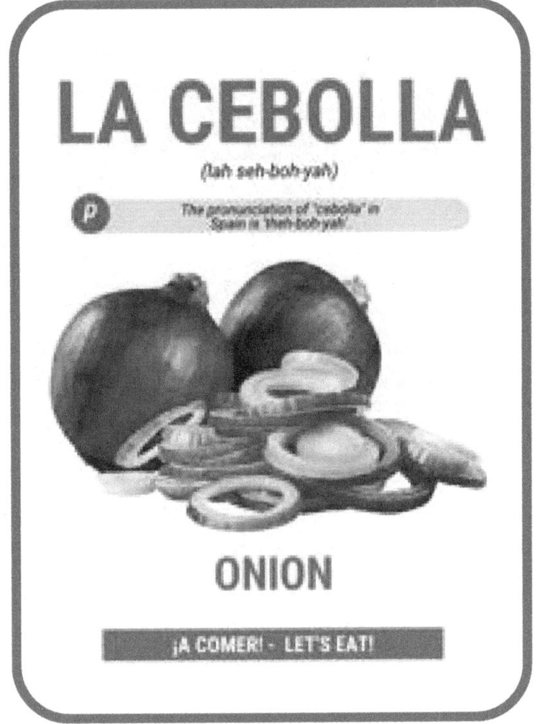
LA CEBOLLA
(lah seh-boh-yah)
P
The pronunciation of 'cebolla' in Spain is 'theh-boh-yah'.
ONION
¡A COMER! - LET'S EAT!

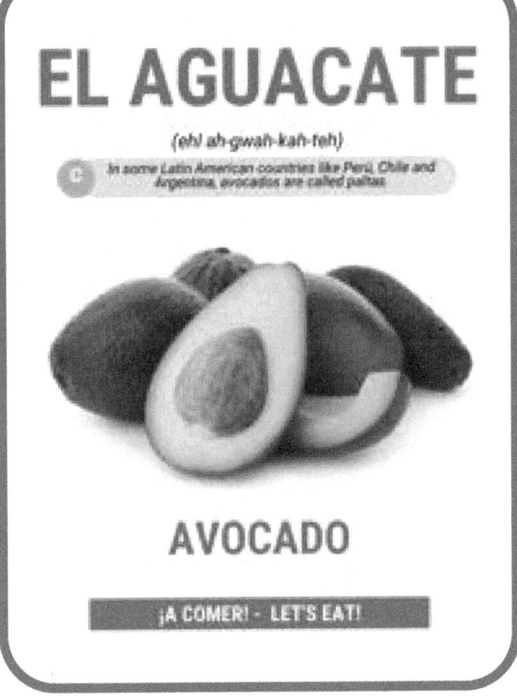
EL AGUACATE
(ehl ah-gwah-kah-teh)
C
In some Latin American countries like Perú, Chile and Argentina, avocados are called paltas.
AVOCADO
¡A COMER! - LET'S EAT!

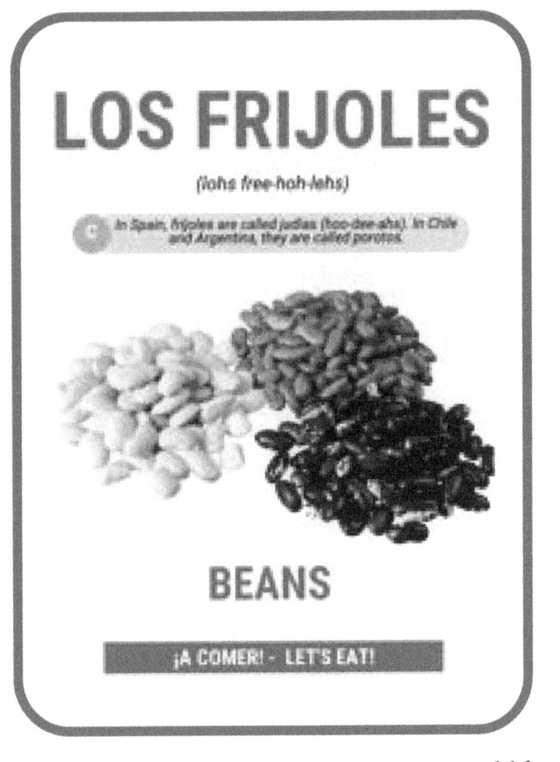
LOS FRIJOLES
(lohs free-hoh-lehs)
C
In Spain, frijoles are called judías (hoo-dee-ahs). In Chile and Argentina, they are called porotos.
BEANS
¡A COMER! - LET'S EAT!

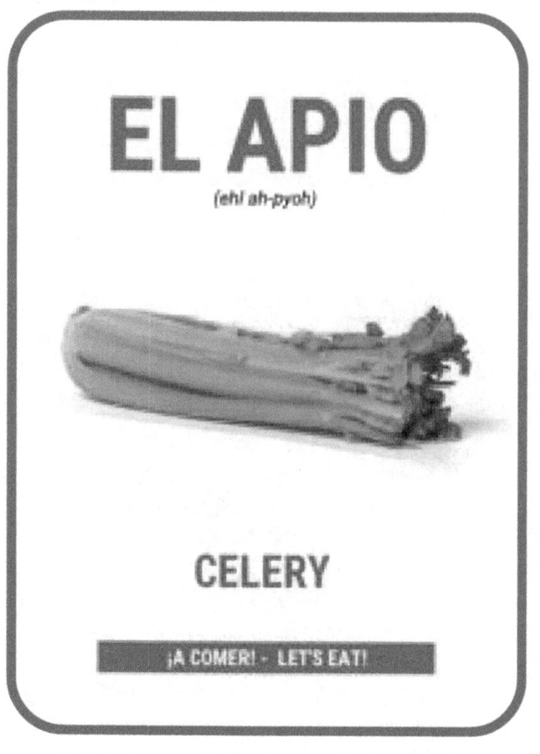
EL APIO
(ehl ah-pyoh)
CELERY
¡A COMER! - LET'S EAT!

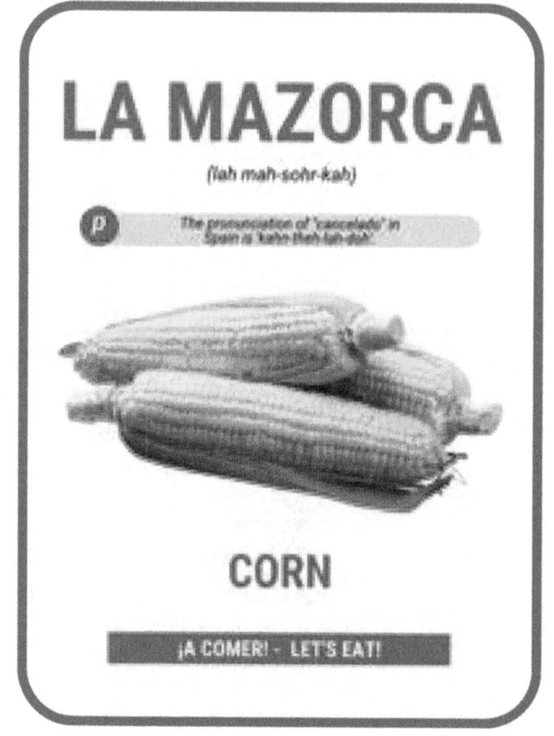
LA MAZORCA
(lah mah-sohr-kah)
p
CORN
¡A COMER! - LET'S EAT!

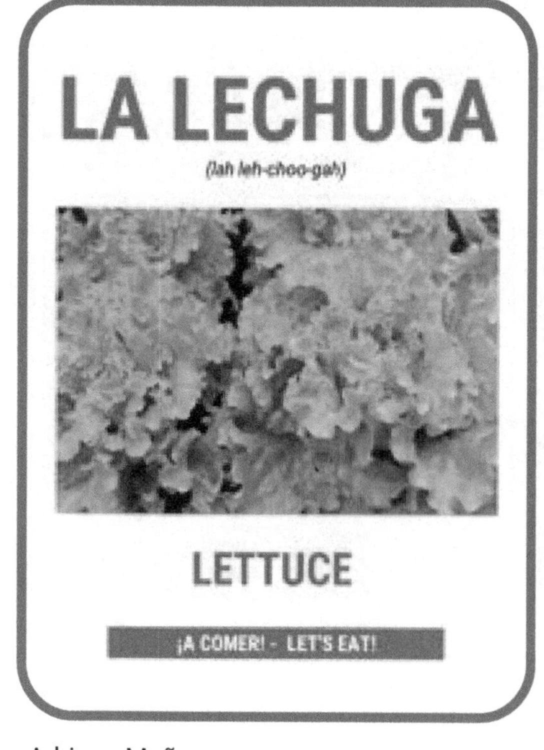
LA LECHUGA
(lah leh-choo-gah)
LETTUCE
¡A COMER! - LET'S EAT!

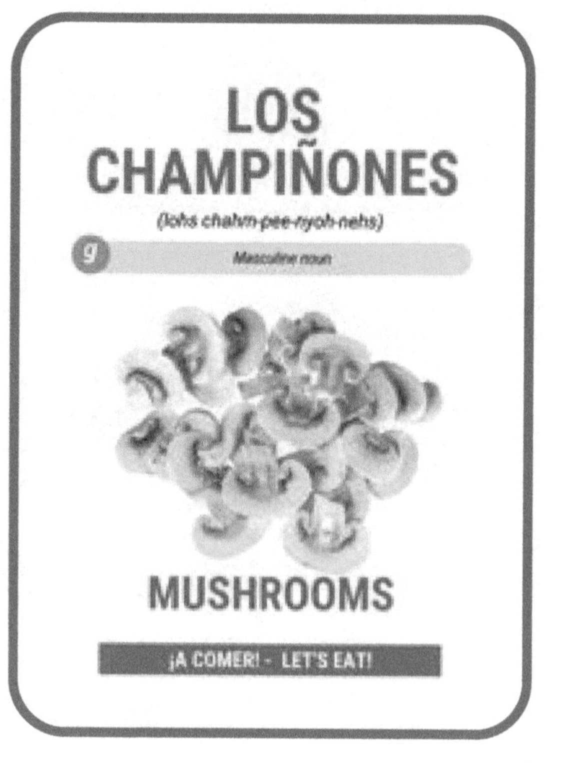
LOS CHAMPIÑONES
(lohs chahm-pee-nyoh-nehs)
g
Masculine noun
MUSHROOMS
¡A COMER! - LET'S EAT!

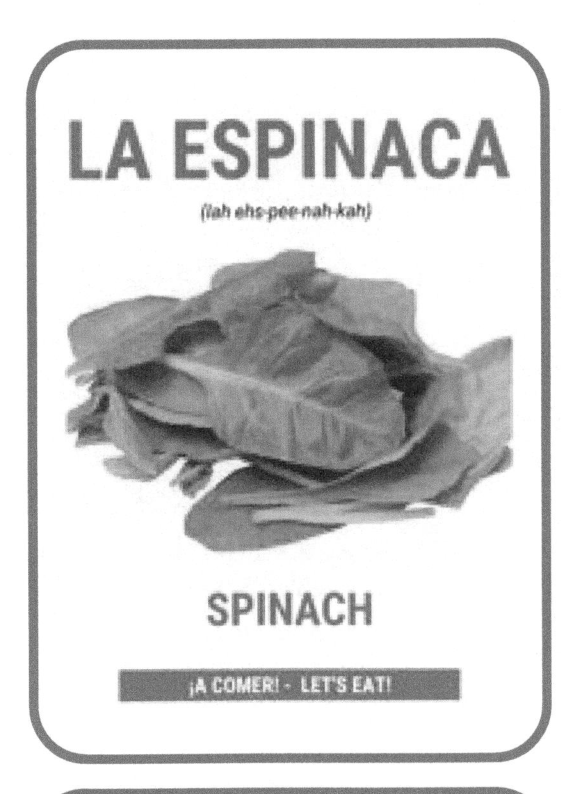
LA ESPINACA
(lah ehs-pee-nah-kah)
SPINACH
¡A COMER! - LET'S EAT!

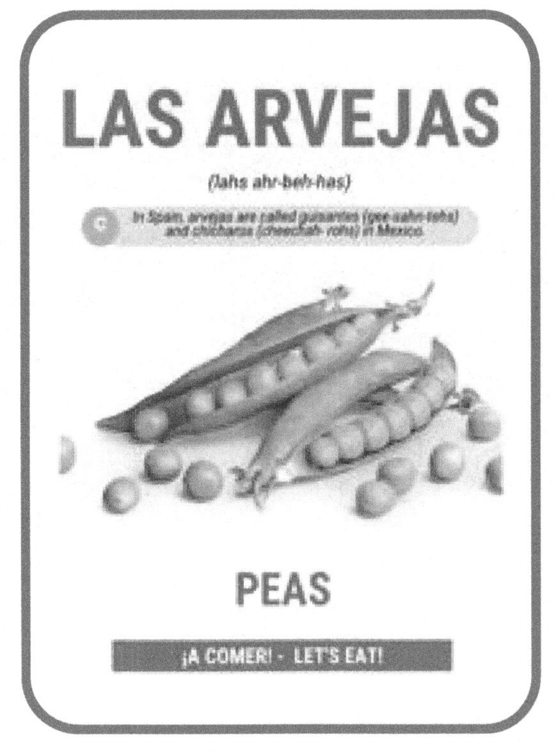
LAS ARVEJAS
(lahs ahr-beh-has)
In Spain, arvejas are called guisantes (gee-sahn-tehs) and chicharos (cheechah- rohs) in Mexico.
PEAS
¡A COMER! - LET'S EAT!

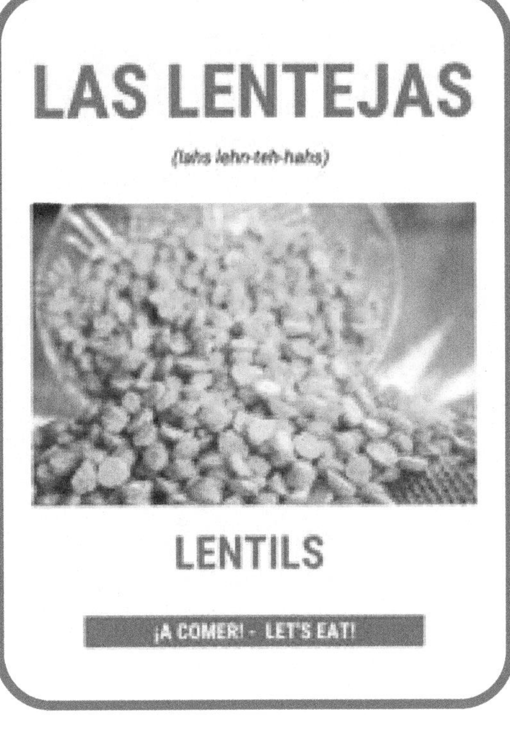
LAS LENTEJAS
(lahs lehn-teh-hahs)
LENTILS
¡A COMER! - LET'S EAT!

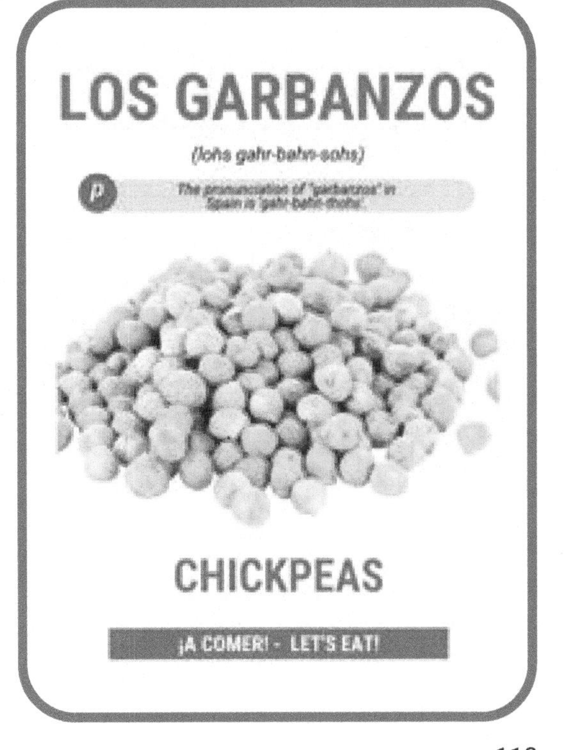
LOS GARBANZOS
(lohs gahr-bahn-sohs)
The pronunciation of "garbanzos" in Spain is 'gahr-bahn-thohs'.
CHICKPEAS
¡A COMER! - LET'S EAT!

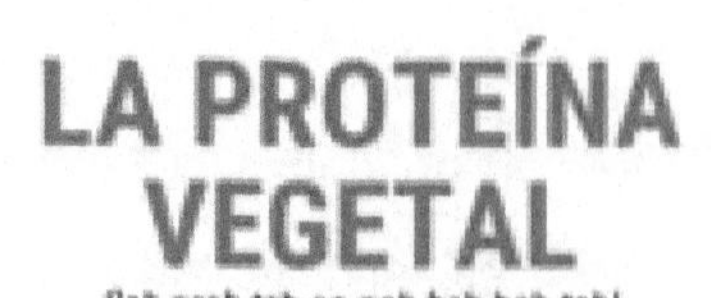

LA PROTEÍNA VEGETAL

(lah proh-teh-ee-nah beh-heh-tahl

VEGETABLE PROTEIN

¡A COMER! - LET'S EAT!

LA SOYA

(lah soh-yah)

SOY

¡A COMER! - LET'S EAT!

LOS PIMIENTOS RELLENOS

(lohs pee-myehn-tohs rreh-yeh-nohs)

STUFFED PEPPERS

¡A COMER! - LET'S EAT!

SIN GLUTEN

(seen gloo-tehn)

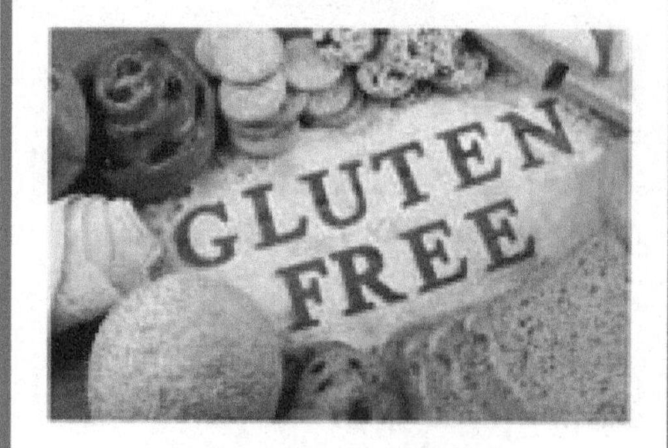

GLUTEN FREE

¡A COMER! - LET'S EAT!

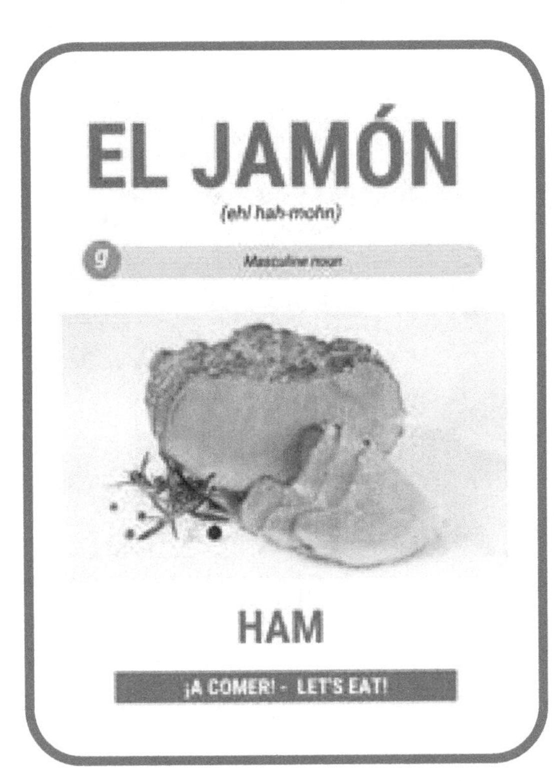
EL JAMÓN
(ehl hah-mohn)
g
Masculine noun
HAM
¡A COMER! - LET'S EAT!

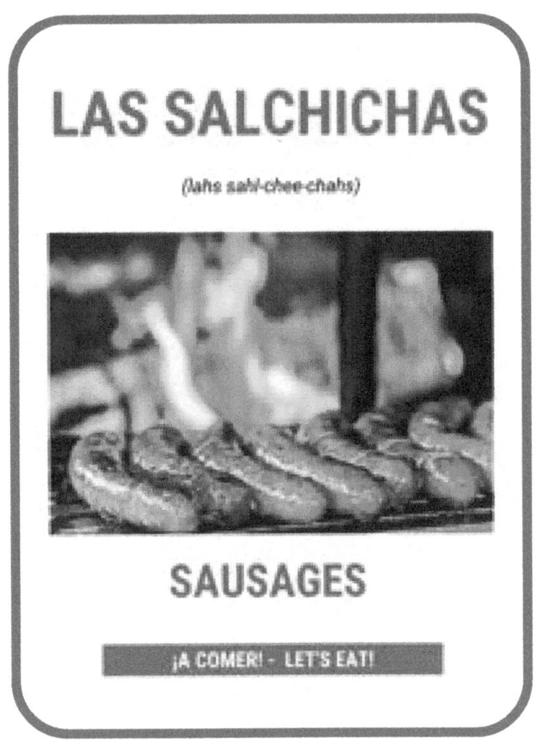
LAS SALCHICHAS
(lahs sahl-chee-chahs)
SAUSAGES
¡A COMER! - LET'S EAT!

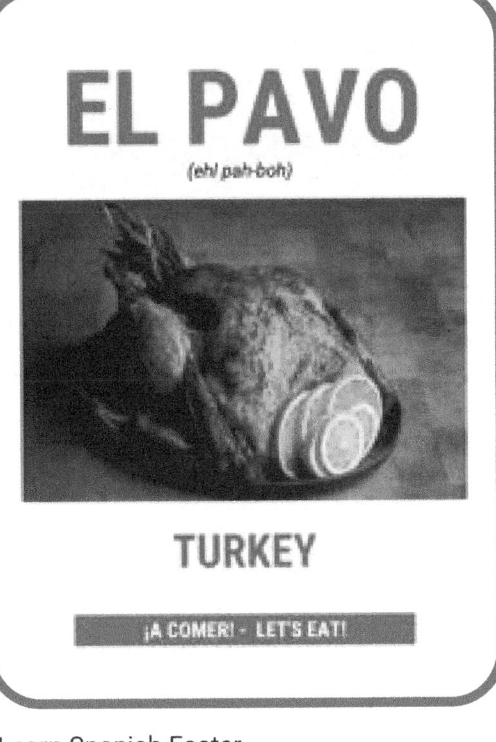
EL PAVO
(ehl pah-boh)
TURKEY
¡A COMER! - LET'S EAT!

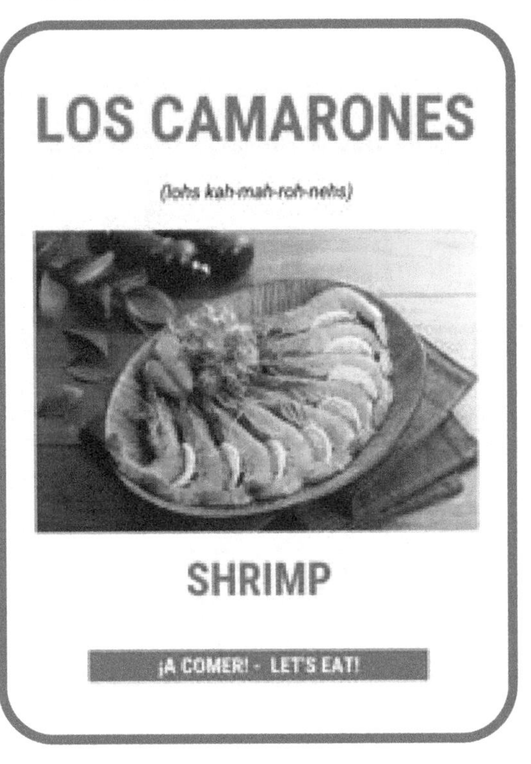
LOS CAMARONES
(lohs kah-mah-roh-nehs)
SHRIMP
¡A COMER! - LET'S EAT!

(ehl sahl-mohn)

SALMON

¡A COMER! - LET'S EAT!

EL ATÚN

(ehl ah-toon)

TUNA

¡A COMER! - LET'S EAT!

LAS OSTRAS

(lahs ohs-trahs

OYSTERS

¡A COMER! - LET'S EAT!

LOS HUEVOS REVUELTOS

(lohs weh-bohs rreh-bwehl-tohs)

SCRAMBLED EGGS

¡A COMER! - LET'S EAT!

LOS HUEVOS FRITOS

(lohs weh-bohs free-tohs)

FRIED EGGS

¡A COMER! - LET'S EAT!

LOS HUEVOS COCIDOS

(lohs weh-bohs koh-see-dohs)

P The pronunciation of 'cocidos' in Spain is 'koh-thee-dohs'.

BOILED EGGS

¡A COMER! - LET'S EAT!

LOS HUEVOS POCHÉ

(lohs weh-bohs poh-che)

POACHED EGGS

¡A COMER! - LET'S EAT!

EL CEREAL

(ehl seh-reh-ahl)

P The pronunciation of "cereal" in Spain is 'theh-reh-ahl'.

CEREAL

¡A COMER! - LET'S EAT!

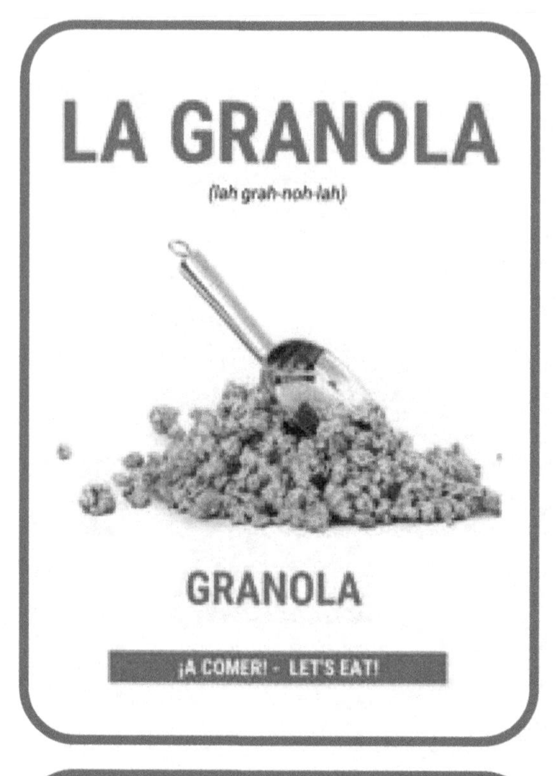
LA GRANOLA
(lah grah-noh-lah)
GRANOLA
¡A COMER! - LET'S EAT!

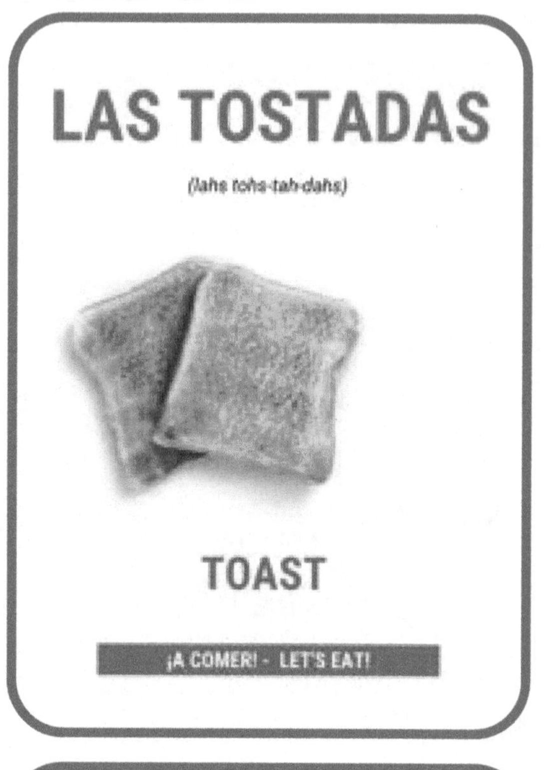
LAS TOSTADAS
(lahs tohs-tah-dahs)
TOAST
¡A COMER! - LET'S EAT!

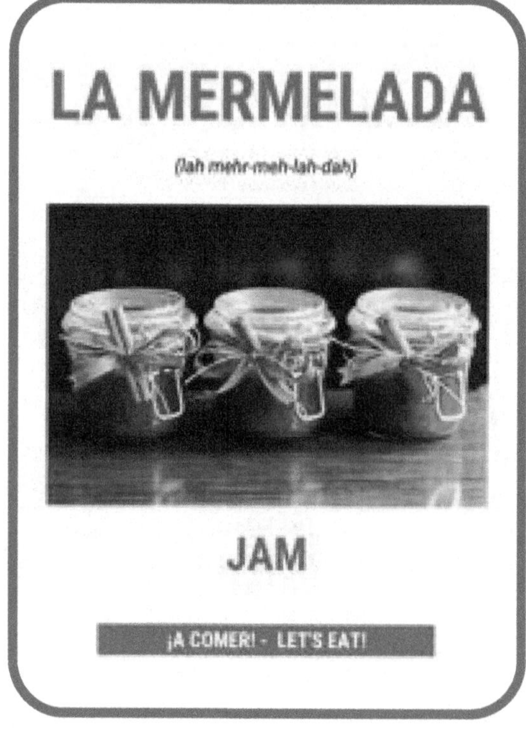
LA MERMELADA
(lah mehr-meh-lah-dah)
JAM
¡A COMER! - LET'S EAT!

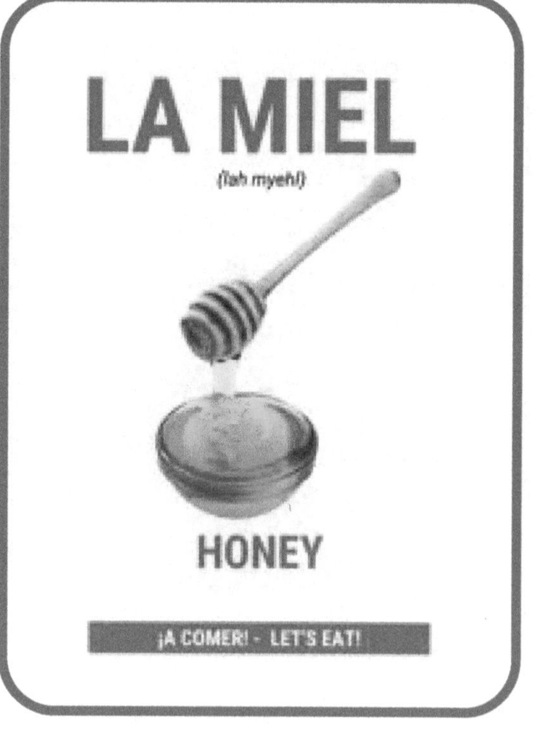
LA MIEL
(lah myehl)
HONEY
¡A COMER! - LET'S EAT!

EL SUPERMERCADO

(ehl soo-pehr-mehr-kah-doh)

SUPERMARKET

DE COMPRAS - SHOPPING

LA TIENDA

(lah tyehn-dah)

STORE

DE COMPRAS - SHOPPING

LA FERIA

(lah feh-ryah)

STREET MARKET

DE COMPRAS - SHOPPING

LA PANADERÍA

(lah pah-nah-deh-ree-ah)

BAKERY

DE COMPRAS - SHOPPING

LA CARNICERÍA

(lah kahr-nee-seh-ree-ah

p The pronunciation of 'carnicería' in Spain is 'kahr-nee-theh-ree-ah'.

BUTCHER'S SHOP

DE COMPRAS - SHOPPING

LA FERRETERÍA

(lah feh-rreh-teh-ree-ah)

HARDWARE STORE

DE COMPRAS - SHOPPING

LA LIBRERÍA

(lah lee-breh-ree-ah)

BOOKSTORE

DE COMPRAS - SHOPPING

LA PAPELERÍA

(lah pah-peh-leh-ree-ah)

OFFICE SUPPLY STORE

DE COMPRAS - SHOPPING

Toy store

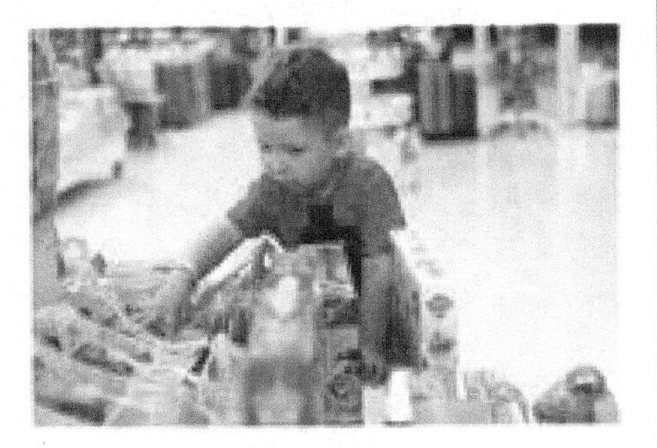

TOY STORE

DE COMPRAS - SHOPPING

LA ZAPATERÍA

(lah sah-pah-teh-ree-ah)

p — *The pronunciation of "zapatería" in Spain is "thah-pah-teh-ree-ah".*

SHOE STORE

DE COMPRAS - SHOPPING

LAS MONEDAS

(lahs moh-neh-dahs)

COINS

DE COMPRAS - SHOPPING

LOS BILLETES

(lohs bee-yeh-tehs)

g — *Masculine noun*

BILLS

DE COMPRAS - SHOPPING

EL PRECIO

(ehl preh-syoh)

The pronunciation of 'precio' in Spain is 'preh-thyoh'.

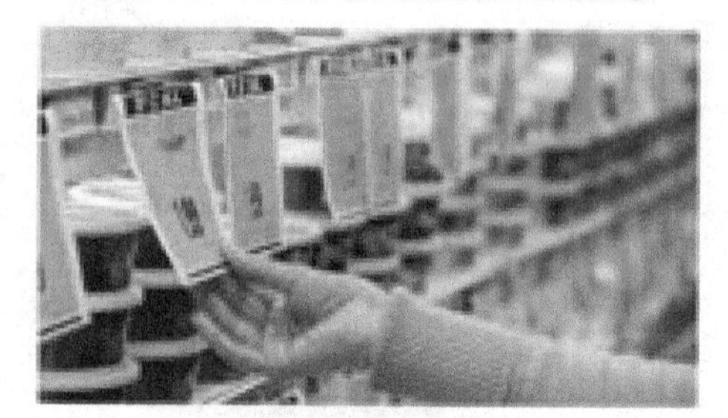

PRICE

DE COMPRAS - SHOPPING

¿TIENE DESCUENTO?

(tyeh-neh dehs-kwehn-toh)

DOES IT HAVE A DISCOUNT?

DE COMPRAS - SHOPPING

¿ESTÁ EN OFERTA?

(ehs-tah ehn oh-fehr-tah)

IS IT ON SALE?

DE COMPRAS - SHOPPING

¡ESTÁ MUY CARO!

(ehs-tah mwee kah-roh)

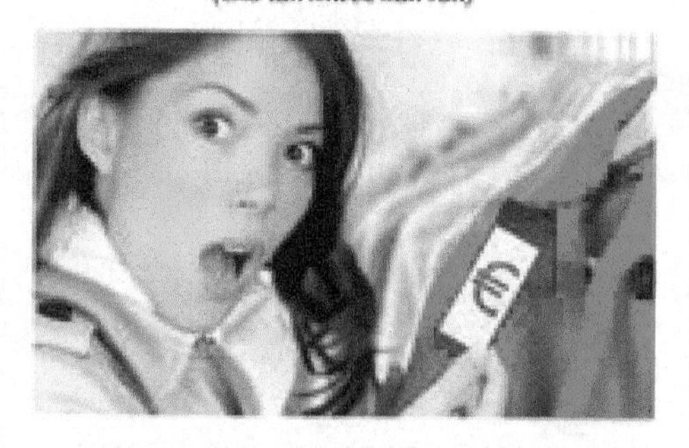

IT'S VERY EXPENSIVE!

DE COMPRAS - SHOPPING

¡ESTÁ MUY BARATO!

(ehs-tah mwee bah-rah-toh)

IT'S VERY CHEAP!

DE COMPRAS - SHOPPING

ES DE BUENA CALIDAD

(ehs deh bweh-nah kah-lee-dad)

g — Say 'es de mala calidad' to express that something is bad quality.

IT'S GOOD QUALITY

DE COMPRAS - SHOPPING

¿ACEPTAN TARJETAS?

(ah-sehp-tahn tahr-heh-tahs)

p — The pronunciation of 'aceptan' in Spain is 'ah-thehp-tahn'.

DO YOU TAKE CARDS?

DE COMPRAS - SHOPPING

EL PROTECTOR SOLAR

(ehl proh-tehk-tohr soh-lahr)

g — Masculine noun

SUNSCREEN

DE COMPRAS - SHOPPING

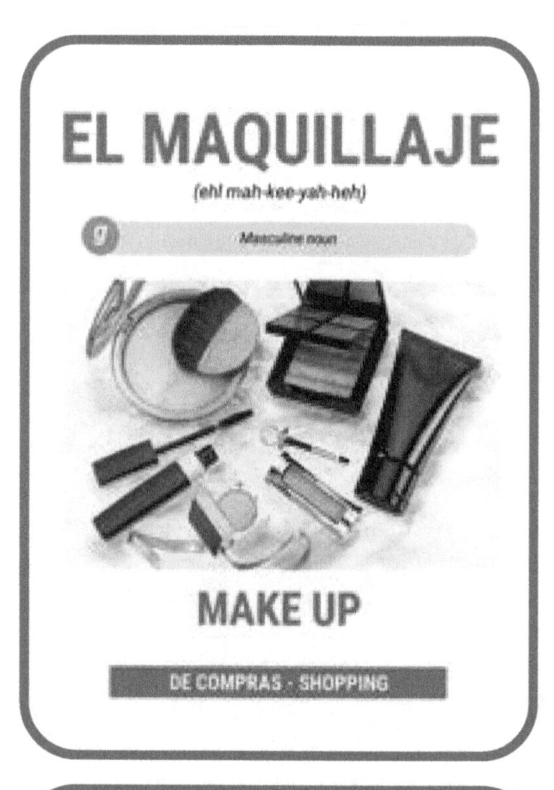
EL MAQUILLAJE
(ehl mah-kee-yah-heh)
g
Masculine noun
MAKE UP
DE COMPRAS - SHOPPING

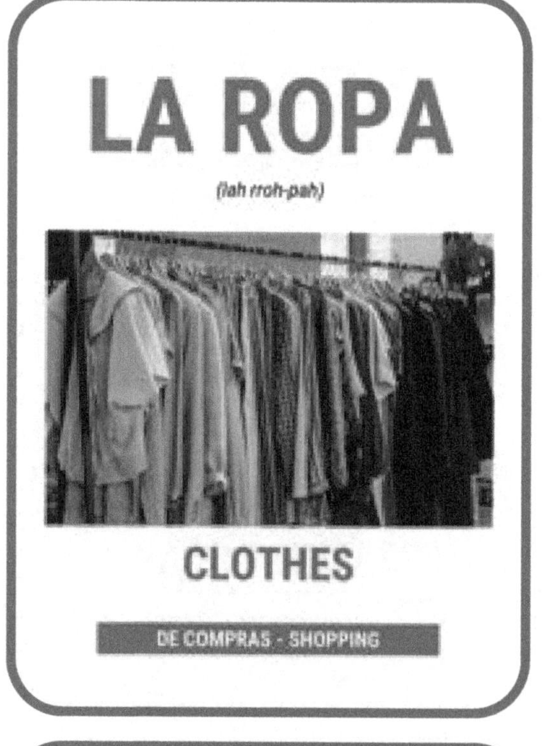
LA ROPA
(lah rroh-pah)
CLOTHES
DE COMPRAS - SHOPPING

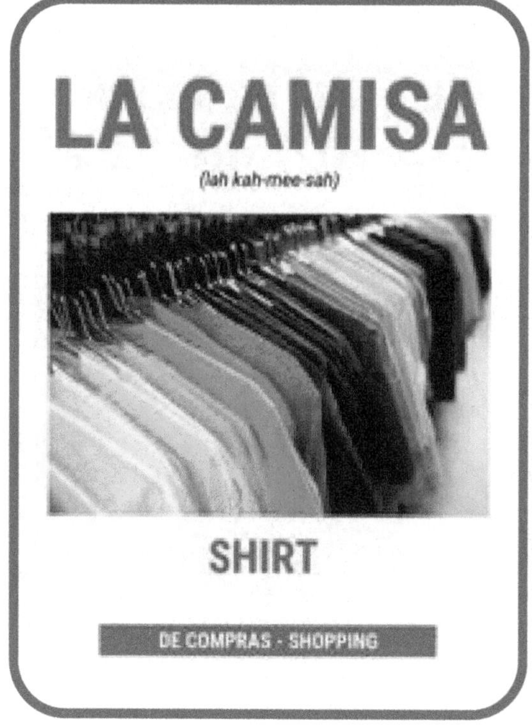
LA CAMISA
(lah kah-mee-sah)
SHIRT
DE COMPRAS - SHOPPING

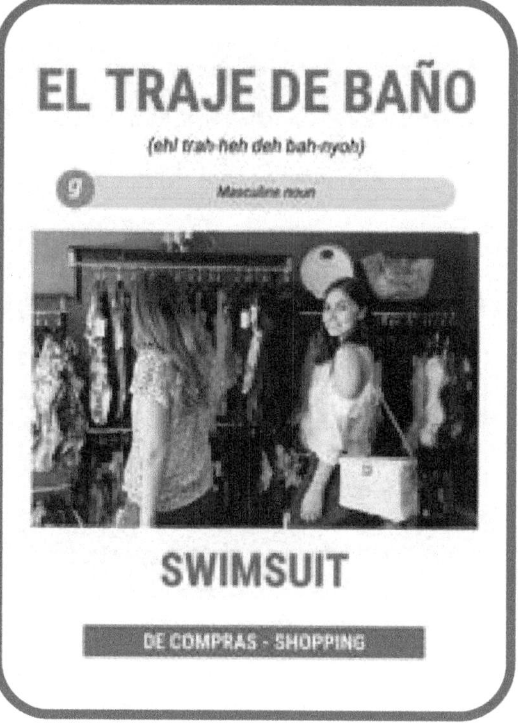
EL TRAJE DE BAÑO
(ehl trah-heh deh bah-nyoh)
g
Masculine noun
SWIMSUIT
DE COMPRAS - SHOPPING

(ehl sohm-breh-roh)

HAT

DE COMPRAS - SHOPPING

LOS ZAPATOS

(lohs sah-pah-tohs)

P The pronunciation of "zapatos" in Spain is 'thah-pah-tohs'.

SHOES

DE COMPRAS - SHOPPING

LOS JUGUETES

(lohs hoo-geh-tehs)

 *Masculine noun*

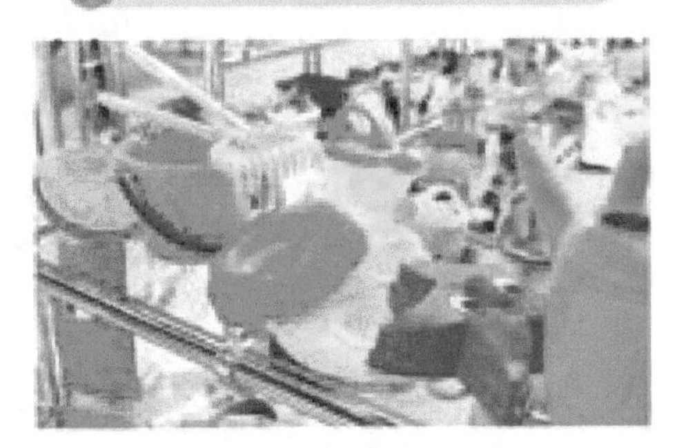

TOYS

DE COMPRAS - SHOPPING

LAS ARTESANÍAS

(lahs ahr-teh-sah-nee-ahs)

CRAFTS

DE COMPRAS - SHOPPING

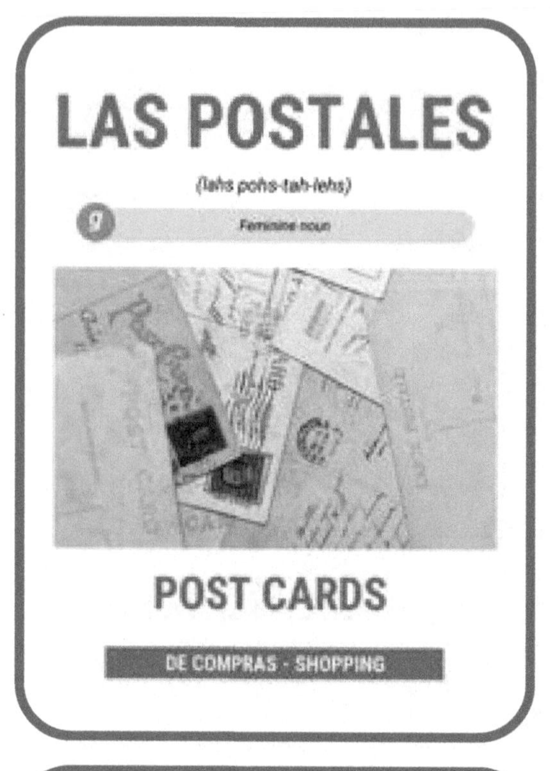
LAS POSTALES
(lahs pohs-tah-lehs)
g
Feminine noun
POST CARDS
DE COMPRAS - SHOPPING

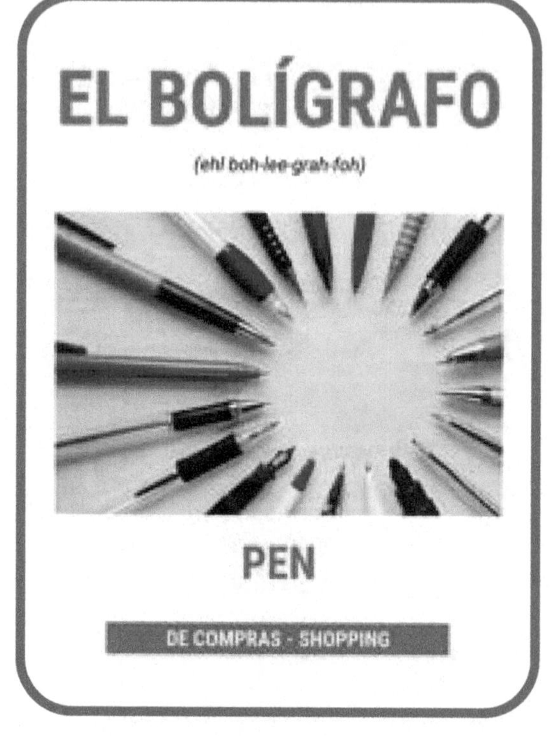
EL BOLÍGRAFO
(ehl boh-lee-grah-foh)
PEN
DE COMPRAS - SHOPPING

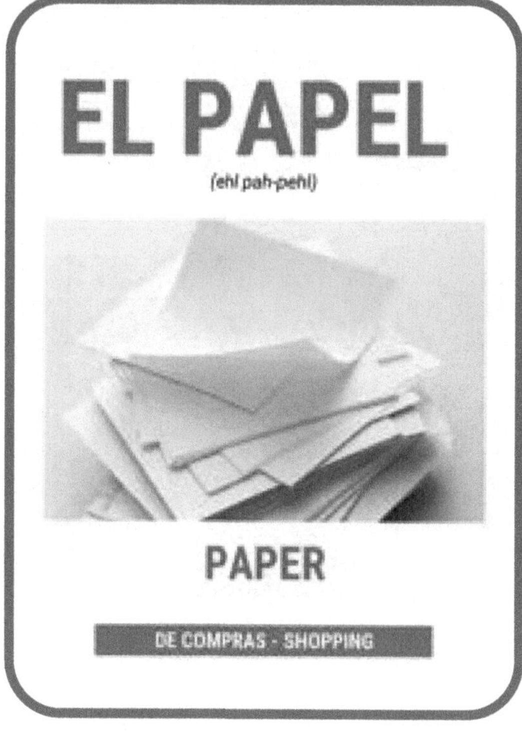
EL PAPEL
(ehl pah-pehl)
PAPER
DE COMPRAS - SHOPPING

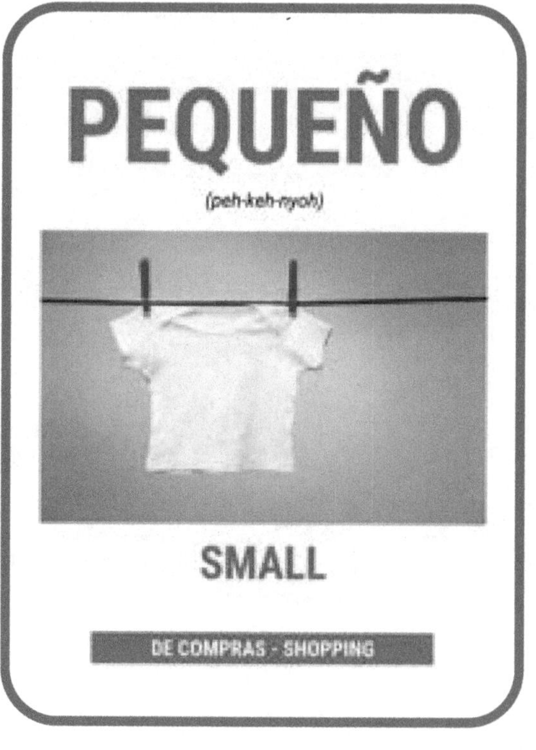
PEQUEÑO
(peh-keh-nyoh)
SMALL
DE COMPRAS - SHOPPING

MEDIANO

(meh-dyah-noh)

MEDIUM

DE COMPRAS - SHOPPING

GRANDE

(grahn-deh)

LARGE

DE COMPRAS - SHOPPING

EXTRAGRANDE

(ehks-trah-grahn-deh)

EXTRA LARGE

DE COMPRAS - SHOPPING

ME GUSTA

(meh goos-tah)

I LIKE IT

DE COMPRAS - SHOPPING

NO ME GUSTA

(noh meh goos-tah)

I DON'T LIKE IT

DE COMPRAS - SHOPPING

¿TE GUSTA?

(teh goos-tah)

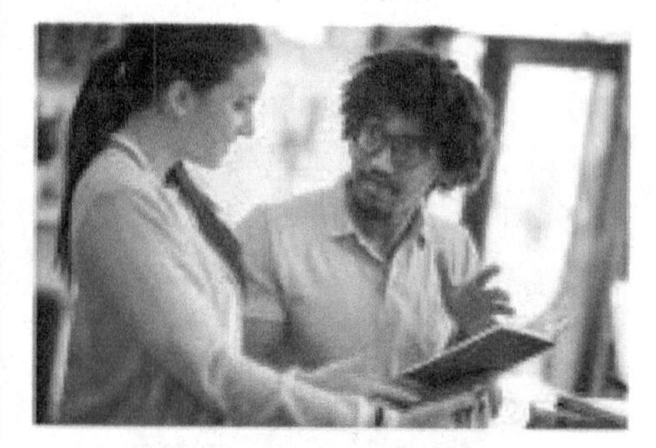

DO YOU LIKE IT?

DE COMPRAS - SHOPPING

LA CAJA

(lah kah-hah)

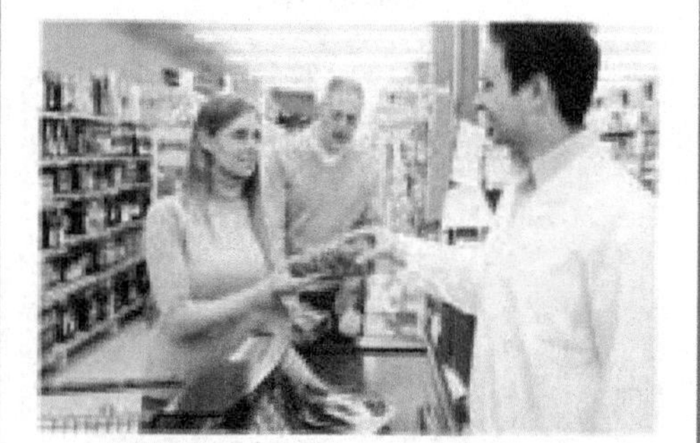

CHECKOUT COUNTER

DE COMPRAS - SHOPPING

EL MOSTRADOR

(ehl mohs-trah-dohr)

COUNTER

DE COMPRAS - SHOPPING

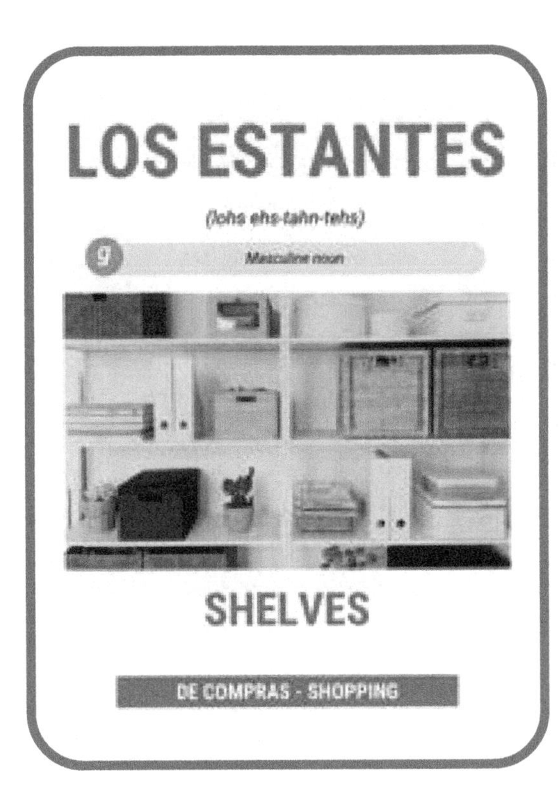
LOS ESTANTES
(lohs ehs-tahn-tehs)
g
Masculine noun
SHELVES
DE COMPRAS - SHOPPING

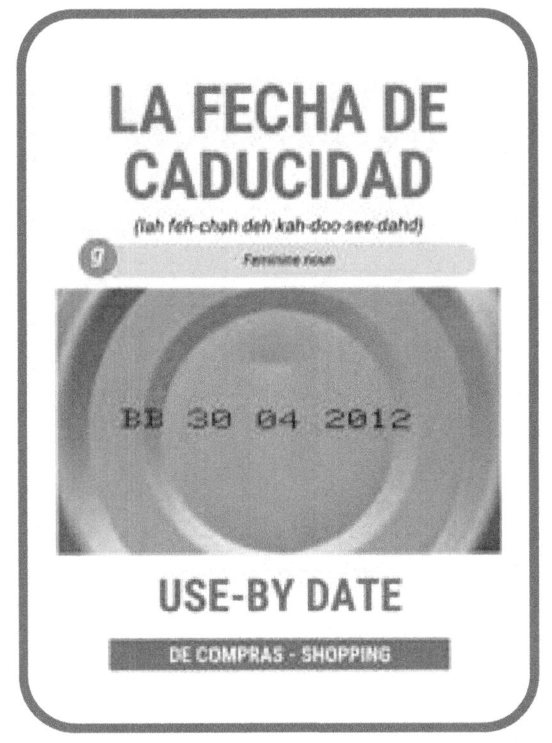
LA FECHA DE CADUCIDAD
(lah feh-chah deh kah-doo-see-dahd)
g
Feminine noun
BB 30 04 2012
USE-BY DATE
DE COMPRAS - SHOPPING

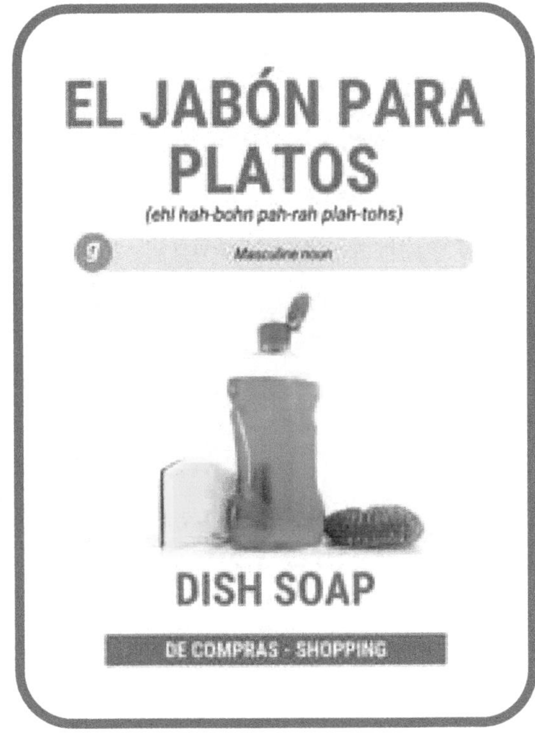
EL JABÓN PARA PLATOS
(ehl hah-bohn pah-rah plah-tohs)
g
Masculine noun
DISH SOAP
DE COMPRAS - SHOPPING

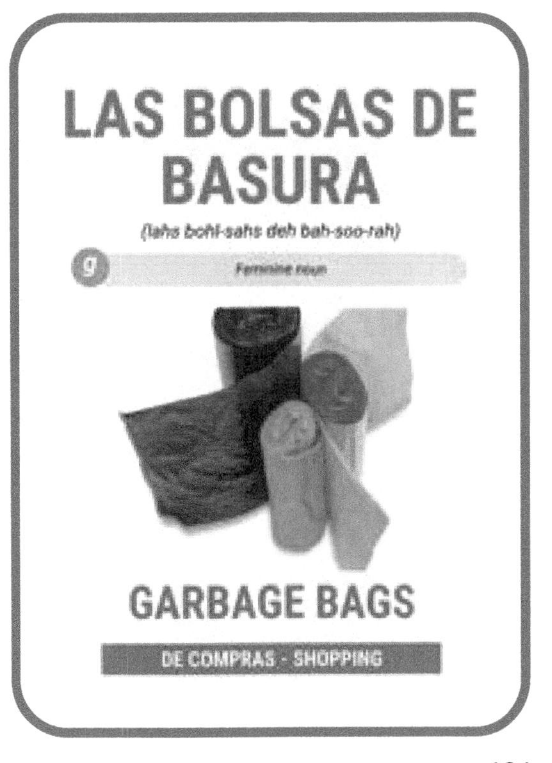
LAS BOLSAS DE BASURA
(lahs bohl-sahs deh bah-soo-rah)
g
Feminine noun
GARBAGE BAGS
DE COMPRAS - SHOPPING

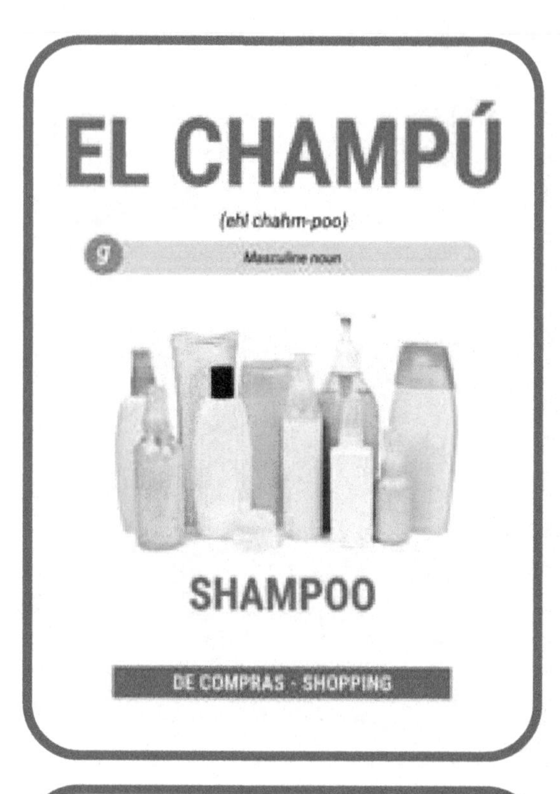
EL CHAMPÚ
(ehl chahm-poo)
g
Masculine noun
SHAMPOO
DE COMPRAS - SHOPPING

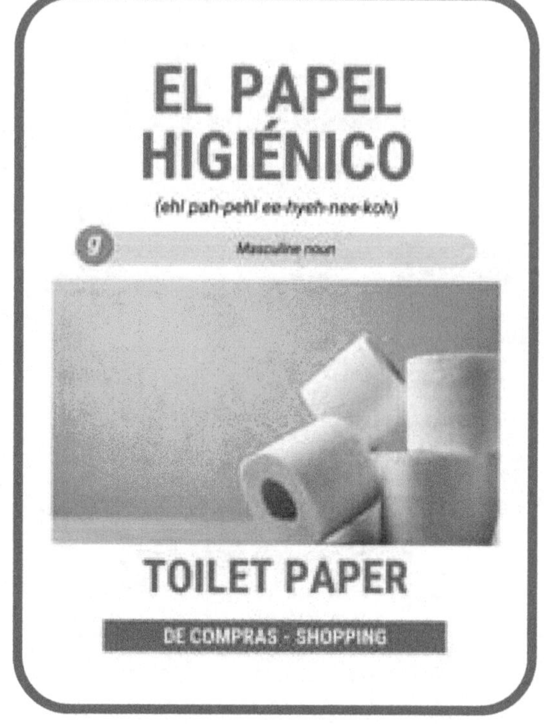
EL PAPEL HIGIÉNICO
(ehl pah-pehl ee-hyeh-nee-koh)
g
Masculine noun
TOILET PAPER
DE COMPRAS - SHOPPING

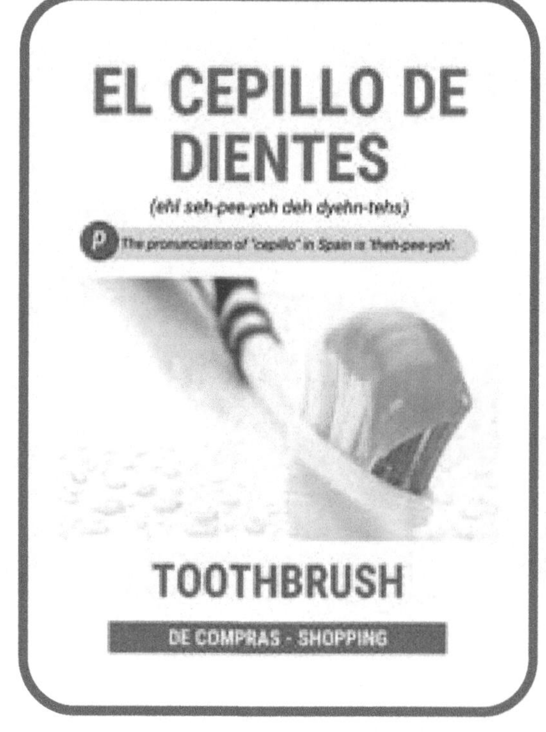
EL CEPILLO DE DIENTES
(ehl seh-pee-yoh deh dyehn-tehs)
p
TOOTHBRUSH
DE COMPRAS - SHOPPING

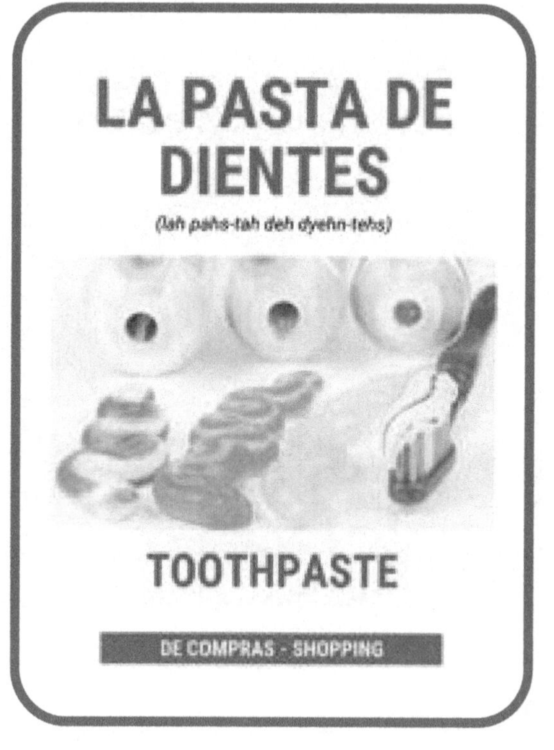
LA PASTA DE DIENTES
(lah pahs-tah deh dyehn-tehs)
TOOTHPASTE
DE COMPRAS - SHOPPING

LA PESCADERÍA

(lah pehs-kah-deh-ree-ah)

FISH MARKET

DE COMPRAS - SHOPPING

LA LAVANDERÍA

(lah lah-bahn-deh-ree-ah)

LAUNDROMAT

DE COMPRAS - SHOPPING

LA ENTRADA

(lah ehn-trah-dah)

ENTRANCE

DE COMPRAS - SHOPPING

LA SALIDA

(lah sah-lee-dah)

EXIT

DE COMPRAS - SHOPPING

ABIERTO

(ah-byehr-toh)

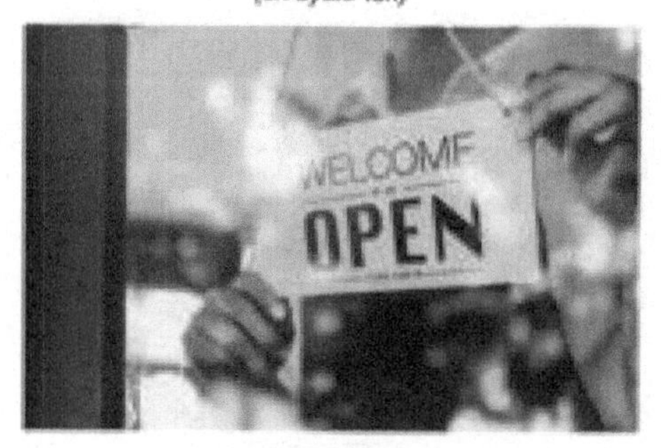

OPEN

DE COMPRAS - SHOPPING

CERRADO

(seh-rrah-doh)

P *The pronunciation of "cerrado" in Spain is 'theh-rrah-doh'.*

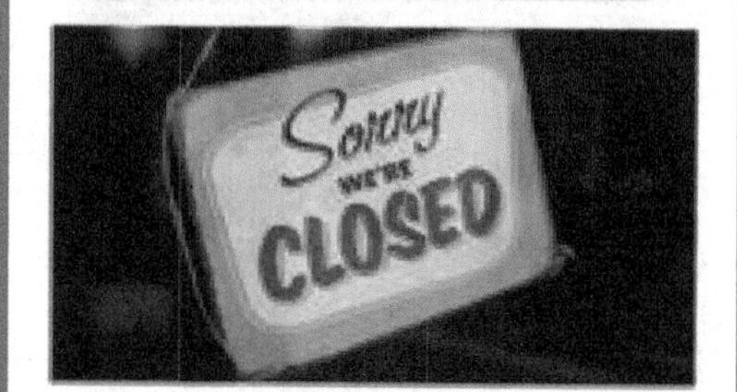

CLOSED

DE COMPRAS - SHOPPING

HORARIO DE ATENCIÓN

(oh-rah-ryoh deh ah-tehn-syohn)

P *The pronunciation of "atención" in Spain is 'ah-tehn-thyohn'.*

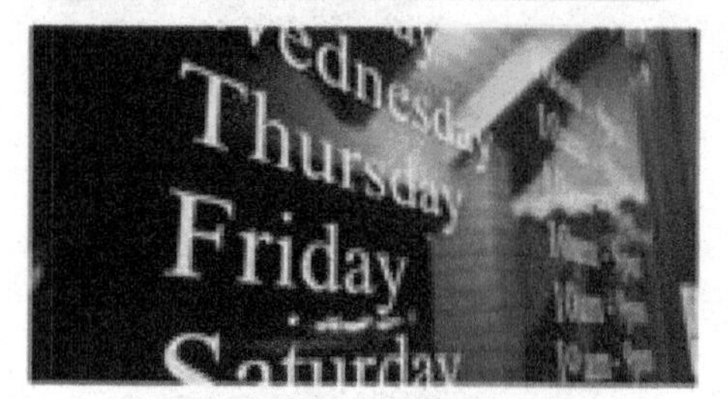

BUSINESS HOURS

DE COMPRAS - SHOPPING

EMPUJE

(ehm-poo-heh)

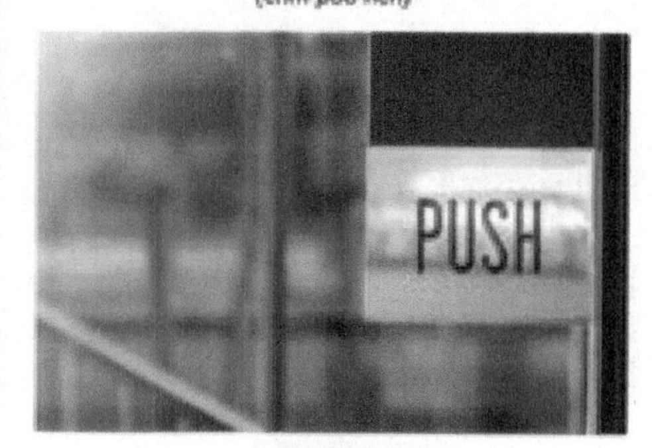

PUSH

DE COMPRAS - SHOPPING

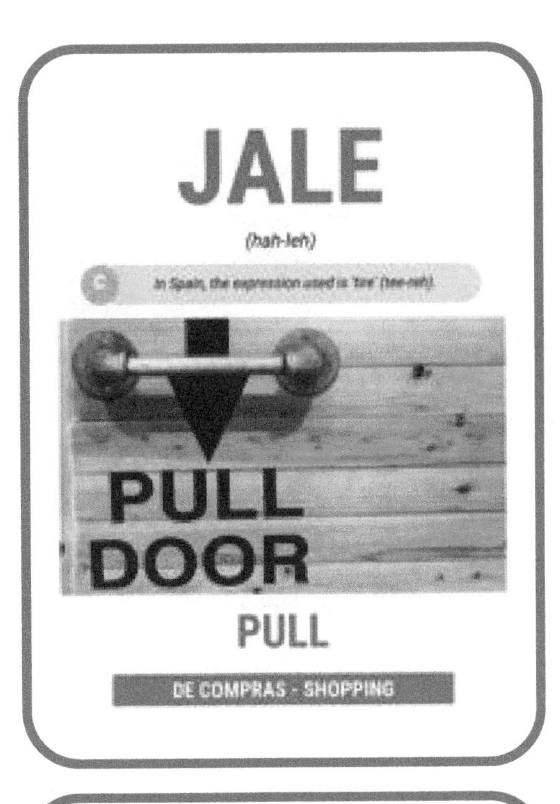
JALE
(hah-leh)
In Spain, the expression used is 'tire' (tee-reh).
PULL
DOOR
PULL
DE COMPRAS - SHOPPING

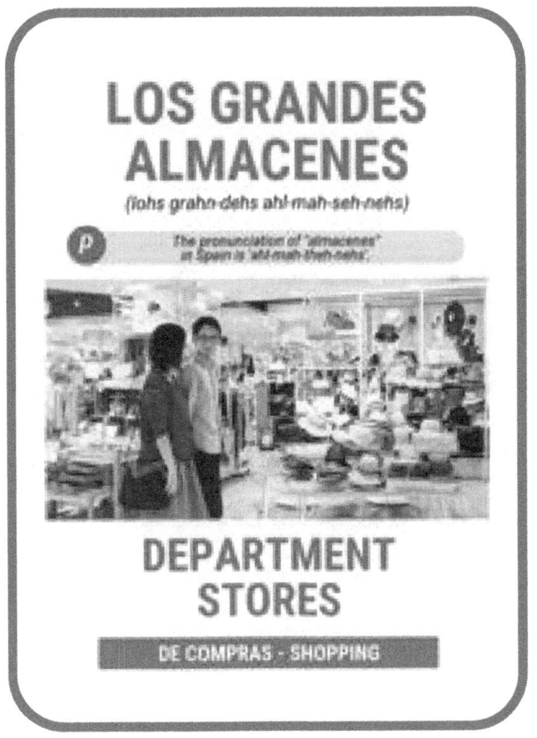
LOS GRANDES ALMACENES
(lohs grahn-dehs ahl-mah-seh-nehs)
P
The pronunciation of "almacenes" in Spain is 'ahl-mah-theh-nehs'.
DEPARTMENT STORES
DE COMPRAS - SHOPPING

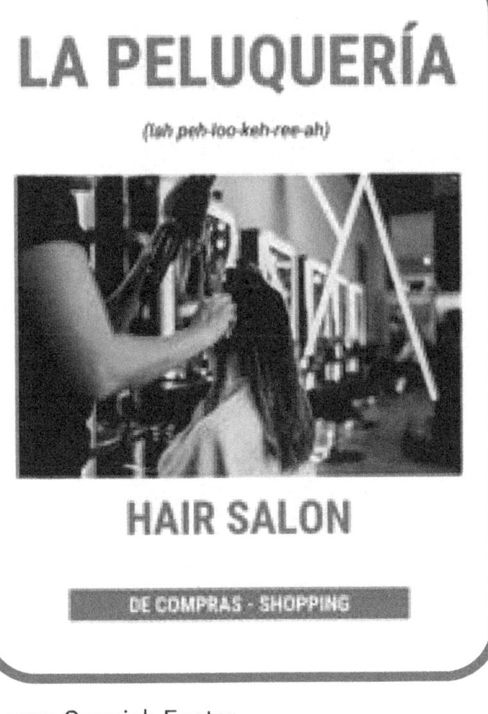
LA PELUQUERÍA
(lah peh-loo-keh-ree-ah)
HAIR SALON
DE COMPRAS - SHOPPING

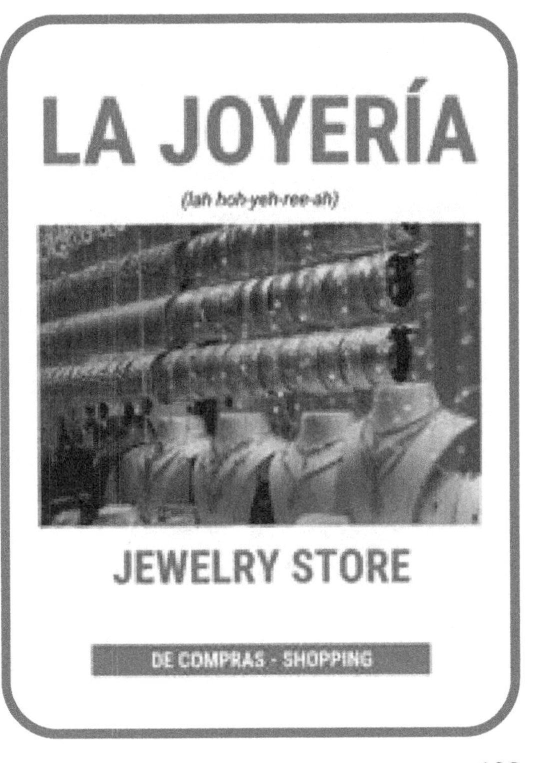
LA JOYERÍA
(lah hoh-yeh-ree-ah)
JEWELRY STORE
DE COMPRAS - SHOPPING

TIENDA DE DEPORTES

(tyehn-dah deh deh-pohr-tehs)

SPORTS STORE

DE COMPRAS - SHOPPING

GASOLINERA

(gah-soh-lee-neh-rah)

GAS STATION

DE COMPRAS - SHOPPING

IR DE COMPRAS

(eer deh kohm-prahs)

¡Vámonos de compras!
Let's go shopping!

TO GO SHOPPING

DE COMPRAS - SHOPPING

¿LO PUEDO VER?

(loh pweh-doh behr)

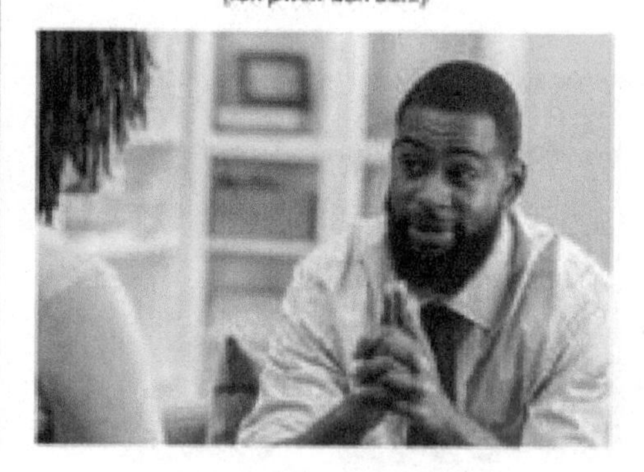

CAN I SEE IT?

DE COMPRAS - SHOPPING

LA ROPA

(lah rroh-pah)

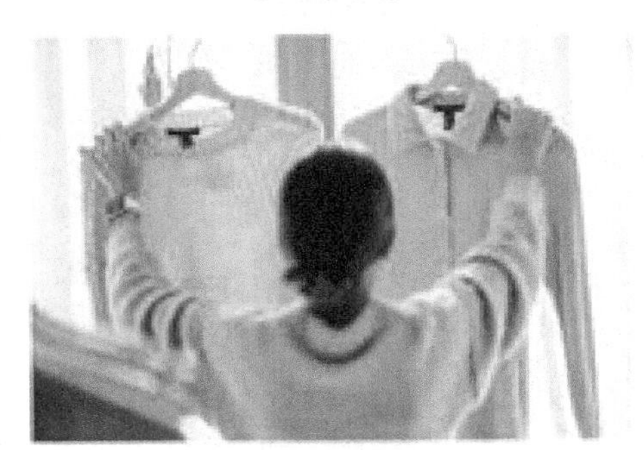

CLOTHES

DE COMPRAS - SHOPPING

LOS ACCESORIOS

(lohs ahk-seh-soh-ryohs)

P The pronunciation of "accesorios" in Spain is 'ahk-theh-soh-ryohs'.

ACCESORIES

DE COMPRAS - SHOPPING

¿TIENE OTRA TALLA?

(tyeh-neh oh-trah tah-yah)

DO YOU HAVE A DIFFERENT SIZE?

DE COMPRAS - SHOPPING

¿TIENE OTRO COLOR?

(tyeh-neh oh-troh koh-lohr)

DO YOU HAVE A DIFFERENT COLOR?

DE COMPRAS - SHOPPING

¿TIENE OTRO MODELO?

(tyeh-neh oh-troh moh-deh-loh)

DO YOU HAVE A DIFFERENT MODEL?

DE COMPRAS - SHOPPING

NO NOS QUEDA

(noh nohs keh-dah)

WE RAN OUT OF IT

DE COMPRAS - SHOPPING

¿ME LO PUEDO PROBAR?

(meh loh pweh-doh proh-bahr)

CAN I TRY IT ON?

DE COMPRAS - SHOPPING

ME QUEDA GRANDE

(meh keh-dah grahn-deh)

IT'S TOO BIG

DE COMPRAS - SHOPPING

ME QUEDA PEQUEÑO

(meh keh-dah peh-keh-nyoh)

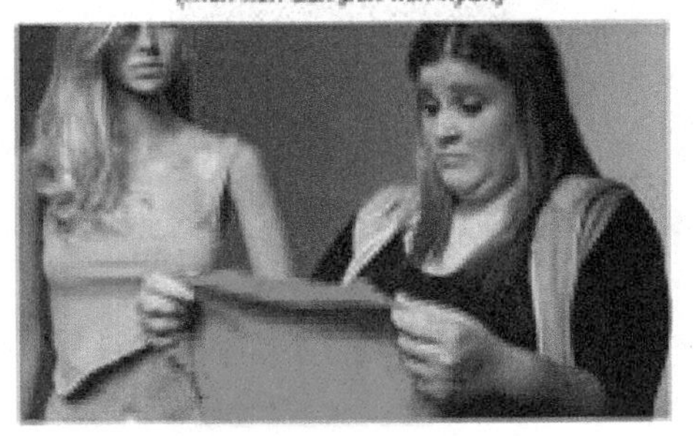

IT'S TOO SMALL

DE COMPRAS - SHOPPING

ME QUEDA APRETADO

(meh keh-dah ah-preh-tah-doh)

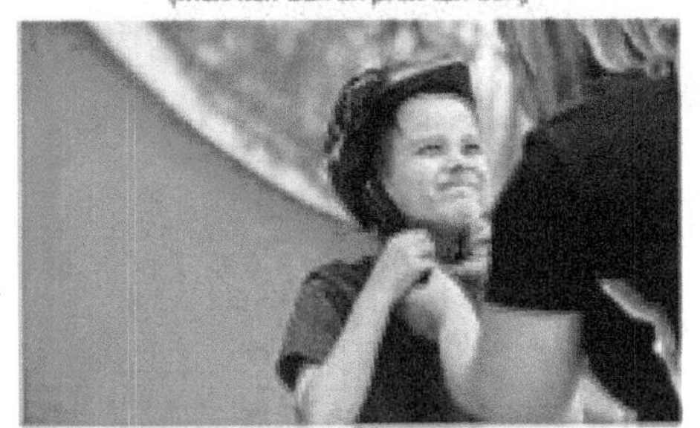

IT'S TOO TIGHT

DE COMPRAS - SHOPPING

¿TIENE OTRA MARCA?

(tyeh-neh oh-trah mahr-kah)

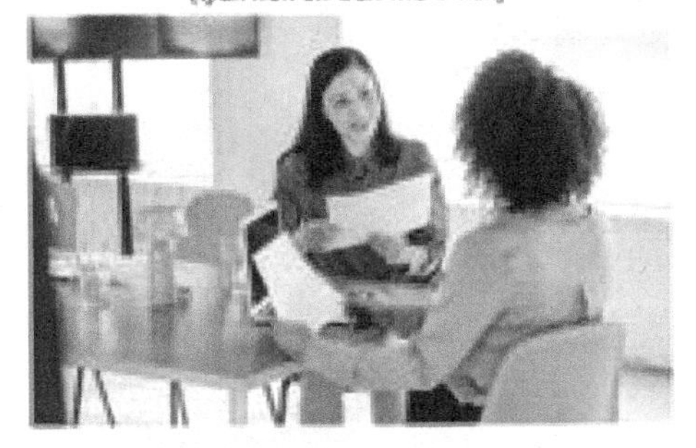

DO YOU HAVE A DIFFERENT BRAND?

DE COMPRAS - SHOPPING

¿TIENE OTRO MÁS BARATO?

(tyeh-neh oh-troh mahs bah-rah-toh)

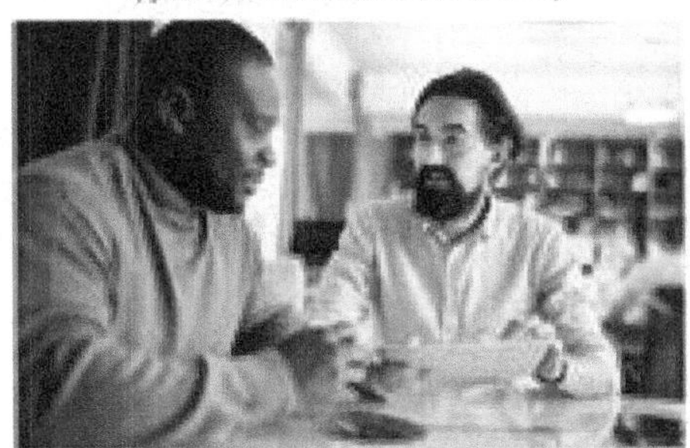

DO YOU HAVE A CHEAPER ONE?

DE COMPRAS - SHOPPING

¿A QUÉ HORA ABREN?

(ah keh oh-rah ah-breh)

WHAT TIME DO THEY OPEN?

DE COMPRAS - SHOPPING

¿A QUÉ HORA CIERRAN?

(ah keh oh-rah syeh-rrahn)

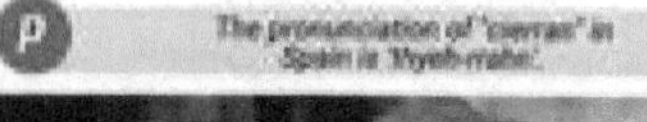

WHAT TIME DO THEY CLOSE?

DE COMPRAS - SHOPPING

QUISIERA PROBÁRMELO

(kee-syeh-rah proh-bahr-meh-loh)

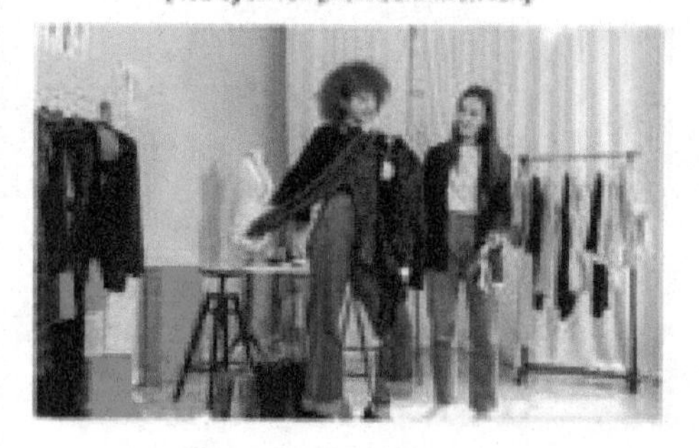

I'D LIKE TO TRY IT ON

DE COMPRAS - SHOPPING

LO QUIERO

(loh kyeh-roh)

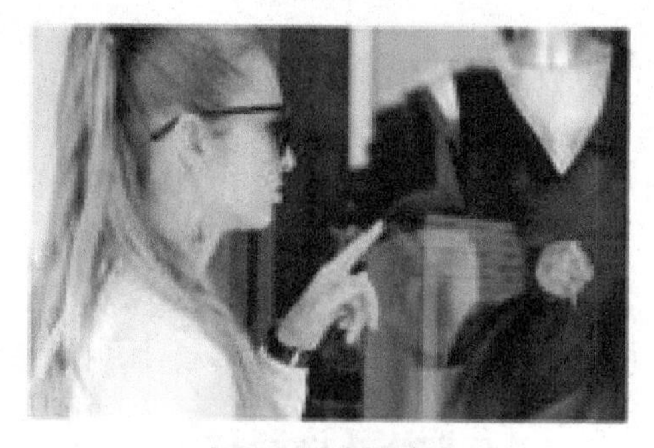

I WANT IT

DE COMPRAS - SHOPPING

NO LO QUIERO

(noh loh kyeh-roh)

I DON'T WANT IT

DE COMPRAS - SHOPPING

VOY A PENSARLO

(boy ah pehn-sahr-loh)

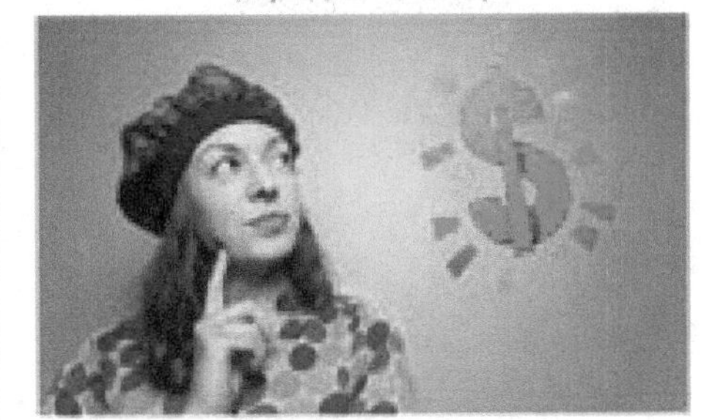

I'M GOING TO THINK ABOUT IT

DE COMPRAS - SHOPPING

SOLO ESTOY MIRANDO

(soh-loh ehs-toy mee-rahn-doh)

I'M JUST LOOKING

DE COMPRAS - SHOPPING

VUELVO MÁS TARDE

(bwehl-boh mahs tahr-deh)

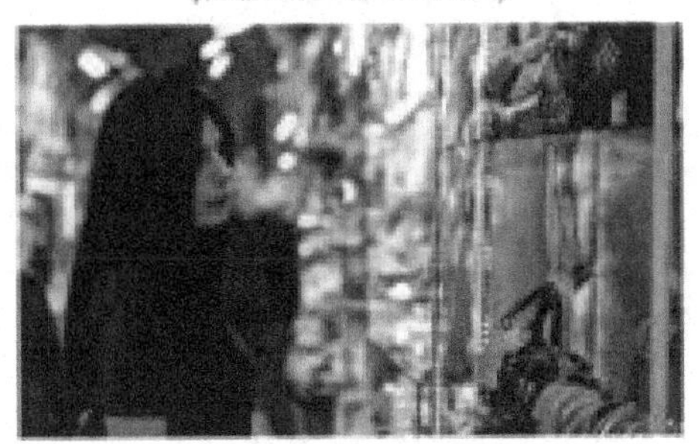

I'LL COME BACK LATER

DE COMPRAS - SHOPPING

COMPRAR

(kohm-prahr)

Compré fruta en el supermercado.
I bought fruit at the supermarket

TO BUY

DE COMPRAS - SHOPPING

VENDER

(behn-dehr)

Vendo productos hechos en casa.
I sell homemade products.

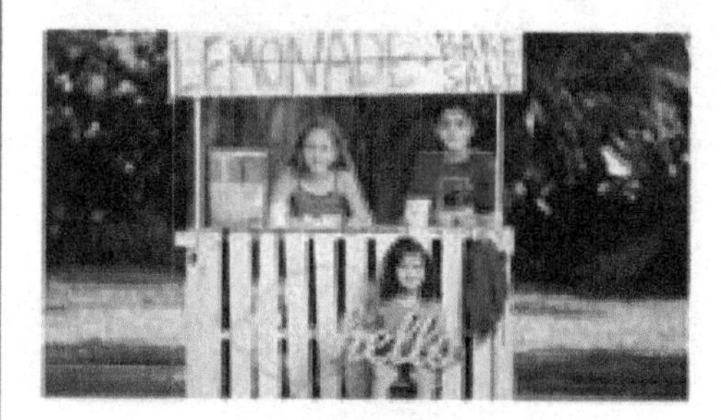

TO SELL

DE COMPRAS - SHOPPING

¿CUÁNTO VALE?

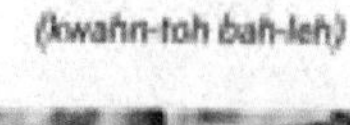

(kwahn-toh bah-leh)

HOW MUCH IS IT?

DE COMPRAS - SHOPPING

EL VENDEDOR

(ehl behn-deh-dohr)

For the female version, change the article and the ending: "la vendedora."

SELLER

DE COMPRAS - SHOPPING

LA REBAJA
(lah reh-bah-hah)
10%
DISCOUNT
DISCOUNT
DE COMPRAS - SHOPPING

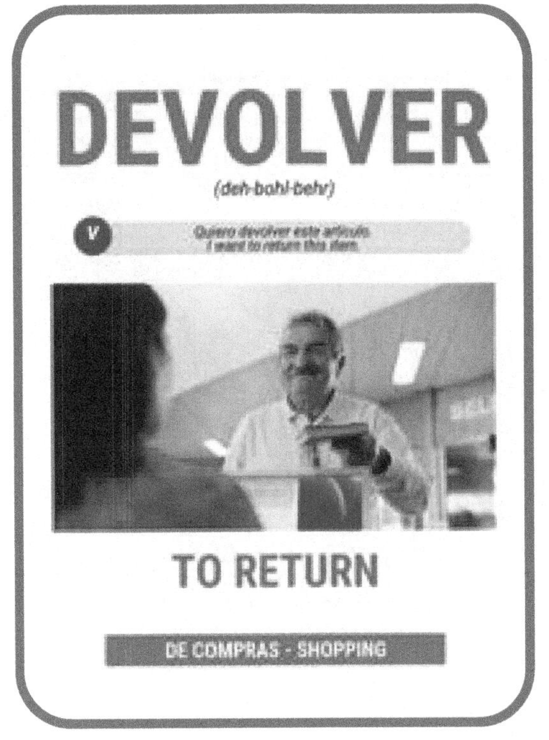
DEVOLVER
(deh-bohl-behr)
V
Quiero devolver este artículo.
I want to return this item.
TO RETURN
DE COMPRAS - SHOPPING

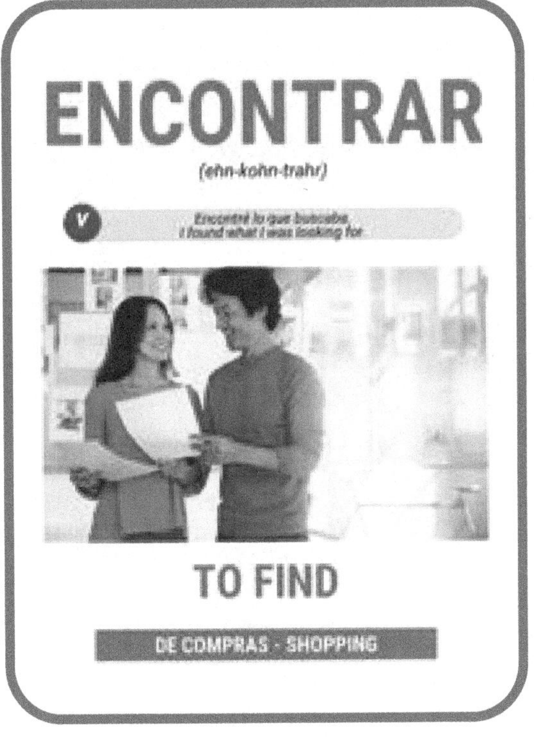
ENCONTRAR
(ehn-kohn-trahr)
V
Encontré lo que buscaba.
I found what I was looking for.
TO FIND
DE COMPRAS - SHOPPING

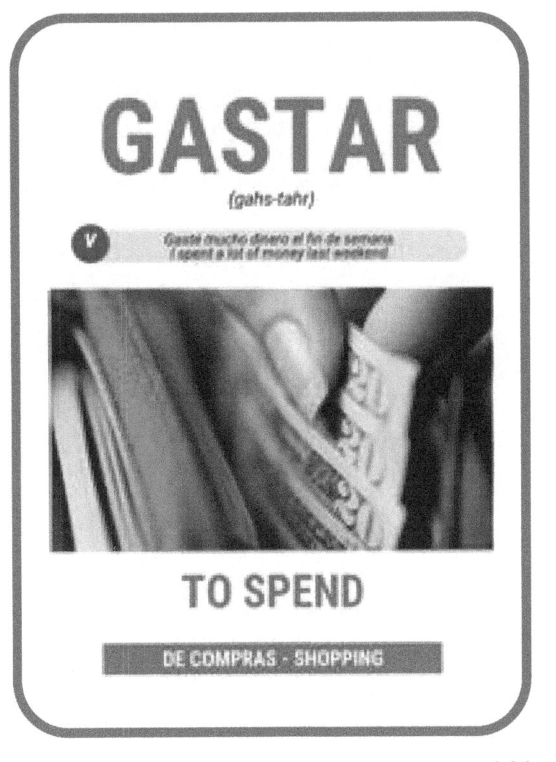
GASTAR
(gahs-tahr)
V
Gasté mucho dinero el fin de semana.
I spent a lot of money last weekend.
TO SPEND
DE COMPRAS - SHOPPING

MIRAR VITRINAS

(mee-rahr bee-tree-nahs)

Pasamos la tarde mirando vitrinas.
We spent the afternoon window shopping.

WINDOW SHOPPING

DE COMPRAS - SHOPPING

UNA MUESTRA

(oo-nah mwehs-trah)

A SAMPLE

DE COMPRAS - SHOPPING

UNA BOLSA

(oo-nah bohl-sah)

A BAG

DE COMPRAS - SHOPPING

EL RECIBO

(ehl reh-see-boh)

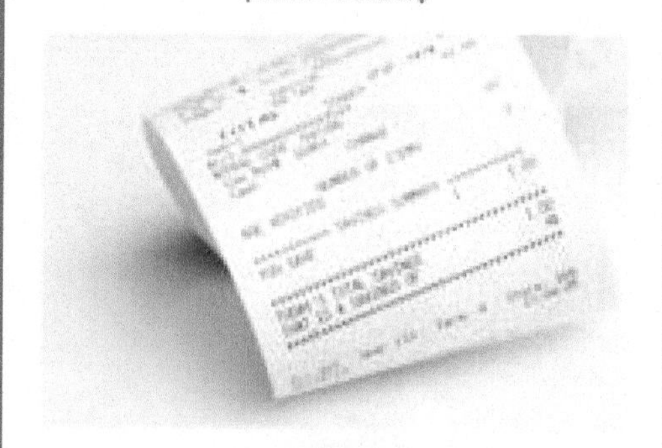

RECEIPT

DE COMPRAS - SHOPPING

EL CAJERO

(ehl kah-heh-roh)

g For the female version, change the article and the ending: 'la cajera.'

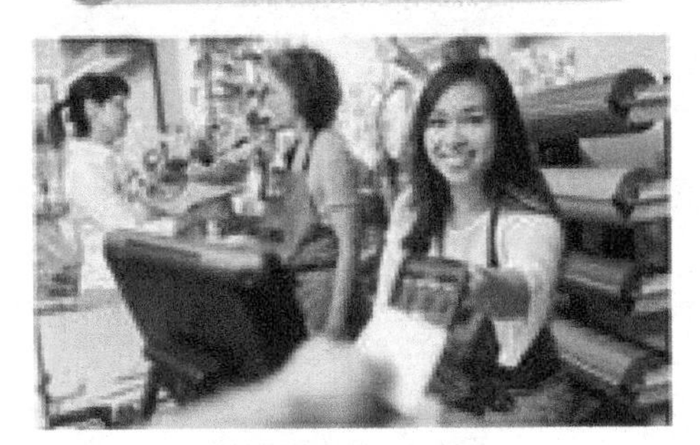

CASHIER

DE COMPRAS - SHOPPING

¿HAY...?

(ay)

g Say 'Hay...' followed by the item or items you are looking for.

IS THERE...? / ARE THERE...?

DE COMPRAS - SHOPPING

EL ABRIGO

(ehl ah-bree-goh)

COAT

DE COMPRAS - SHOPPING

LA CHAQUETA

(lah chah-keh-tah)

JACKET

DE COMPRAS - SHOPPING

EL IMPERMEABLE

(ehl eem-pehr-meh-ah-bleh)

RAINCOAT

DE COMPRAS - SHOPPING

LA PIYAMA

(lah pee-yah-mah)

PIJAMAS

DE COMPRAS - SHOPPING

EL PANTALÓN

(ehl pahn-tah-lohn)

PANTS

DE COMPRAS - SHOPPING

LOS PANTALONES CORTOS

(lohs pahn-tah-loh-nehs kohr-tohs)

SHORTS

DE COMPRAS - SHOPPING

(ehl sweh-tehr)

SWEATER

DE COMPRAS - SHOPPING

LA CAMISETA

(lah kah-mee-seh-tah)

T-SHIRT

DE COMPRAS - SHOPPING

LAS MEDIAS

(lahs meh-dyahs)

SOCKS

DE COMPRAS - SHOPPING

LAS BOTAS

(lahs boh-tahs)

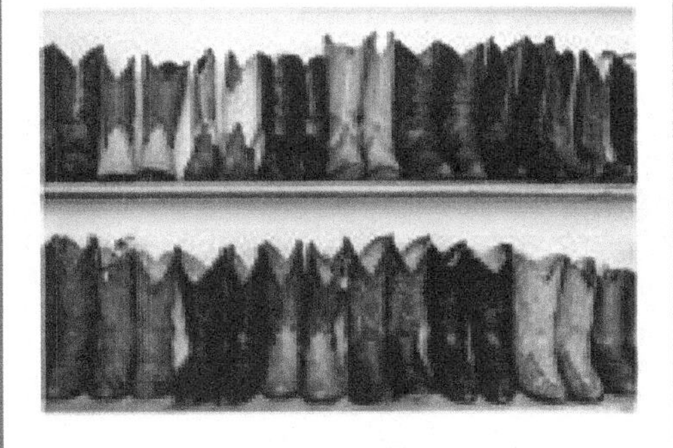

BOOTS

DE COMPRAS - SHOPPING

LAS SANDALIAS

(lahs sahn-dah-lyahs)

SANDALS

DE COMPRAS - SHOPPING

LOS ZAPATOS DE TACÓN

(lohs sah-pah-tohs deh tah-kohn)

P The pronunciation of "zapatos" in Spain is 'thah-pah-tohs'.

HIGH-HEELED SHOES

DE COMPRAS - SHOPPING

LOS TENIS

(lohs teh-nees)

In Spain and other Spanish speaking countries, these are also known as zapatillas deportivas.

SNEAKERS

DE COMPRAS - SHOPPING

UNA BLUSA

(oo-nah bloo-sah)

A BLOUSE

DE COMPRAS - SHOPPING

UNA FALDA

(oo-nah fahl-dah)

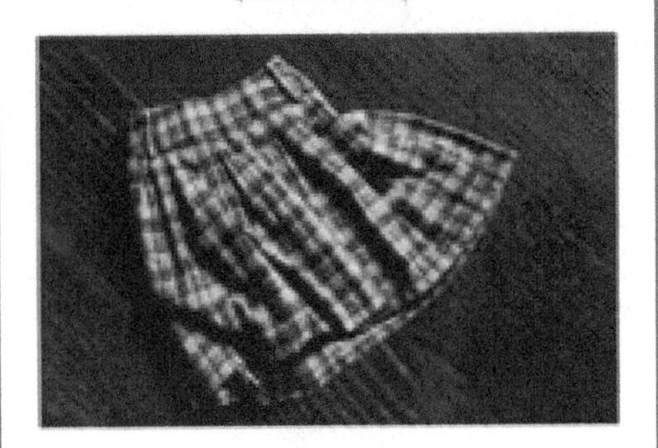

A SKIRT

DE COMPRAS - SHOPPING

UNA MINIFALDA

(oo-nah mee-nee-fahl-dah)

A MINISKIRT

DE COMPRAS - SHOPPING

UN TRAJE

(oon trah-heh)

g *Masculine noun*

A SUIT

DE COMPRAS - SHOPPING

UNA BUFANDA

(oo-nah boo-fahn-dah)

A SCARF

DE COMPRAS - SHOPPING

UN CINTURÓN
(oon seen-too-rohn)
A BELT
DE COMPRAS - SHOPPING

UN RELOJ
(oon reh-lohh)
g
Masculine noun
A WATCH
DE COMPRAS - SHOPPING

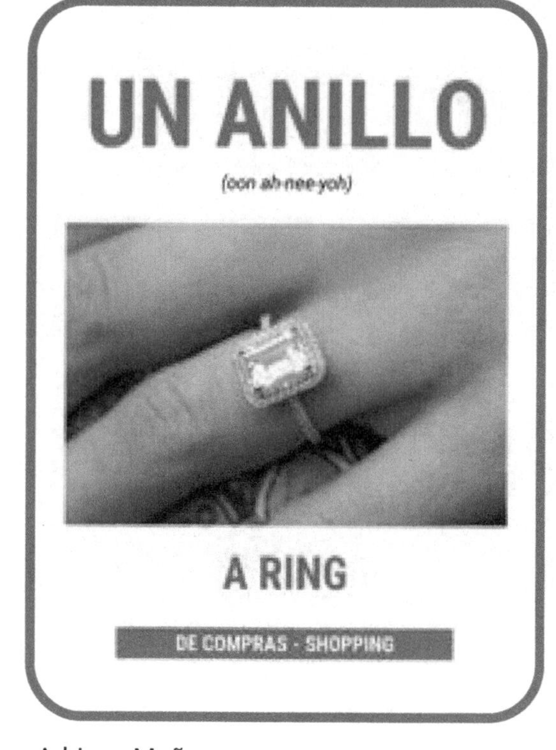

UN ANILLO
(oon ah-nee-yoh)
A RING
DE COMPRAS - SHOPPING

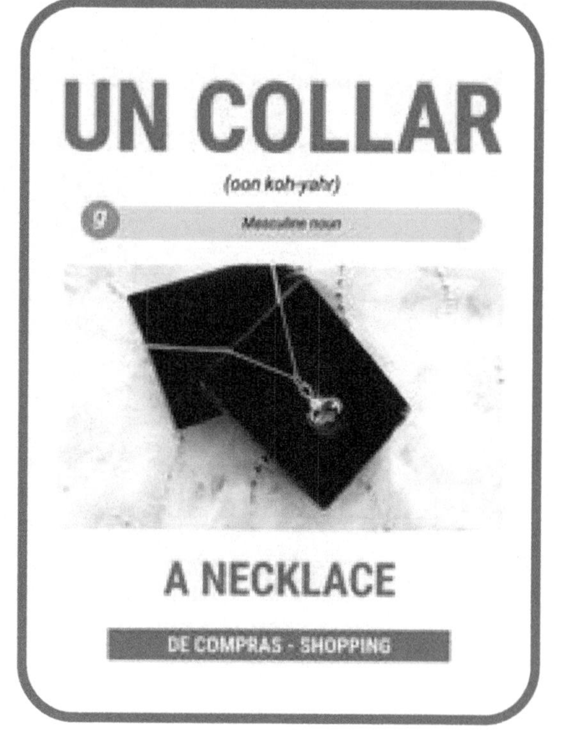

UN COLLAR
(oon koh-yahr)
g
Masculine noun
A NECKLACE
DE COMPRAS - SHOPPING

UNA PULSERA

(oo-nah pool-seh-rah)

A BRACELET

DE COMPRAS - SHOPPING

LAS GAFAS

(lahs gah-fahs)

GLASSES

DE COMPRAS - SHOPPING

LAS GAFAS DE SOL

(lahs gah-fahs deh sohl)

g Masculine noun

SUNGLASSES

DE COMPRAS - SHOPPING

LOS GUANTES

(lohs gwahn-tehs)

g Masculine noun

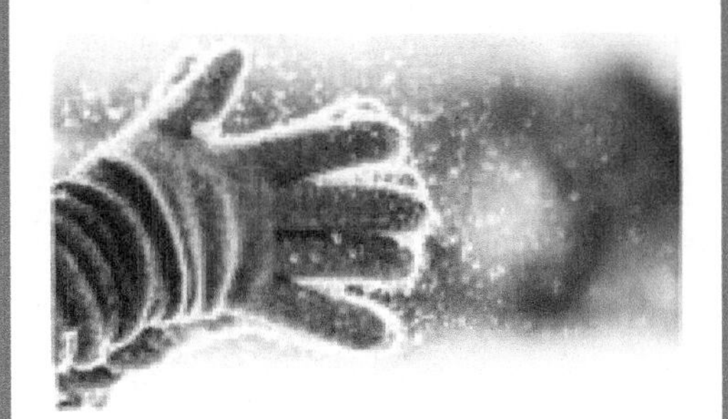

GLOVES

DE COMPRAS - SHOPPING

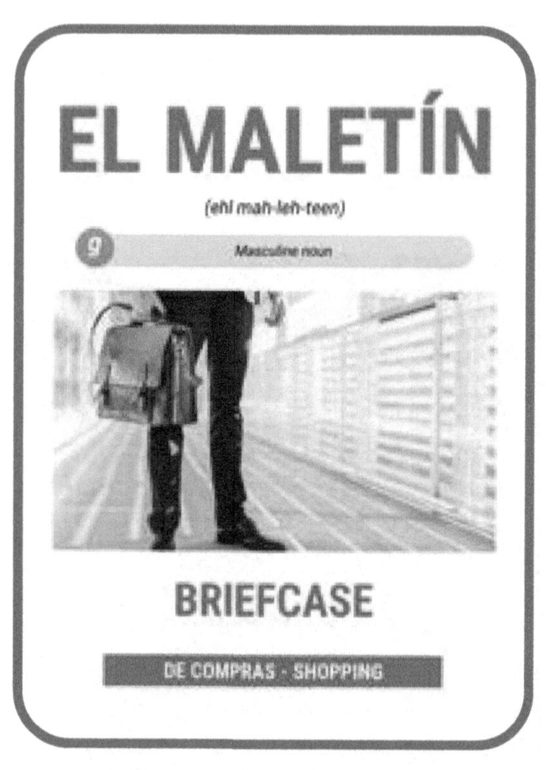
EL MALETÍN
(ehl mah-leh-teen)
g
Masculine noun
BRIEFCASE
DE COMPRAS - SHOPPING

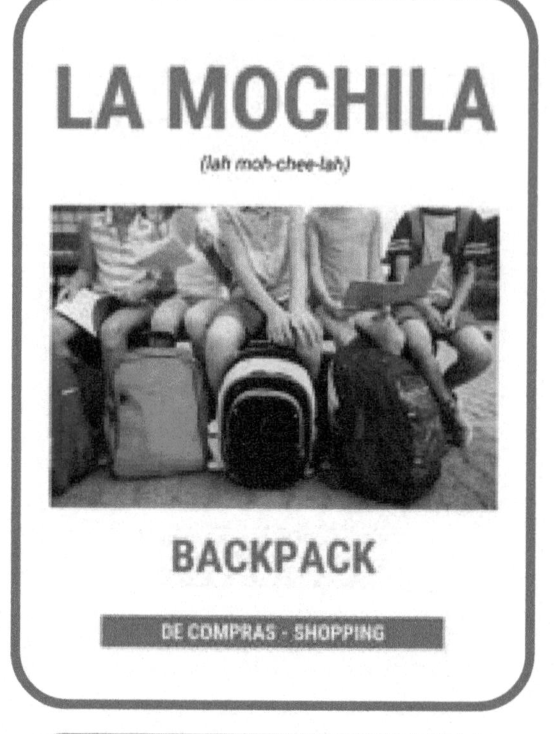
LA MOCHILA
(lah moh-chee-lah)
BACKPACK
DE COMPRAS - SHOPPING

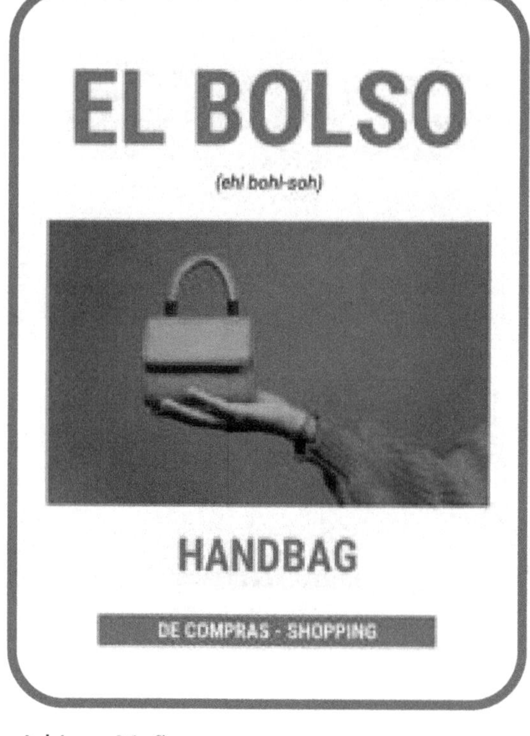
EL BOLSO
(ehl bohl-soh)
HANDBAG
DE COMPRAS - SHOPPING

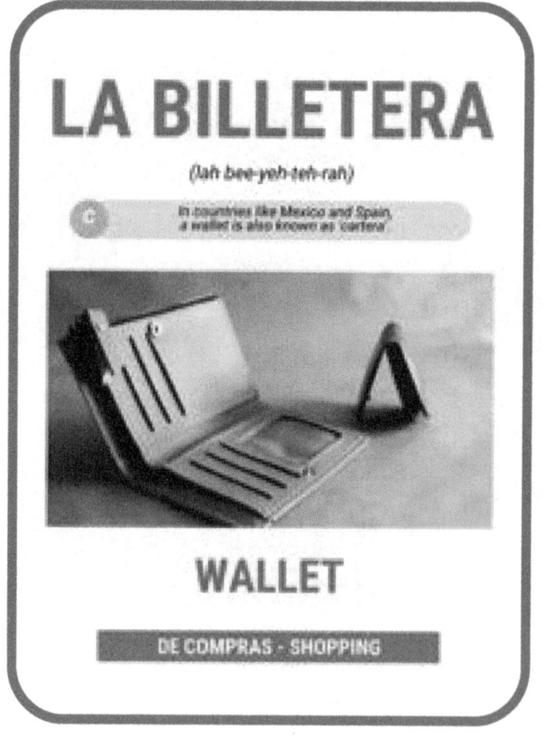
LA BILLETERA
(lah bee-yeh-teh-rah)
In countries like Mexico and Spain, a wallet is also known as 'cartera'
WALLET
DE COMPRAS - SHOPPING

EL PARAGUAS
(ehl pah-rah-gwahs)
UMBRELLA
DE COMPRAS - SHOPPING

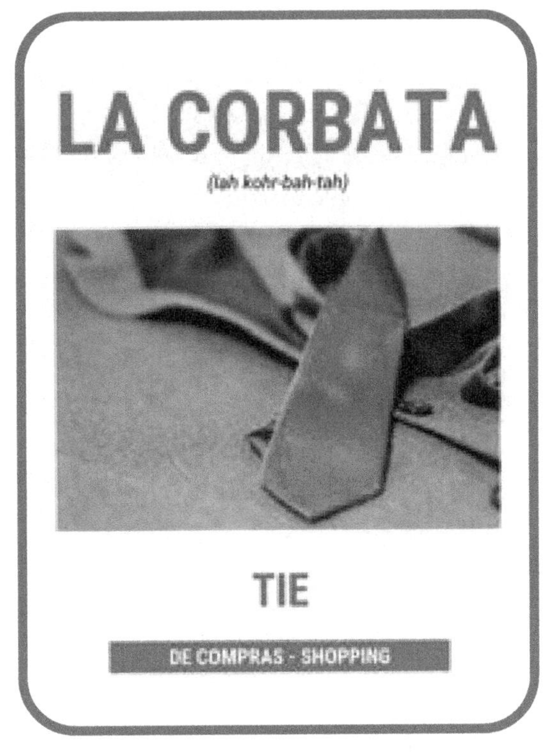
LA CORBATA
(lah kohr-bah-tah)
TIE
DE COMPRAS - SHOPPING

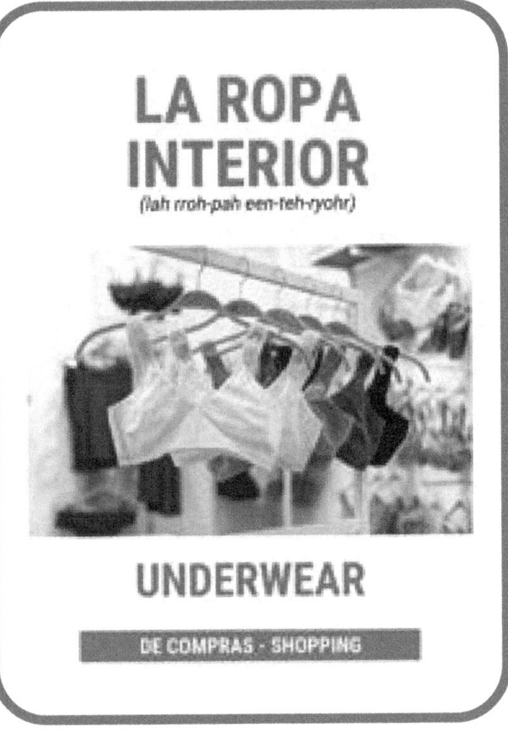
LA ROPA INTERIOR
(lah rroh-pah een-teh-ryohr)
UNDERWEAR
DE COMPRAS - SHOPPING

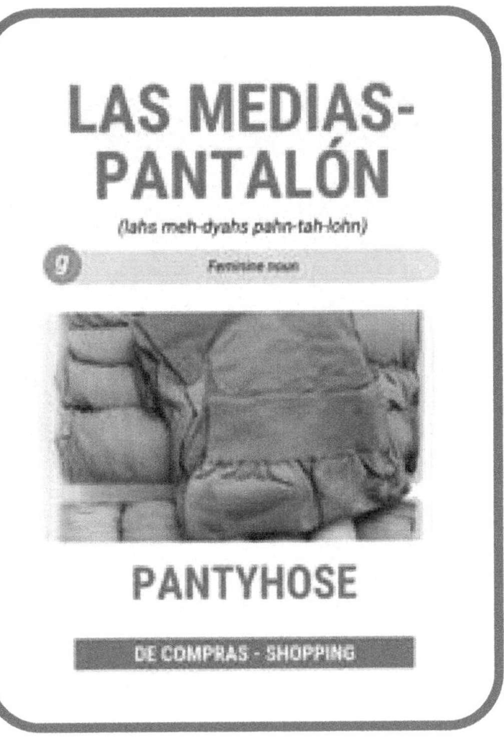
LAS MEDIAS-PANTALÓN
(lahs meh-dyahs pahn-tah-lohn)
g
Feminine noun
PANTYHOSE
DE COMPRAS - SHOPPING

EL SOSTÉN

(ehl sohs-tehn)

In Spain it is known as sujetador. En Colombia and Mexico as brasier, and in Argentina as corpiño.

BRA

DE COMPRAS - SHOPPING

LAS BRAGAS

(lahs brah-gahs)

PANTIES

DE COMPRAS - SHOPPING

LOS BÓXERS

(lohs bohk-sehrs)

BOXER SHORTS

DE COMPRAS - SHOPPING

¿DE QUÉ MATERIAL ES?

(deh keh mah-teh-ryahl es)

WHAT MATERIAL IS IT?

DE COMPRAS - SHOPPING

ES DE ALGODÓN

(ehs deh ahl-goh-dohn)

IT'S MADE OF COTTON

DE COMPRAS - SHOPPING

ES DE CUERO

(ehs deh kweh-roh)

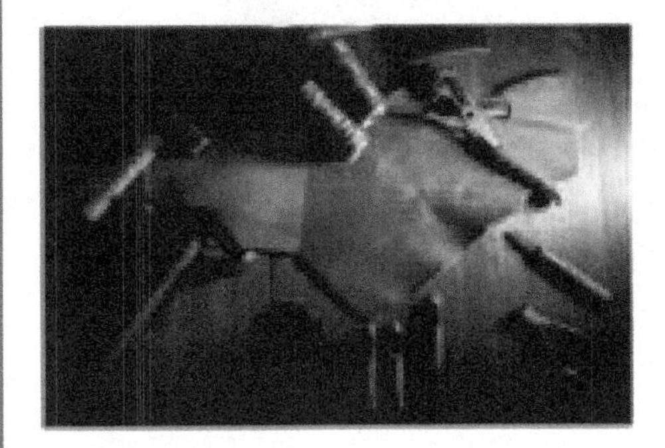

IT'S MADE OF LEATHER

DE COMPRAS - SHOPPING

ES DE TELA

(ehs deh teh-lah)

IT'S FABRIC

DE COMPRAS - SHOPPING

ES HECHO EN CASA

(ehs eh-choh ehn kah-sah)

IT'S HOMEMADE

DE COMPRAS - SHOPPING

ES HECHO A MANO

(ehs eh-choh ah mah-noh)

IT'S HANDMADE

DE COMPRAS - SHOPPING

ES TALLADO

(ehs tah-yah-doh)

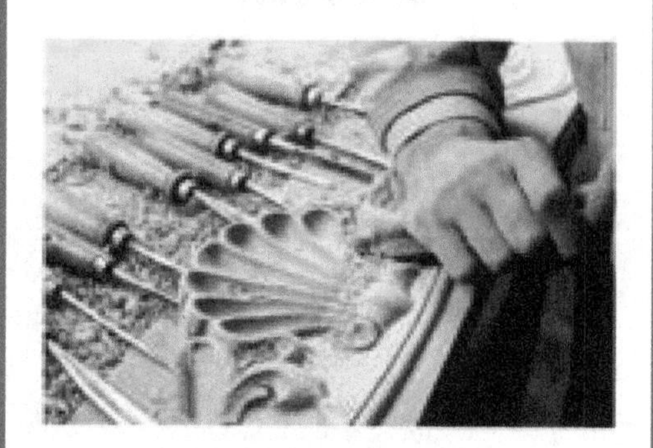

IT'S CARVED

DE COMPRAS - SHOPPING

ES COSIDO

(ehs koh-see-doh)

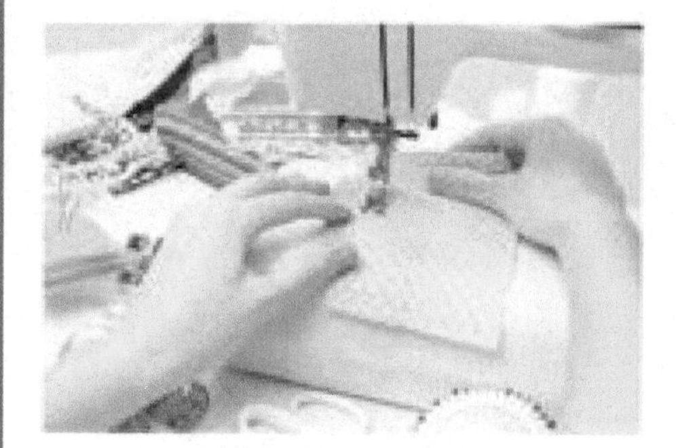

IT'S SEWN

DE COMPRAS - SHOPPING

ES TEJIDO

(ehs teh-hee-doh)

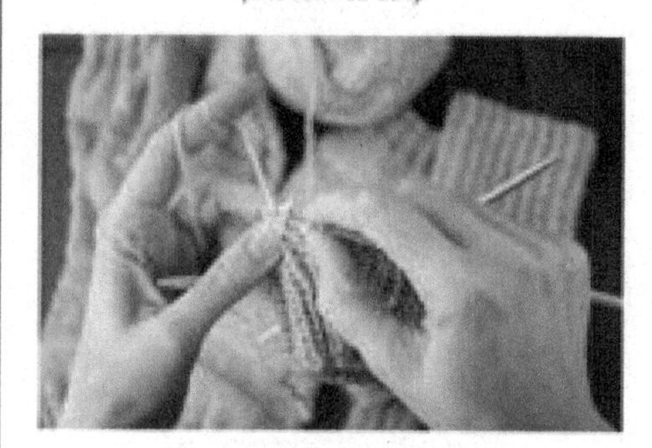

IT'S KNITTED

DE COMPRAS - SHOPPING

ES DE CERÁMICA

(ehs deh seh-rah-mee-kah)

IT'S MADE OF CERAMIC

DE COMPRAS - SHOPPING

ES DE PORCELANA

(ehs deh pohr-seh-lah-nah)

IT'S MADE OF PORCELAIN

DE COMPRAS - SHOPPING

¡ESTÁ BONITO!

(ehs-tah boh-nee-toh)

IT'S PRETTY!

DE COMPRAS - SHOPPING

¡ESTÁ FEO!

(ehs-tah feh-oh)

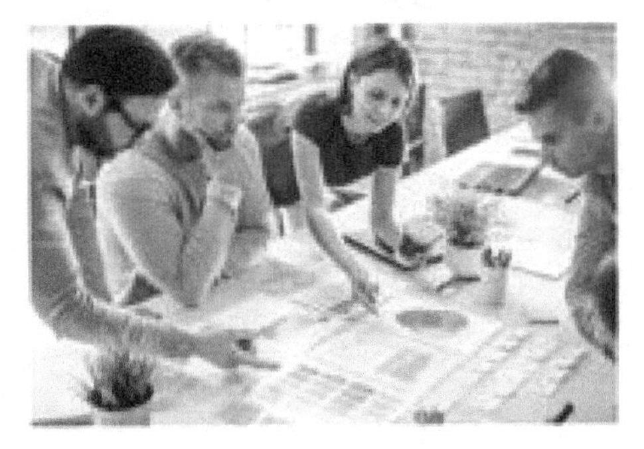

IT'S UGLY!

DE COMPRAS - SHOPPING

ESTÁ ECONÓMICO

(ehs-tah eh-koh-noh-mee-koh)

IT'S AFFORDABLE

DE COMPRAS - SHOPPING

ESTÁ ELEGANTE

(ehs-tah eh-leh-gahn-teh)

IT'S ELEGANT

DE COMPRAS - SHOPPING

ESTÁ ROTO

(ehs-tah roh-toh)

IT'S BROKEN

DE COMPRAS - SHOPPING

ESTÁ DAÑADO

(ehs-tah dah-nyah-doh)

IT'S DAMAGED

DE COMPRAS - SHOPPING

NO SIRVE

(noh seer-beh)

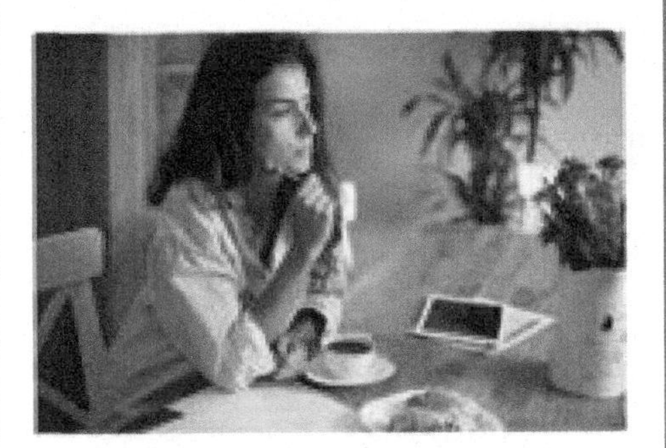

IT DOESN'T WORK

DE COMPRAS - SHOPPING

¿PUEDE REPARARLO?

(pweh-deh rreh-pah-rahr-loh)

CAN YOU FIX IT?

DE COMPRAS - SHOPPING

IR EN BICICLETA

(eer ehn bee-see-kleh-tah)

Me gusta ir en bicicleta.
I like to go cycling.

TO GO CYCLING

PASATIEMPOS - LEISURE ACTIVITIES

JUGAR AJEDREZ

(hoo-gahr ah-heh-drehs)

Juego ajedrez con mi hermana.
I play chess with my sister.

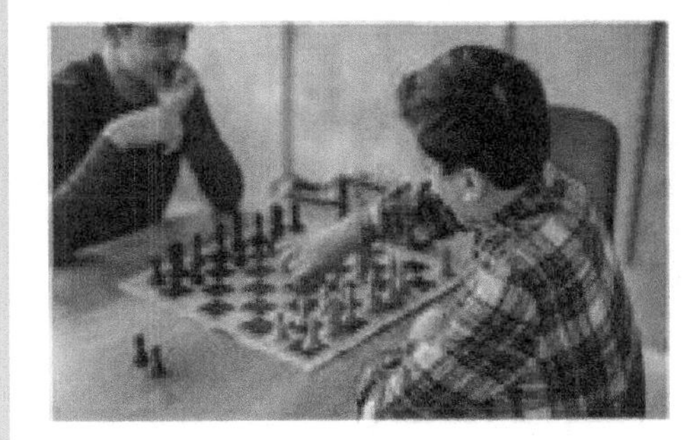

TO PLAY CHESS

PASATIEMPOS - LEISURE ACTIVITIES

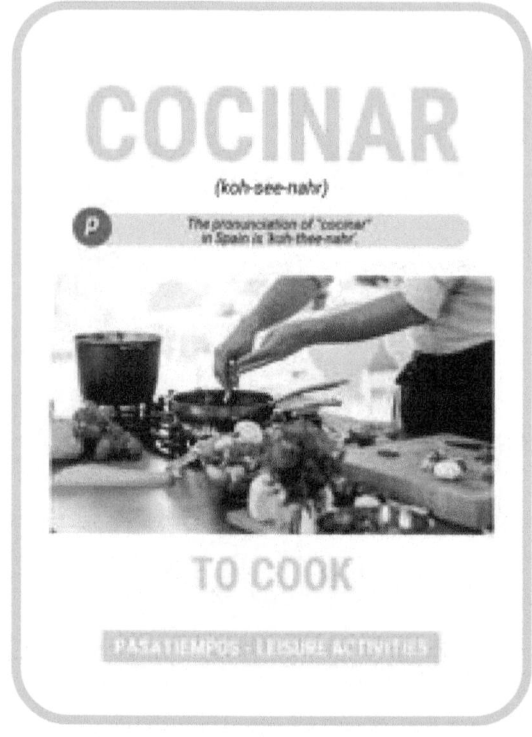
COCINAR
(koh-see-nahr)
p
The pronunciation of "cocinar" in Spain is 'koh-thee-nahr'.
TO COOK
PASATIEMPOS - LEISURE ACTIVITIES

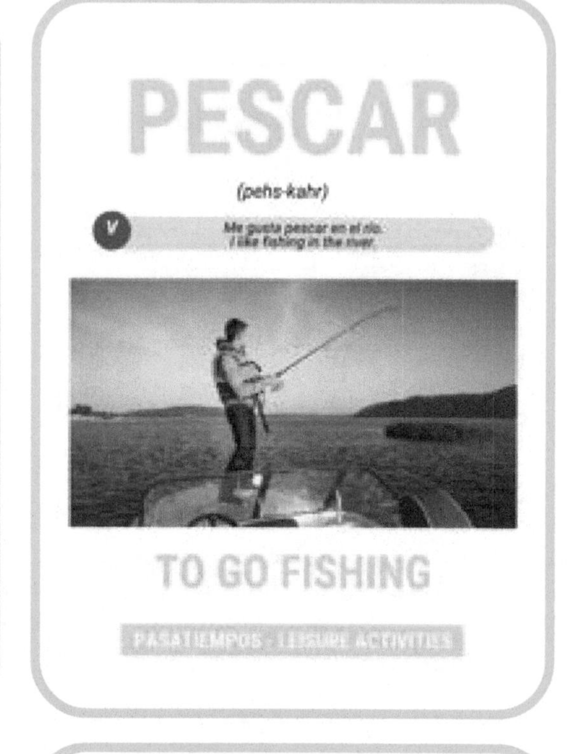
PESCAR
(pehs-kahr)
v
Me gusta pescar en el río.
I like fishing in the river.
TO GO FISHING
PASATIEMPOS - LEISURE ACTIVITIES

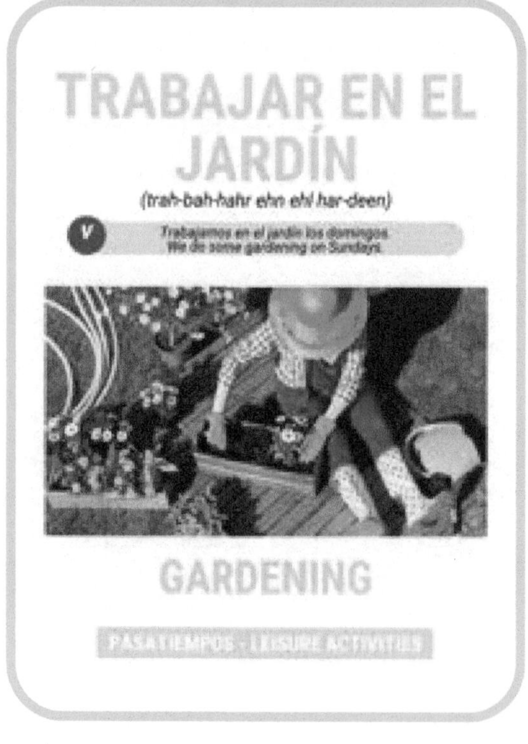
TRABAJAR EN EL JARDÍN
(trah-bah-hahr ehn ehl har-deen)
v
Trabajamos en el jardín los domingos.
We do some gardening on Sundays.
GARDENING
PASATIEMPOS - LEISURE ACTIVITIES

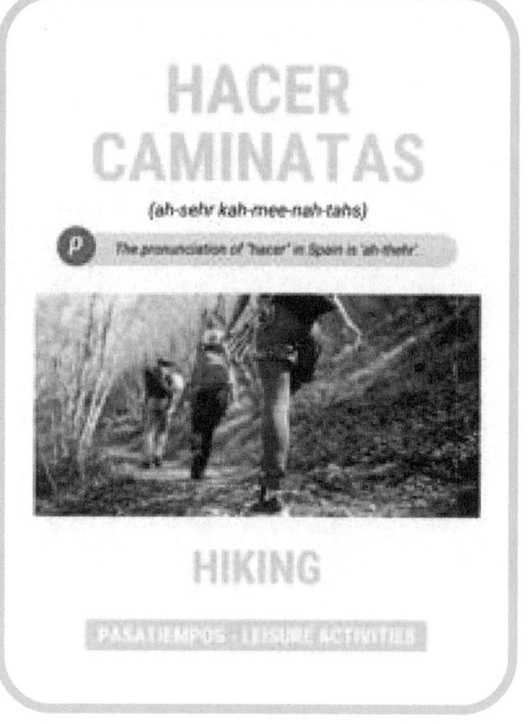
HACER CAMINATAS
(ah-sehr kah-mee-nah-tahs)
p
The pronunciation of "hacer" in Spain is 'ah-thehr'.
HIKING
PASATIEMPOS - LEISURE ACTIVITIES

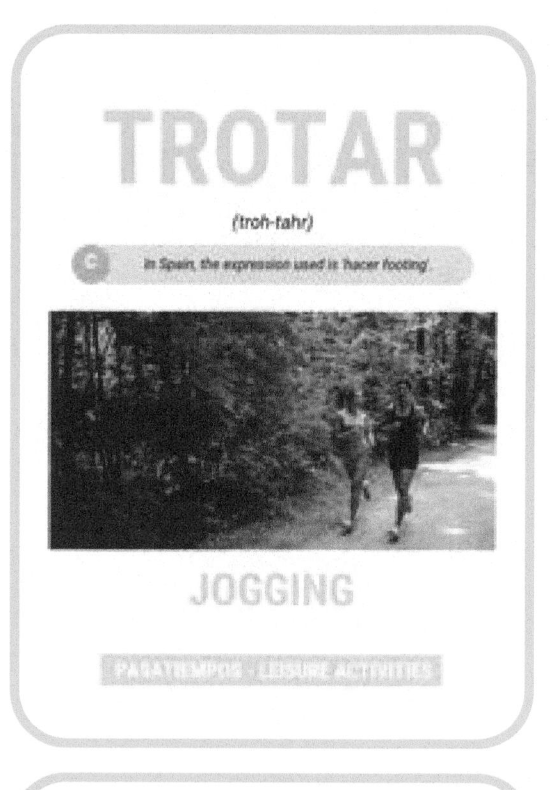
TROTAR
(troh-tahr)
C
In Spain, the expression used is 'hacer footing'.
JOGGING
PASATIEMPOS - LEISURE ACTIVITIES

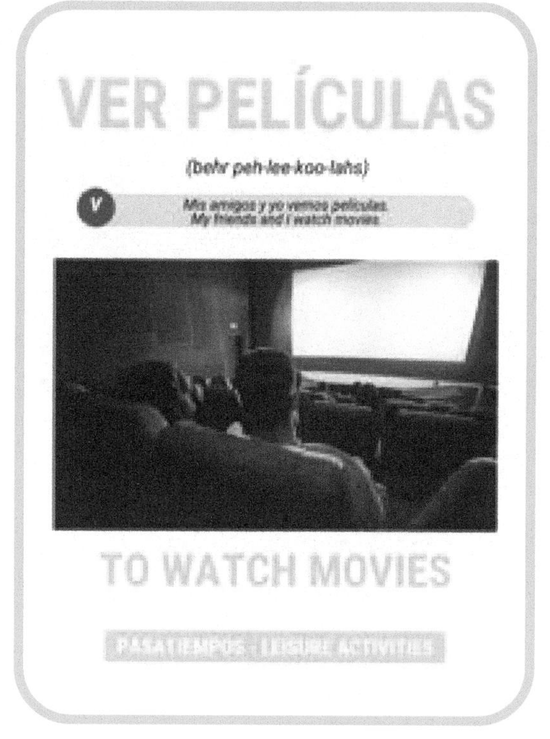
VER PELÍCULAS
(behr peh-lee-koo-lahs)
V
Mis amigos y yo vemos películas.
My friends and I watch movies.
TO WATCH MOVIES
PASATIEMPOS - LEISURE ACTIVITIES

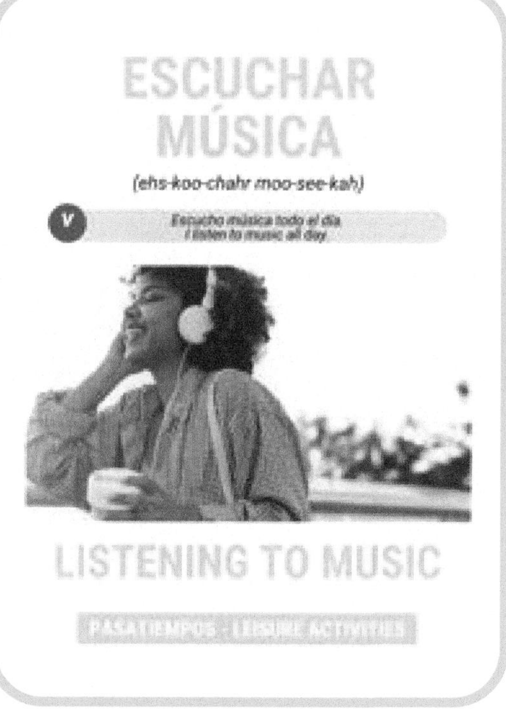
ESCUCHAR MÚSICA
(ehs-koo-chahr moo-see-kah)
V
Escucho música todo el día.
I listen to music all day.
LISTENING TO MUSIC
PASATIEMPOS - LEISURE ACTIVITIES

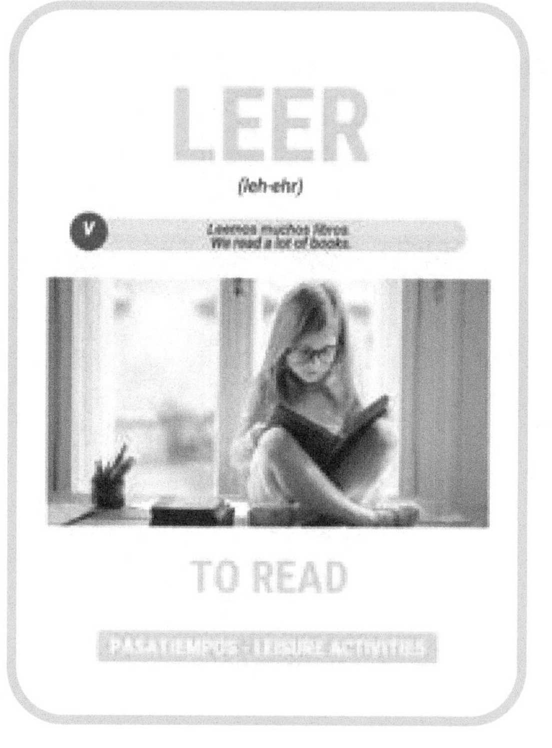
LEER
(leh-ehr)
V
Leemos muchos libros.
We read a lot of books.
TO READ
PASATIEMPOS - LEISURE ACTIVITIES

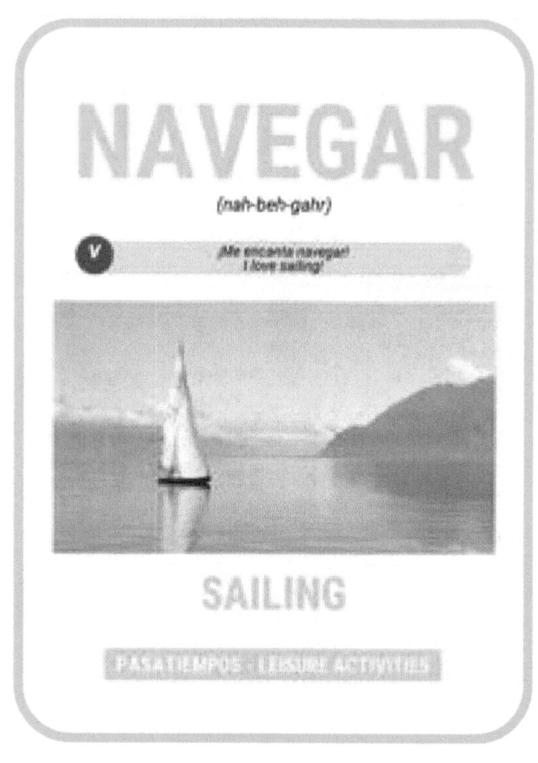
NAVEGAR
(nah-beh-gahr)
V
SAILING
PASATIEMPOS - LEISURE ACTIVITIES

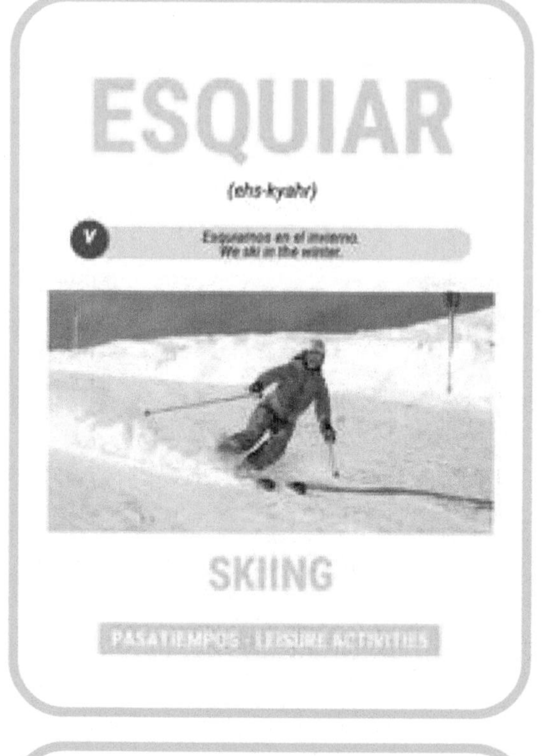
ESQUIAR
(ehs-kyahr)
V
SKIING
PASATIEMPOS - LEISURE ACTIVITIES

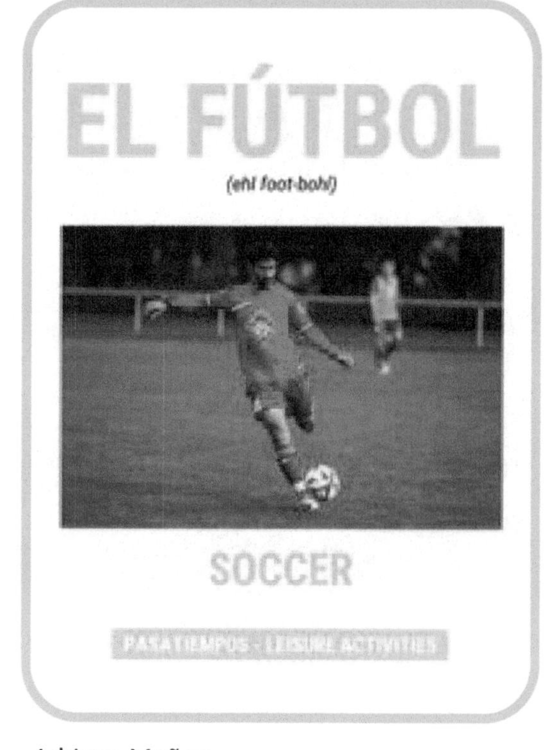
EL FÚTBOL
(ehl foot-bohl)
SOCCER
PASATIEMPOS - LEISURE ACTIVITIES

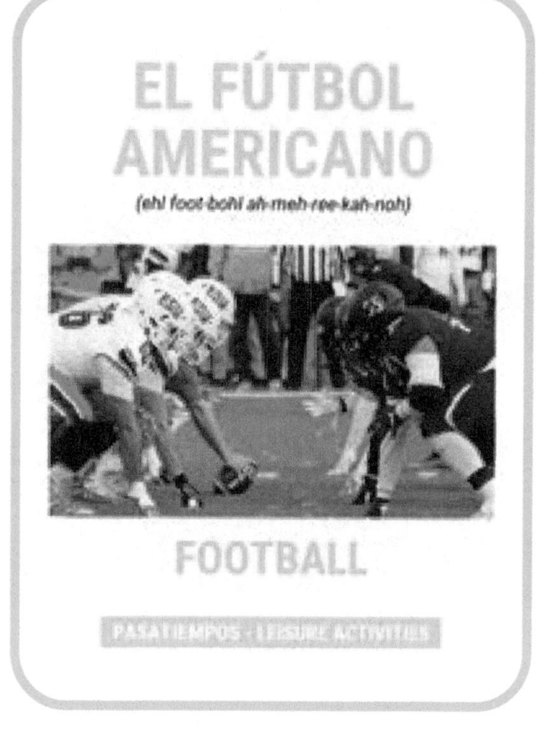
EL FÚTBOL AMERICANO
(ehl foot-bohl ah-meh-ree-kah-noh)
FOOTBALL
PASATIEMPOS - LEISURE ACTIVITIES

LA NATACIÓN

(lah nah-tah-syohn)

The pronunciation of 'natación' in Spain is 'nah-tah-thyohn'.

SWIMMING

PASATIEMPOS - LEISURE ACTIVITIES

EL TENIS

(ehl teh-nees)

Masculine noun

TENNIS

PASATIEMPOS - LEISURE ACTIVITIES

LA LUCHA LIBRE

(lah loo-chah lee-breh)

WRESTLING

PASATIEMPOS - LEISURE ACTIVITIES

VER LA TELE

(behr lah teh-leh)

Por la noche vemos la tele.
We watch TV at night.

TO WATCH TV

PASATIEMPOS - LEISURE ACTIVITIES

LAS ARTES MARCIALES

(lahs ahr-tehs mahr-syah-lehs)

Feminine noun

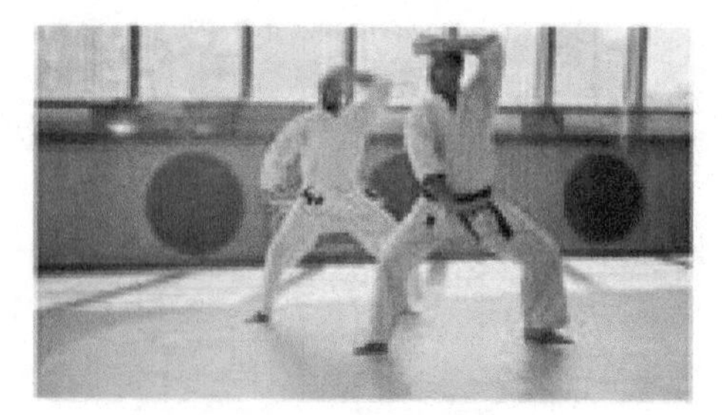

MARTIAL ARTS

PASATIEMPOS - LEISURE ACTIVITIES

LOS DEPORTES EXTREMOS

(lohs deh-pohr-tehs ehks-treh-mohs)

EXTREME SPORTS

PASATIEMPOS - LEISURE ACTIVITIES

LOS DEPORTES DE INVIERNO

(lohs deh-pohr-tehs deh een-byehr-noh)

WINTER SPORTS

PASATIEMPOS - LEISURE ACTIVITIES

EL POLO ACUÁTICO

(ehl poh-loh ah-kwah-tee-koh)

WATER POLO

PASATIEMPOS - LEISURE ACTIVITIES

EL BÁDMINTON
(ehl bahd-meen-tohn)
g
Masculine noun
BADMINTON
PASATIEMPOS - LEISURE ACTIVITIES

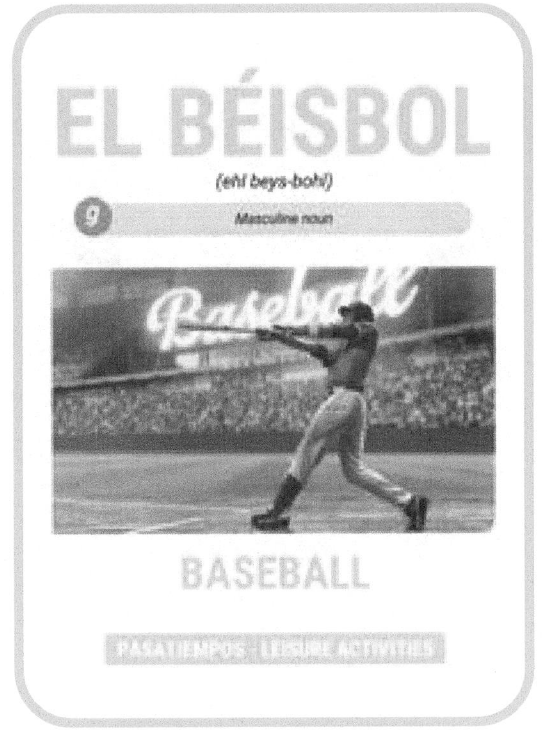
EL BÉISBOL
(ehl beys-bohl)
g
Masculine noun
Baseball
BASEBALL
PASATIEMPOS - LEISURE ACTIVITIES

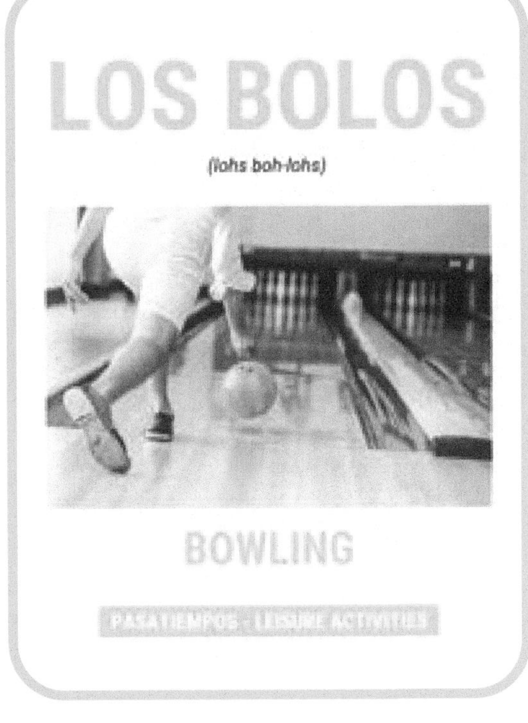
LOS BOLOS
(lohs boh-lohs)
BOWLING
PASATIEMPOS - LEISURE ACTIVITIES

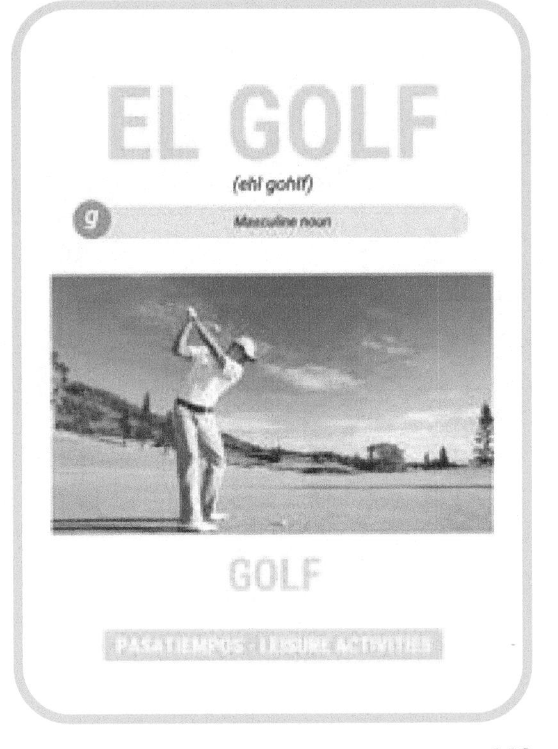
EL GOLF
(ehl gohlf)
g
Masculine noun
GOLF
PASATIEMPOS - LEISURE ACTIVITIES

EL POLO

(ehl poh-loh)

POLO

PASATIEMPOS - LEISURE ACTIVITIES

EL RUGBY

(ehl rroog-bee)

g Masculine noun

RUGBY

PASATIEMPOS - LEISURE ACTIVITIES

EL VOLEIBOL

(ehl boh-ley-bohl)

VOLLEYBALL

PASATIEMPOS - LEISURE ACTIVITIES

EL TENIS DE MESA

(ehl teh-nees deh meh-sah)

g Masculine noun

TABLE TENNIS

PASATIEMPOS - LEISURE ACTIVITIES

EL TIRO CON ARCO

(ehl tee-roh kohn ahr-koh)

g Masculine noun

ARCHERY

PASATIEMPOS - LEISURE ACTIVITIES

EL ATLETISMO

(ehl aht-leh-tees-moh)

ATHLETICS

PASATIEMPOS - LEISURE ACTIVITIES

EL PIRAGÜISMO

(ehl pee-rah-gwees-moh)

CANOEING

PASATIEMPOS - LEISURE ACTIVITIES

LA ESCALADA

(lah ehs-kah-lah-dah)

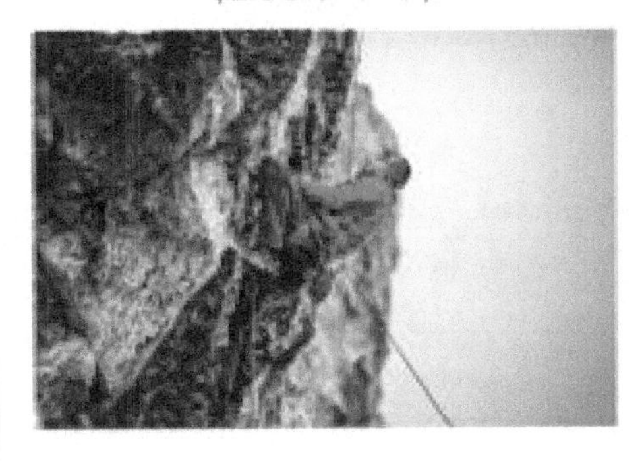

CLIMBING

PASATIEMPOS - LEISURE ACTIVITIES

EL BUCEO

(ehl boo-seh-oh)

P The pronunciation of "buceo" in Spain is 'boo-theh-oh'.

SCUBA DIVING

PASATIEMPOS - LEISURE ACTIVITIES

LA ESGRIMA

(lah ehs-gree-mah)

FENCING

PASATIEMPOS - LEISURE ACTIVITIES

LA GIMNASIA

(lah heem-nah-syah)

GYMNASTICS

PASATIEMPOS - LEISURE ACTIVITIES

LA EQUITACIÓN

(lah eh-kee-tah-syohn)

P The pronunciation of "equitación" in Spain is 'eh-kee-tah-thyohn'.

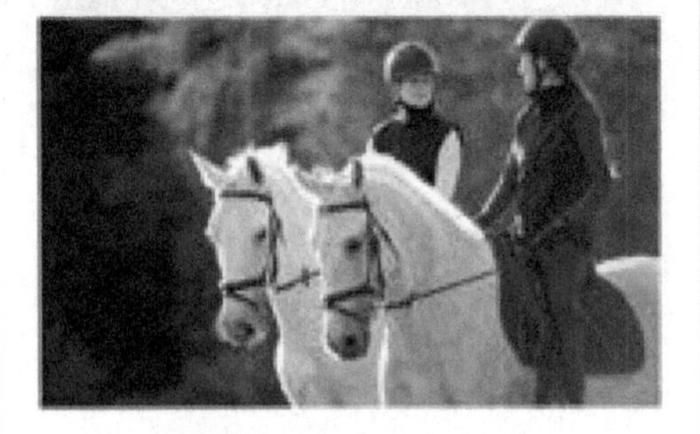

HORSE RIDING

PASATIEMPOS - LEISURE ACTIVITIES

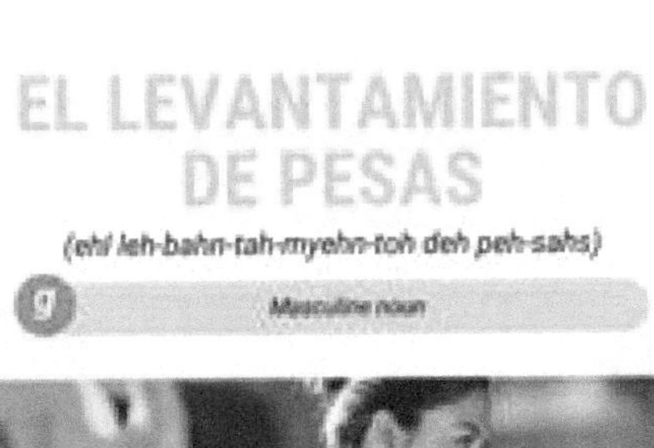

EL LEVANTAMIENTO DE PESAS

(ehl leh-bahn-tah-myehn-toh deh peh-sahs)

g — Masculine noun

WEIGHT LIFTING

PASATIEMPOS - LEISURE ACTIVITIES

EL YUDO

(ehl yoo-doh)

JUDO

PASATIEMPOS - LEISURE ACTIVITIES

EL KARATE

(ehl kah-rah-teh)

g — Masculine noun

KARATE

PASATIEMPOS - LEISURE ACTIVITIES

LAS ARTES MARCIALES MIXTAS

(lahs ahr-tehs mahr-syah-lehs meeks-tahs)

p — The pronunciation of "marciales" in Spain is 'mahr-thyah-lehs'.

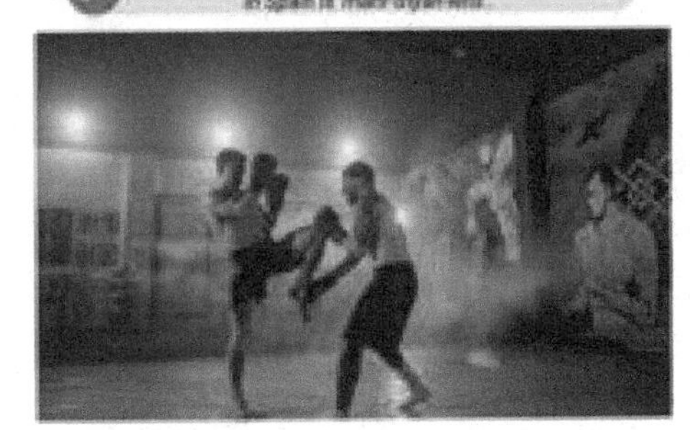

MIXED MARTIAL ARTS (MMA)

PASATIEMPOS - LEISURE ACTIVITIES

EL TAEKWONDO

(ehl taheh-kwohn-doh)

TAEKWONDO

PASATIEMPOS - LEISURE ACTIVITIES

EL PATINAJE ARTÍSTICO

(ehl pah-tee-nah-heh ahr-tees-tee-koh)

Masculine noun

FIGURE SKATING

PASATIEMPOS - LEISURE ACTIVITIES

EL HOCKEY SOBRE HIELO

(el hoh-kee soh-breh yeh-loh)

ICE HOCKEY

PASATIEMPOS - LEISURE ACTIVITIES

EL PATINAJE SOBRE NIEVE

(ehl pah-tee-nah-heh soh-breh nyeh-beh)

Masculine noun

SNOWBOARDING

PASATIEMPOS - LEISURE ACTIVITIES

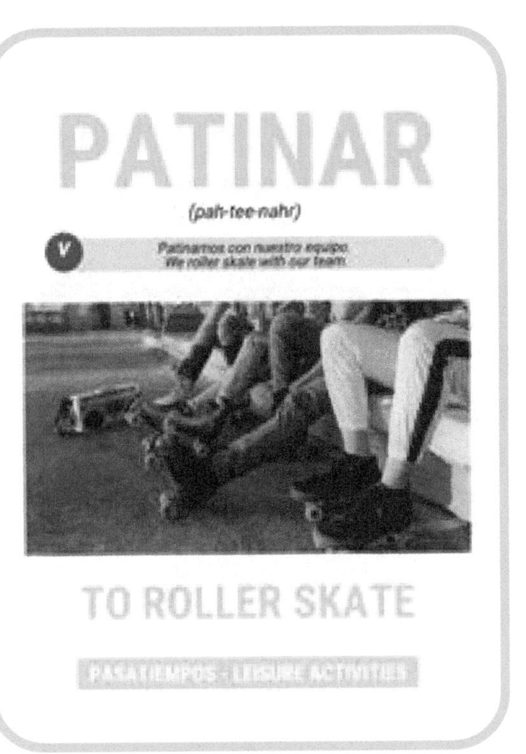
PATINAR
(pah-tee-nahr)
v
Patinamos con nuestro equipo.
We roller skate with our team.
TO ROLLER SKATE
PASATIEMPOS - LEISURE ACTIVITIES

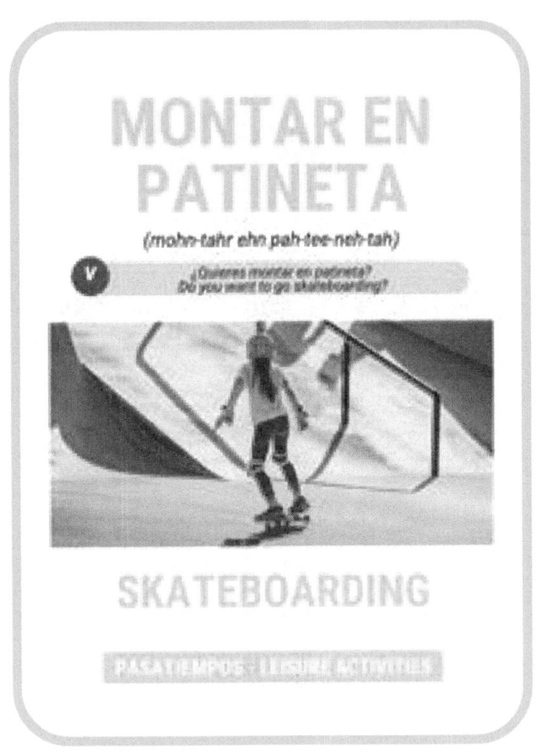
MONTAR EN PATINETA
(mohn-tahr ehn pah-tee-neh-tah)
v
¿Quieres montar en patineta?
Do you want to go skateboarding?
SKATEBOARDING
PASATIEMPOS - LEISURE ACTIVITIES

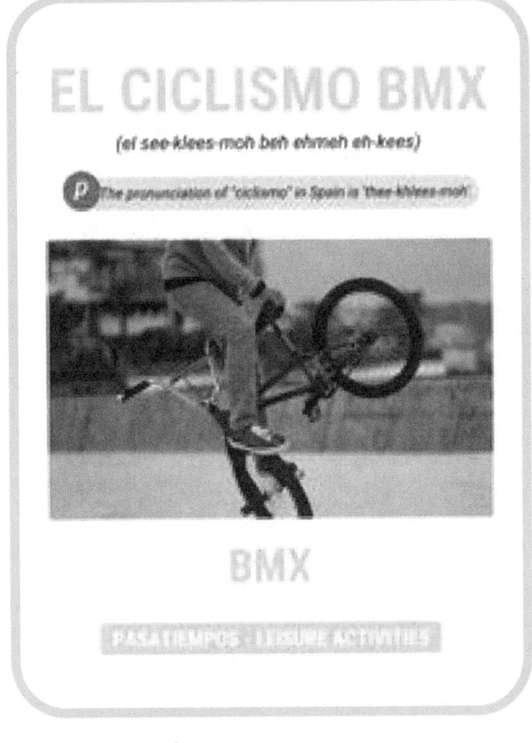
EL CICLISMO BMX
(el see-klees-moh beh ehmeh eh-kees)
p
The pronunciation of "ciclismo" in Spain is 'thee-klees-moh'.
BMX
PASATIEMPOS - LEISURE ACTIVITIES

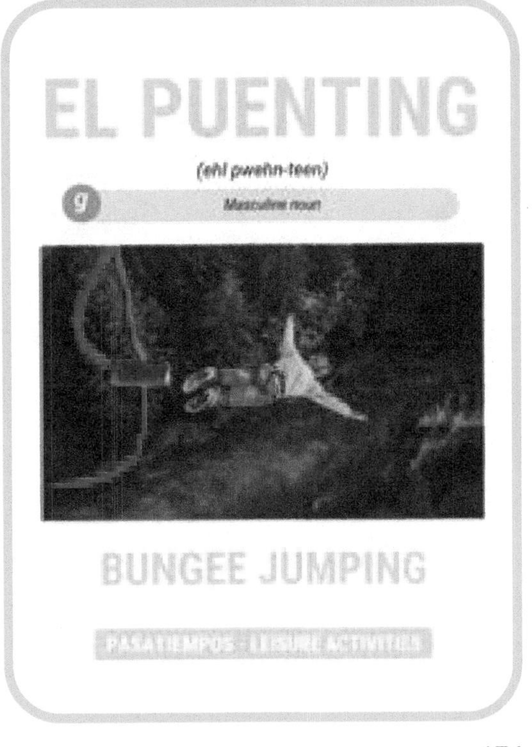
EL PUENTING
(ehl pwehn-teen)
g
Masculine noun
BUNGEE JUMPING
PASATIEMPOS - LEISURE ACTIVITIES

(ehl pah-rah-kay-dees-moh)

PARACHUTING

PASATIEMPOS - LEISURE ACTIVITIES

EL PARAPENTE

(ehl pah-rah-pehn-teh)

g Masculine noun

PARAGLIDING

PASATIEMPOS - LEISURE ACTIVITIES

EL ESNÓRQUEL

(ehl ehs-nohr-kehl)

g — *Masculine noun*

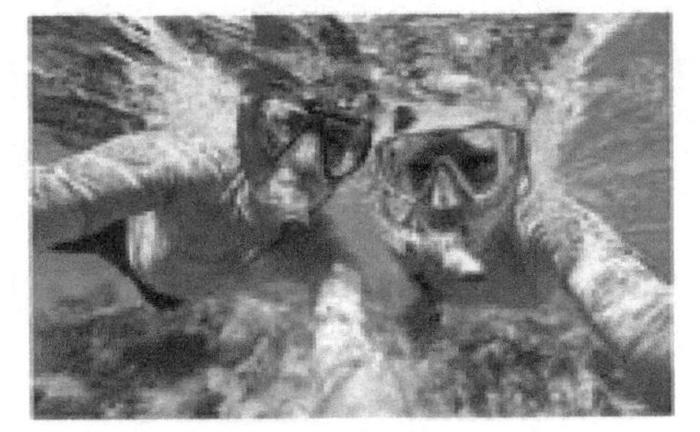

SNORKEL

PASATIEMPOS - LEISURE ACTIVITIES

EL TANQUE DE OXÍGENO

(ehl tahn-keh deh ohk-see-heh-noh)

OXYGEN TANK

PASATIEMPOS - LEISURE ACTIVITIES

EL PARACAÍDAS

(ehl pah-rah-kah-ee-dahs)

g — *Masculine noun*

PARACHUTE

PASATIEMPOS - LEISURE ACTIVITIES

EL KAYAK

(ehl kah-yahk)

g — *Masculine noun*

KAYAK

PASATIEMPOS - LEISURE ACTIVITIES

EL ARNÉS

(ehl ahr-nehs)

Masculine noun

HARNESS

PASATIEMPOS - LEISURE ACTIVITIES

LAS RODILLERAS

(lahs rroh-dee-yeh-rahs)

KNEE PADS

PASATIEMPOS - LEISURE ACTIVITIES

LAS CODERAS

(lahs koh-deh-rahs)

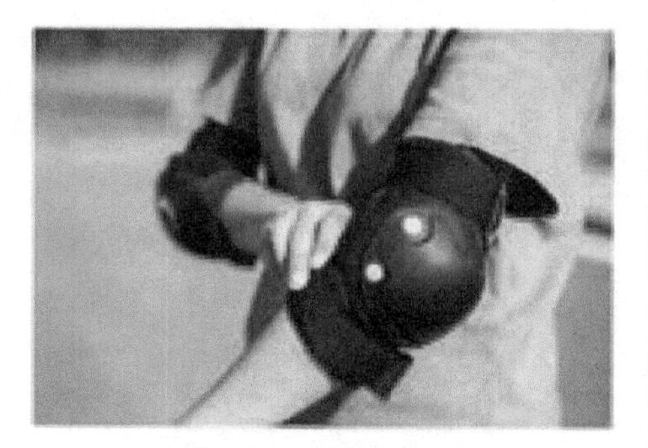

ELBOW PADS

PASATIEMPOS - LEISURE ACTIVITIES

LAS ESPINILLERAS

(lahs ehs-pee-nee-yeh-rahs)

SHIN GUARDS

PASATIEMPOS - LEISURE ACTIVITIES

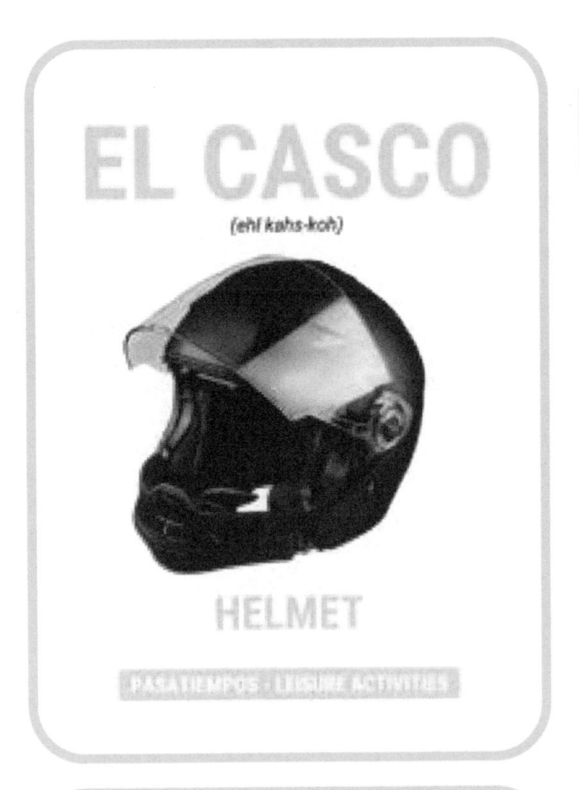
EL CASCO
(ehl kahs-koh)
HELMET
PASATIEMPOS - LEISURE ACTIVITIES

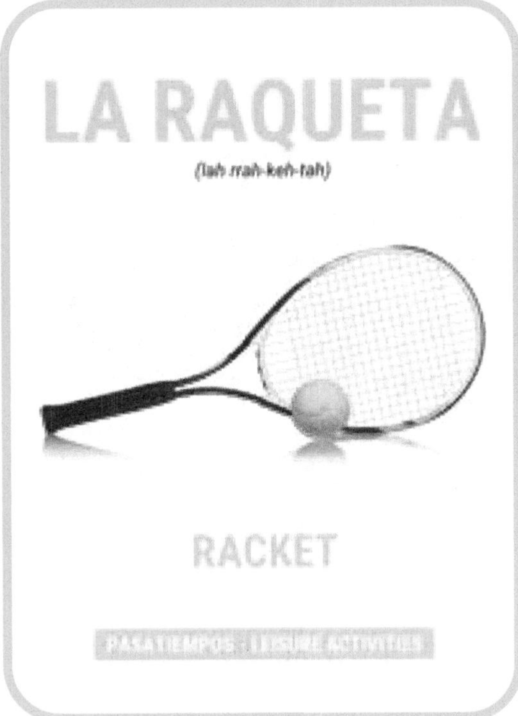
LA RAQUETA
(lah rrah-keh-tah)
RACKET
PASATIEMPOS - LEISURE ACTIVITIES

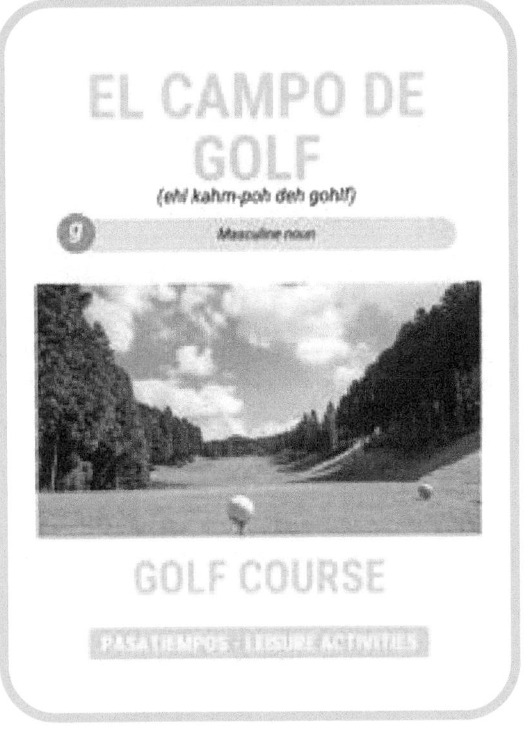
EL CAMPO DE GOLF
(ehl kahm-poh deh gohlf)
g
Masculine noun
GOLF COURSE
PASATIEMPOS - LEISURE ACTIVITIES

LA PISCINA
(lah pee-see-nah)
p
The pronunciation of "piscina" in Spain is 'pees-thee-nah'.
SWIMMING POOL
PASATIEMPOS - LEISURE ACTIVITIES

EL ESTADIO

(ehl ehs-tah-dyoh)

STADIUM

PASATIEMPOS - LEISURE ACTIVITIES

LA CANCHA DE TENIS

(lah kahn-chah deh teh-nees)

g — *Feminine noun*

TENNIS COURT

PASATIEMPOS - LEISURE ACTIVITIES

JUGAR

(hoo-gahr)

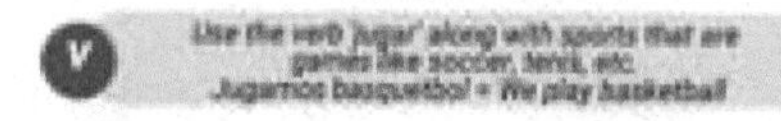

v — *Use the verb 'jugar' along with sports that are games like soccer, tenis, etc.*
Jugamos basquetbol = We play basketball

TO PLAY (A SPORT)

PASATIEMPOS - LEISURE ACTIVITIES

PRACTICAR

(prahk-tee-kahr)

v — *Use the verb 'practicar' along with sports that are disciplines like gymnastics, fencing, scuba diving, etc.*
Practicamos el boxeo = We practice boxing

TO PRACTICE

PASATIEMPOS - LEISURE ACTIVITIES

¡GANÉ!

(gah-neh)

I WON!

PASATIEMPOS - LEISURE ACTIVITIES

¡PERDISTE!

(pehr-dees-teh)

YOU LOST!

PASATIEMPOS - LEISURE ACTIVITIES

¿QUIERES JUGAR CONMIGO?

(kyeh-rehs hoo-gahr kohn-mee-goh)

DO YOU WANT TO PLAY WITH ME?

PASATIEMPOS - LEISURE ACTIVITIES

¡JUGUEMOS OTRA VEZ!

(hoo-geh-mohs oh-trah behs)

LET'S PLAY AGAIN!

PASATIEMPOS - LEISURE ACTIVITIES

EL ARTE
(ehl ahr-teh)
g
Masculine noun
ART
PASATIEMPOS - LEISURE ACTIVITIES

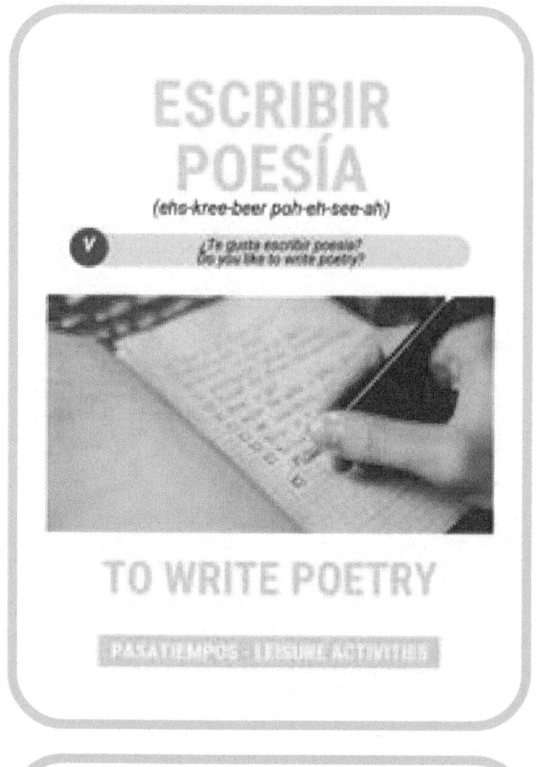
ESCRIBIR POESÍA
(ehs-kree-beer poh-eh-see-ah)
v
¿Te gusta escribir poesía?
Do you like to write poetry?
TO WRITE POETRY
PASATIEMPOS - LEISURE ACTIVITIES

VISITAR MUSEOS
(ehs-kree-beer poh-eh-see-ah)
v
Visitamos el Museo del Prado.
We visited the Prado Museum.
TO VISIT MUSEUMS
PASATIEMPOS - LEISURE ACTIVITIES

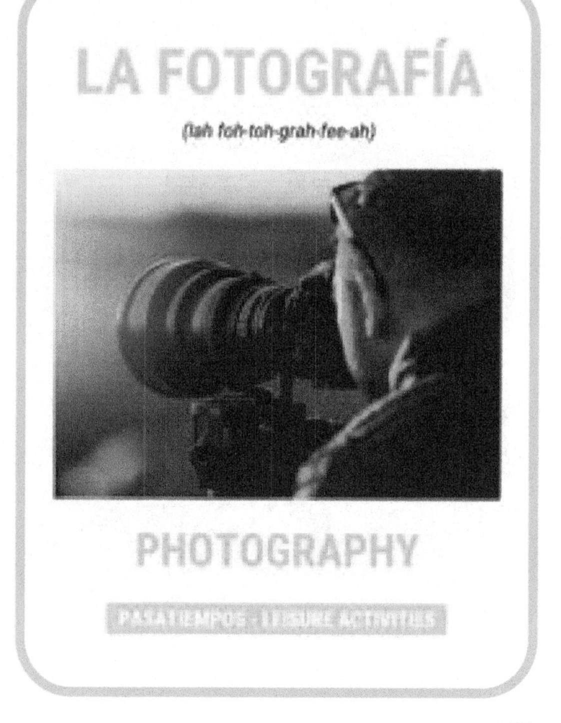
LA FOTOGRAFÍA
(lah foh-toh-grah-fee-ah)
PHOTOGRAPHY
PASATIEMPOS - LEISURE ACTIVITIES

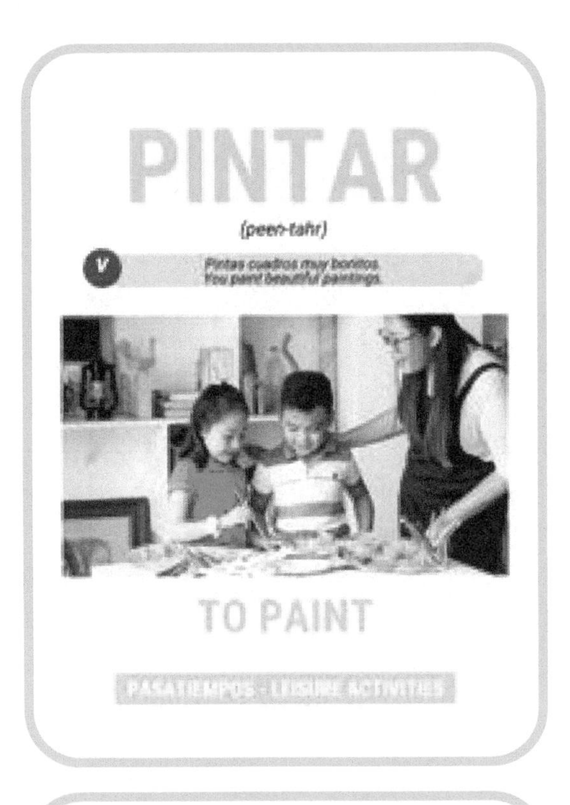
PINTAR
(peen-tahr)
V
Pintas cuadros muy bonitos.
You paint beautiful paintings.
TO PAINT
PASATIEMPOS - LEISURE ACTIVITIES

DIBUJAR
(dee-boo-hahr)
V
Él dibuja muy bien.
He draws very well.
TO DRAW
PASATIEMPOS - LEISURE ACTIVITIES

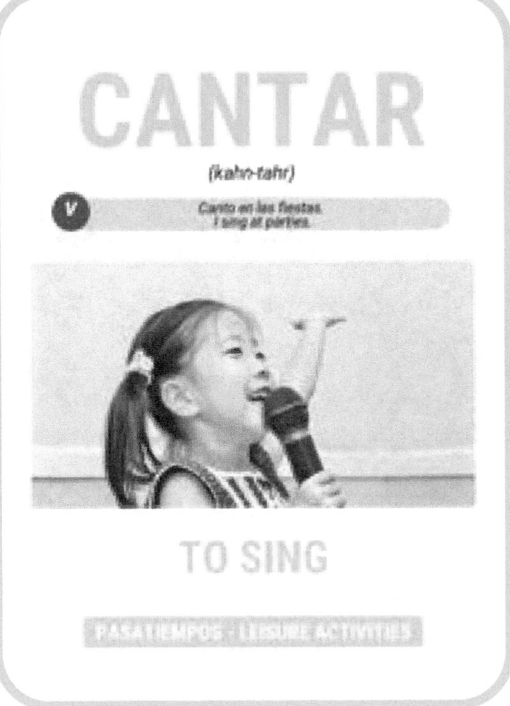
CANTAR
(kahn-tahr)
V
Canto en las fiestas.
I sing at parties.
TO SING
PASATIEMPOS - LEISURE ACTIVITIES

COMPONER CANCIONES
(kohm-poh-nehr kahn-syoh-nehs)
V
Componer canciones me hace feliz.
Writing songs makes me happy.
SONGWRITING
PASATIEMPOS - LEISURE ACTIVITIES

TOCAR LA GUITARRA

(toh-kahr lah gee-tah-rrah)

In Spanish, the verb used to say you play an instrument is 'tocar'. Toco la guitarra = I play the guitar.

TO PLAY THE GUITAR

PASATIEMPOS - LEISURE ACTIVITIES

TOCAR EL PIANO

(toh-kahr ehl pyah-noh)

Me gusta tocar el piano.
I like to play the piano.

TO PLAY THE PIANO

PASATIEMPOS - LEISURE ACTIVITIES

EL BAJO

(ehl bah-hoh)

BASS GUITAR

PASATIEMPOS - LEISURE ACTIVITIES

LA BATERÍA

(lah bah-teh-ree-ah)

DRUMS

PASATIEMPOS - LEISURE ACTIVITIES

EL VIOLÍN
(ehl byoh-leen)
g
Masculine noun
VIOLIN
PASATIEMPOS - LEISURE ACTIVITIES

LA FLAUTA
(lah flow-tah)
FLUTE
PASATIEMPOS - LEISURE ACTIVITIES

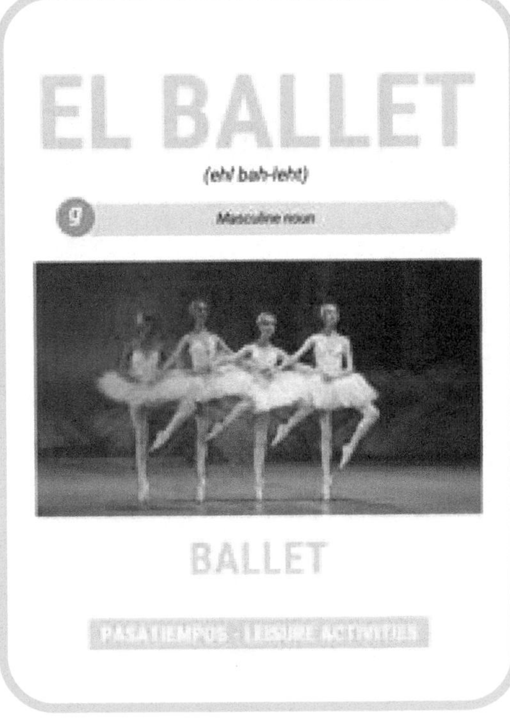
EL BALLET
(ehl bah-leht)
g
Masculine noun
BALLET
PASATIEMPOS - LEISURE ACTIVITIES

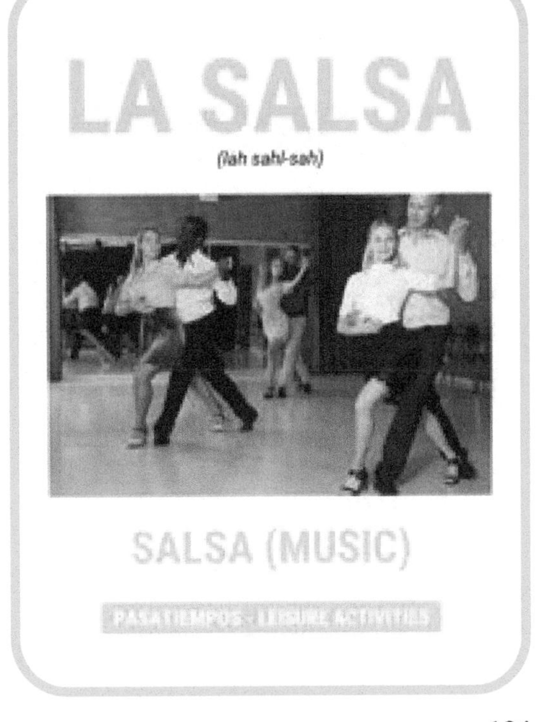
LA SALSA
(lah sahl-sah)
SALSA (MUSIC)
PASATIEMPOS - LEISURE ACTIVITIES

TANGO

PASATIEMPOS - LEISURE ACTIVITIES

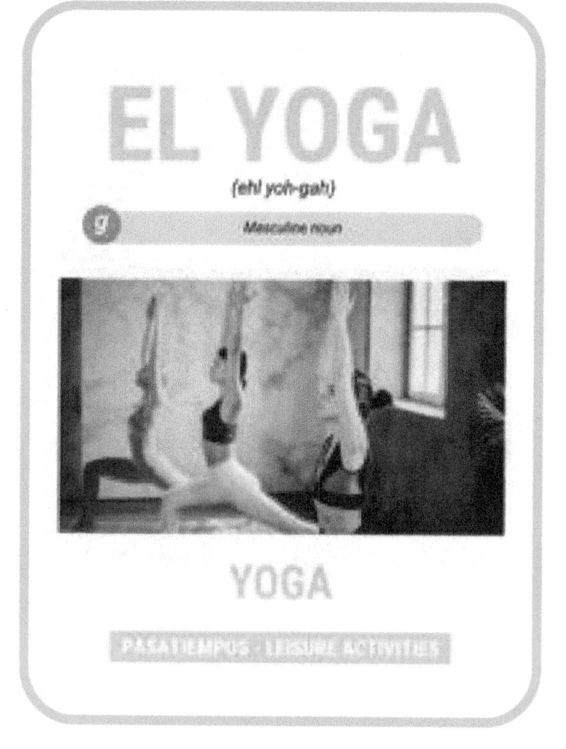

LA MÚSICA LATINA

(lah moo-see-kah lah-tee-nah)

C Some examples of Latin music styles are: salsa, bachata, cumbia, merengue, samba, and reggaeton.

LATIN MUSIC

PASATIEMPOS - LEISURE ACTIVITIES

LOS VIDEOJUEGOS

(lohs bee-deh-oh-hweh-gohs)

VIDEOGAMES

PASATIEMPOS - LEISURE ACTIVITIES

JUGAR CARTAS

(hoo-gahr kahr-tahs)

Los viernes jugamos cartas.
We play cards on Fridays.

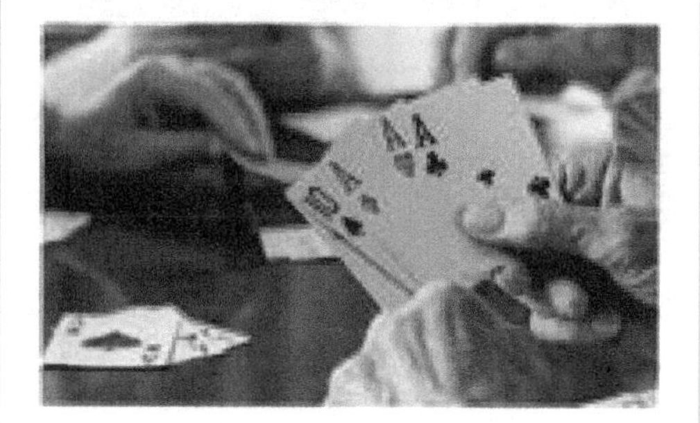

TO PLAY CARDS

PASATIEMPOS - LEISURE ACTIVITIES

CHATEAR

(chah-teh-ahr)

Está siempre chateando en su móvil.
He's always chatting on his phone.

CHATTING

PASATIEMPOS - LEISURE ACTIVITIES

IR AL GIMNASIO

(eer ahl heem-nah-syoh)

v Nos gusta mucho ir al gimnasio. We really like going to the gym.

TO GO TO THE GYM

PASATIEMPOS · LEISURE ACTIVITIES

LA CARPINTERÍA

(lah kahr-peen-teh-ree-ah)

CARPENTRY

PASATIEMPOS · LEISURE ACTIVITIES

EL ARTISTA

(ehl ahr-tees-tah)

g For the female version, simply replace the article: La artista

ARTIST

PASATIEMPOS · LEISURE ACTIVITIES

LA CREATIVIDAD

(lah kreh-ah-tee-bee-dahd)

g Feminine noun

CREATIVITY

PASATIEMPOS · LEISURE ACTIVITIES

LA ESCULTURA

(lah ehs-kool-too-rah)

SCULPTURE

PASATIEMPOS - LEISURE ACTIVITIES

EL ARTE MODERNO

(ehl ahr-teh moh-dehr-noh)

g — *Masculine noun*

MODERN ART

PASATIEMPOS - LEISURE ACTIVITIES

LA EXHIBICIÓN

(lah ehk-see-bee-syohn)

p — *The pronunciation of 'exhibición' in Spain is 'ehk-see-bee-thyohn'.*

EXHIBITION

PASATIEMPOS - LEISURE ACTIVITIES

EL PINTOR

(ehl peen-tohr)

g — For the female version, simply replace the article and the noun's ending: La pintora

PAINTER

PASATIEMPOS - LEISURE ACTIVITIES

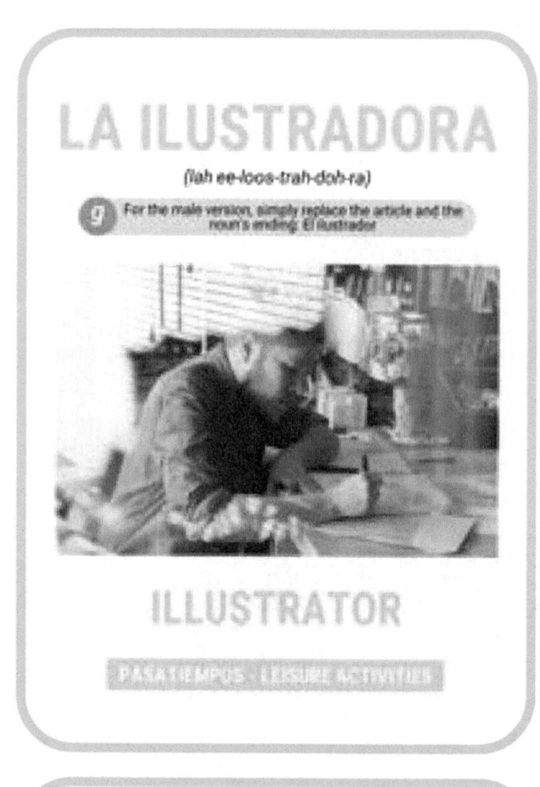
LA ILUSTRADORA
(lah ee-loos-trah-doh-ra)
g
For the male version, simply replace the article and the noun's ending: El ilustrador
ILLUSTRATOR
PASATIEMPOS - LEISURE ACTIVITIES

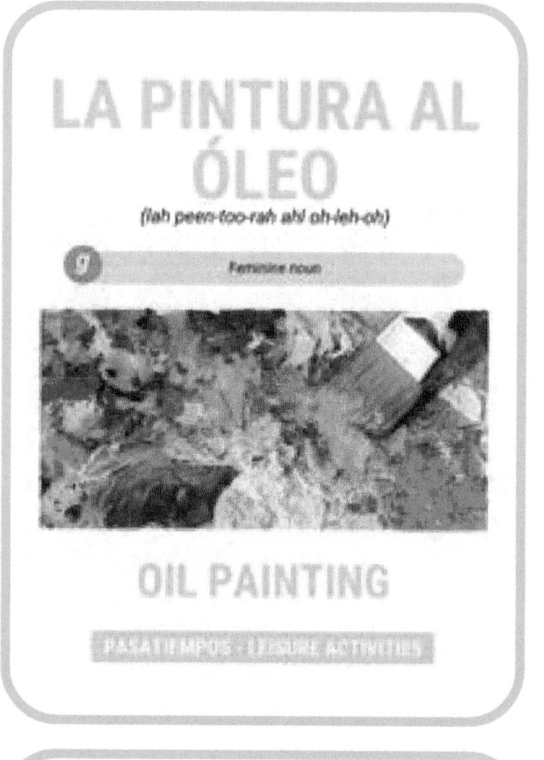
LA PINTURA AL ÓLEO
(lah peen-too-rah ahl oh-leh-oh)
g
Feminine noun
OIL PAINTING
PASATIEMPOS - LEISURE ACTIVITIES

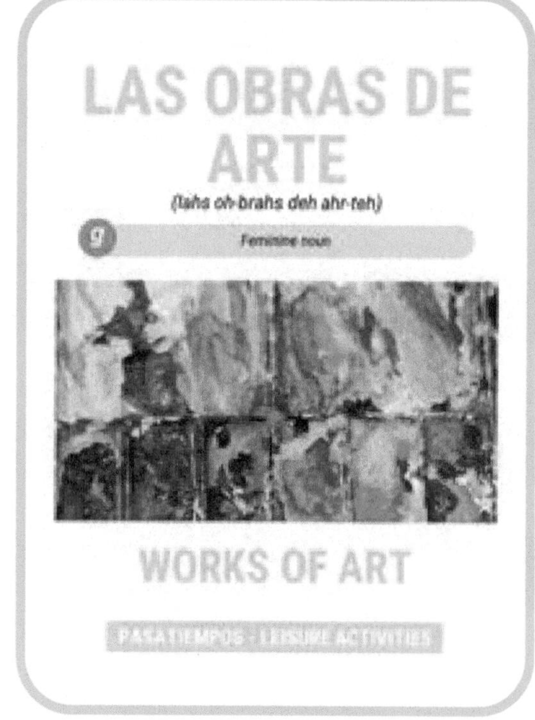
LAS OBRAS DE ARTE
(lahs oh-brahs deh ahr-teh)
g
Feminine noun
WORKS OF ART
PASATIEMPOS - LEISURE ACTIVITIES

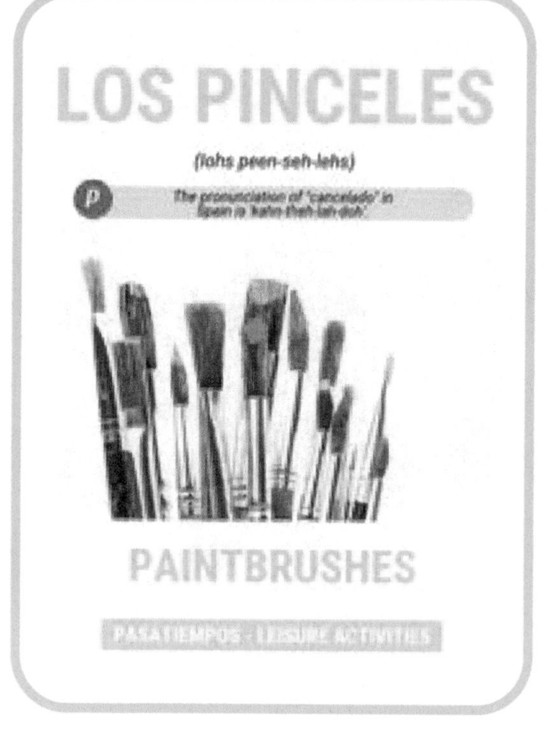
LOS PINCELES
(lohs peen-seh-lehs)
p
The pronunciation of "cancelado" in Spain is 'kahn-theh-lah-doh'
PAINTBRUSHES
PASATIEMPOS - LEISURE ACTIVITIES

EL LIENZO
(ehl lyehn-soh)
p
The pronunciation of "lienzo" in Spain is 'lyehn-thoh'.
CANVAS
PASATIEMPOS - LEISURE ACTIVITIES

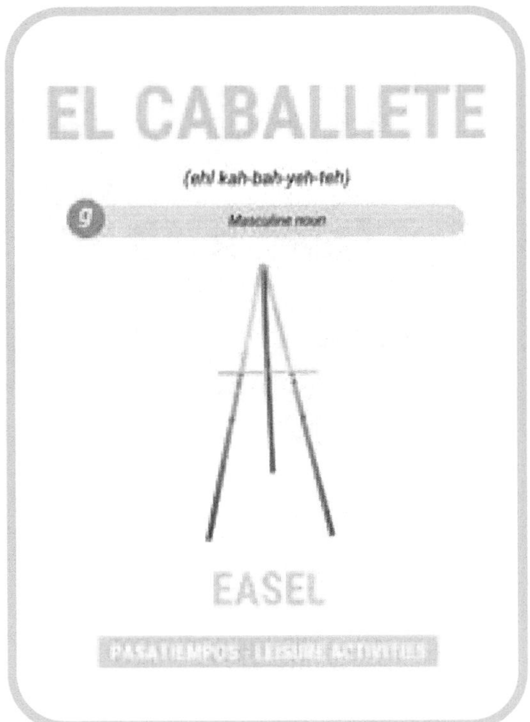
EL CABALLETE
(ehl kah-bah-yeh-teh)
g
Masculine noun
EASEL
PASATIEMPOS - LEISURE ACTIVITIES

EL MARCO
(ehl mahr-koh)
FRAME
PASATIEMPOS - LEISURE ACTIVITIES

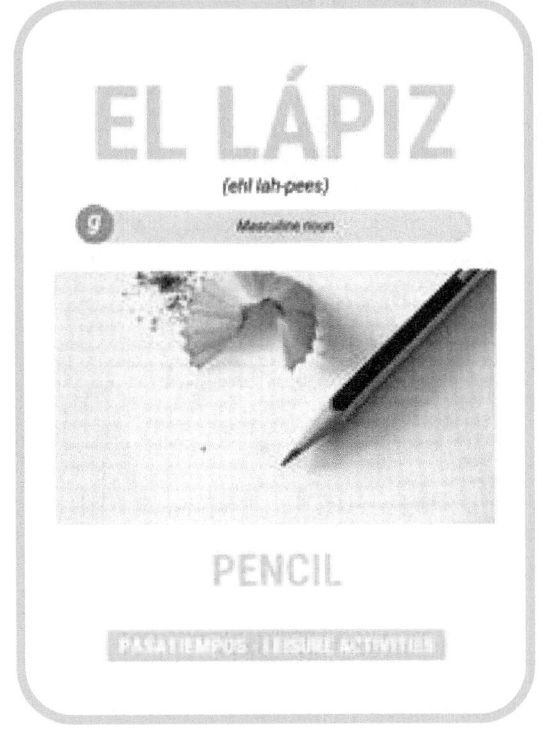
EL LÁPIZ
(ehl lah-pees)
g
Masculine noun
PENCIL
PASATIEMPOS - LEISURE ACTIVITIES

LA ESPONJA

(lah ehs-pohn-hah)

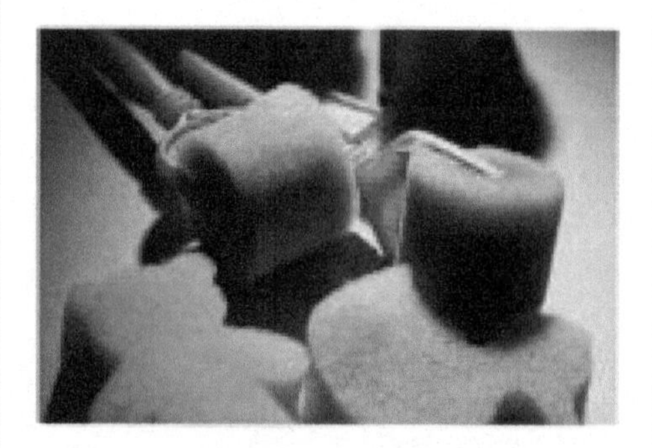

SPONGE

PASATIEMPOS - LEISURE ACTIVITIES

EL BORRADOR

(ehl boh-rrah-dohr)

Masculine noun

ERASER

PASATIEMPOS - LEISURE ACTIVITIES

LAS PLANTILLAS

(lahs plahn-tee-yahs)

STENCILS

PASATIEMPOS - LEISURE ACTIVITIES

LA ACUARELA

(lah ah-kwah-reh-lah)

WATERCOLOR

PASATIEMPOS - LEISURE ACTIVITIES

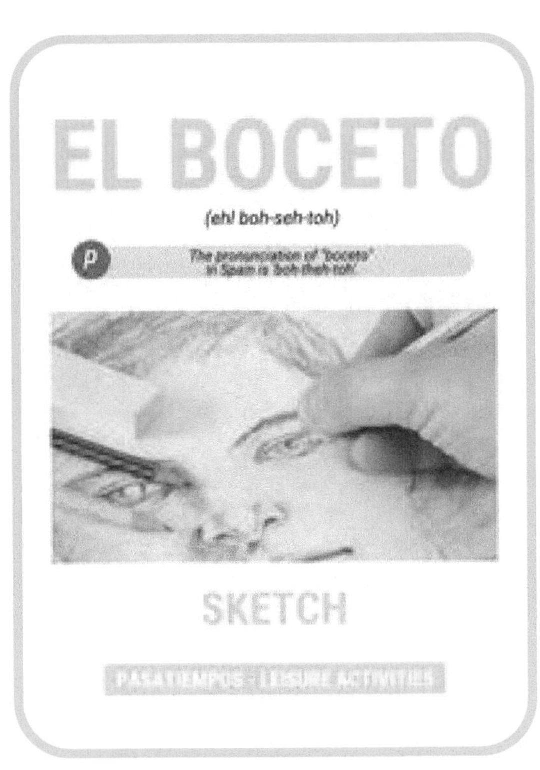

EL BOCETO
(ehl boh-seh-toh)
p
The pronunciation of 'boceto'
in Spain is 'boh-theh-toh'
SKETCH
PASATIEMPOS - LEISURE ACTIVITIES

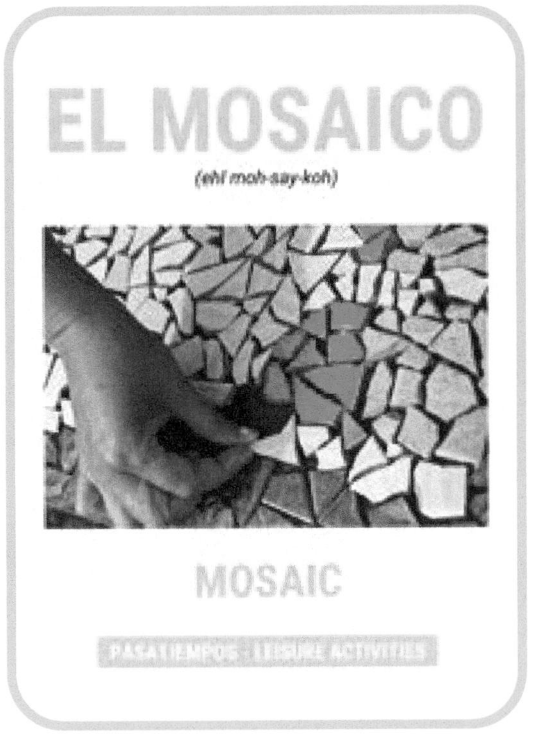

EL MOSAICO
(ehl moh-say-koh)
MOSAIC
PASATIEMPOS - LEISURE ACTIVITIES

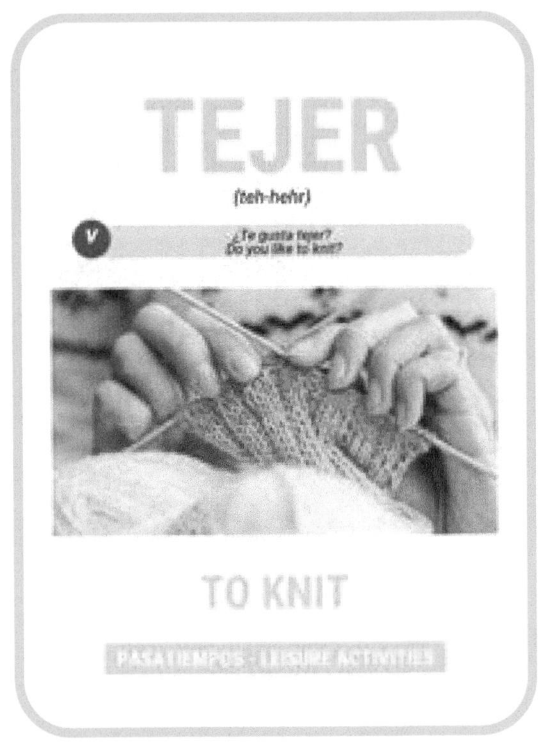

TEJER
(teh-hehr)
v
¿Te gusta tejer?
Do you like to knit?
TO KNIT
PASATIEMPOS - LEISURE ACTIVITIES

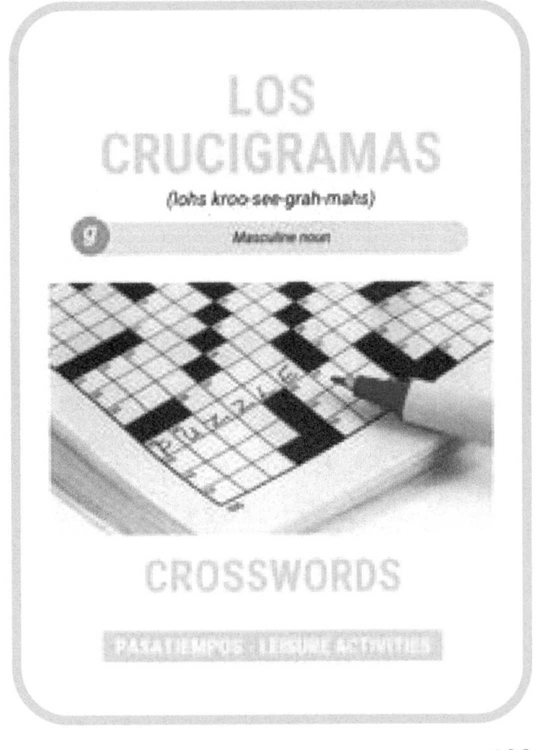

LOS
CRUCIGRAMAS
(lohs kroo-see-grah-mahs)
g
Masculine noun
CROSSWORDS
PASATIEMPOS - LEISURE ACTIVITIES

(lah soh-pah deh leh-trahs)

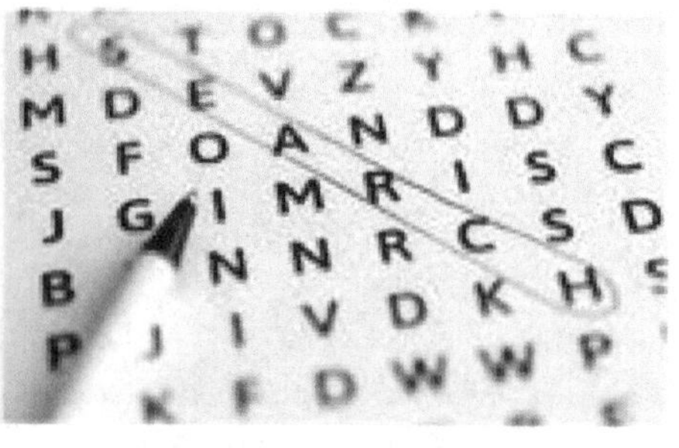

WORD SEARCH

PASATIEMPOS - LEISURE ACTIVITIES

EL DOMINÓ

(ehl doh-mee-noh)

DOMINOES

PASATIEMPOS - LEISURE ACTIVITIES

COLECCIONAR

(koh-lehk-syoh-nahr)

TO COLLECT

PASATIEMPOS - LEISURE ACTIVITIES

EL TEATRO

(ehl teh-ah-troh)

THEATER

PASATIEMPOS - LEISURE ACTIVITIES

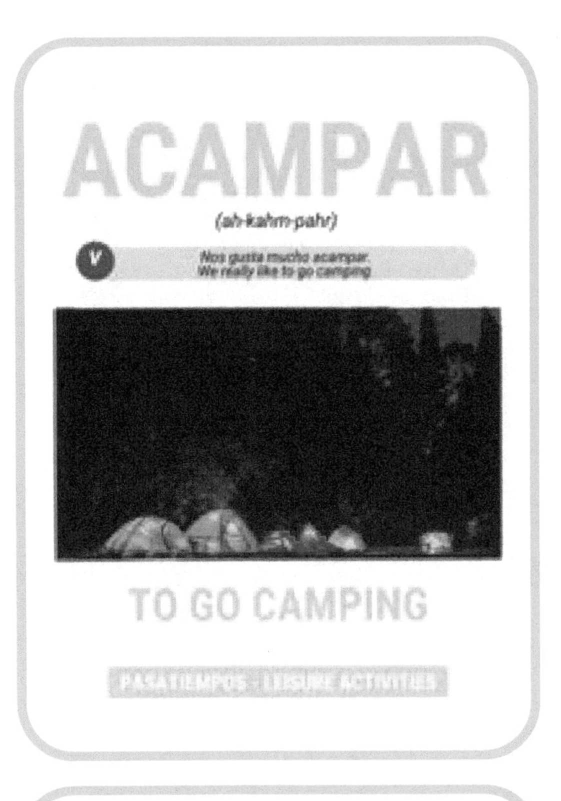
ACAMPAR
(ah-kahm-pahr)
V
Nos gusta mucho acampar.
We really like to go camping
TO GO CAMPING
PASATIEMPOS - LEISURE ACTIVITIES

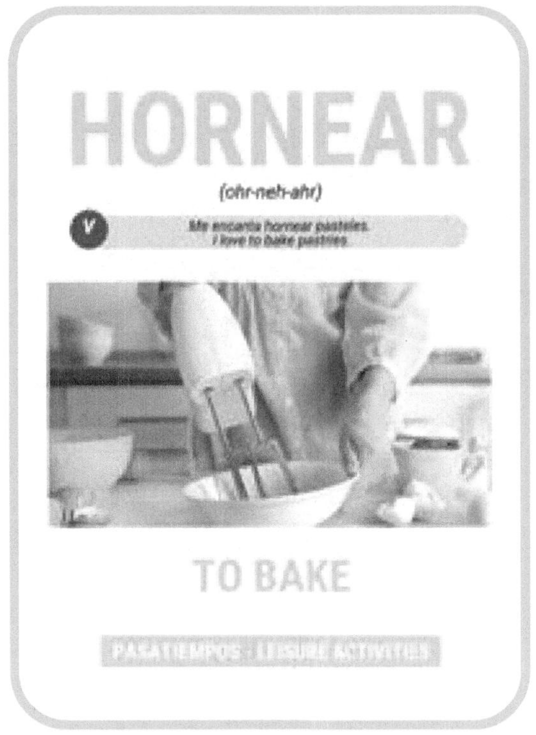
HORNEAR
(ohr-neh-ahr)
V
Me encanta hornear pasteles.
I love to bake pastries.
TO BAKE
PASATIEMPOS - LEISURE ACTIVITIES

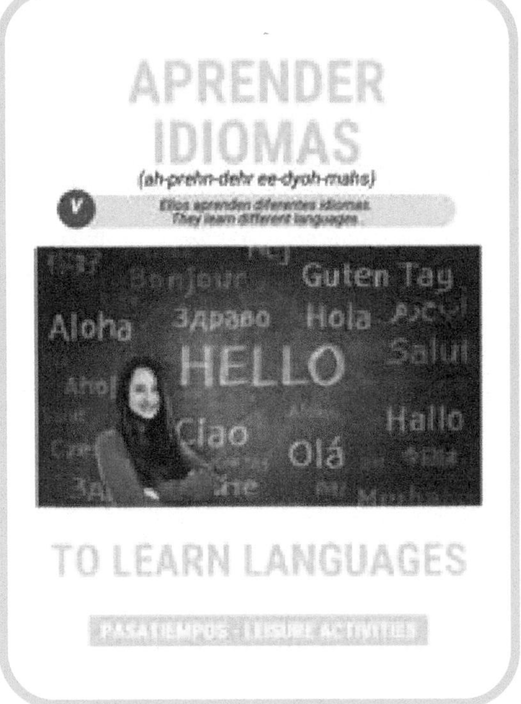
APRENDER IDIOMAS
(ah-prehn-dehr ee-dyoh-mahs)
V
Ellos aprenden diferentes idiomas.
They learn different languages.
Bonjour
Guten Tag
Aloha
Здраво
Hola
Salut
HELLO
Ciao
Hallo
Olá
TO LEARN LANGUAGES
PASATIEMPOS - LEISURE ACTIVITIES

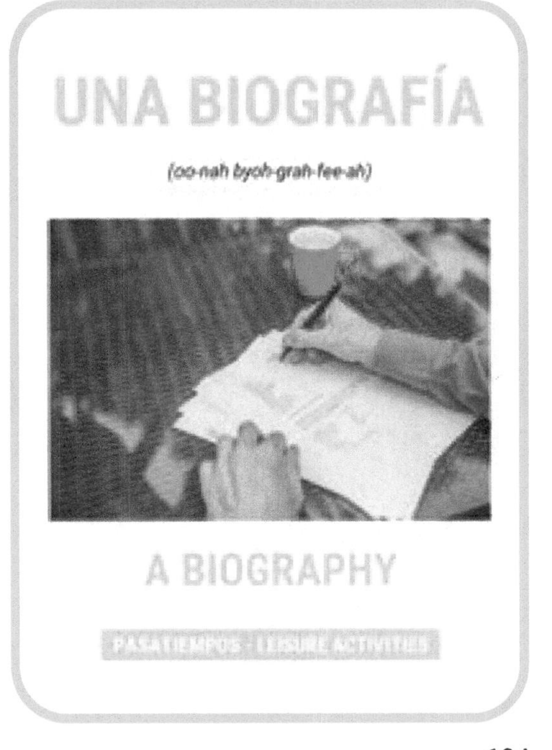
UNA BIOGRAFÍA
(oo-nah byoh-grah-fee-ah)
A BIOGRAPHY
PASATIEMPOS - LEISURE ACTIVITIES

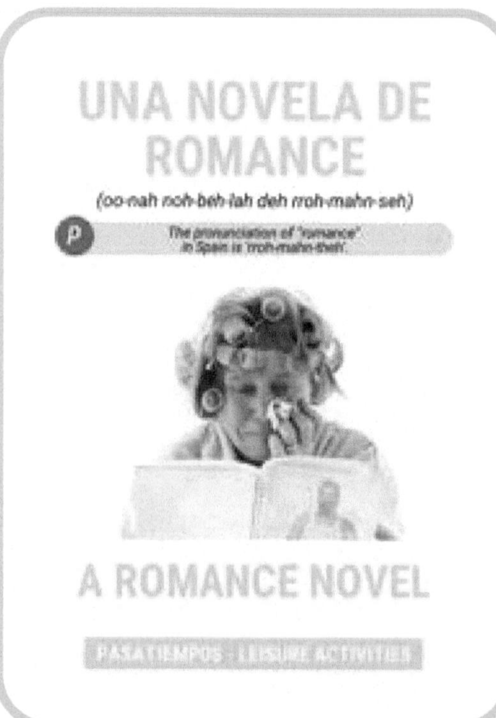
UNA NOVELA DE ROMANCE
(oo-nah noh-beh-lah deh rroh-mahn-seh)
p
The pronunciation of "romance" in Spain is 'rroh-mahn-theh'.
A ROMANCE NOVEL
PASATIEMPOS - LEISURE ACTIVITIES

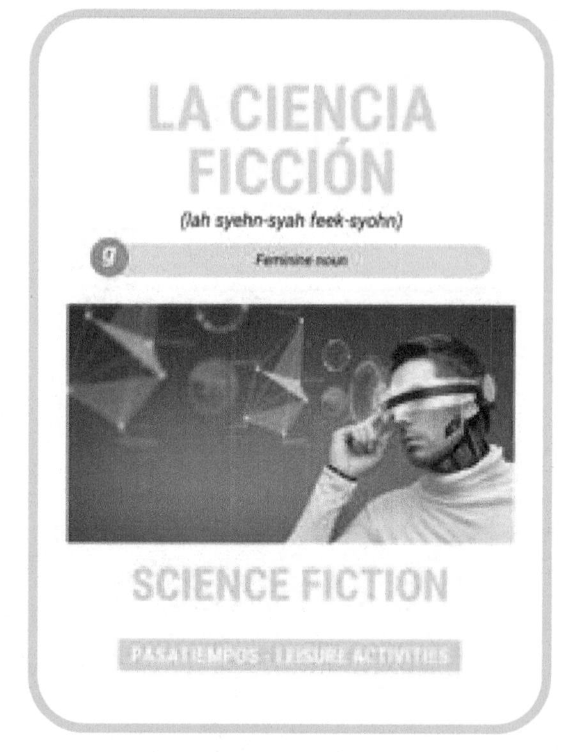
LA CIENCIA FICCIÓN
(lah syehn-syah feek-syohn)
g
Feminine noun
SCIENCE FICTION
PASATIEMPOS - LEISURE ACTIVITIES

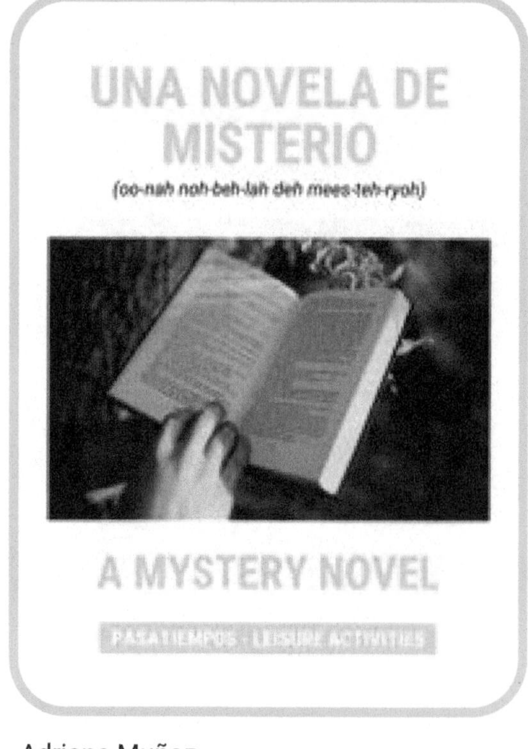
UNA NOVELA DE MISTERIO
(oo-nah noh-beh-lah deh mees-teh-ryoh)
A MYSTERY NOVEL
PASATIEMPOS - LEISURE ACTIVITIES

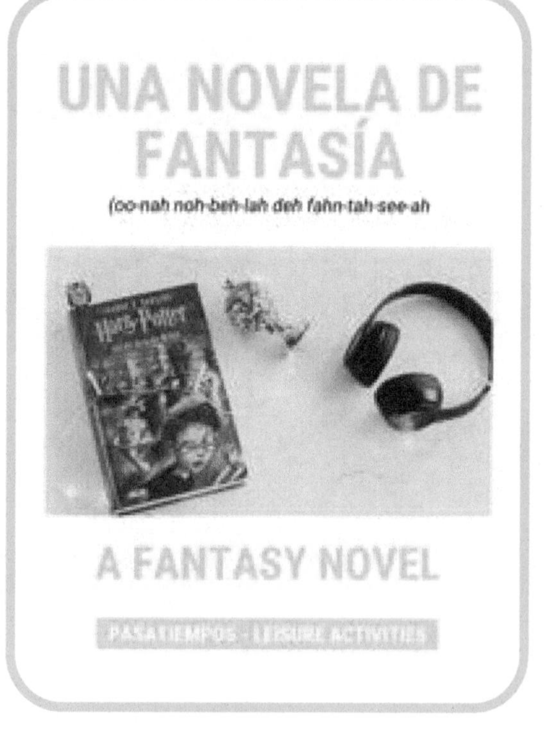
UNA NOVELA DE FANTASÍA
(oo-nah noh-beh-lah deh fahn-tah-see-ah
Harry Potter
A FANTASY NOVEL
PASATIEMPOS - LEISURE ACTIVITIES

IR A LA DISCOTECA

(eer ah lah dees-koh-teh-kah)

¿Quieres ir a la discoteca?
Do you want to go to the disco?

TO GO TO THE DISCO

PASATIEMPOS - LEISURE ACTIVITIES

ME INTERESA...

(meh een-teh-reh-sah)

g

Say 'me interesa...' followed by the activity or object of your interest: Me interesa aprender idiomas = I'm interested in learning languages. Me interesa el arte moderno = I'm interested inmodern art.

I'M INTERESTED IN...

PASATIEMPOS - LEISURE ACTIVITIES

MI PASATIEMPO FAVORITO ES...

(mee pah-sah-tyehm-poh fah-boh-ree-toh ehs)

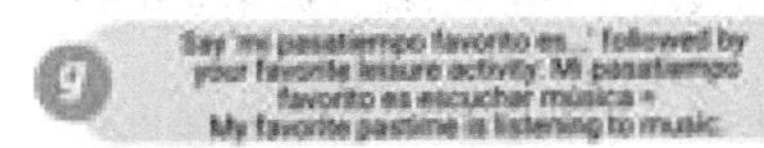

g

Say 'mi pasatiempo favorito es...' followed by your favorite leisure activity: Mi pasatiempo favorito es escuchar música =
My favorite pastime is listening to music.

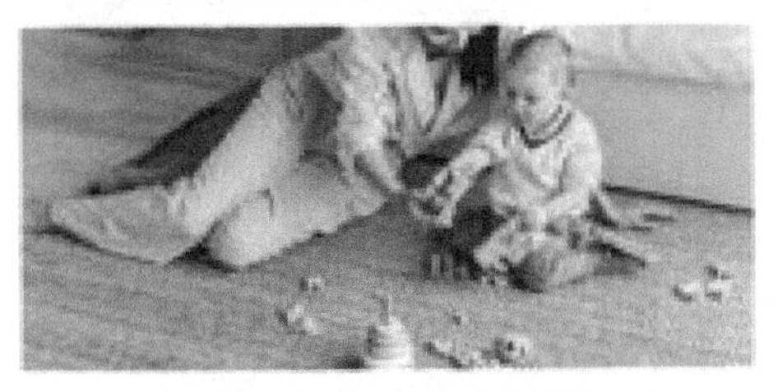

MY FAVORITE PASTIME IS...

PASATIEMPOS - LEISURE ACTIVITIES

¿TE GUSTA...?

(teh goos-tah)

g

Ask '¿Te gusta...' followed by an object or activity to find out if another person likes it:
¿Te gusta jugar poker? = Do you like to play poker?

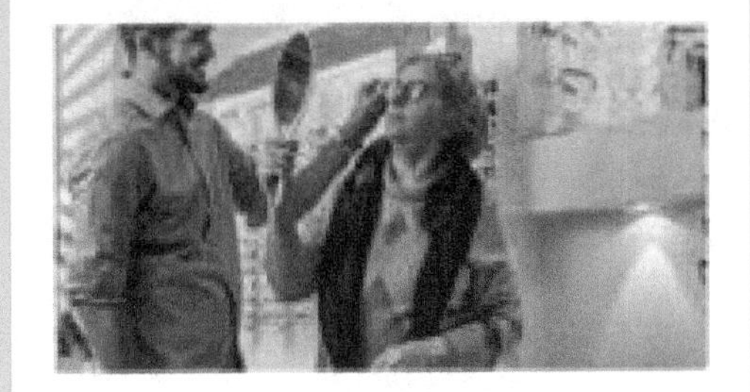

DO YOU LIKE...?

PASATIEMPOS - LEISURE ACTIVITIES

¿QUÉ TE GUSTA HACER EL FIN DE SEMANA?

(keh teh goos-tah ah-sehr ehl feen deh seh-mah-nah)

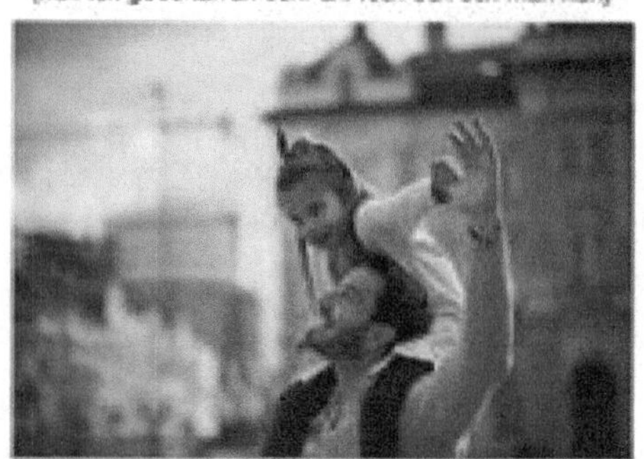

WHAT DO YOU LIKE TO DO ON WEEKENDS?

PASATIEMPOS - LEISURE ACTIVITIES

ME ENCANTA...

(meh ehn-kahn-tah)

g Say 'me encanta...' followed by an object or activity you really love: ¡Me encanta el cine! = I love the cinema!

I LOVE...

PASATIEMPOS - LEISURE ACTIVITIES

EL PADRE

(ehl pah-dreh)

c Another popular word for father is 'papá' (pah-pah).

FATHER

EN EL HOGAR - HOME LIFE

LA MADRE

(lah mah-dreh)

c Another popular word for mother is 'mamá' (mah-mah).

MOTHER

EN EL HOGAR - HOME LIFE

EL HIJO

(ehl ee-hoh)

SON

EN EL HOGAR - HOME LIFE

LA HERMANA

(lah ehr-mah-nah)

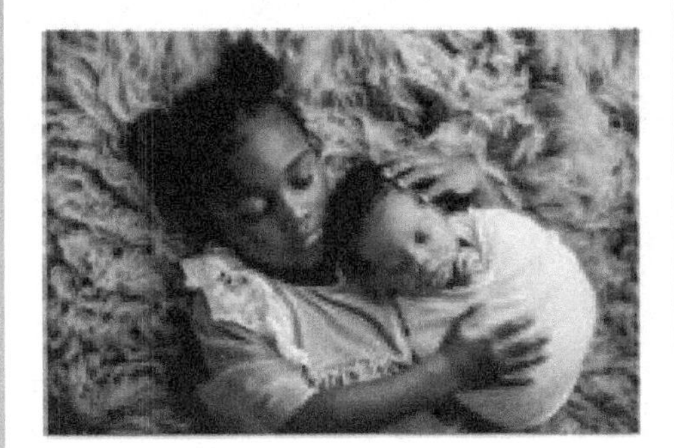

SISTER

EN EL HOGAR - HOME LIFE

EL NIÑO

(ehl nee-nyoh)

BOY

EN EL HOGAR - HOME LIFE

LA HIJA

(lah ee-hah)

DAUGHTER

EN EL HOGAR - HOME LIFE

EL HERMANO

(ehl ehr-mah-noh)

BROTHER

EN EL HOGAR - HOME LIFE

LA NIÑA

(lah nee-nyah)

GIRL

EN EL HOGAR - HOME LIFE

LA ABUELA

(lah ah-bweh-lah)

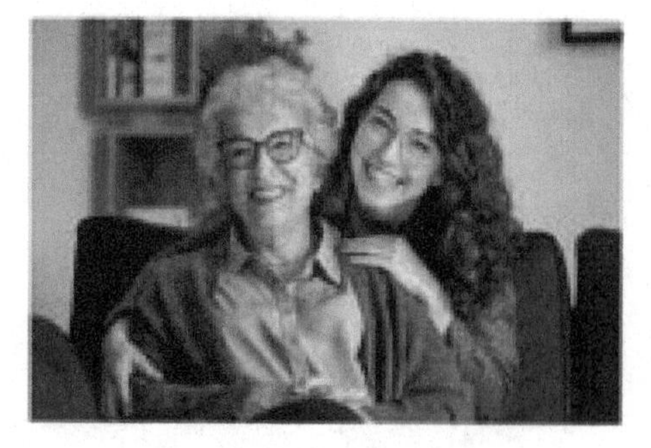

GRANDMOTHER

EN EL HOGAR - HOME LIFE

EL ABUELO

(ehl ah-bweh-loh)

GRANDFATHER

EN EL HOGAR - HOME LIFE

LA BISABUELA

(lah bee-sah-bweh-lah)

GREAT-GRANDMOTHER

EN EL HOGAR - HOME LIFE

EL BISABUELO

(ehl bee-sah-bweh-loh)

GREAT-GRANDFATHER

EN EL HOGAR - HOME LIFE

LA TÍA

(lah tee-ah)

g For the male version, simply replace the article and the noun's ending: El tío.

AUNT

EN EL HOGAR - HOME LIFE

EL PRIMO

(ehl pree-moh)

g For the female version, simply replace the article and the noun's ending: La prima.

COUSIN

EN EL HOGAR - HOME LIFE

LA FAMILIA

(lah fah-mee-lyah)

FAMILY

EN EL HOGAR - HOME LIFE

LOS AMIGOS

(lohs ah-mee-gohs)

g The male version works for male friends, as well as for a mixed gender group. For a group of only female friends, say: las amigas.

FRIENDS

EN EL HOGAR - HOME LIFE

LA ESPOSA

(lah ehs-poh-sah)

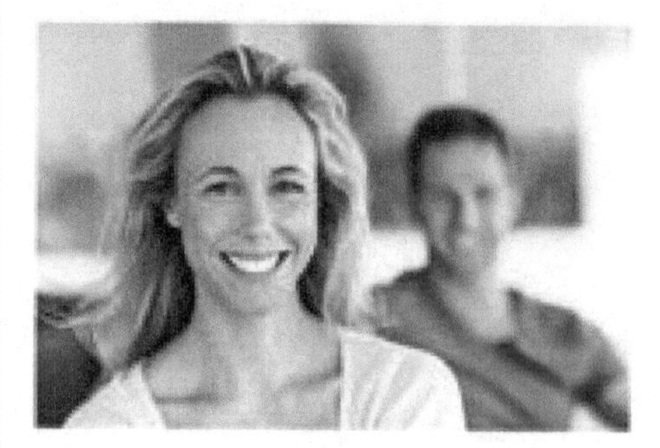

WIFE

EN EL HOGAR - HOME LIFE

EL ESPOSO

(ehl ehs-poh-soh)

Another popular word for husband is 'marido' (mah-ree-doh).

HUSBAND

EN EL HOGAR - HOME LIFE

LOS GEMELOS

(lohs heh-meh-lohs)

g The male version works for boys, as well as for mixed gender twins. For twin girls, say: las gemelas.

TWINS

EN EL HOGAR - HOME LIFE

LA HERMANASTRA

(lah ehr-mah-nahs-trah)

g For the male version, simply replace the article and the noun's ending. El hermanastro.

STEPSISTER

EN EL HOGAR - HOME LIFE

LA MADRASTA

(lah mah-drahs-trah)

STEPMOTHER

EN EL HOGAR - HOME LIFE

EL PADRASTRO

(ehl pah-drahs-troh)

STEPFATHER

EN EL HOGAR - HOME LIFE

LOS NIETOS

(lohs nyeh-tohs)

g The male version works for grandsons, as well as for mixed gender grandchildren. For granddaughters, say: las nietas.

GRANDCHILDREN

EN EL HOGAR - HOME LIFE

EL SOBRINO

(ehl soh-bree-noh)

NEPHEW

EN EL HOGAR - HOME LIFE

LA SOBRINA

(lah soh-bree-nah)

NIECE

EN EL HOGAR - HOME LIFE

EL HUÉRFANO

(ehl wehr-fah-noh)

g For the female version, simply replace the article and the noun's ending: La huérfana.

ORPHAN

EN EL HOGAR - HOME LIFE

EL HIJO ÚNICO

(ehl ee-hoh oo-nee-koh)

g For the female version, simply replace the article and the endings: La hija única.

ONLY CHILD

EN EL HOGAR - HOME LIFE

EL HERMANO MAYOR

(ehl ehr-mah-noh mah-yohr)

g For the female version, simply replace the article and the noun's ending: La hermana mayor.

OLDER BROTHER

EN EL HOGAR - HOME LIFE

LA HERMANA MENOR

(lah ehr-mah-nah meh-nohr)

 For the male version, simply replace the article and the noun's endings: El hermano menor.

YOUNGER SISTER

EN EL HOGAR - HOME LIFE

LA HIJA ADOPTIVA

(lah ee-hah ah-dohp-tee-bah)

g For the male version, simply replace the article and the endings: El hijo adoptivo.

ADOPTED DAUGHTER

EN EL HOGAR - HOME LIFE

LA MADRINA
(lah mah-dree-nah)

GODMOTHER

EN EL HOGAR - HOME LIFE

EL PADRINO
(ehl pah-dree-noh)

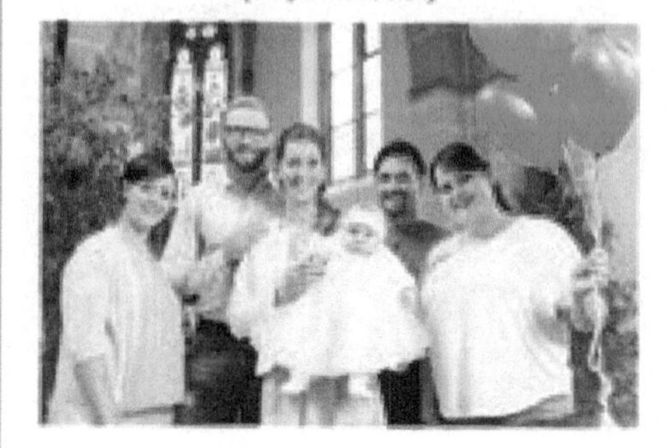

GODFATHER

EN EL HOGAR - HOME LIFE

LA NUERA
(lah nweh-rah)

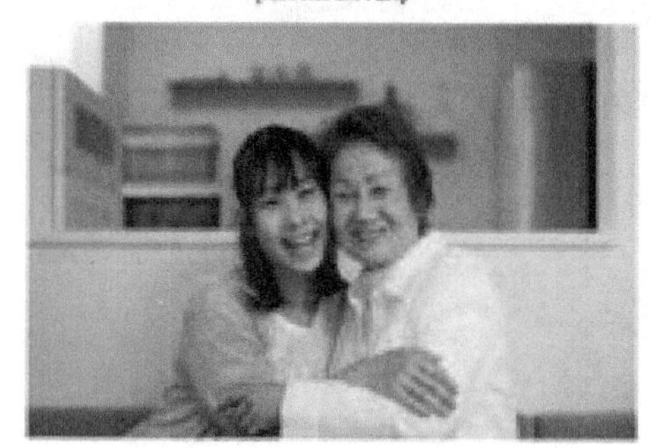

DAUGHTER-IN-LAW

EN EL HOGAR - HOME LIFE

EL YERNO
(ehl yehr-noh)

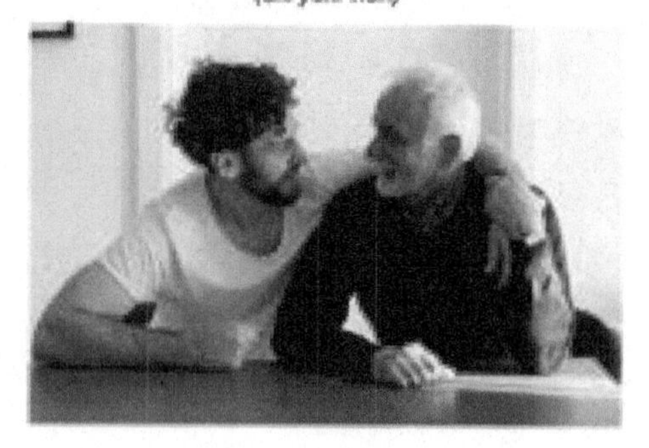

SON-IN-LAW

EN EL HOGAR - HOME LIFE

EL SUEGRO

(ehl sweh-groh)

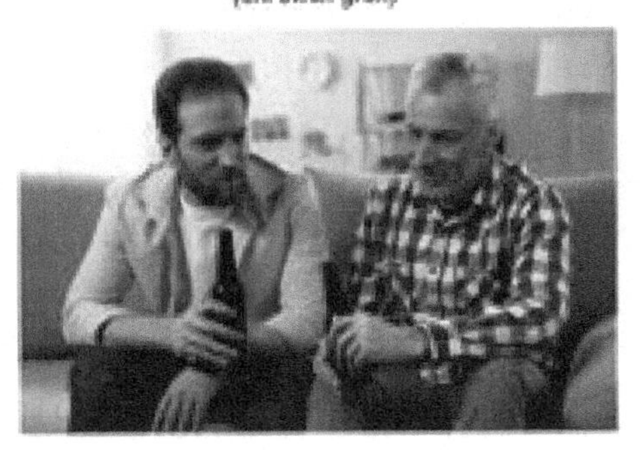

FATHER-IN-LAW

EN EL HOGAR - HOME LIFE

LA SUEGRA

(lah sweh-grah)

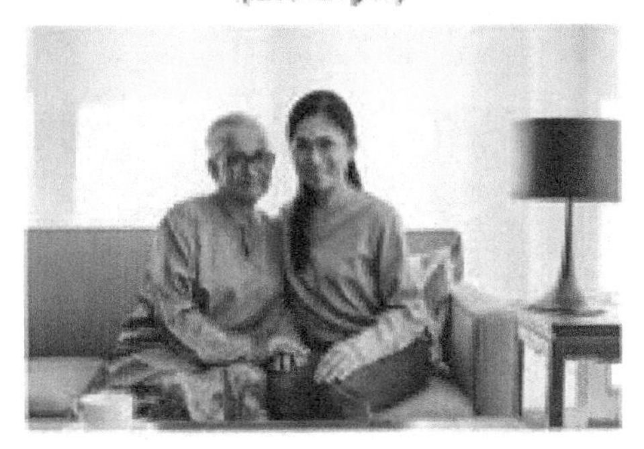

MOTHER-IN-LAW

EN EL HOGAR - HOME LIFE

LA VIUDA

(lah byoo-dah)

g For widower, simply replace the article and the noun's ending: El viudo.

WIDOW

EN EL HOGAR - HOME LIFE

EL CUÑADO

(ehl koo-nyah-doh)

g For the female version, simply replace the article and the noun's ending: La cuñada.

BROTHER-IN-LAW

EN EL HOGAR - HOME LIFE

LOS VECINOS

(lohs beh-see-nohs)

g The male version works for male neighbors, as well as for mixed gender neighbors. For female neighbors only, say: las vecinas.

NEIGHBORS

EN EL HOGAR - HOME LIFE

LOS PARIENTES

(lohs pah-ryehn-tehs)

c Another popular word for relatives is 'familiares' (fah-mee-lyah-rehs).

RELATIVES

EN EL HOGAR - HOME LIFE

LA CASA

(lah kah-sah)

HOUSE

EN EL HOGAR - HOME LIFE

EL APARTAMENTO

(ehl ah-pahr-tah-mehn-toh)

c In Spain, the word for apartment is 'piso' (pee-soh).

APARTMENT

EN EL HOGAR - HOME LIFE

EL EDIFICIO

(ehl eh-dee-fee-syoh)

The pronunciation of "edificio" in Spain is 'eh-dee-fee-thyoh'.

BUILDING

EN EL HOGAR - HOME LIFE

LA GRANJA

(lah grahn-hah)

FARM

EN EL HOGAR - HOME LIFE

LA HABITACIÓN

(lah ah-bee-tah-syohn)

The pronunciation of "habitación" in Spain is 'ah-bee-tah-thyohn'.

BEDROOM

EN EL HOGAR - HOME LIFE

LA SALA

(lah sah-lah)

LIVING ROOM

EN EL HOGAR - HOME LIFE

EL COMEDOR

(ehl koh-meh-dohr)

g — *Masculine noun*

DINING ROOM

EN EL HOGAR - HOME LIFE

LA COCINA

(lah koh-see-nah)

p — The pronunciation of "cocina" in Spain is 'koh-thee-nah'.

KITCHEN

EN EL HOGAR - HOME LIFE

EL BAÑO

(ehl bah-nyoh)

BATHROOM

EN EL HOGAR - HOME LIFE

LA DUCHA

(lah doo-chah)

SHOWER

EN EL HOGAR - HOME LIFE

EL PASILLO

(ehl pah-see-yoh)

HALLWAY

EN EL HOGAR - HOME LIFE

EL SÓTANO

(ehl soh-tah-noh)

BASEMENT

EN EL HOGAR - HOME LIFE

LA CAMA

(lah kah-mah)

BED

EN EL HOGAR - HOME LIFE

LA LUZ

(lah loos)

P *The pronunciation of "luz" in Spain is 'looth'.*

LIGHT

EN EL HOGAR - HOME LIFE

LA LÁMPARA

(lah lahm-pah-rah)

LAMP

EN EL HOGAR - HOME LIFE

LAS SÁBANAS

(lahs sah-bah-nahs)

SHEETS

EN EL HOGAR - HOME LIFE

LAS MANTAS

(lahs mahn-tahs)

BLANKETS

EN EL HOGAR - HOME LIFE

LAS CORTINAS

(lahs kohr-tee-nahs)

CURTAINS

EN EL HOGAR - HOME LIFE

LA ALMOHADA

(lah ahl-moh-ah-dah)

PILLOW

EN EL HOGAR - HOME LIFE

LA FUNDA

(lah foon-dah)

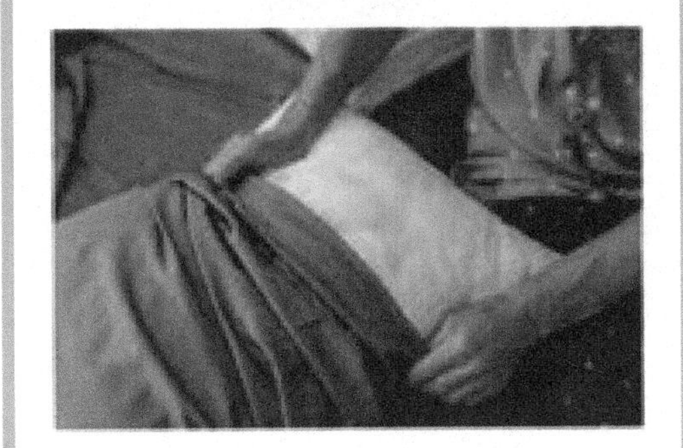

PILLOWCASE

EN EL HOGAR - HOME LIFE

LA TOALLA

(lah toh-ah-yah)

TOWEL

EN EL HOGAR - HOME LIFE

LOS COJINES

(los koh-hee-nehs)

g Masculine noun

CUSHIONS

EN EL HOGAR - HOME LIFE

CLOSET

EN EL HOGAR - HOME LIFE

EL CAJÓN

(ehl kah-hohn)

g Masculine noun

DRAWER

EN EL HOGAR - HOME LIFE

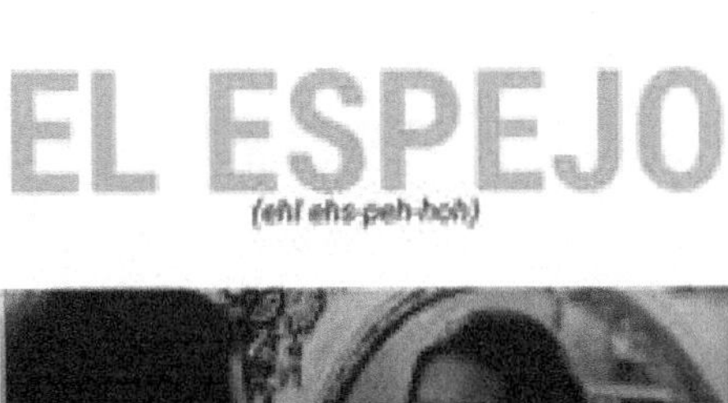

EL ESPEJO

(ehl ehs-peh-hoh)

MIRROR

EN EL HOGAR - HOME LIFE

EL INTERRUPTOR DE LA LUZ

(ehl een-teh-rroop-tohr deh lah loos)

p — The pronunciation of "luz" in Spain is 'looth'.

LIGHT SWITCH

EN EL HOGAR - HOME LIFE

EL COLCHÓN

(ehl kohl-chohn)

g — Masculine noun

MATRESS

EN EL HOGAR - HOME LIFE

EL GANCHO

(ehl gahn-choh)

HANGER

EN EL HOGAR - HOME LIFE

LA ALFOMBRA

(lah ahl-fohm-brah)

RUG

EN EL HOGAR - HOME LIFE

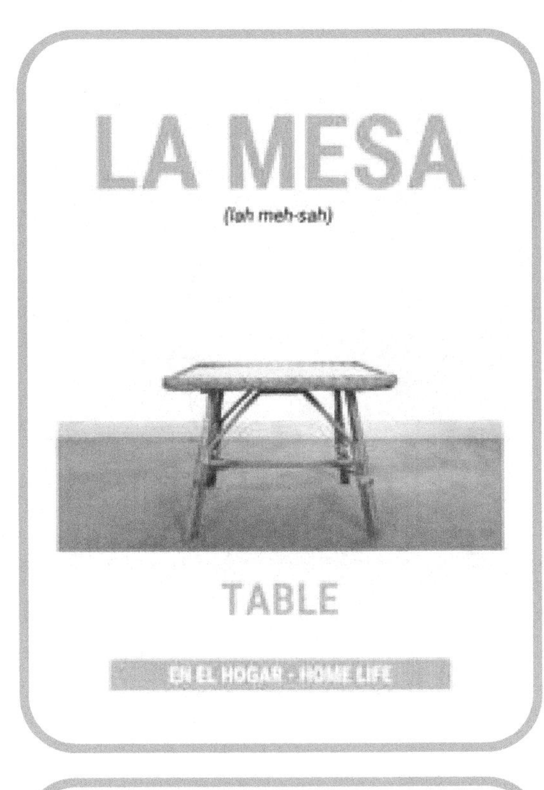
LA MESA
(lah meh-sah)
TABLE
EN EL HOGAR - HOME LIFE

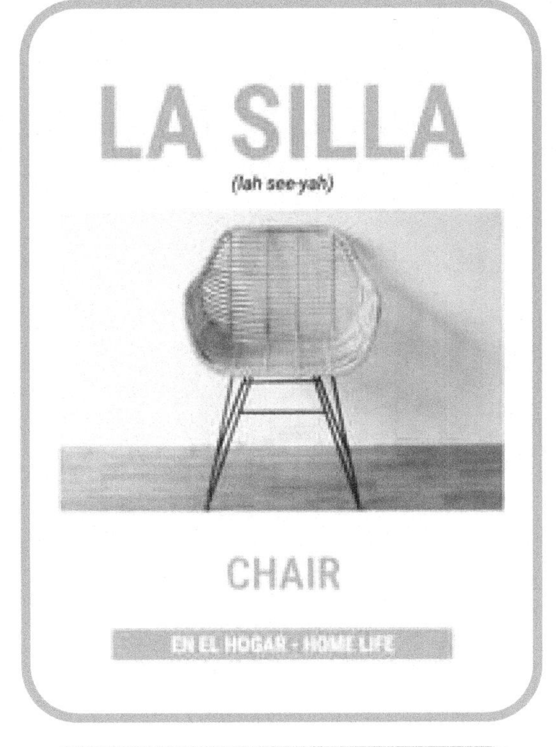
LA SILLA
(lah see-yah)
CHAIR
EN EL HOGAR - HOME LIFE

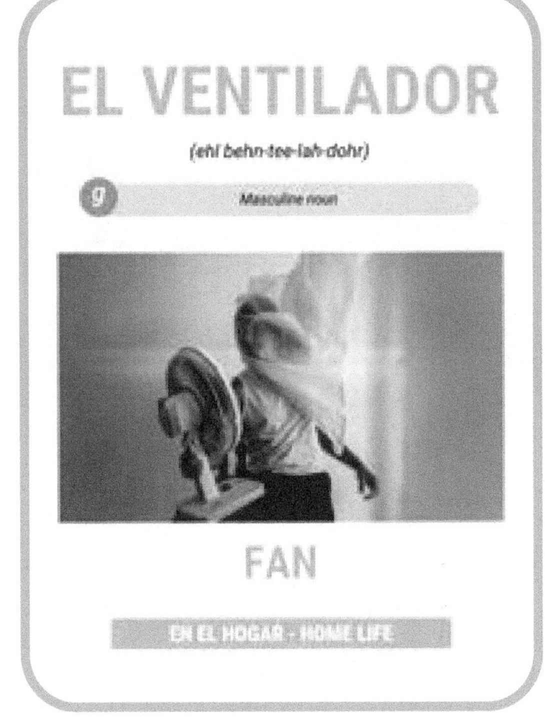
EL VENTILADOR
(ehl behn-tee-lah-dohr)
g
Masculine noun
FAN
EN EL HOGAR - HOME LIFE

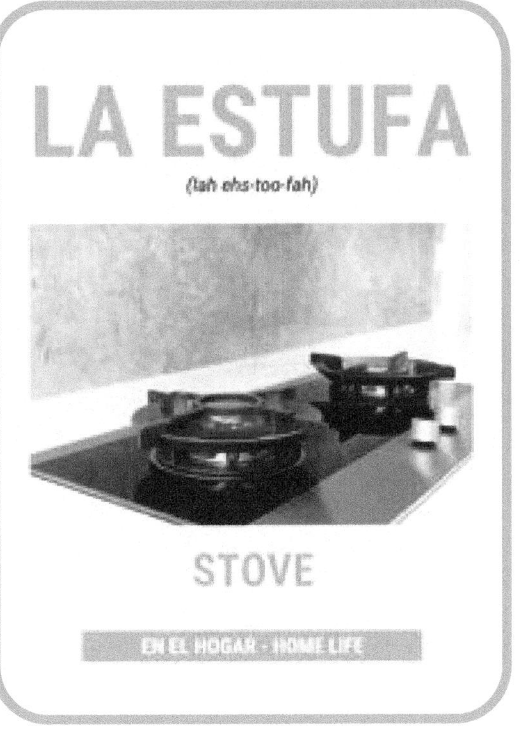
LA ESTUFA
(lah ehs-too-fah)
STOVE
EN EL HOGAR - HOME LIFE

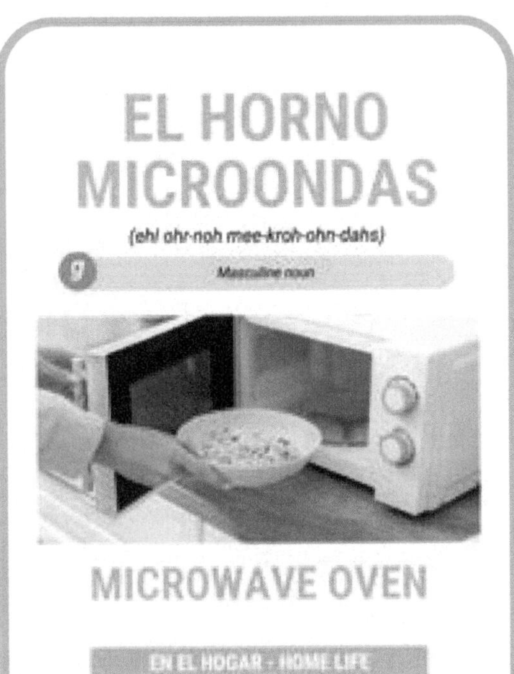

EL HORNO MICROONDAS

(ehl ohr-noh mee-kroh-ohn-dahs)

g Masculine noun

MICROWAVE OVEN

EN EL HOGAR - HOME LIFE

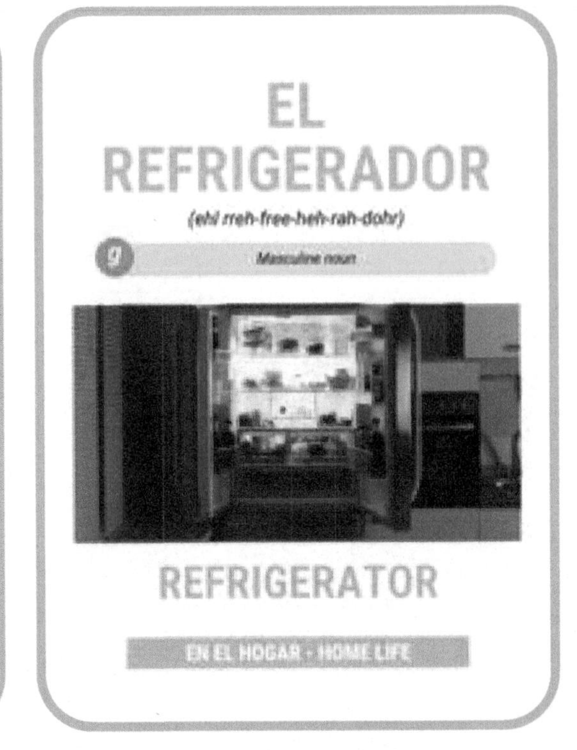

EL REFRIGERADOR

(ehl rreh-free-heh-rah-dohr)

g Masculine noun

REFRIGERATOR

EN EL HOGAR - HOME LIFE

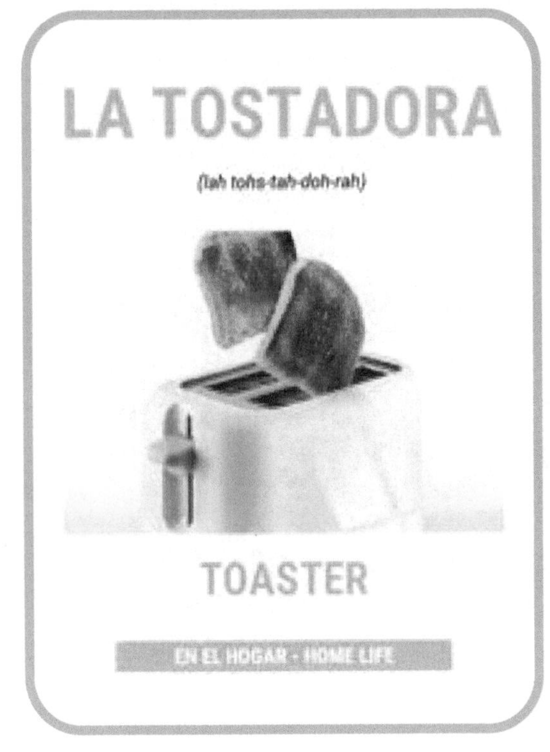

LA TOSTADORA

(lah tohs-tah-doh-rah)

TOASTER

EN EL HOGAR - HOME LIFE

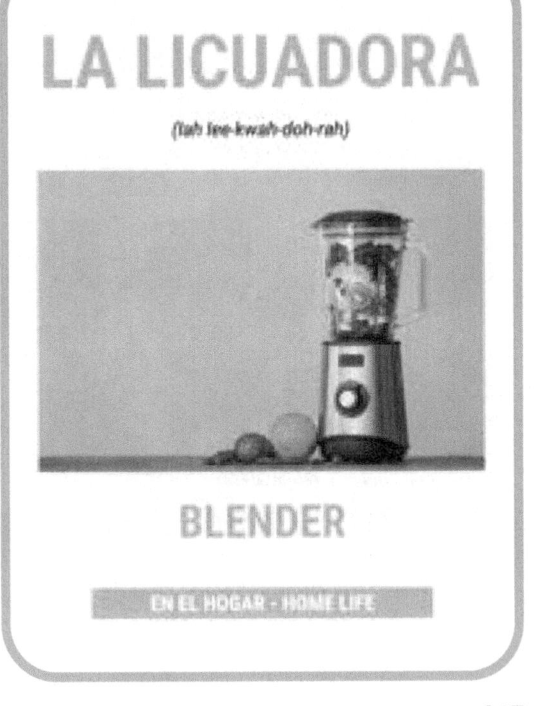

LA LICUADORA

(lah lee-kwah-doh-rah)

BLENDER

EN EL HOGAR - HOME LIFE

EL LAVAPLATOS AUTOMÁTICO

(ehl lah-bah plah-tohs ow-toh-mah-tee-koh)

DISHWASHER

EN EL HOGAR - HOME LIFE

LA LAVADORA

(lah lah-bah-doh-rah)

WASHING MACHINE

EN EL HOGAR - HOME LIFE

EL TELEVISOR

(ehl teh-leh-bee-sohr)

TV SET

EN EL HOGAR - HOME LIFE

EL COMPUTADOR

(ehl kohm-poo-tah-dohr)

COMPUTER

EN EL HOGAR - HOME LIFE

LAS MASCOTAS

(lahs mahs-koh-tahs)

PETS

LA NATURALEZA - NATURE

UN PÁJARO

(oon pah-hah-roh)

A BIRD

LA NATURALEZA - NATURE

UN CANARIO

(oon kah-nah-ryoh)

A CANARY

LA NATURALEZA - NATURE

UN GATO

(oon gah-toh)

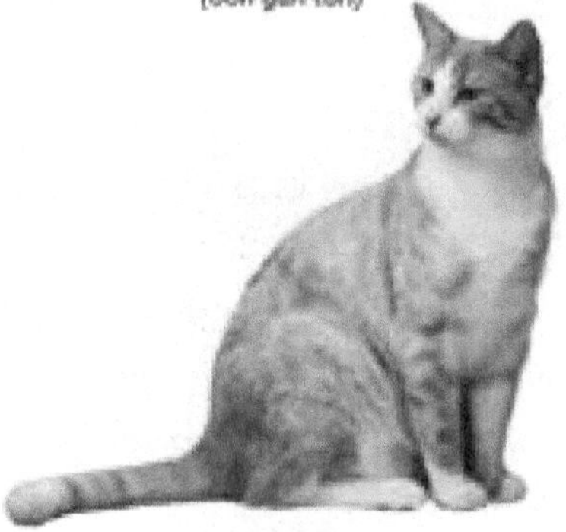

A CAT

LA NATURALEZA - NATURE

UN PERRO

(oon peh-rroh)

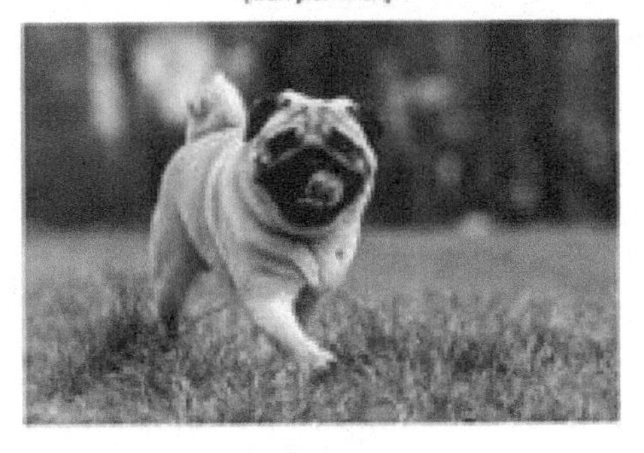

A DOG

LA NATURALEZA - NATURE

UN HURÓN

(oon oo-rohn)

A FERRET

LA NATURALEZA - NATURE

UN PEZ

(oon pehs)

P The pronunciation of 'pez' in Spain is 'pehth'.

A FISH

LA NATURALEZA - NATURE

UN HÁMSTER

(oon hahms-tehr)

A HAMSTER

LA NATURALEZA - NATURE

UN CABALLO

(oon kah-bah-yoh)

A HORSE

LA NATURALEZA - NATURE

UNA LAGARTIJA

(oo-nah lah-gahr-tee-hah)

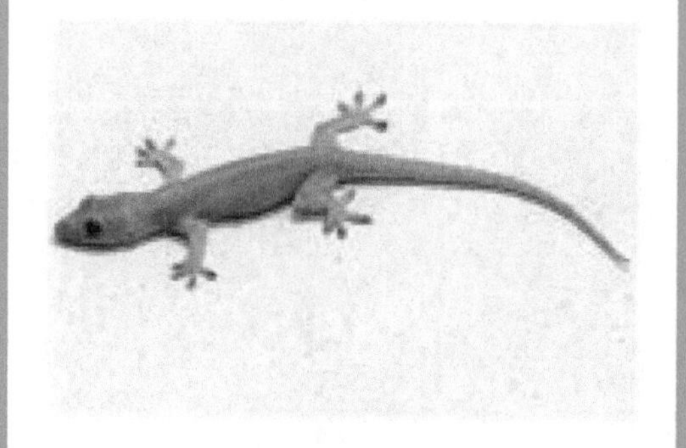

A LIZARD

LA NATURALEZA - NATURE

UN RATÓN

(oon rrah-tohn)

A MOUSE

LA NATURALEZA - NATURE

UN LORO

(oon loh-roh)

A PARROT

LA NATURALEZA - NATURE

UN CERDO

(oon sehr-doh)

A PIG

LA NATURALEZA - NATURE

UN CONEJO

(oon koh-neh-hoh)

A RABBIT

LA NATURALEZA - NATURE

UNA SERPIENTE

(oo-nah sehr-pyehn-teh)

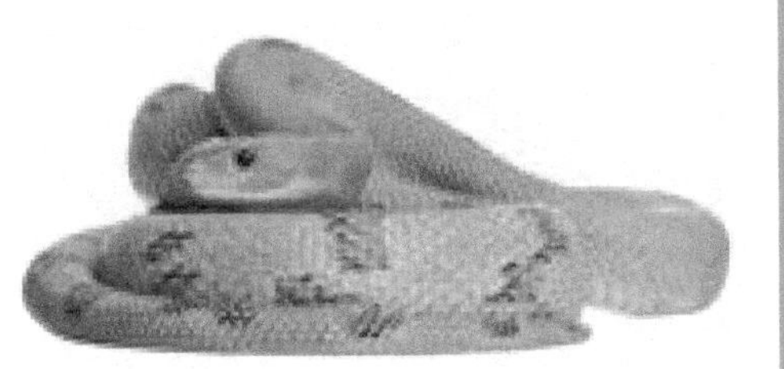

A SNAKE

LA NATURALEZA - NATURE

UNA TORTUGA

(oo-nah tohr-too-gah)

A TURTLE

LA NATURALEZA - NATURE

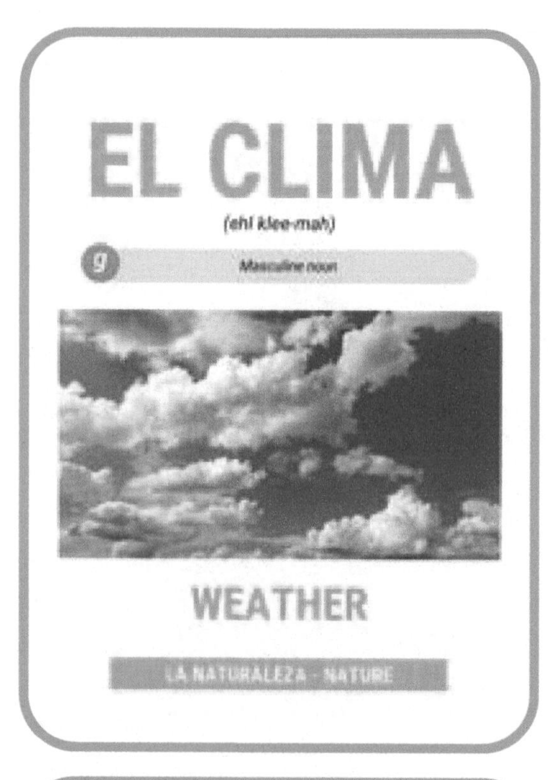
EL CLIMA
(ehl klee-mah)
g
Masculine noun
WEATHER
LA NATURALEZA - NATURE

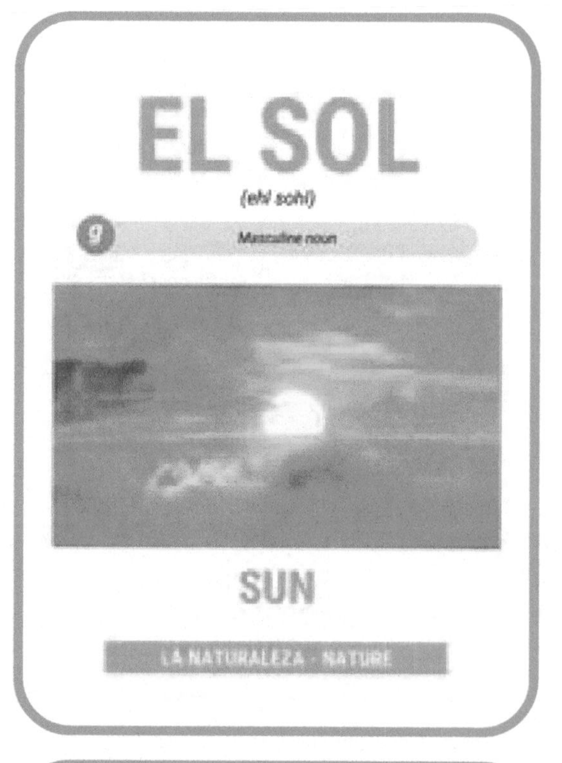
EL SOL
(ehl sohl)
g
Masculine noun
SUN
LA NATURALEZA - NATURE

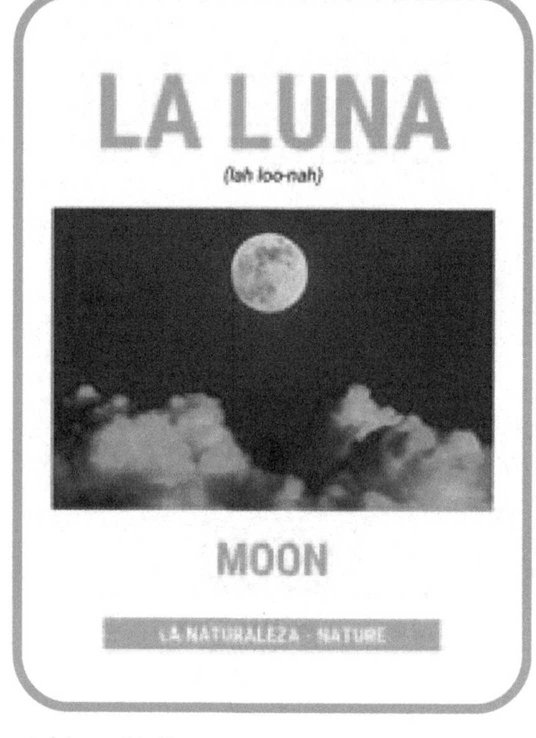
LA LUNA
(lah loo-nah)
MOON
LA NATURALEZA - NATURE

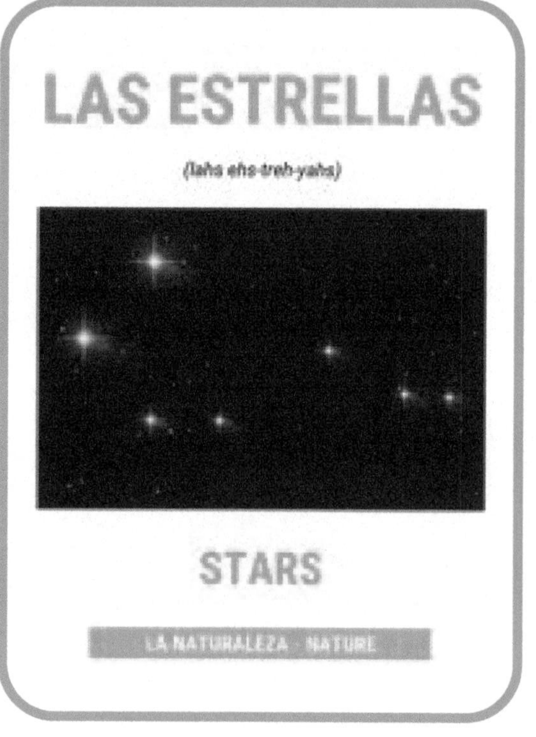
LAS ESTRELLAS
(lahs ehs-treh-yahs)
STARS
LA NATURALEZA - NATURE

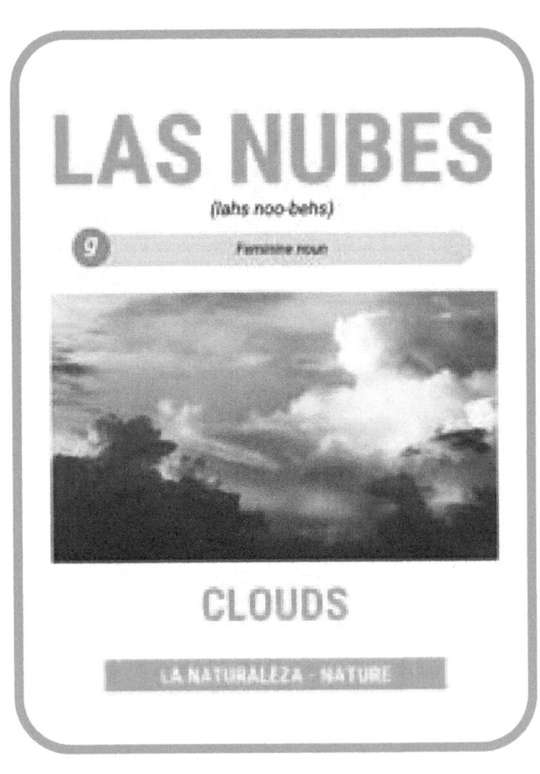
LAS NUBES
(lahs noo-behs)
CLOUDS
LA NATURALEZA - NATURE

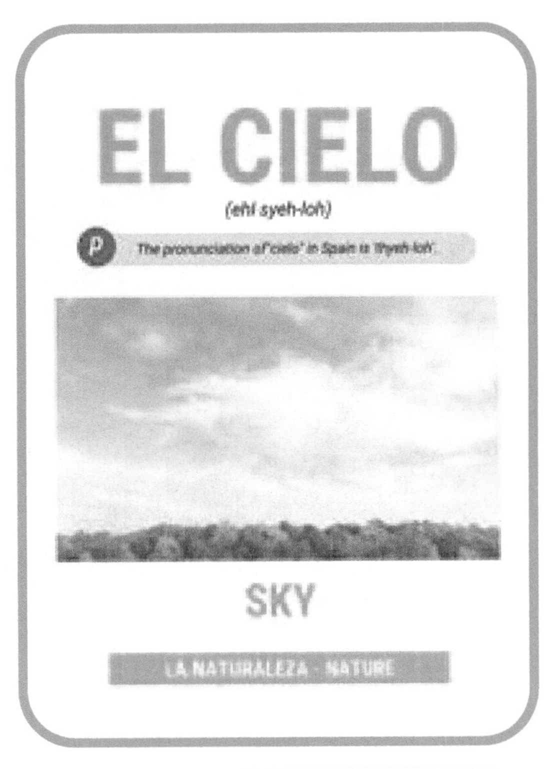
EL CIELO
(ehl syeh-loh)
SKY
LA NATURALEZA - NATURE

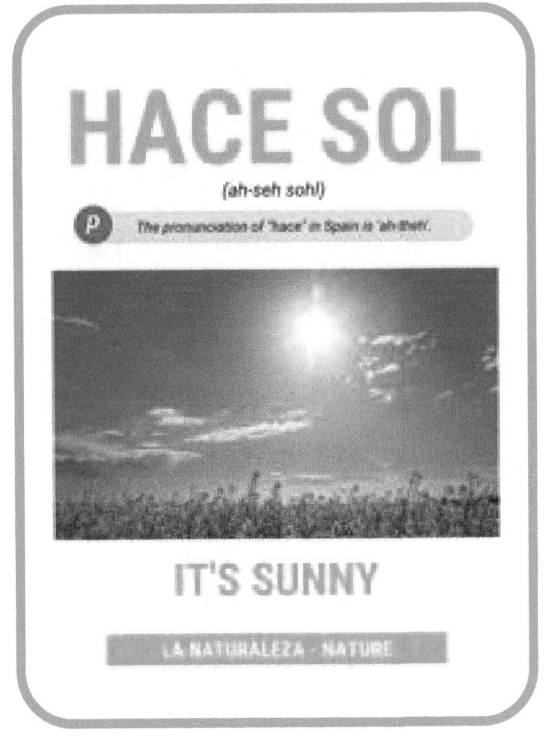
HACE SOL
(ah-seh sohl)
IT'S SUNNY
LA NATURALEZA - NATURE

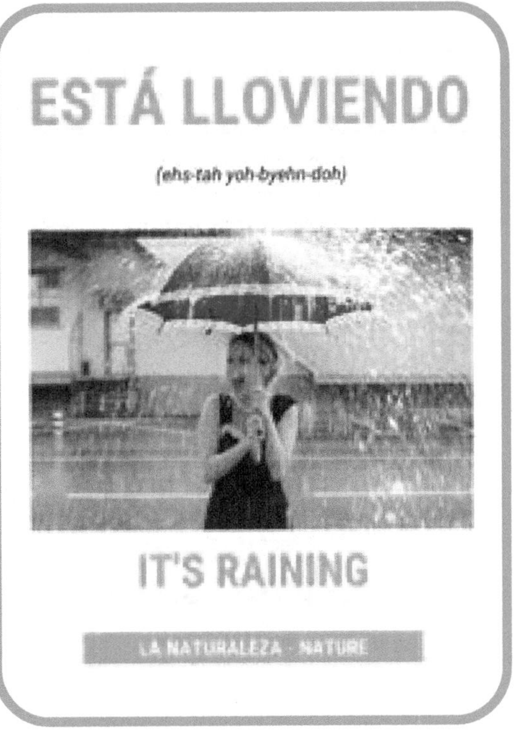
ESTÁ LLOVIENDO
(ehs-tah yoh-byehn-doh)
IT'S RAINING
LA NATURALEZA - NATURE

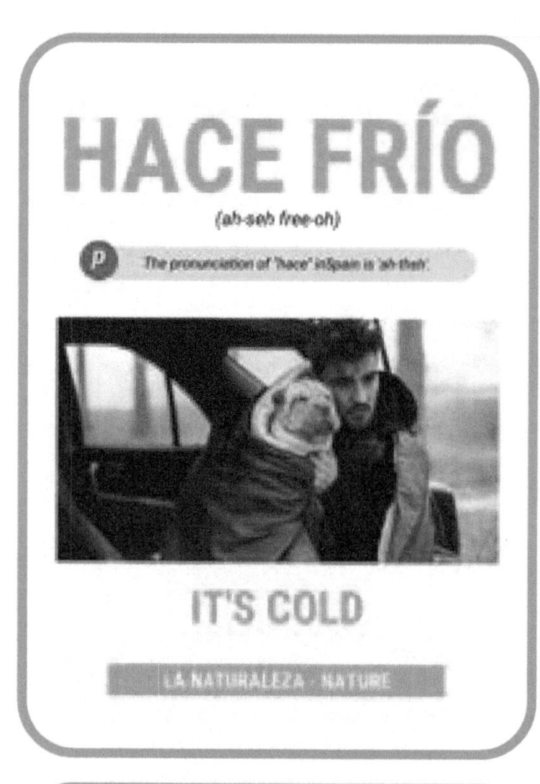
HACE FRÍO
(ah-seh free-oh)
P
The pronunciation of 'hace' inSpain is 'ah-theh'.
IT'S COLD
LA NATURALEZA - NATURE

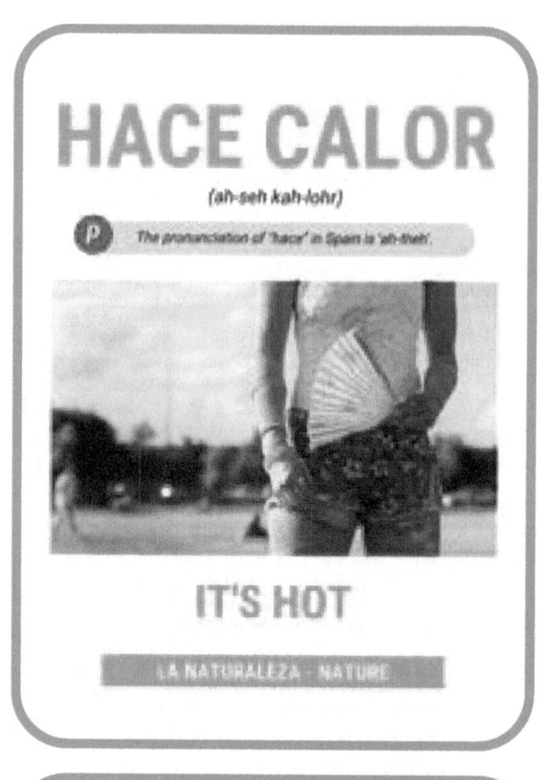
HACE CALOR
(ah-seh kah-lohr)
P
The pronunciation of 'hace' in Spain is 'ah-theh'.
IT'S HOT
LA NATURALEZA - NATURE

ESTÁ FRESCO
(ehs-tah frehs-koh)
IT'S COOL
(TEMPERATURE)
LA NATURALEZA - NATURE

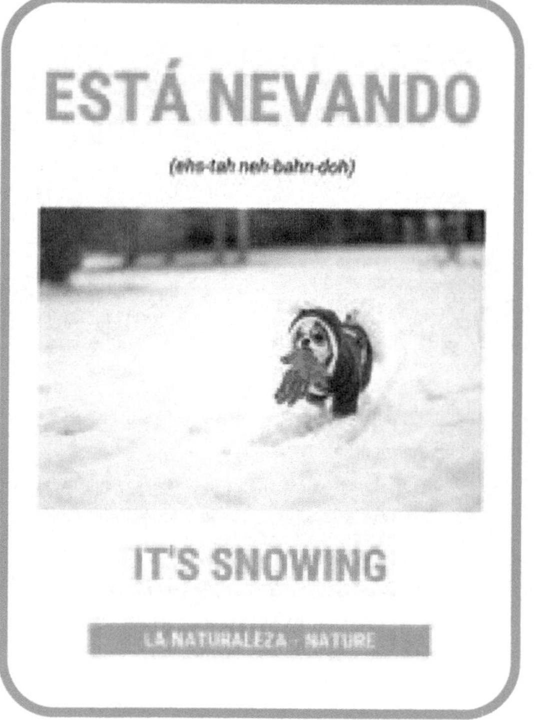
ESTÁ NEVANDO
(ehs-tah neh-bahn-doh)
IT'S SNOWING
LA NATURALEZA - NATURE

ESTÁ GRANIZANDO

(ehs-tah grah-nee-sahn-doh)

P The pronunciation of "granizando" in Spain is 'grah-nee-thahn-doh'.

IT'S HAILING

LA NATURALEZA - NATURE

HAY VIENTO

(ay byehn-toh)

IT'S WINDY

LA NATURALEZA - NATURE

HAY UNA TORMENTA

(ay oo-nah tohr-mehn-tah)

THERE'S A STORM

LA NATURALEZA - NATURE

EL HURACÁN

(ehl oo-rah-kahn)

HURRICANE

LA NATURALEZA - NATURE

ESTÁ NUBLADO

(ehs-tah noo-blah-doh)

IT'S CLOUDY

LA NATURALEZA - NATURE

ESTÁ DESPEJADO

(ehs-tah dehs-peh-hah-doh)

THE SKY IS CLEAR

LA NATURALEZA - NATURE

LAS ESTACIONES

(lahs ehs-tah-syoh-nehs)

The pronunciation of "estaciones" in Spain is 'ehs-tah-thyoh-nehs'.

SEASONS

LA NATURALEZA - NATURE

EL VERANO

(ehl beh-rah-noh)

SUMMER

LA NATURALEZA - NATURE

LA PRIMAVERA

(lah pree-mah-beh-rah)

SPRING

LA NATURALEZA - NATURE

EL OTOÑO

(ehl oh-toh-nyoh)

FALL

LA NATURALEZA - NATURE

EL INVIERNO

(ehl een-byehr-noh)

WINTER

LA NATURALEZA - NATURE

LA TORMENTA ELÉCTRICA

(lah tohr-mehn-tah eh-lehk-tree-kah)

THUNDERSTORM

LA NATURALEZA - NATURE

LA NIEBLA

(lah nyeh-blah)

FOG

LA NATURALEZA - NATURE

UN ARCOÍRIS

(oon ahr-koh-ee-rees)

A RAINBOW

LA NATURALEZA - NATURE

AMARILLO

(ah-mah-ree-yoh)

g Adjectives that end in a vowel change their ending according to the gender of the noun they describe: La camisa amarilla / El pantalón amarillo.

YELLOW

PALABRAS ÚTILES - USEFUL WORDS
ADJECTIVES

AZUL

(ah-sool)

p *The pronunciation of azul" in Spain is 'ah-thool'.*

BLUE

PALABRAS ÚTILES - USEFUL WORDS
ADJECTIVES

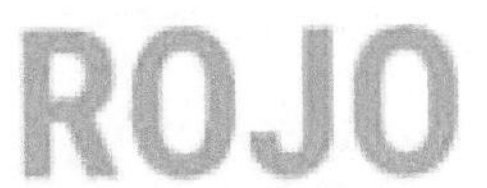

(rroh-hoh)

g Adjectives that end -a or -o change their ending according to the gender of the noun they describe: La casa roja / El abrigo rojo.

RED

PALABRAS ÚTILES - USEFUL WORDS

ADJECTIVES

VERDE

(behr-deh)

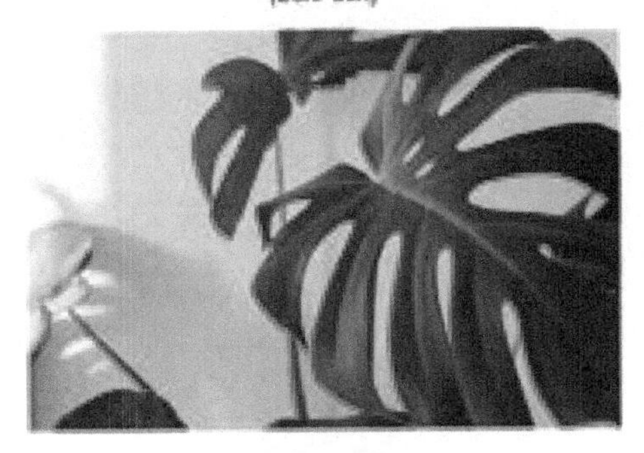

GREEN

PALABRAS ÚTILES - USEFUL WORDS

ADJECTIVES

NEGRO

(neh-groh)

g Adjectives that end -a or -o change their ending according to the gender of the noun they describe: La mesa negra / El casco negro.

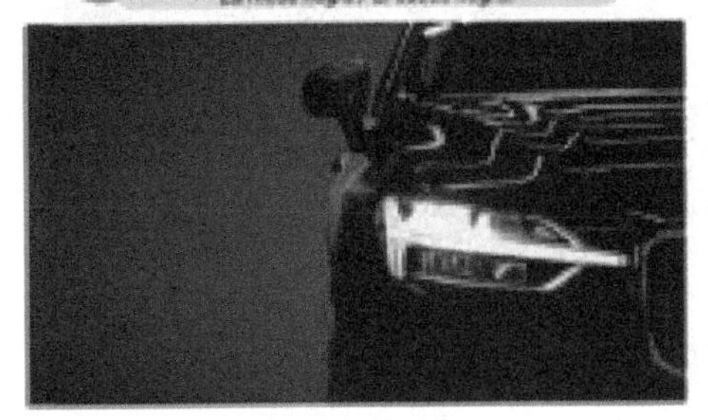

BLACK

PALABRAS ÚTILES - USEFUL WORDS

ADJECTIVES

BLANCO

(blahn-koh)

g Adjectives that end -a or -o change their ending according to the gender of the noun they describe: La ropa blanca / El saco blanco.

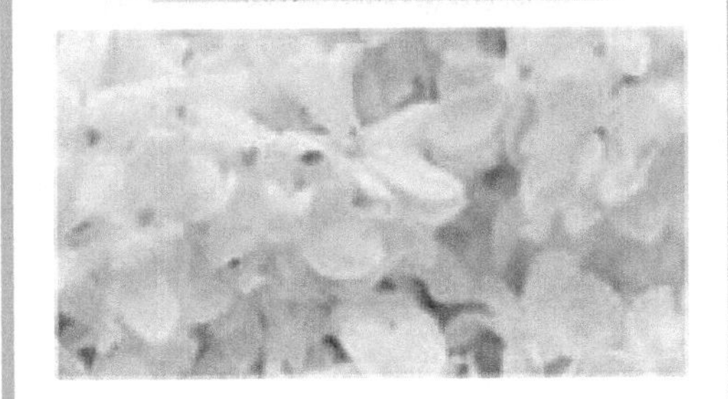

WHITE

PALABRAS ÚTILES - USEFUL WORDS

ADJECTIVES

NARANJA

(nah-rahn-hah)

g **Naranja** is an exception and it does not change its ending: La blusa naranja / El zapato naranja.

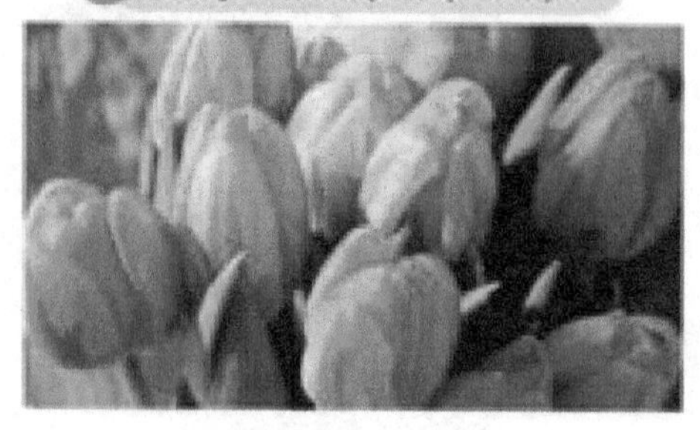

ORANGE

PALABRAS ÚTILES - USEFUL WORDS

ADJECTIVES

CAFÉ

(kah-feh)

Another word for brown is 'marrón' (mah-rrohn).

BROWN

PALABRAS ÚTILES - USEFUL WORDS

ADJECTIVES

MORADO

(moh-rah-doh)

g Adjectives that end -a or -o change their ending according to the gender of the noun they describe: **La** llave morada / **El** carro morado.

PURPLE

PALABRAS ÚTILES - USEFUL WORDS

ADJECTIVES

GRIS

(grees)

GRAY

PALABRAS ÚTILES - USEFUL WORDS

ADJECTIVES

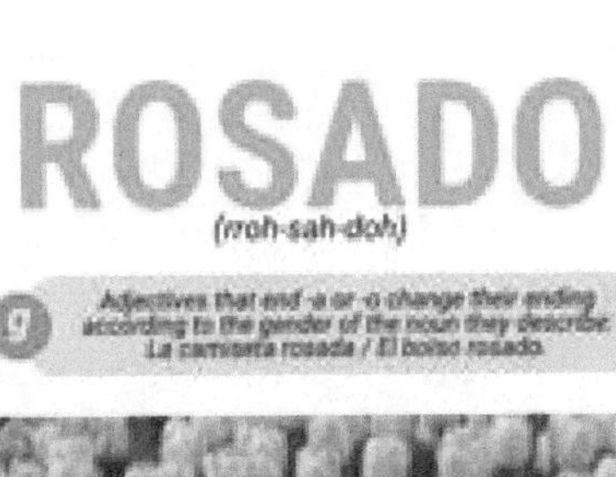

ROSADO

(rroh-sah-doh)

g — *Adjectives that end -a or -o change their ending according to the gender of the noun they describe. La camiseta rosada / El bolso rosado.*

PINK

PALABRAS ÚTILES - USEFUL WORDS

ADJECTIVES

TRANSPARENTE

(trahns-pah-rehn-teh)

TRANSPARENT

PALABRAS ÚTILES - USEFUL WORDS

ADJECTIVES

CLARO

(klah-roh)

g — *Use claro to specify that a color is light in shade: Me gusta el azul claro = I like light blue.*

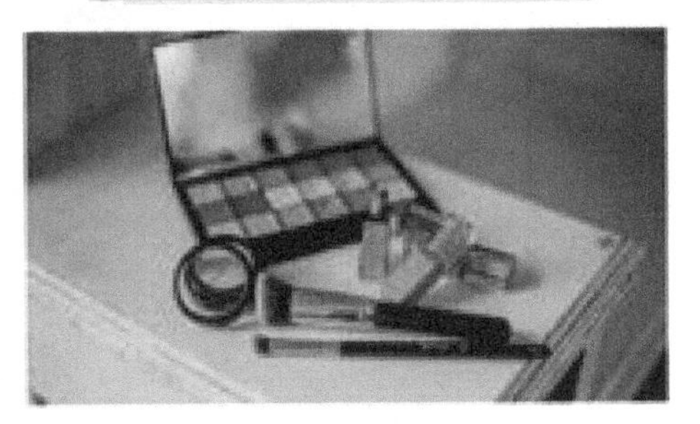

LIGHT

PALABRAS ÚTILES - USEFUL WORDS

ADJECTIVES

OSCURO

(ohs-koo-roh)

g — *Use oscuro to specify that a color is dark in shade: No me gusta el verde oscuro = I don't like dark green.*

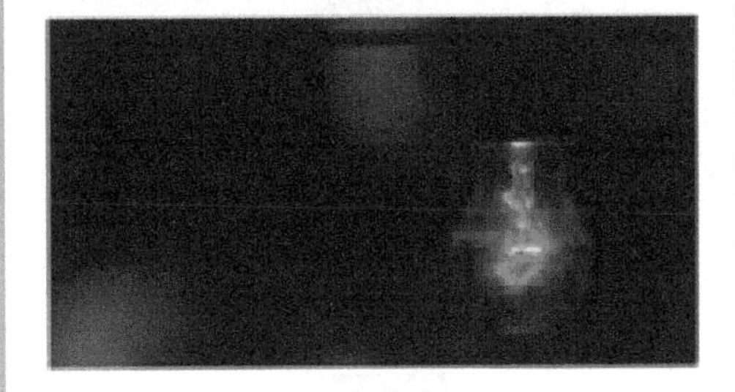

DARK

PALABRAS ÚTILES - USEFUL WORDS

ADJECTIVES

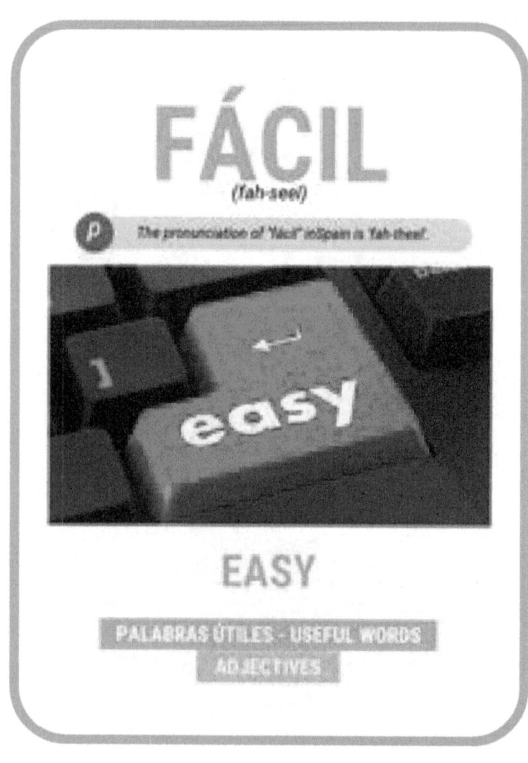
FÁCIL
(fah-seel)
The pronunciation of 'fácil' in Spain is 'fah-theel'.
easy
EASY
PALABRAS ÚTILES - USEFUL WORDS
ADJECTIVES

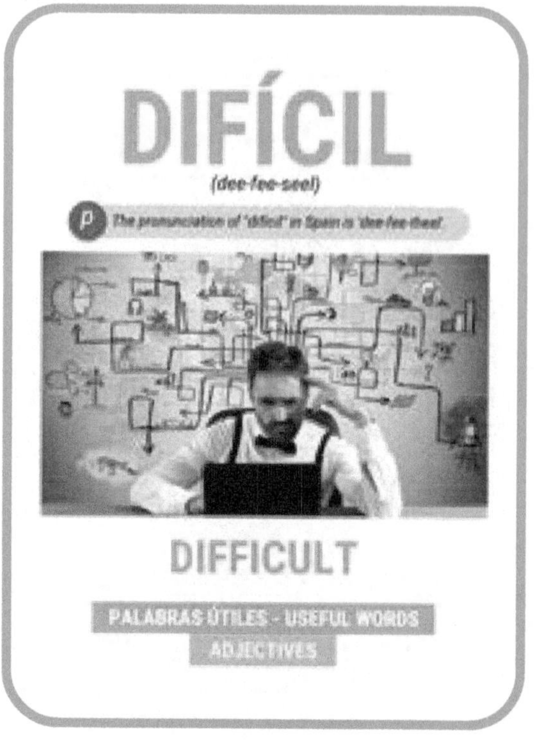
DIFÍCIL
(dee-fee-seel)
The pronunciation of 'difícil' in Spain is 'dee-fee-theel'.
DIFFICULT
PALABRAS ÚTILES - USEFUL WORDS
ADJECTIVES

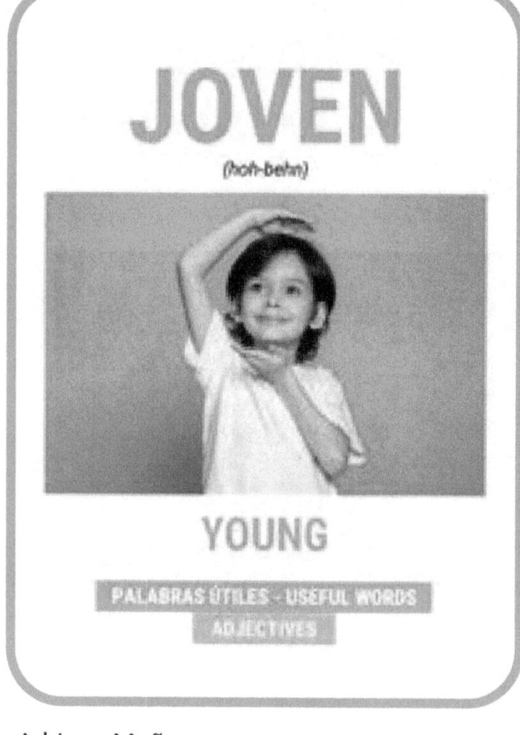
JOVEN
(hoh-behn)
YOUNG
PALABRAS ÚTILES - USEFUL WORDS
ADJECTIVES

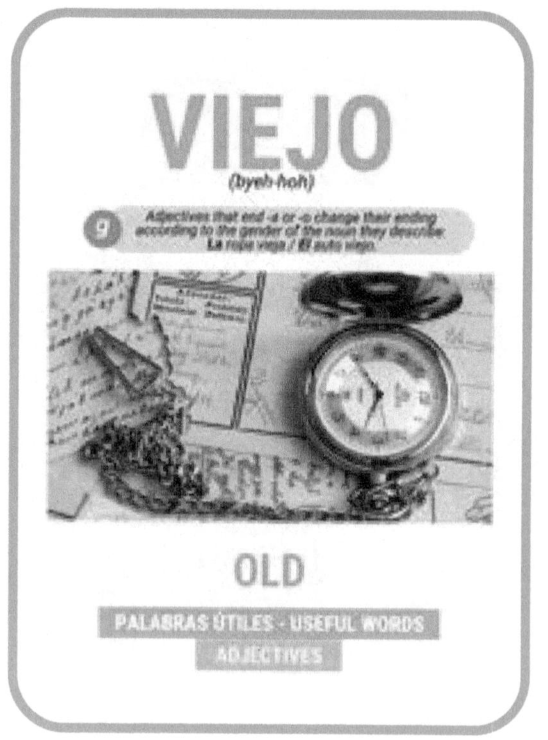
VIEJO
(byeh-hoh)
Adjectives that end -a or -o change their ending according to the gender of the noun they describe:
La ropa vieja / El auto viejo.
OLD
PALABRAS ÚTILES - USEFUL WORDS
ADJECTIVES

(nweh-boh)

g Adjectives that end -a or -o change their ending according to the gender of the noun they describe: **La** ropa vieja / **El** auto viejo.

NEW

PALABRAS ÚTILES - USEFUL WORDS

ADJECTIVES

ÚTIL

(oo-teel)

USEFUL

PALABRAS ÚTILES - USEFUL WORDS

ADJECTIVES

FELIZ

(feh-lees)

p The pronunciation of "feliz" in Spain is 'feh-leeth'.

HAPPY

PALABRAS ÚTILES - USEFUL WORDS

ADJECTIVES

TRISTE

(trees-teh)

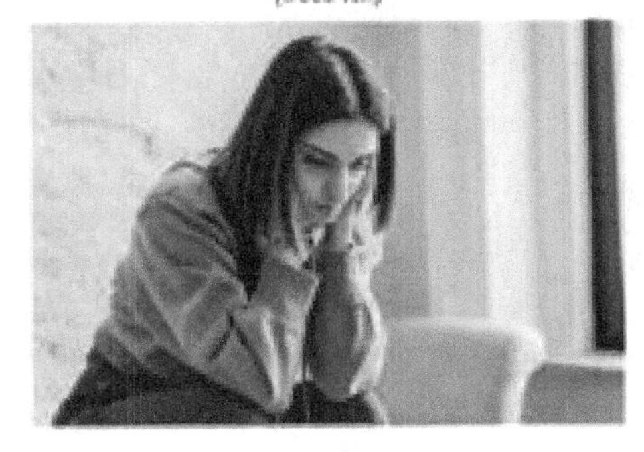

SAD

PALABRAS ÚTILES - USEFUL WORDS

ADJECTIVES

GRANDE

(grahn-deh)

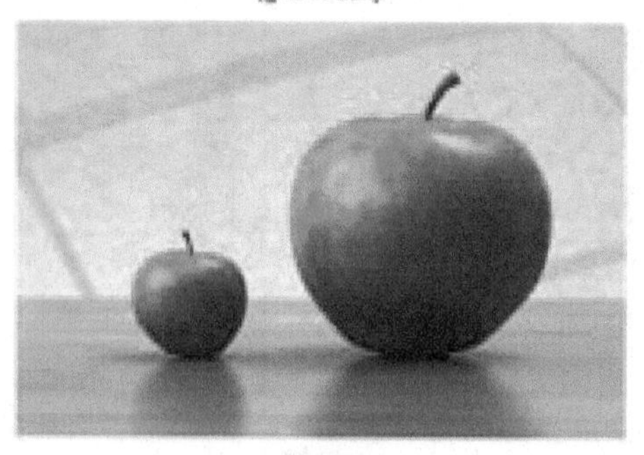

BIG

PALABRAS ÚTILES - USEFUL WORDS

ADJECTIVES

PEQUEÑO

(peh-keh-nyoh)

g Adjectives that end -a or -o change their ending according to the gender of the noun they describe: La tortuga pequeña / El pájaro pequeño.

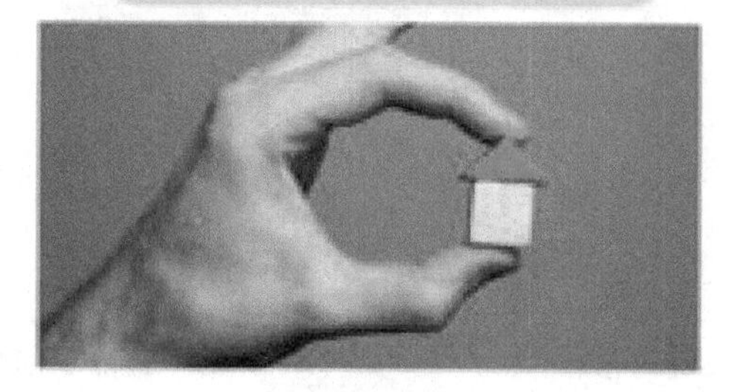

SMALL

PALABRAS ÚTILES - USEFUL WORDS

ADJECTIVES

INTERESANTE

(een-teh-reh-sahn-teh)

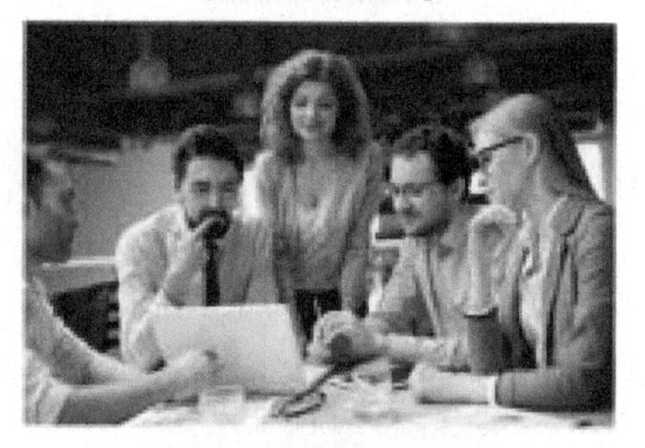

INTERESTING

PALABRAS ÚTILES - USEFUL WORDS

ADJECTIVES

ABURRIDO

(ah-boo-rree-doh)

g Adjectives that end -a or -o change their ending according to the gender of the noun they describe: La obra es aburrida / El libro es aburrido.

BORING

PALABRAS ÚTILES - USEFUL WORDS

ADJECTIVES

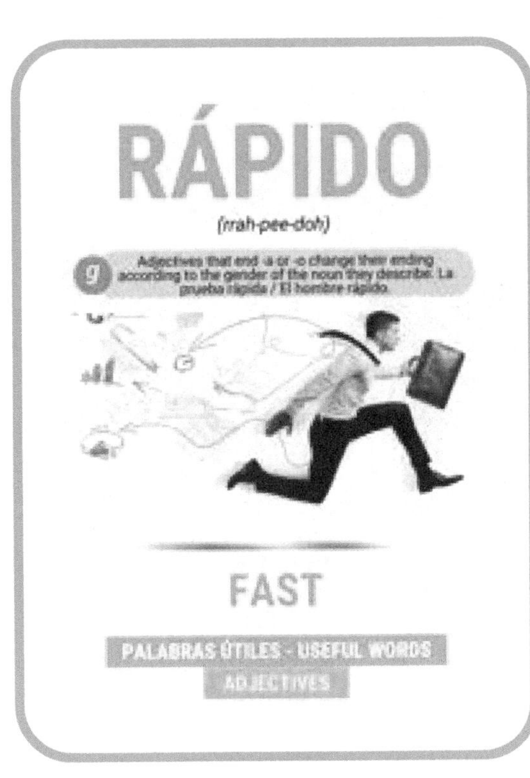

RÁPIDO
(rrah-pee-doh)
Adjectives that end -a or -o change their ending according to the gender of the noun they describe. La prueba rápida / El hombre rápido.
FAST
PALABRAS ÚTILES - USEFUL WORDS
ADJECTIVES

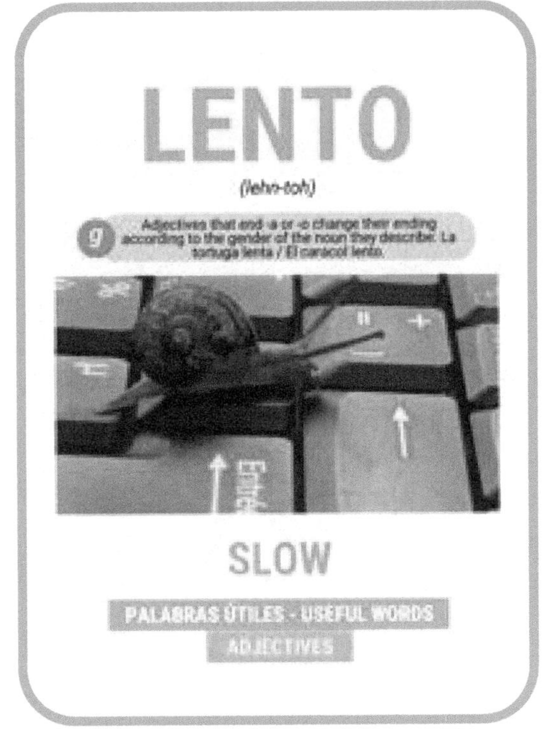

LENTO
(lehn-toh)
Adjectives that end -a or -o change their ending according to the gender of the noun they describe. La tortuga lenta / El caracol lento.
SLOW
PALABRAS ÚTILES - USEFUL WORDS
ADJECTIVES

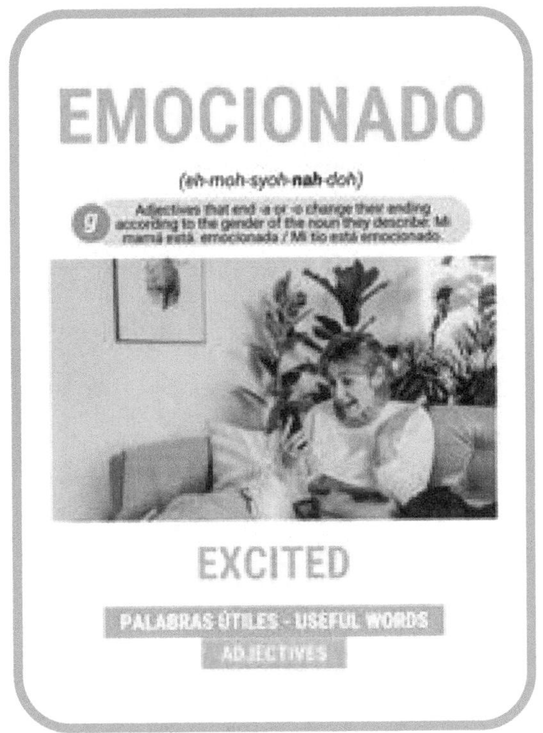

EMOCIONADO
(eh-moh-syoh-nah-doh)
Adjectives that end -a or -o change their ending according to the gender of the noun they describe. Mi mamá está emocionada / Mi tío está emocionado.
EXCITED
PALABRAS ÚTILES - USEFUL WORDS
ADJECTIVES

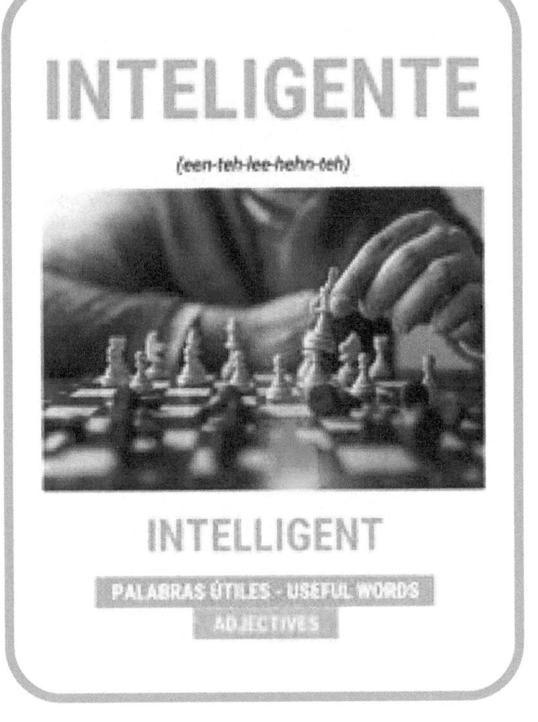

INTELIGENTE
(een-teh-lee-hehn-teh)
INTELLIGENT
PALABRAS ÚTILES - USEFUL WORDS
ADJECTIVES

EL HOMBRE

(ehl ohm-breh)

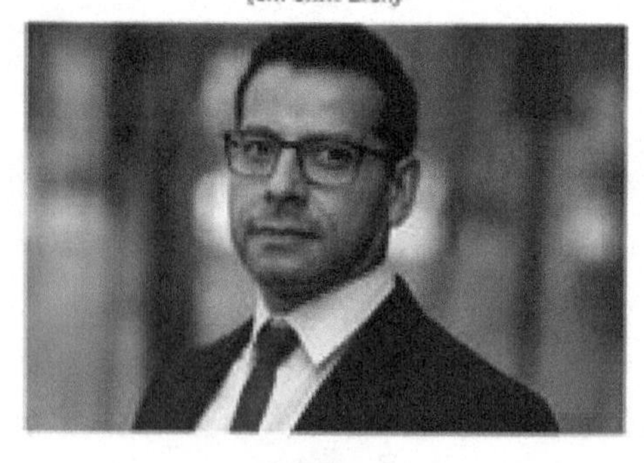

MAN

PALABRAS ÚTILES - USEFUL WORDS

NOUNS

LA MUJER

(lah moo-hehr)

WOMAN

PALABRAS ÚTILES - USEFUL WORDS

NOUNS

EL MUNDO

(ehl moon-doh)

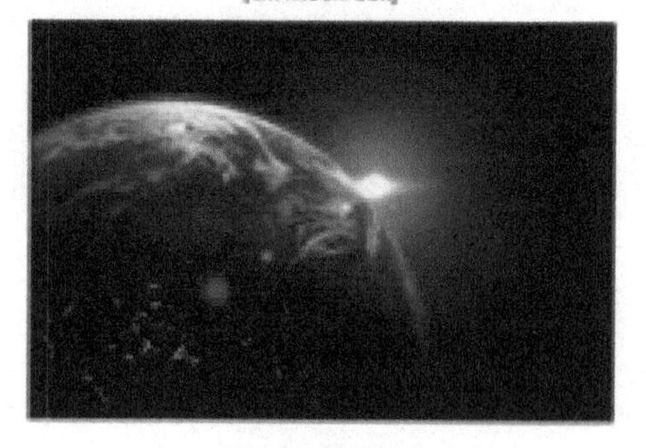

WORLD

PALABRAS ÚTILES - USEFUL WORDS

NOUNS

EL DÍA

(ehl dee-ah)

g Masculine noun

DAY

PALABRAS ÚTILES - USEFUL WORDS

NOUNS

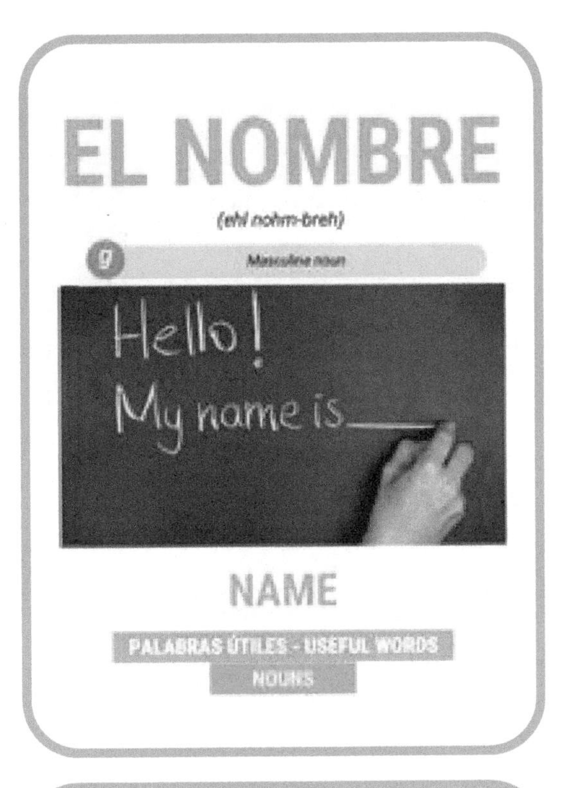
EL NOMBRE
(ehl nohm-breh)
g
Masculine noun
Hello!
My name is___
NAME
PALABRAS ÚTILES - USEFUL WORDS
NOUNS

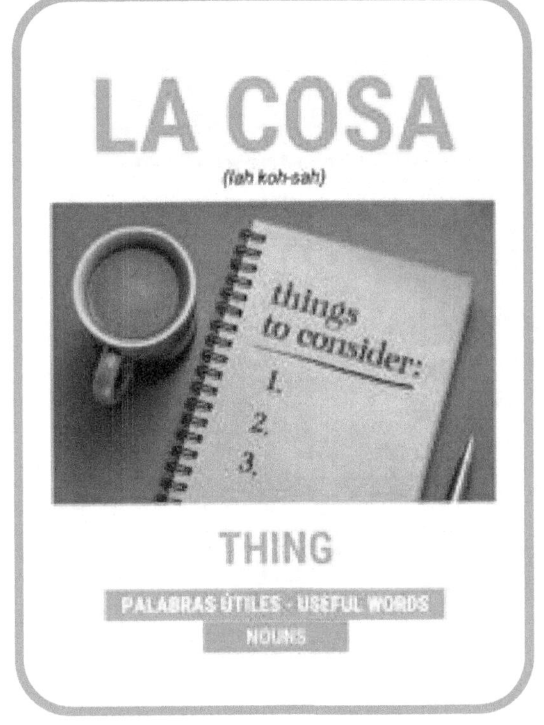
LA COSA
(lah koh-sah)
things to consider:
1.
2.
3.
THING
PALABRAS ÚTILES - USEFUL WORDS
NOUNS

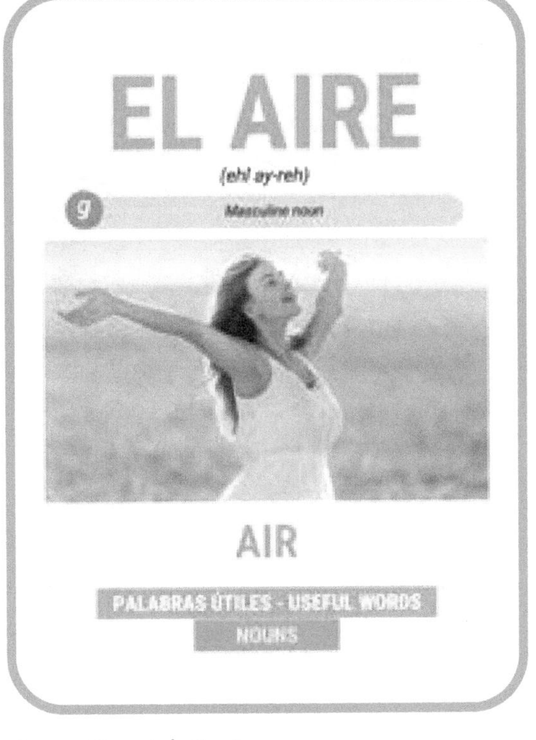
EL AIRE
(ehl ay-reh)
g
Masculine noun
AIR
PALABRAS ÚTILES - USEFUL WORDS
NOUNS

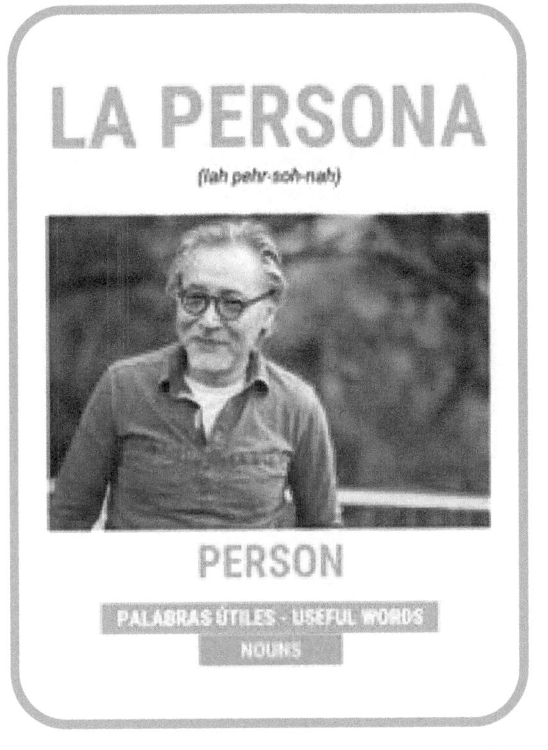
LA PERSONA
(lah pehr-soh-nah)
PERSON
PALABRAS ÚTILES - USEFUL WORDS
NOUNS

(lah pah-lah-brah)

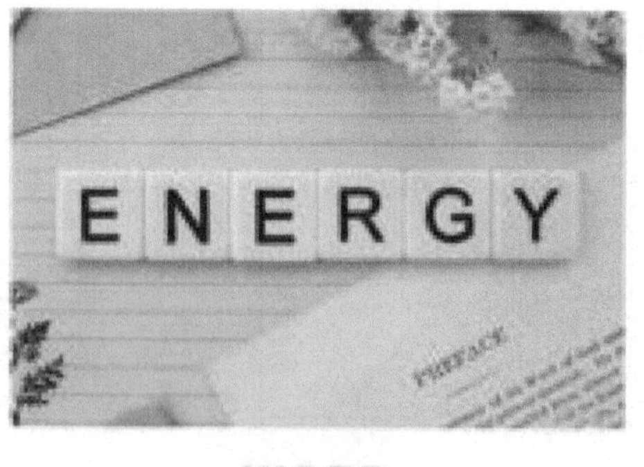

WORD

PALABRAS ÚTILES - USEFUL WORDS

NOUNS

LA PÁGINA

(lah pah-hee-nah)

PAGE

PALABRAS ÚTILES - USEFUL WORDS

NOUNS

HOY

(oy)

TODAY

PALABRAS ÚTILES - USEFUL WORDS

NOUNS

MAÑANA

(mah-nyah-nah)

TOMORROW

PALABRAS ÚTILES - USEFUL WORDS

NOUNS

(lah oh-rah)

HOUR

PALABRAS ÚTILES - USEFUL WORDS

NOUNS

EL AÑO

(ehl ah-nyoh)

YEAR

PALABRAS ÚTILES - USEFUL WORDS

NOUNS

LA SEMANA

(lah seh-mah-nah)

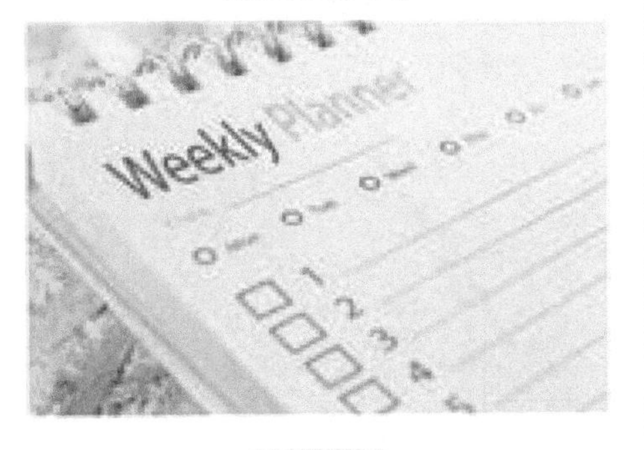

WEEK

PALABRAS ÚTILES - USEFUL WORDS

NOUNS

EL TIEMPO

(ehl tyehm-poh)

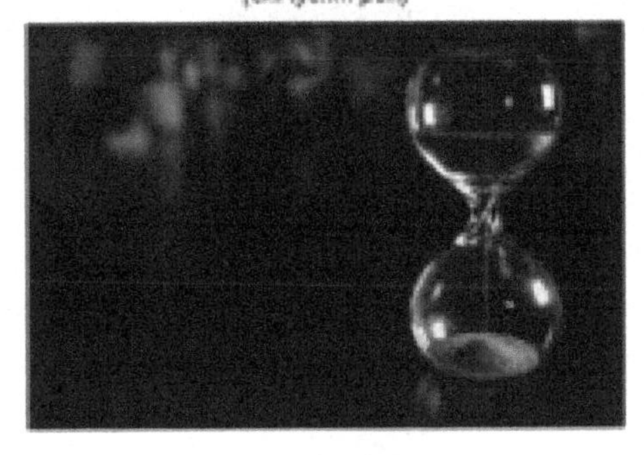

TIME

PALABRAS ÚTILES - USEFUL WORDS

NOUNS

EL PAÍS

(ehl pah-ees)

g Masculine noun

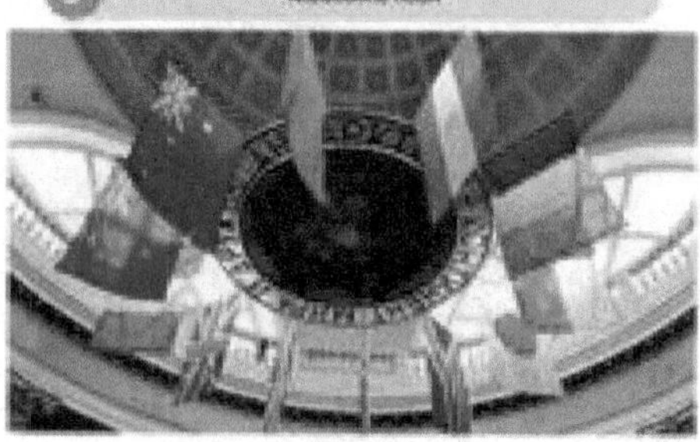

COUNTRY

PALABRAS ÚTILES - USEFUL WORDS

NOUNS

LA CIUDAD

(lah syoo-dahd)

p The pronunciation of 'ciudad' in Spain is 'thyoo-dahd'

CITY

PALABRAS ÚTILES - USEFUL WORDS

NOUNS

LA FORMA

(lah fohr-mah)

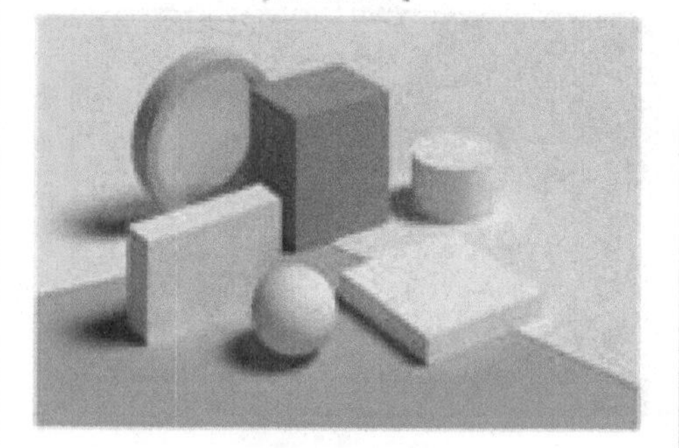

SHAPE

PALABRAS ÚTILES - USEFUL WORDS

NOUNS

NADA

(nah-dah)

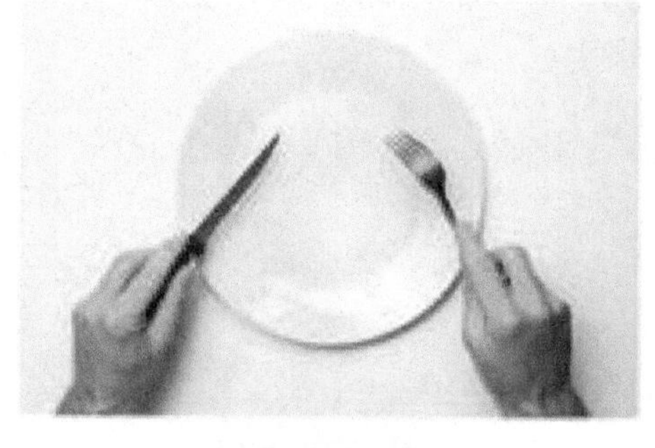

NOTHING

PALABRAS ÚTILES - USEFUL WORDS

NOUNS

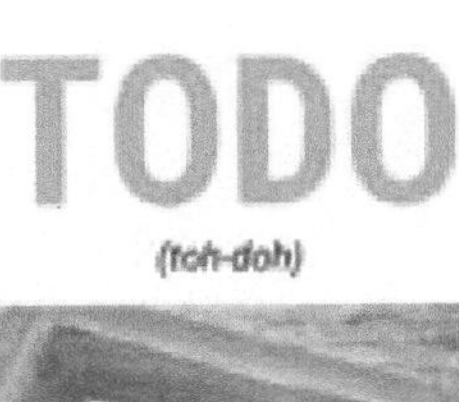

TODO

(toh-doh)

EVERYTHING

PALABRAS ÚTILES - USEFUL WORDS

NOUNS

LA PREGUNTA

(lah preh-goon-tah)

QUESTION

PALABRAS ÚTILES - USEFUL WORDS

NOUNS

LA RESPUESTA

(lah rrehs-pwehs-tah)

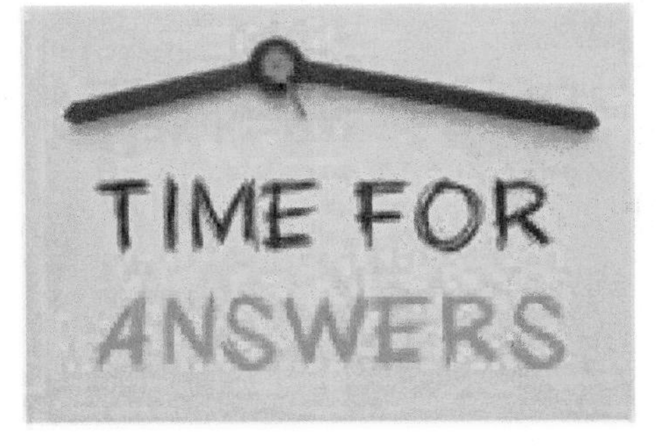

ANSWER

PALABRAS ÚTILES - USEFUL WORDS

NOUNS

EL COMIENZO

(ehl koh-myehn-soh)

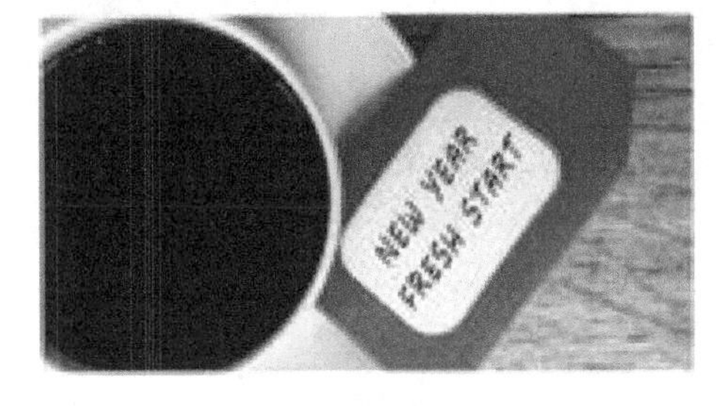

START

PALABRAS ÚTILES - USEFUL WORDS

NOUNS

EL FINAL

(ehl fee-nahl)

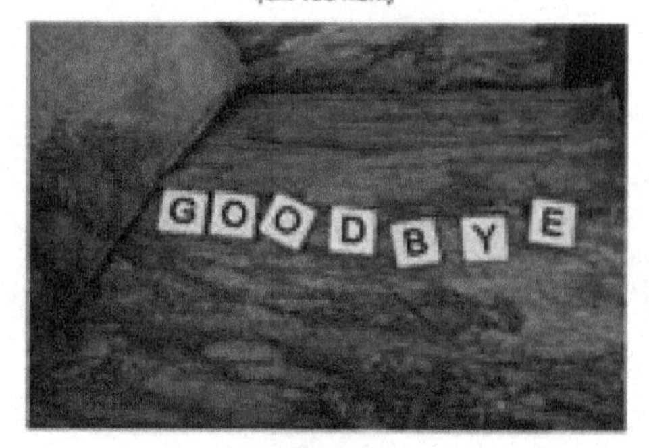

END

PALABRAS ÚTILES - USEFUL WORDS

NOUNS

LA VIDA

(lah bee-dah)

LIFE

PALABRAS ÚTILES - USEFUL WORDS

NOUNS

EL GOBIERNO

(ehl goh-byehr-noh)

GOVERNMENT

PALABRAS ÚTILES - USEFUL WORDS

NOUNS

LAVAR

(lah-bahr)

V Regular verb

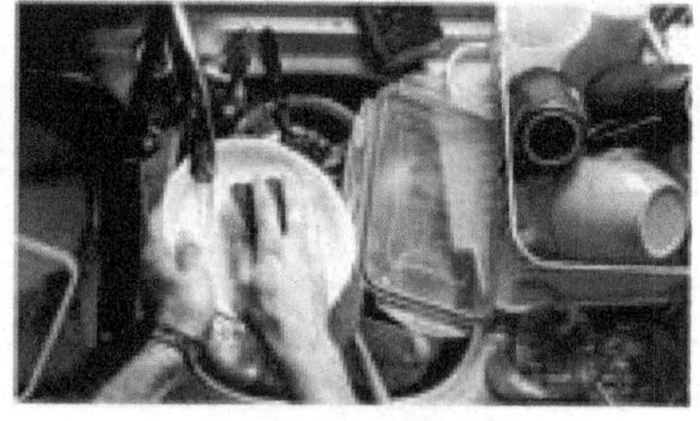

TO WASH

PALABRAS ÚTILES - USEFUL WORDS

VERBS

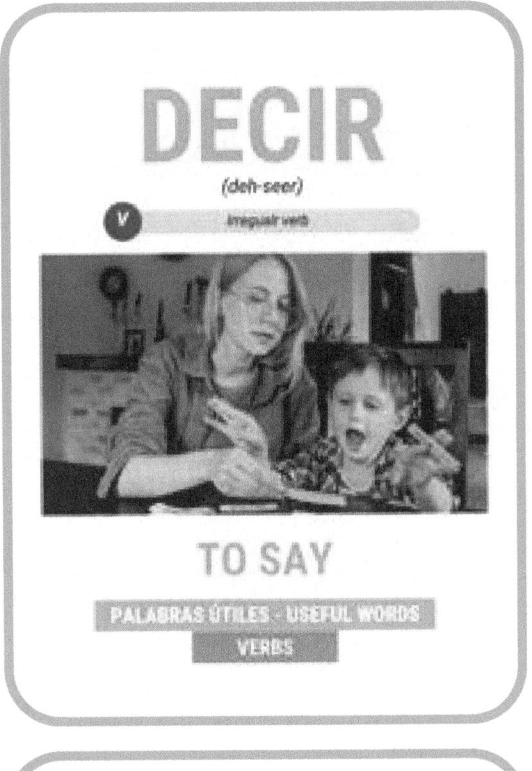
DECIR
(deh-seer)
V
TO SAY
PALABRAS ÚTILES - USEFUL WORDS
VERBS

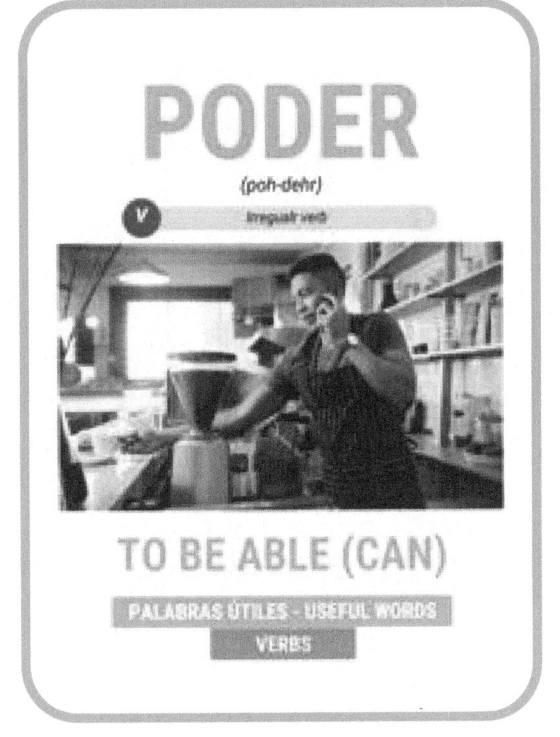
PODER
(poh-dehr)
V
TO BE ABLE (CAN)
PALABRAS ÚTILES - USEFUL WORDS
VERBS

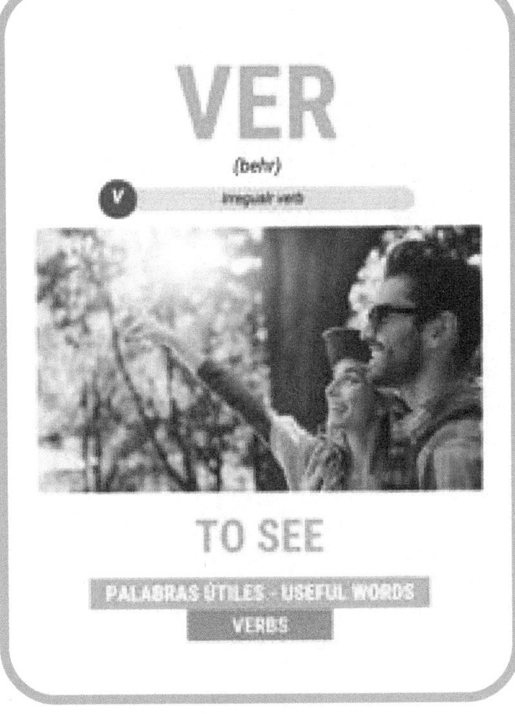
VER
(behr)
V
TO SEE
PALABRAS ÚTILES - USEFUL WORDS
VERBS

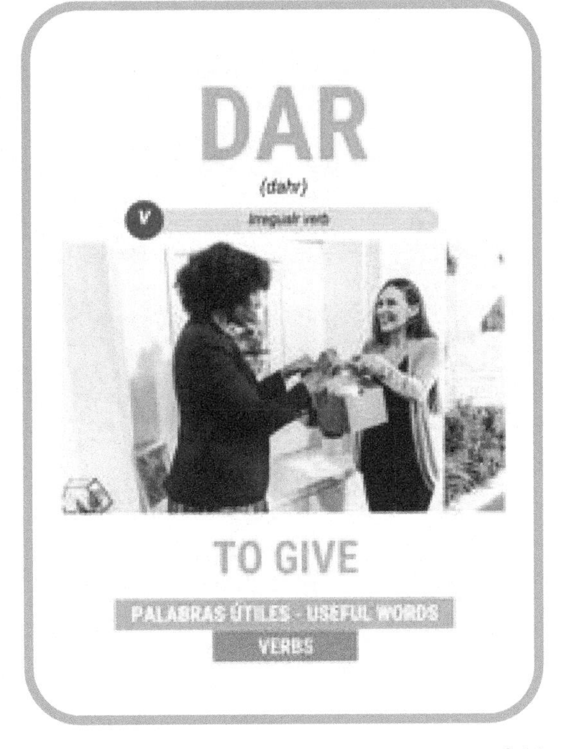
DAR
(dahr)
V
TO GIVE
PALABRAS ÚTILES - USEFUL WORDS
VERBS

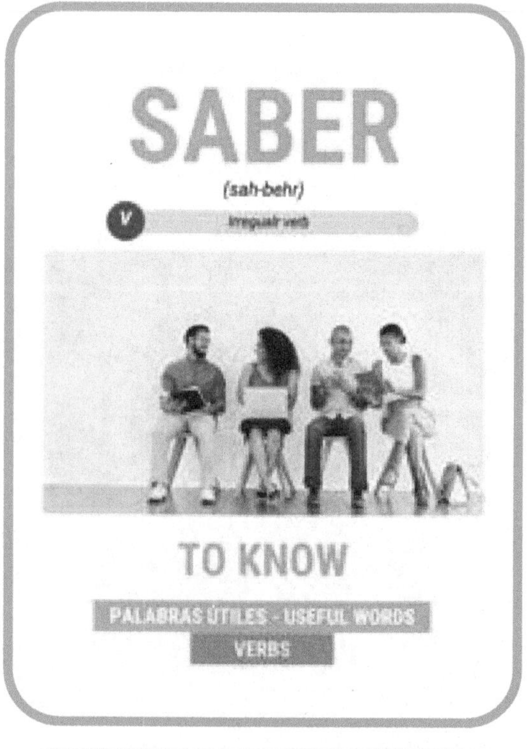
SABER
(sah-behr)
V
TO KNOW
PALABRAS ÚTILES - USEFUL WORDS
VERBS

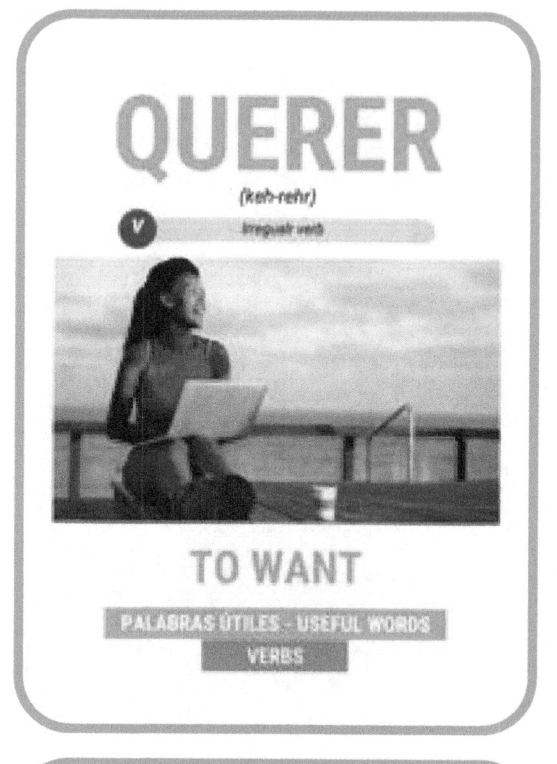
QUERER
(keh-rehr)
V
TO WANT
PALABRAS ÚTILES - USEFUL WORDS
VERBS

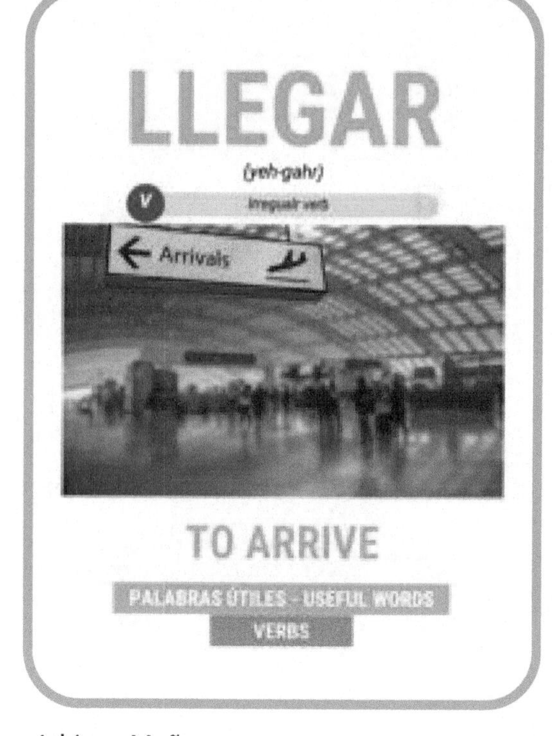
LLEGAR
(yeh-gahr)
V
Arrivals
TO ARRIVE
PALABRAS ÚTILES - USEFUL WORDS
VERBS

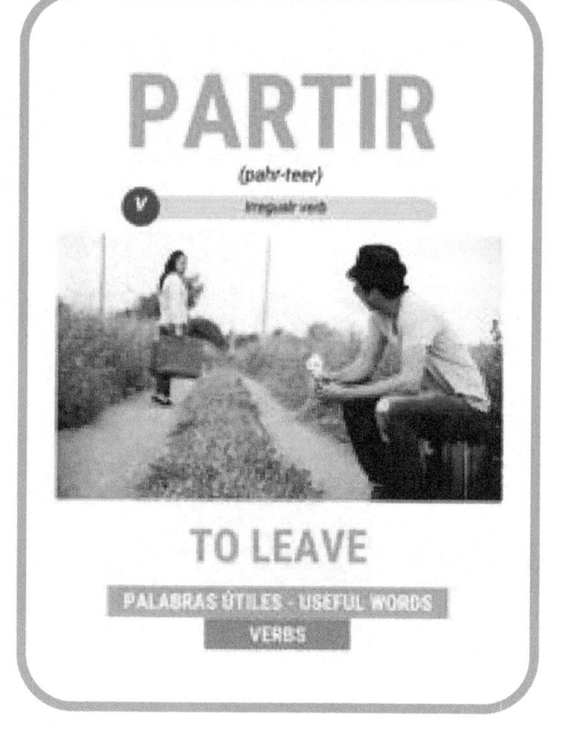
PARTIR
(pahr-teer)
V
TO LEAVE
PALABRAS ÚTILES - USEFUL WORDS
VERBS

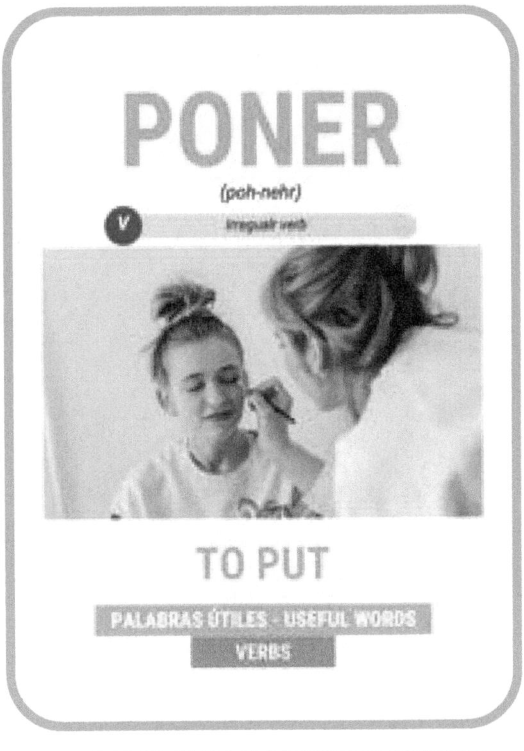
PONER
(poh-nehr)
V
TO PUT
PALABRAS ÚTILES - USEFUL WORDS
VERBS

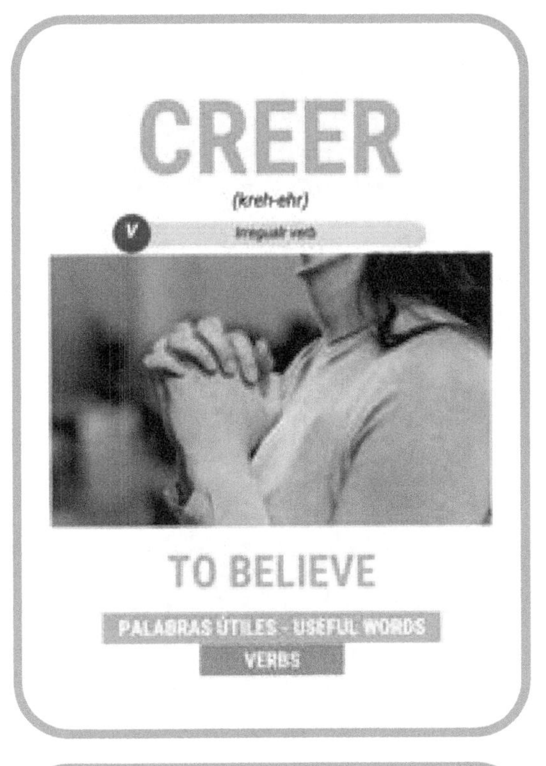
CREER
(kreh-ehr)
V
TO BELIEVE
PALABRAS ÚTILES - USEFUL WORDS
VERBS

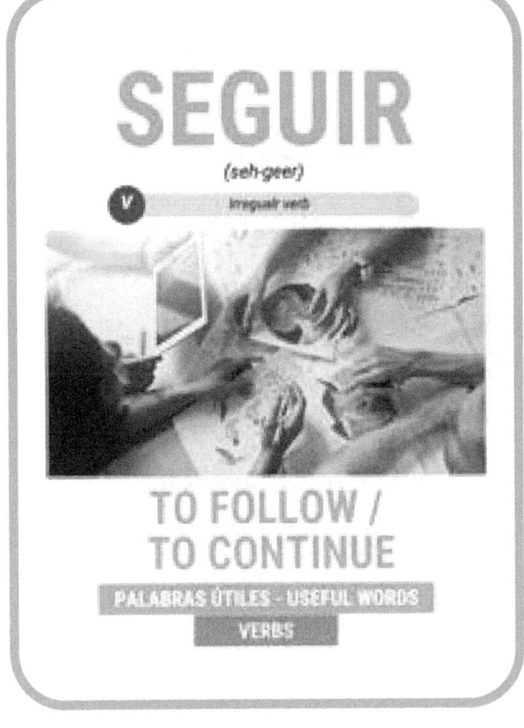
SEGUIR
(seh-geer)
V
TO FOLLOW /
TO CONTINUE
PALABRAS ÚTILES - USEFUL WORDS
VERBS

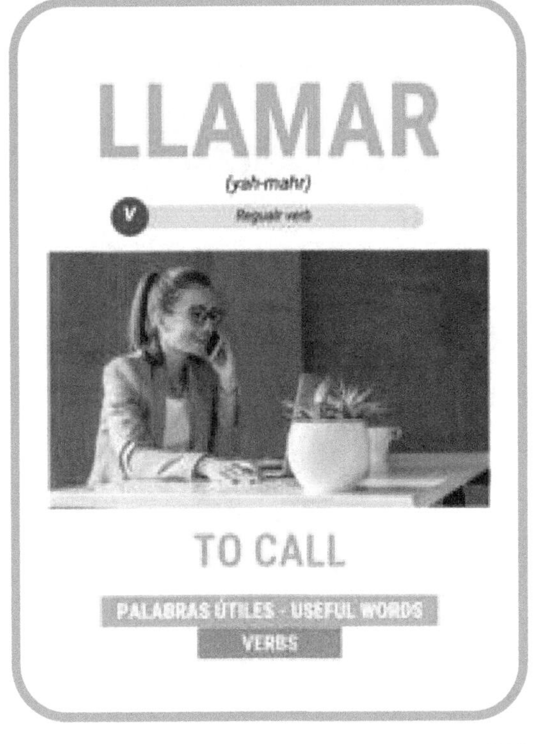
LLAMAR
(yah-mahr)
V
TO CALL
PALABRAS ÚTILES - USEFUL WORDS
VERBS

VENIR
(beh-neer)
V
TO COME
PALABRAS ÚTILES - USEFUL WORDS
VERBS

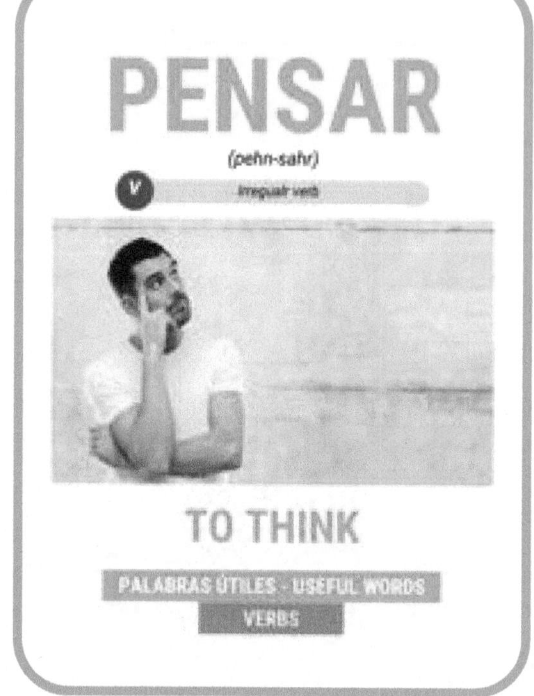
PENSAR
(pehn-sahr)
V
TO THINK
PALABRAS ÚTILES - USEFUL WORDS
VERBS

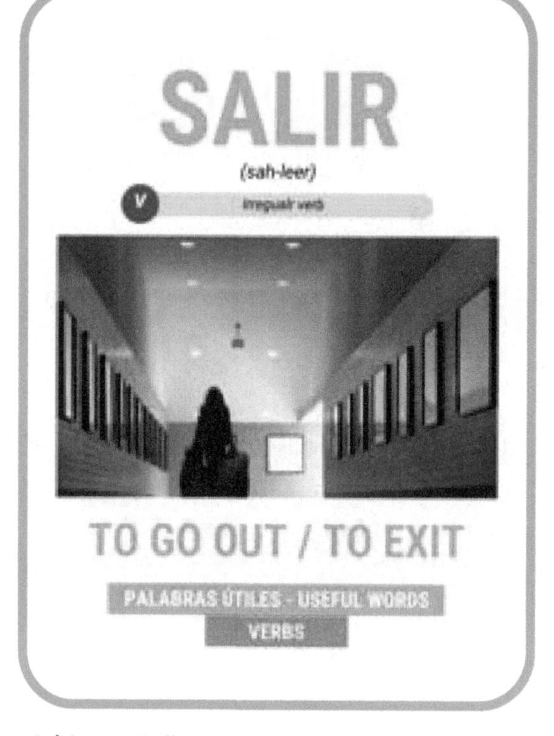
SALIR
(sah-leer)
V
TO GO OUT / TO EXIT
PALABRAS ÚTILES - USEFUL WORDS
VERBS

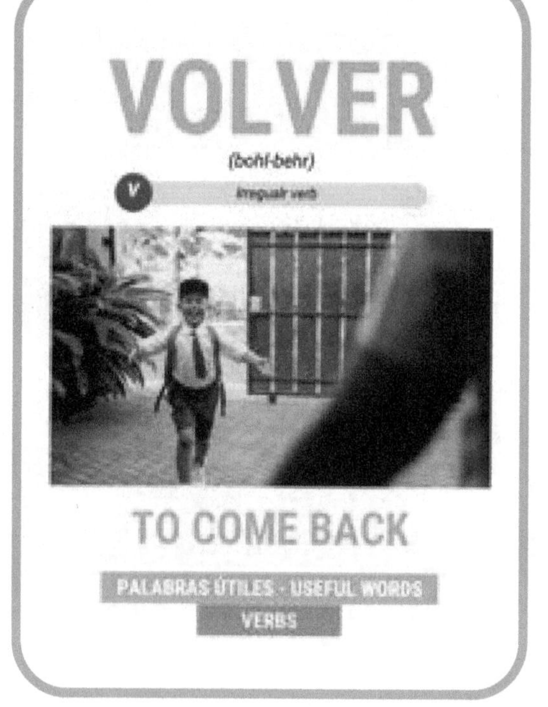
VOLVER
(bohl-behr)
V
TO COME BACK
PALABRAS ÚTILES - USEFUL WORDS
VERBS

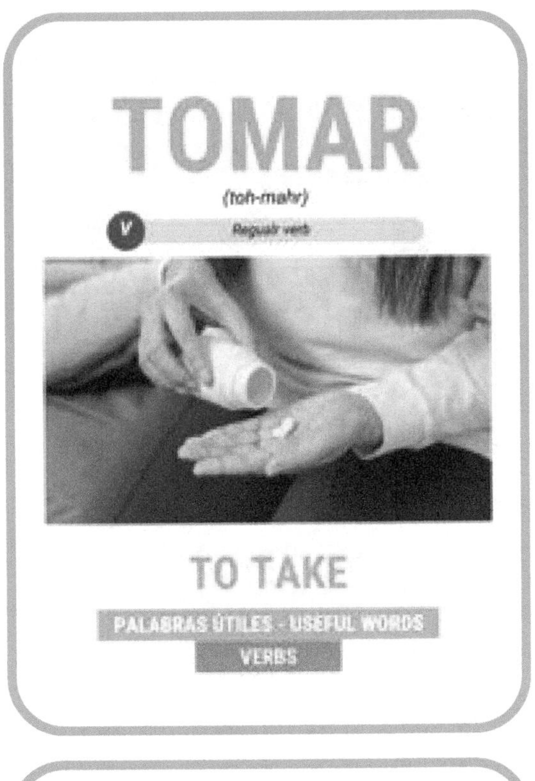
TOMAR
(toh-mahr)
V
TO TAKE
PALABRAS ÚTILES - USEFUL WORDS
VERBS

SENTIR
(sehn-teer)
V
TO FEEL
PALABRAS ÚTILES - USEFUL WORDS
VERBS

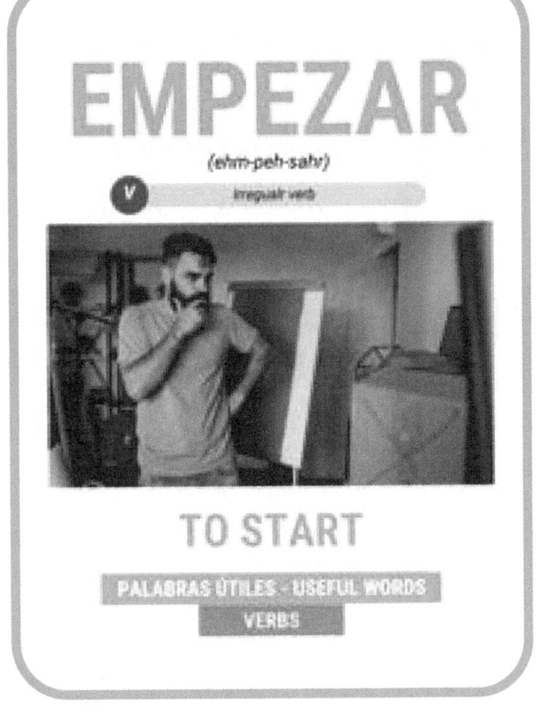
EMPEZAR
(ehm-peh-sahr)
V
TO START
PALABRAS ÚTILES - USEFUL WORDS
VERBS

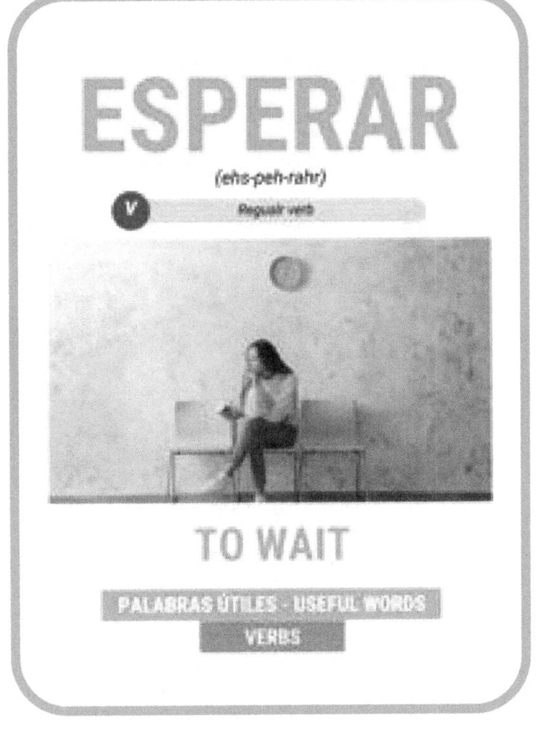
ESPERAR
(ehs-peh-rahr)
V
TO WAIT
PALABRAS ÚTILES - USEFUL WORDS
VERBS

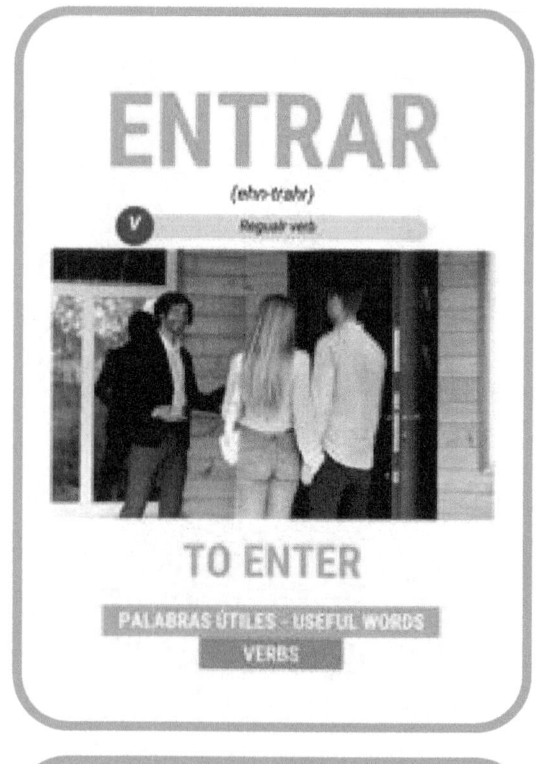
ENTRAR
(ehn-trahr)
V
TO ENTER
PALABRAS ÚTILES - USEFUL WORDS
VERBS

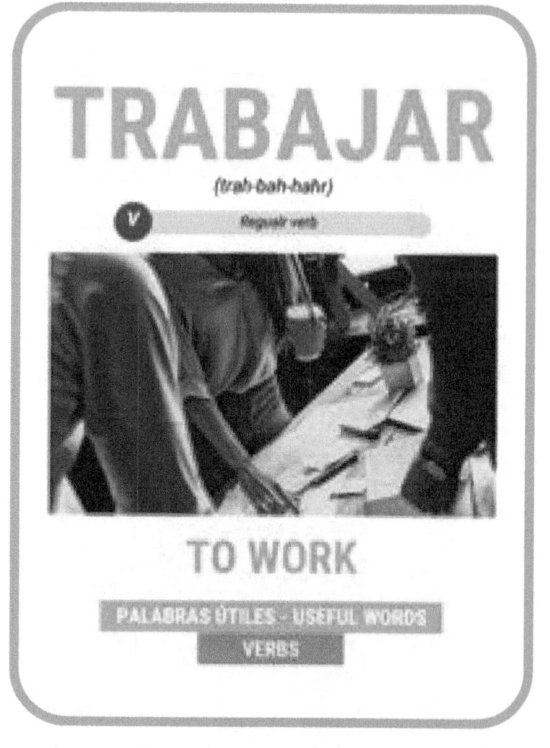
TRABAJAR
(trah-bah-hahr)
V
TO WORK
PALABRAS ÚTILES - USEFUL WORDS
VERBS

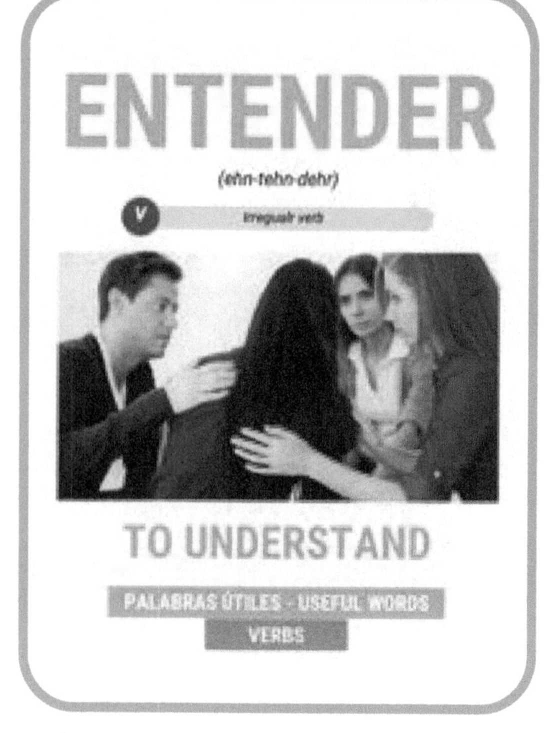
ENTENDER
(ehn-tehn-dehr)
V
TO UNDERSTAND
PALABRAS ÚTILES - USEFUL WORDS
VERBS

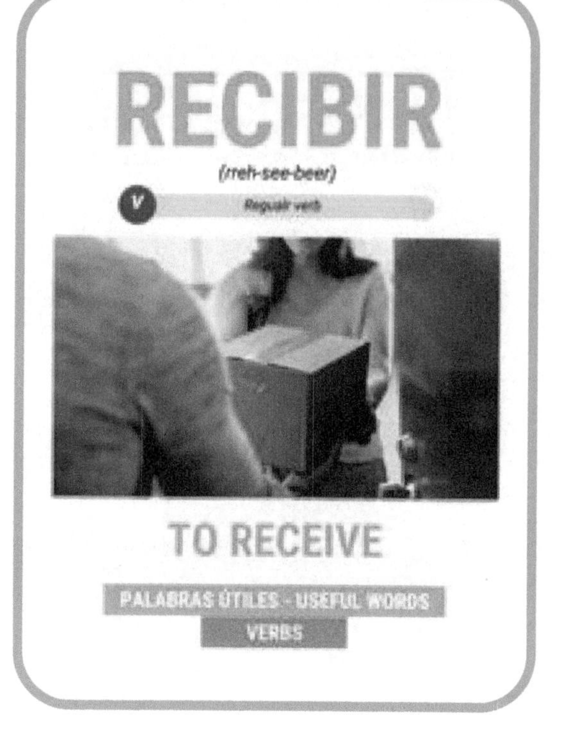
RECIBIR
(rreh-see-beer)
V
TO RECEIVE
PALABRAS ÚTILES - USEFUL WORDS
VERBS

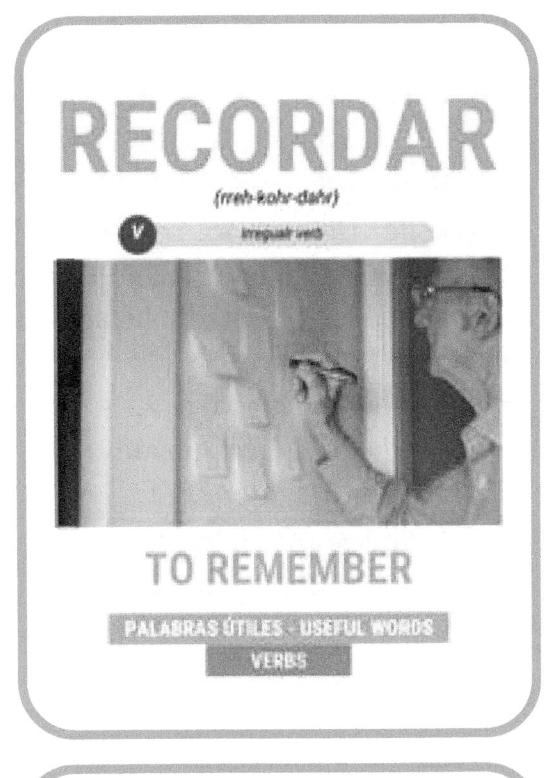
RECORDAR
(rreh-kohr-dahr)
V
TO REMEMBER
PALABRAS ÚTILES - USEFUL WORDS
VERBS

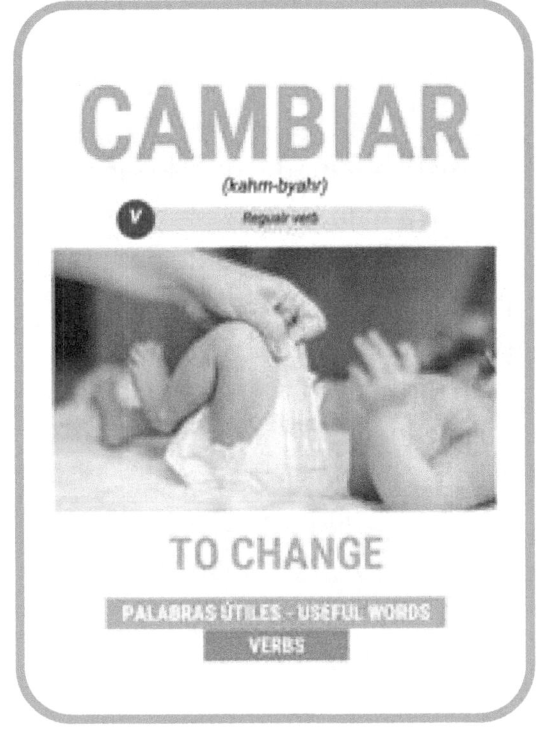
CAMBIAR
(kahm-byahr)
V
TO CHANGE
PALABRAS ÚTILES - USEFUL WORDS
VERBS

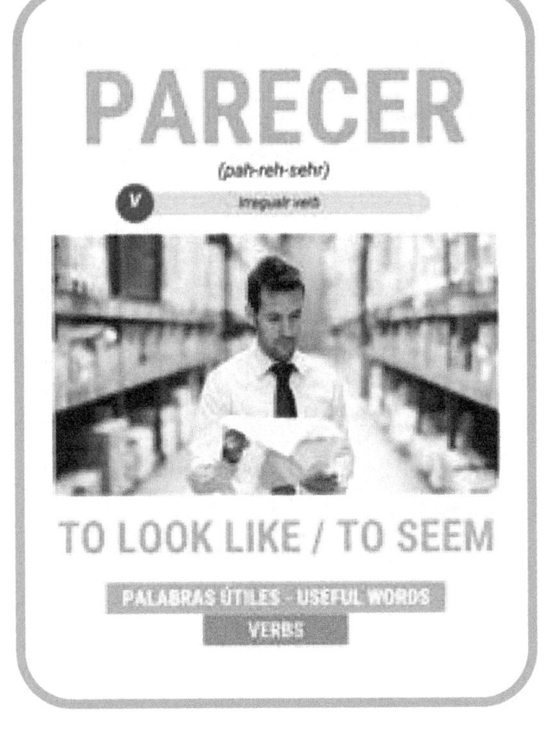
PARECER
(pah-reh-sehr)
V
TO LOOK LIKE / TO SEEM
PALABRAS ÚTILES - USEFUL WORDS
VERBS

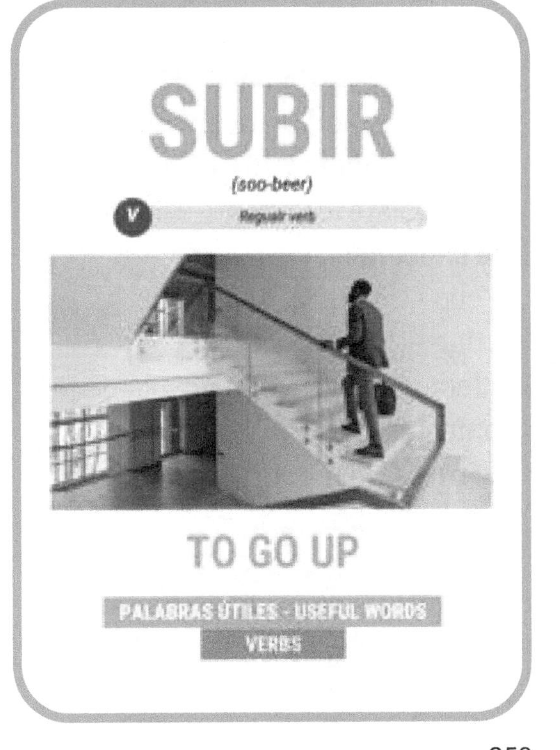
SUBIR
(soo-beer)
V
TO GO UP
PALABRAS ÚTILES - USEFUL WORDS
VERBS

INDEX - INDICES

A

INDEX - INDICES

INDEX - INDICES

INDEX - INDICES

INDEX - INDICES

INDEX - INDICES

INDEX - INDICES

INDEX - INDICES

INDEX - INDICES

INDEX - INDICES

INDEX - INDICES

INDEX - INDICES

INDEX - INDICES

INDEX - INDICES

INDEX - INDICES

INDEX - INDICES

INDEX - INDICES

INDEX - INDICES

INDEX - INDICES

INDEX - INDICES

INDEX - INDICES

INDEX - INDICES

Y

Z

AUTHOR BIO

Adriana Muñoz loves languages.

As a Spanish-American, she served as a linguist for six years in the United States Navy before continuing her language proficiencies by teaching others who want to learn them as a second language or improve on their native tongue.

She's fluent in Spanish, Portuguese, French, English, and Arabic.

Adrian grew up in Spain and now resides in America with her family, and publishes language learning books to help those traveling or just wanting to learn another language.

Made in the USA
Las Vegas, NV
14 April 2023